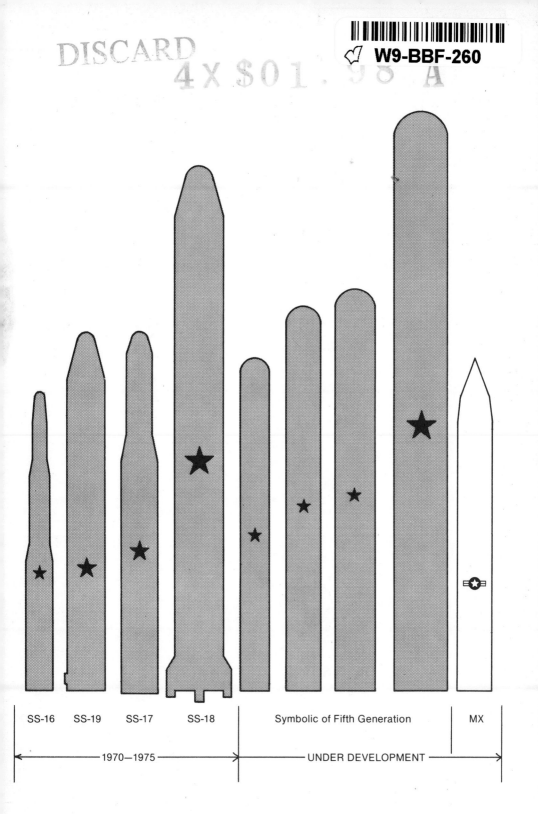

SS-16   SS-19   SS-17   SS-18   Symbolic of Fifth Generation   MX

1970—1975   UNDER DEVELOPMENT

ENDGAME

Books by Strobe Talbott

Endgame: The Inside Story of SALT II

Translated and Edited

Khrushchev Remembers (1970)

Khrushchev Remembers: The Last Testament (1974)

ENDGAME

THE INSIDE STORY OF SALT II

Strobe Talbott

HARPER & ROW, PUBLISHERS

NEW YORK, HAGERSTOWN

SAN FRANCISCO

LONDON

ENDGAME: THE INSIDE STORY OF SALT II.

Copyright © 1979 by Strobe Talbott.

All rights reserved. Printed in the United States of America. No part of this book may be used or reproduced in any manner whatsoever without written permission except in the case of brief quotations embodied in critical articles and reviews. For information address Harper & Row, Publishers, Inc., 10 East 53rd Street, New York, N.Y. 10022. Published simultaneously in Canada by Fitzhenry & Whiteside Limited, Toronto.

Published simultaneously in Great Britain by Harper & Row Ltd., 28 Tavistock Street, London WC2E 7PN and in Australia and New Zealand by Harper & Row (Australasia) Pty. Ltd., P.O. Box 226, Artarmon, New South Wales 2064.

FIRST EDITION

Designer: Sidney Feinberg

Library of Congress Cataloging in Publication Data

Talbott, Strobe.
  Endgame: the inside story of SALT II.
  Includes index.
  1. Strategic Arms Limitation Talks.
I. Title.
JX1974.75.T34 1979   327'.174   79-2238
ISBN 0-06-014213-8

79 80 81 82 83 10 9 8 7 6 5 4 3 2 1

For my parents, Josephine and Nelson Talbott

Contents

Foreword

I have traced the evolution of the strategic arms limitation talks up to the signing of the SALT II agreement by Jimmy Carter and Leonid Brezhnev at their meeting in Vienna, June 15–18, 1979. With that summit, one phase of SALT, involving primarily negotiations between the United States and the Soviet Union, came to an end. Another phase was about to begin. It would involve a vigorous public debate in the U.S. over the merits of the agreement and an intense, probably prolonged political struggle between the Carter administration and the Senate over whether the treaty should be ratified as submitted, substantially amended in ways that might require renegotiation, or rejected as incompatible with American national interests. The Senate would exercise its constitutional duty to advise and consent on the treaty, declaring whether this most elaborate, most esoteric of deals between two great powers should become law. Only when that decision was rendered could SALT III begin in earnest, to be followed perhaps by SALT IV, V and so on. Its proponents hope that SALT will be a story without end. The story told here ends at that critical moment in the course of arms control when the Soviet-American negotiations were, in effect, adjourned to accommodate the American democratic process. Public and congressional judgments about whether the treaty signed in Vienna should be ratified in the Senate and whether SALT II should have its sequels would depend partly on questions of history: who conceded what to whom when in exchange for what? What actually happened in the negotiations and why? What was said in the talks and what did it mean at the time? Helping to answer such questions is one of the goals of this book.

I carried out the reporting and writing while SALT II was in progress. Official records of many events described here will remain classified, and participants constrained from freely discussing their roles, for years to come. Therefore most of the people I interviewed spoke to me on the condition that they would not be identified as sources of the information necessary to assemble a narrative account of the negotiations and the accompanying deliberations within the American government. They included numerous officials in various departments and agencies of the executive branch during the Carter administration, as well as some from the Nixon and Ford administrations; senators, representatives and members of their staffs; Soviets in Washington, Moscow and a number of cities in between; and West European diplomats. To all of them—for their time, their candor and their trust—I am grateful.

A number of colleagues at *Time* magazine helped me along the way. Among them I would like to thank Henry Muller, Bruce Nelan, Burt Pines, and Don Sider. Chris Ogden has been my closest professional partner on SALT as on so many other stories we have covered together. Murray Gart and his successor as chief of correspondents, Richard Duncan, supported me when I undertook to prepare an article for *Time* on the history of SALT II. I am additionally indebted to Dick Duncan for encouraging me to expand that article into this book and for making it possible for me to do so. My appreciation also to Robert Dean, Eugene Linden, Priscilla Johnson McMillan and William Shawcross for spurring me on at an early stage, and to Paul Nitze and Herbert Scoville, whose opinions differ widely but whose expertise and fairness served me well on a number of occasions.

To three people who read the manuscript and helped me to improve it, I wish to acknowledge special gratitude: my wife, Brooke Shearer, who is one of my best editors; Jan Lodal and Michael Mandelbaum, who generously, patiently and lucidly shared with me their wisdom about the technology and theology of SALT.

Finally, thanks to Jim Moore, my literary agent; to Gail Lynch, who assisted me with such good cheer and great skill in the research and typing of the book; and to Erwin Glikes and Barbara Grossman at Harper & Row.

S.T.

Washington, June 22, 1979

How many angels can dance on the point of a very fine needle
without jostling each other?

> —Isaac D'Israeli, 1823, paraphrasing
> an idea from *Summa Theologiae*
> by the thirteenth-century scholastic
> Saint Thomas Aquinas

How many MIRVs can they put on top of a booster?

> —Senator John Glenn, November 3, 1977,
> questioning Secretary of State Cyrus Vance
> during hearings in executive session on
> SALT II

ENDGAME

1   The Summit

The second weekend in June 1979 Jimmy Carter went up to the presidential retreat at Camp David in the Catoctin Mountains of Maryland to prepare for his meeting with Leonid Brezhnev a week later in Vienna. It was to be the first encounter between the two men and the first face-to-face meeting between a Soviet and an American leader since Gerald Ford saw Brezhnev in Helsinki in 1975. Both governments hoped the upcoming summit would end a protracted period of mistrust and misunderstanding between the superpowers. Ever since the presidential campaign of 1976 that had elevated Carter to the White House, Soviet-American relations had been deteriorating. The relationship could no longer be described as one of détente, or what the Soviets called "the relaxation of tensions." There were old tensions over the Middle East and Africa, exacerbated by recent developments in both areas, and new tensions over China and human rights. But underlying these and other differences of regional politics and ideology, there were new and ominous strains in the strategic relationship between the U.S. and the Soviet Union. Each country felt it had good reason to question the long-range intentions of the other. Each felt threatened by the other's nuclear arsenal and its presumed geopolitical designs. In the U.S., words like "vulnerability," "survivability" and "destabilization" no longer had quite the same ring of think-tank jargon that they had had earlier. They were becoming commonplaces of political rhetoric and journalistic commentary, and they were ringing in Jimmy Carter's ears as he settled down to do his homework for his meeting with Brezhnev.

The National Security Council ordered up briefing papers from all over the government. The State Department provided summaries of U.S. policy on a variety of bilateral issues between the U.S. and the Soviet Union. The Departments of Treasury, Agriculture, Energy and Commerce reviewed the Soviet domestic economy and offered projections for grain crops and energy output and the outlook for foreign trade. The Central Intelligence Agency assembled potted biographies of the Soviet leadership and synthesized the most authoritative, yet still highly equivocal, speculation about who would succeed Brezhnev. The CIA also updated its analysis of Soviet military and clandestine political mischief-making around the world. The Defense Department and Joint Chiefs of Staff surveyed the strength of Soviet and Warsaw Pact forces. Carter's mounting stack of paperwork contained highlights of past summits, including the one previously held in Vienna between John F. Kennedy and Nikita Khrushchev in 1961. It was a cautionary tale: Kennedy had come into the meeting with conflicting guidance from his advisers; he struck Khrushchev as inexperienced and unsure of himself, and the Soviet leader subsequently attempted to exploit what he perceived to be Kennedy's uncertainty in the crises over Berlin and Cuba. The National Security Council boiled down this mass of paper into thick black ring-binders, tabbed by topic, for Carter to take with him to Camp David. He pored over these by the swimming pool and in his study at Aspen Lodge, the main cabin on the compound. When he came down from Camp David on Monday, June 11, the briefing books were dog-eared and the margins filled with jottings in green ink. Carter also reviewed his notes from earlier meetings with West German Chancellor Helmut Schmidt, French President Valéry Giscard d'Estaing and former British Prime Minister James Callaghan, all of whom had coached the American president on what to expect at the summit. Director of Central Intelligence Stansfield Turner played for Carter videotapes of Richard Nixon's and Gerald Ford's meetings with Brezhnev. Carter consulted with Nixon by phone, and invited Ford to come by the White House to advise him in person. Brezhnev could be expected to bluster and browbeat, said Ford; Carter should be polite but not give an inch.

Carter's appetite for homework seemed insatiable. He kept calling for more papers, more briefings—on the background and ramifications of any subject that might conceivably come up at the summit. He had always tended to immerse himself in the detail of any task. He had a compulsive desire—and, indeed, a prodigious ability—to master the most technical aspects of his job. Even some of his most loyal supporters and assistants felt that in this respect he was a conscientious to a fault, that he wasted time and energy on minutiae, that there was an obsessive quality to his meticulousness. It was as though he thought he could beat any problem simply by understanding it to death. But in this case, there may well have been an extra—and uncharacteristic—element of apprehension, even insecurity, in his over-preparation. The talks with Brezhnev at the end of the week promised to be a critical test of Carter's much-criticized competence as president.

Far and away the most important batch of papers in Carter's pile of homework was the text of the SALT II agreement. It was still incomplete and still classified TOP SECRET. In a week it would be finished and public. The agreement was a bundle of forbiddingly titled documents, different in form and duration. There was a Treaty on the Limitation of Strategic Offensive Arms, to expire in 1985; a Protocol, to expire at the end of 1981; a Joint Statement of Principles and Basic Guidelines for Subsequent Negotiations on the Limitation of Strategic Arms (SALT III); Agreed Statements and Common Understandings Regarding the Treaty; a Memorandum of Understanding Regarding the Establishment of Data Base of Numbers of Strategic Offensive Arms; a Statement of Data on the Numbers of Strategic Offensive Arms as of the Date of Signature of the Treaty. There were also separate exchanges between the governments on the Soviet deployment of the Backfire bomber and the use of code in missile tests. It was this package of more than a hundred pages that occasioned the summit. Carter and Brezhnev would sign the treaty and other accords at the climax of their four-day meeting on Monday, June 18. While the SALT II agreement was the longest and most complicated single item in the mass of paper Carter had to study, it was also the one he knew best. He had been living and struggling with it for two and a half years. He had participated in many of the deliberations and made many of the decisions that determined its evolution and its present contents. He had intervened to resolve many of the interagency squabbles within the U.S. government over the formulation of various provisions. At key moments along the way, he had personally negotiated with Brezhnev's emissaries in Washington. He knew intimately the baffling terminology, the hierarchy of numbers, the convolutions of legalese, the artful and arcane definitions and disclaimers. He could cite chapter and verse any of the nineteen articles of the treaty, any of the four articles of the protocol, and many of the scores of agreed statements and common understandings. He knew the negotiating history of every important issue addressed in the treaty, going back in some cases many years to the Nixon administration. He knew the sensitivities of the uniformed military and the intelligence community on each of the many points about which they felt strongly. As an Annapolis graduate, a nuclear submariner, a quick study and a stickler for detail, he knew backwards and forwards the SALT-related technology of warfare and espionage. He understood the hardware and doctrine, both Soviet and American.

But what he did not know was whether the treaty he had helped negotiate and was now preparing to sign would ever be the law of the land. He did not know if this immensely complicated document, in which he and his two predecessors had invested so much of their prestige and effort, would survive the scrutiny of the United States Senate, which must ratify it by a two-thirds majority. For Jimmy Carter's presidency was in trouble, and so, largely for that reason, was SALT II.

Clouds over Air Force One

Rather than sallying forth on the diplomatic high road, Carter seemed almost to be beating a hasty retreat from a politically hostile home front. High inflation and long lines at gas stations had become debilitating fixtures in the American economy, and Carter was held largely to blame. Moreover, the low-key, ingenuous, anti-establishmentarian style that had served him so well as an aspirant to the presidency was proving a bane to him as an incumbent. With an eye to the 1980 presidential elections, a number of Republicans, and some potential usurpers among his fellow Democrats, were finding Carter most vulnerable on the amorphous but potent issue of leadership. His approval rating in some national public-opinion polls had slipped to 30 percent, near the nadir of Richard Nixon's standing at the time of his resignation. The Congress, even though it was dominated by his own party, seemed in a frenzy of defiance that amounted to a vote of no confidence. Almost every day brought a new setback, a new instance of the law-makers' seeking to block or reverse administration initiatives, particularly in foreign policy. In the two days before Carter's departure for Vienna, the Senate tried to thwart his recently announced policy of maintaining economic sanctions against the government of Rhodesia, and the House of Representatives threatened to block the legislation necessary to implement the Panama Canal treaties, which had been narrowly ratified in 1977 in the administration's first big fight with Congress. There was also renewed resistance in the House to an administration effort to extend military aid to Turkey— a NATO ally whose long border with the U.S.S.R. made it an important host country for U.S. bases from which to monitor Soviet compliance with SALT.

On the very eve of Carter's departure, Senator Henry Jackson of Washington, the most prominent critic of SALT II, delivered to an audience of conservative Democrats his most extreme attack to date on the President and the agreement. By going to Vienna to sign SALT II with Leonid Brezhnev, said Jackson, Carter would be following in the footsteps of Neville Chamberlain's ignominious journey to Munich in 1938: "To enter a treaty which favors the Soviets as this one does on the ground that we will be in a worse position without it, is appeasement in its purest form. . . . Against overwhelming evidence of a continuing Soviet strategic and conventional military buildup, there has been a flow of official administration explanations, extenuations, excuses. It is all ominously reminiscent of Great Britain in the 1930s, when one government pronouncement after another was issued to assure the British public that Hitler's Germany would never achieve military equality—let alone superiority. The failure to face reality today, like the failure to do so then—that is the mark of appeasement." Jackson cast his invidious comparison in terms so broad that they included the two previous, Republican administrations; Richard Nixon, Gerald Ford and Henry Kissinger were all, in his view, accessories before the fact in the act Carter was about to commit in Vienna. The bipartisan sweep of Jackson's charge made it no less infuriating to the Carter administration. The harshness and timing of the speech led Thomas P. O'Neill, the Speaker of the House, to release a statement warning that no one should misinterpret squabbling between Carter and the Congress as a sign of American lack of resolve or consensus. O'Neill's protestation unintentionally served only to underscore precisely what he was trying to mitigate—the danger that the discord generated by the American governing process could severely impede American diplomacy.

Nor was opposition to Carter's SALT policy confined to the legislative branch of the government. He faced it within the executive branch as well. Indeed, he faced it within the delegation that had carried out his—and his predecessors'—instructions at the negotiating table in Geneva. Shortly after the American and Soviet SALT teams put the finishing touches on the text of the agreement in the early hours of the morning that Carter was to fly to Vienna, Lieutenant General Edward Rowny, the representative of the Joint Chiefs of Staff, "respectfully declined" the President's invitation to attend the signing ceremony. He intended the gesture as a protest over what he considered to be unwarranted and dangerous American concessions in the course of the negotiations. The debate over the treaty in the Senate would turn on many factors, but an important one would be the attitude of the military establishment in general and the Joint Chiefs in particular. That meant the fate of the treaty could very well depend in large measure on whether Rowny was isolated as a spoiler, a defector from the responsible military to the hard-line opposition, or whether his criticism of the treaty, voiced in public speeches and congressional testimony, became an echo of the more muted misgivings of the Joint Chiefs themselves. In one last effort to assuage those misgivings before he signed the treaty, Carter summoned the Chiefs to the White House for what a presidential aide called a "hand-holding session." Then he helicoptered to Andrews Air Force Base in Maryland to board Air Force One.

At planeside, Carter attempted to put his mission into a historical context. He did so in a way that said much about his state of mind. He noted that he would be seeing Brezhnev thirty-four years after Harry Truman met with Joseph Stalin at Potsdam. During that earlier summit, recalled Carter, "a brief message was brought to President Truman: just before dawn, on the desert of Alamogordo, the first atomic bomb had been exploded. Man had unleashed the power of matter itself and changed the world forever." The reference to Truman, Potsdam and Alamogordo seemed to be significant in a number of ways for Carter, some calculated, some perhaps subconscious. By reminding the world that it was the U.S. that had unleashed the destructive power of the atom, he was implying that the U.S. had a unique responsibility to control that power. He seemed also to be bolstering the claim that American presidents, in their eleven encounters with Soviet leaders since Potsdam, have traditionally been able to negotiate from strength—that the technological superiority manifest at Alamogordo in 1945 still sustained the U.S. in 1979. Also, it had become the administration's main theme that SALT had at least as much to do with defense as with disarmament. The purpose of the negotiations was "to avoid nuclear war while maintaining the security of our nation," as Carter put it before his departure for Vienna. It was a somewhat defensive theme, intended to refute the accusation made by Jackson and others that Carter was a naïve and sentimental enthusiast of arms control for its own sake. Finally, by evoking the memory of Harry Truman, Carter seemed to be reaching out, in a time of his own political travail, for a consoling comparison with another president who had been beleaguered in office but was highly esteemed in retrospect; a president who had stood up effectively to the Russians despite widespread unpopularity among the American people and congressional doubts about his statesmanship. So stung was Carter by Jackson's denunciation of him as a latter-day Neville Chamberlain that he ordered no umbrellas on his arrival in Vienna, where it was raining. "I'd rather drown than carry an umbrella," he said.

The Last Compromise

Even as Carter took off across the Atlantic, the document that he and Brezhnev were to sign was still in the final stages of preparation in Geneva. There the permanent Soviet and American SALT delegations had been working virtually nonstop for years, but with redoubled urgency since the White House and Kremlin announced agreement in principle five weeks before. A host of drafting and definitional problems kept the negotiators in meetings that often ran until the small hours of the morning. With the deadline of the June 18 signing date approaching, the full delegations had come together twenty times in the last ten days. The final half dozen sticking points were, or should have been, as minor and as readily solvable as they were complex and esoteric. But because they were the last points of contention, on which concession or at least compromise would be required, they had become issues of principle, especially in the eyes of the military overseers of both delegations. They were invested with symbolic importance out of all proportion to their political and strategic significance. This phenomenon, a common feature throughout SALT but particularly in its later phases, made it all the harder for the negotiators to complete the document.

One problem, unresolved until the last moment, concerned whether the delineation of various restrictions on different kinds of cruise missiles should be spelled out in the main text of the agreement or in the accompanying apparatus of footnotes, the so-called agreed statements and common understandings. This was the last twitch in what had often seemed like a life-and-death struggle between the Soviet and American military over the treatment in SALT of a weapon that represented the most conspicuous American technological advantage. Even though the footnotes were to have exactly the same legal force as the main text, the Joint Chiefs of Staff back in Washington made a last stand on this drafting detail. The Chiefs were concerned that whatever the validity of the footnotes, they might seem less binding than clauses in the main text. As a matter of political appearances, definitions contained in the footnotes might seem somehow incidental to the agreement itself, in a way that the Soviets could exploit later as they tried to stretch the scope of SALT's restrictions on cruise missiles in the next round of talks, SALT III. Therefore the Chiefs wanted the text proper—and not "some goddamn stapled-on throw-away," as one military official put it—to stipulate that the restrictions in the long-term treaty applied only to one form of cruise missile (air-launched) and not to others (ground-launched and sea-launched). Another problem involved the treaty language used to define a certain refinement of a multiple-warhead missile test that the Soviets had conducted in the final months of the negotiations but that they had already agreed would not be allowed under SALT II.* Here the American military and intelligence communities wanted a precise definition while the Soviets wanted a general one. The more precise the definition, the easier it would be for the U.S. to claim it was entitled to intercept electronic test data in order to monitor Soviet compliance with this particular provision of SALT—and thus the less code the Soviets might be allowed to use in transmitting those data. It was a matter on which the Soviet General Staff felt just as strongly, and held out just as stubbornly, as the U.S. Joint Chiefs did on the last-minute drafting details concerning cruise missiles. And the solution was a classic SALT trade-off: the U.S. got its way on where the treaty delineated restrictions on cruise missiles, and the Soviets got their way on a general definition of the prohibited missile test.

That compromise fell into place on Wednesday, June 13, the day before Carter's departure from Washington. Other wrangles over treaty language and an exact count of what was to be covered by SALT kept the negotiators hard at it until three o'clock the next morning. When they had finally finished, the weary chief negotia-

---

*The test in question entailed "release simulations," explained in Chapter 14.

tors, Ralph Earle and Victor Karpov, opened a bottle of champagne, toasted each other, and went home to bed. For some of their colleagues, however, a new round of tedious work could only just now begin. The entire agreement had to be typed in four versions: an English original with the United States named first at every mention of the two countries, an English *alternat* with the Soviet Union named first, a Russian original, and a Russian *alternat.* Thus neither side would enjoy even the most symbolic primacy in either language. For the Soviet delegation, typing the two Russian-language versions was a tedious task, to be accomplished on old-fashioned manual typewriters and coarse, red-bordered treaty paper as unwieldy as cardboard. A single typographical error meant starting a page over. The job of typing the two English versions was easier for the American delegation, since it had the benefit of a modern word-processing machine. Editing and correcting could be done instantaneously on a cathode-ray-tube screen. Thursday evening Earle and Karpov met again at the American SALT headquarters to initial each page of all four versions—nearly 300 pages in all. Then, in the standard concluding ritual at such occasions, they exchanged pens and shook hands, to the applause of the assembled Soviet negotiators and virtually the entire staff of the American delegation, including secretaries, translators and communications specialists. General Rowny was there and joined in the applause, though with noticeably less enthusiasm than his colleagues. At about that time, Secretary of State Cyrus Vance, en route to Vienna aboard Air Force One, was talking to reporters in the back of the plane and called Earle and his fellow negotiators the "unsung heroes" of SALT.

The next day, Friday, Rowny flew back to the U.S., while Earle and other members of the delegation flew to Vienna. A representative of the State Department was assigned to hand-carry the document. He did so in a nondescript black attaché case without any official markings on it. As the group prepared to board an Austrian Airlines DC-9 at Geneva airport, he placed the case on a conveyor belt at a security check for hand luggage. Other passengers for the flight crowded behind him, and there emerged from the X-ray machine four nearly identical briefcases. In some anxiety, the State Department officer was not able to open the lock on the case and check the contents until he was already on board. Only then was he absolutely sure he was still carrying the SALT II document.

High-Level Ailments

During the previous two and a half years of bickering between his administration and the Soviet leadership, Carter had said from time to time that "if only I could get my hands" on Brezhnev, it would surely do some good. The President had for a long time nurtured the conviction that much of the bad blood between Washington and Moscow could be cured by personal diplomacy. He had been confident that the seemingly insurmountable obstacles of SALT would fall away if only he and Brezhnev could sit down and reason together, look each other in the eye and talk man to man about the problems of war and peace. Brezhnev was having none of that. He and his colleagues in the Soviet leadership were deeply suspicious of Carter in his guise as a political faith healer. They had resisted a meeting with him until they were sure that the centerpiece of the event, SALT II, would be ready for signature. In addition to mistrusting an American politician they saw as disconcertingly naïve, the Soviets were concerned about the unpredictability and fragility of their own man. Brezhnev was seventy-two years old. Over the years he had eaten too much starchy food, smoked too many cigarettes, drunk too much vodka and undergone too much stress. Now he suffered from a variety of chronic respiratory, circulatory and neurological ailments that had slurred his speech, slowed his movement and drained his energy. He had his bad days and his good days. No one knew in advance whether his four-day meeting with Carter would find him up or down. During the visit of French President Giscard to Moscow two months before, Brezhnev had barely been able to conduct his side of the conversation. He seemed to have bounced back somewhat a few weeks later when Yugoslavia's Josip Broz Tito—fourteen years his senior but considerably more vigorous—had come to call. Brezhnev made a perfunctory trip to Budapest for talks with the Hungarian leader János Kádár two weeks before the Vienna summit. The purpose appeared to be, as much as anything, to show the world he was still fit to travel. Many observers seemed less interested in what Brezhnev said in Budapest than in the difficulty with which he said it. Ambassadors in a receiving line compared notes afterward on his flaccid handshake and the shuffle with which he mounted a speaker's platform. Brezhnev's public appearances were rapidly becoming opportunities to examine the patient.

The very site of the Soviet-American summit was, in effect, a medical dispensation for the Russian leader. Since Richard Nixon had traveled to Moscow in 1974 and Gerald Ford to Vladivostok later that same year, protocol required that this time the American president play host. But, as Ambassador Anatoly Dobrynin had explained to Secretary of State Vance in arranging the summit, Brezhnev's doctors and colleagues on the Politburo worried that "the long journey" of a transatlantic flight might be too much for him. The agenda for the Vienna meeting was kept as flexible as possible to allow Brezhnev maximum time for naps and ministrations by the doctors in his entourage. Now that Carter's chance to "get my hands on Brezhnev" had finally arrived, the American officials stage-managing the summit and fine-tuning its atmospherics decided to minimize all reference in arrival statements, toasts and communiqués to "personal diplomacy." As one of the summit planners put it bluntly, "There's no point in stressing the personal relationship with a guy who is on his last legs. Better to pitch this thing so that we are looking forward, beyond Brezhnev, to binding agreements and institutionalized contacts."

That suited the Soviets fine, although for different reasons. They were looking beyond Carter, whose political health they saw to be at least as precarious as Brezhnev's physical health. "We read closely what is written in your country about the condition of Carter's presidency," said a Soviet official at the time of the summit." We follow the polls. We read all your eminent columnists who write about the political ineptitude of this White House. We watch the House of Representatives threaten to liquidate the Panama Canal treaties. We see the administration, despite all its commitment to arms control, try to ingratiate itself to the military-industrial complex by deploying new weapons. We see it trying to ingratiate itself to cold warriors. We see all this and we have to wonder. Of course, your system is not a complete mystery to us. We have been studying it for a long time. And besides, it is not without precedent for us to deal with a U.S. president who is politically wounded."

The intended comparison—to Richard Nixon in 1974—was as far-fetched as it was unsubtle. Whatever Jimmy Carter's political tribulations, they were hardly comparable to those facing Nixon at the time of his 1974 summit meeting with Brezhnev in Moscow, when he was in the throes of Watergate, only weeks away from resignation. Carter was under attack for using the powers of his office ineffectively—not for abusing them. Many of the same polls that showed Carter in a deep trough of unpopularity also showed him rated highly for integrity and honesty. But what the Soviets cared about was whether the man whose signature would go alongside Brezhnev's on SALT II could manage the politics of ratification, and on that score there was legitimate doubt in Moscow as well as in Washington. If SALT II was destined to be scuttled by the Senate, the Soviets would do their best to make it look as though the warmongering forces of capitalism had triumphed over those of détente and peaceful coexistence. They would undoubtedly try to make use of the defeat of SALT II in their propaganda. But there would be no way they could avoid sharing with the Carter administration at least some of the embarrassment and the blame in the eyes of what the Russians themselves like to call "world public opinion." The Soviets saw that risk clearly as they prepared for the summit, and possibly one reason they contrived to hold the meeting on neutral ground—quite aside from minimizing the strain on Brezhnev's shaky health—was to avoid the additional political hazard of sending their leader all the way to the U.S. to sign a document that might end up on the trash heap of history. Brezhnev could be forgiven for not wanting to preside in person over the opening of a congressional and public debate in which, even before the ink was dry on the treaty, American politicians, especially presidential candidates, might use the document as a pretext to denounce Soviet repression, militarism and adventurism.

From the beginning of the summit, the physical and political conditions of Brezhnev and Carter respectively were much on everyone's mind. At the first press conference given by Carter's press secretary, Jody Powell, and the chief Soviet spokesman, Leonid Zamyatin, a British television reporter asked about Brezhnev's health. With unconcealed annoyance, Zamyatin replied, "The question is irrelevant. It has nothing to do with the subject matter of our press conference. But still, I will answer. Our president, Leonid Brezhnev, is performing a tremendous volume of state and party work in our country. And foreign policy activities occupy a considerable part of the work he is doing. Here in Vienna you have an opportunity to observe him at work, and this work naturally requires good health. He has no complaints about his health. Reports in your press on this matter are nothing but speculations."

An alert and reciprocity-minded *Izvestia* correspondent leapt to his feet and asked Powell, "Would you mind telling us about the political health of President Carter?"

"About the same," quipped Powell.

Carter did nothing to downplay his own physical vigor in deference to the ailing Brezhnev. He arose early the first morning to jog,
under the watchful eyes of both Secret Service bodyguards and television cameramen. Later that day the President bounded exuberantly
up a long staircase to a gilded anteroom of the Hofburg, the Imperial
Palace of the Habsburgs, for his first meeting with Brezhnev. They
were to pay a joint courtesy call on the host of the summit, Austrian
President Rudolf Kirchschläger. Brezhnev arrived five minutes later
by elevator, looking rheumy, weary and awkward, clutching his spec-
tacles as though they might hold him up if he lost his balance. But
when the photographers pressed forward and asked for handshakes,
Brezhnev seemed to come alive. He responded with a resounding
"Da!" to Carter's opening comment that it had taken them too long
to get together. They walked side by side down a red carpet and
chatted for a few minutes in the same brocaded chairs where Kennedy
and Khrushchev had sat in 1961.

Brezhnev said to Carter, in an obvious reference to the task of arms
control, "God will not forgive us if we fail." The Soviet foreign minister, Andrei Gromyko, sought to make light of his leader's un-Marxian
reference to the deity. Pointing skyward, Gromyko cracked, "He's
that fellow up there." Brezhnev's spokesman Zamyatin later attempted to expunge the religious lapse from the record. What the
General Secretary of the Central Committee of the Communist Party
and Chairman of the Supreme Soviet of the U.S.S.R. had actually said,
explained Zamyatin, was, "Future generations will not forgive us if we
fail." Another Soviet official admitted that Brezhnev had indeed referred to God, but he had done so "simply because he wanted to
express his commitment to SALT in terms that Carter would understand and identify with."

The Last Concession

In all, the two men spent nearly fifteen hours in formal sessions and
working dinners as well as one private, ninety-minute discussion with
only their interpreters present.* For the most part, Brezhnev stuck to

---

*One of the most sensitive subjects of the private session concerned a third country,
Turkey, and the U-2 spy plane, an aircraft that had played such a dramatic and disrup-
tive role when Dwight Eisenhower and Khrushchev met in 1960 at the Paris summit.
Until 1979, the U.S. had relied heavily on intelligence collection posts in Iran to monitor
Soviet missile launches from a test site nearby in Kazakhstan. Having lost the use of the
Iranian facilities with the downfall of the Shah, Washington asked Ankara for permission

reading prepared statements, relying frequently on interjections from his foreign minister, Gromyko, and defense minister, Dimitri Ustinov. There was a fourth member of the Politburo in attendance, Party Secretary Konstantin Chernyenko, making it the most high-powered Soviet delegation at any postwar summit. Also for the first time since World War II, the defense ministers and chiefs of staff of the two sides (Ustinov, Defense Secretary Harold Brown, Marshal Nikolai Ogarkov and JCS Chairman General David Jones) held a meeting of their own. The talks were wide-ranging and studded with disagreement—on human rights, China, the Middle East, and southern Africa.

The handling of the principal item of business, SALT, had been carefully scripted in advance. Still, there was at least one unpleasant surprise. It concerned the Backfire bomber and the form of Soviet assurances restricting its range and rate of production. The Backfire, like the cruise missile, had been a sticking point in SALT for more than four years, and for much the same reason. Its status under SALT—i.e., whether it was a strategic, or intercontinental, weapon—was ambiguous. It had strategic potential but was deployed for shorter range use. As previously arranged, Brezhnev read aloud, and then gave Carter, a statement declaring that the U.S.S.R. "does not intend to give this airplane a capability of operating at intercontinental distances." Carter said he would be signing SALT on the basis of his understanding that this Soviet statement, while couched in terms of intent, was a binding assurance and that any significant increase in the range and payload of the bomber would be inconsistent with the agreement as a whole. Brezhnev's statement on Backfire also contained a promise to freeze production at "the present rate," but without a specific number. The U.S. had come prepared to respond with its own statement identifying the missing number as thirty—a figure the Soviets did not dispute but did not want to volunteer. This rather contorted procedure, involving a Soviet lacuna filled by an American "unilateral interpretation," in turn confirmed by Soviet "non-contradiction," had for a long time been a curious but common feature of the negotiating

---

to conduct U-2 flights along the Turkish-Soviet border in order to supplement data that U.S. intelligence was already intercepting at its ground stations in Turkey. The Turks replied that they would permit U-2s into their airspace only if the Kremlin did not object. When Carter raised the matter with Brezhnev, the Soviet leader's response was noncommittal, but he knew that the loss of the Iranian stations had impaired the U.S.'s ability to verify Soviet compliance with some provisions of SALT II and that the degree of senatorial confidence in verification could well determine whether the treaty was ratified.

ritual in SALT. In this case, however, both sides departed from the script. Carter read aloud the key passages from the prepared American written response to Brezhnev's letter, then asked for confirmation of the figure thirty. Gromyko said no answer was required to that question. As far as he was concerned, the ritual was over. The wrangle continued until the next day, when Carter delivered a table-pounding lecture, saying that he had come to Vienna "in good faith" believing that the Backfire issue had been resolved in advance and that for the Soviets to renege now would be to jeopardize the summit. Vance and Gromyko got into a sharp exchange over who was changing signals on whom. Finally Brezhnev intervened. Throwing up his hands in a gesture meant to convey both impatience and magnanimity, he stated, for the record, that, yes, the reference in the Soviet letter to "present rate" of production meant thirty. "There," concluded Brezhnev, "another Soviet concession!"

Brezhnev Warns the Senate

The accommodation on Backfire was one of a number of provisions that Henry Jackson and other critics of SALT in the Senate were sure to challenge and, if possible, force back to the negotiating table through amendments to the treaty. Article XVIII of the document declared, "Each party may propose amendments to this treaty." But amendments would then have to be agreed to by the other side. In the weeks leading up to the summit, there had been intense speculation in Washington over what amendments, if any, the Soviets might accept. Pro-SALT Senators distinguished between "cosmetic amendments," that would leave the substance of the treaty intact, and "killer amendments" that would require renegotiation and very likely be tantamount to rejection. The Soviets had said repeatedly they were not going to make any further concessions, especially under pressure from politicians like Jackson whom they considered to be "enemies of détente." Most American officials and virtually all Soviet spokesmen were convinced that any Senate initiative further restricting the Backfire would be a sure-fire killer amendment. At the summit, Brezhnev made clear he was aware of, and not unsympathetic toward, Carter's political problems over SALT. "Your system is somewhat different than ours," said the Soviet leader privately. "We really don't have much doubt about the ratification process in our country." But Brezhnev made no such attempt at facetious understatement in his toast at a working dinner Sunday, the evening before the signing. Addressing himself squarely to the U.S. Senate, he said, "Of course [the treaty] is a compromise. It could not be otherwise. Each side would like some parts of the text to be somewhat different, more suitable from its own standpoint. But each side has had to yield something, taking into account the legitimate interests of the other side. Any attempt to shake this elaborate structure which has been so hard to build, to substitute something new for any of its elements, to pull it closer to one's self—would be an unprofitable exercise. The entire structure might then collapse, and that would entail grave and even dangerous consequences for our relations and for the situation in the world as a whole."

The next day Carter and Brezhnev met on a stage beneath the chandeliers of the Redoutensaal, a splendid ballroom in the Hofburg. In front of each president was a leather binder with a gold embossed seal of his country. After signing both sets of the document, the two men stood up, shook hands, and embraced, kissing each other on both cheeks in the Russian fashion. Carter's speech at the end of the ceremony was clearly intended to appeal both to Soviets of Brezhnev's generation, who had lived through World War II, and to Senators back home, who were concerned about reconciling arms control with national defense: "I, as President, am entrusted with the security of the United States of America. I would never take any action that would jeopardize that sacred trust. President Brezhnev, you and I both have children and grandchildren and we want them to live, and to live in peace. We have both worked hard to give our own and our nations' children that security. We realize that no one treaty, no one meeting can guarantee the future safety of our nations. In the end, peace can be won only if we have pursued it and struggled tenaciously to keep the peace all along. Yet this fight for peace has often seemed the most difficult victory to win."

Carter then went straight to Vienna airport, where he boarded Air Force One for the flight home, there to address a more skeptical audience than the assembly of dignitaries in the Redoutensaal. Within two hours after touching down at Andrews Air Force Base, Carter appeared before a joint session of Congress to report on the summit —and to campaign for the ratification of SALT II. He, like his opponents, had already been waging the battle for many months, but now, for the first time, he had a public document to defend—and they had one to attack.

Poker at the Chessboard

Arms control negotiations and the larger diplomatic and strategic enterprise of which they are a part have invited comparison to games of all sorts. In the nuclear age, to think about war in terms of games is to make it easier to think about at all. Game theory, as applied to the politics of nuclear weaponry, is in part a hedge against the fundamental horror of the subject. Thinking about how to avoid war requires pondering the way a war would come about, what winning—or losing—it would mean, "how it would play out." The clichés of SALT, therefore, are liberally interspersed with colloquialisms from games of skill and chance. Participants in the process have often been called, and have often called themselves, players. Poker is a favorite metaphor of SALT: both sides have bluffed, upped the ante, raised the stakes, and, from time to time, tipped their hands. But by and large, the players themselves have most preferred that SALT be compared to chess. Chess pieces move solely at the command of human intelligence—they are not shuffled, they do not fall where they may. A chess player can be lucky only if his opponent makes a stupid mistake, unnecessarily endangering a piece or overlooking an opportunity. The intellectual exercise involves the continued reassessment of the correlation of forces on both sides. There must be constant anticipation and planning for contingencies. The outcome may well depend on how many moves in advance a player is thinking when he touches a piece.

Surveying the agenda for what would prove to be nearly another full year of SALT II, Paul Warnke, Ralph Earle's predecessor as chief negotiator, remarked in the summer of 1978 that the negotiating table was like a chess board at the beginning of the endgame—the phase when both players have been reduced to a small but comparable number of pieces. Each surviving piece becomes more valuable, its sacrifice more painful, stratagems to protect it more elaborate, and calculations over whether to trade, say, a bishop for a knight become more complex, more fraught with risk. Relaxing and reminiscing the evening after his return from Vienna, Carter's special assistant for national security affairs, Zbigniew Brzezinski, picked up the metaphor, likening the summit to "the last moves of the endgame."

Only up to a point, however, does SALT lend itself to comparisons to chess or poker or any other game. The defect of any such analogy is that in these games, the object is victory. A chess player is trying to

checkmate his opponent, a poker player to win the whole pot—a
warrior to defeat his enemy. In SALT, however, the object has not
been for one player to beat the other. While taking some pawns along
the way perhaps limiting the freedom of movement of the other's
queen, neither side has sought to check the other's king—that is, to
imperil its self-perceived vital national interest. To play to win would
be to seek "unilateral advantage" or "strategic superiority." It would
be to violate the rules of parity and stability. In SALT, the object of
the game is a draw. In the endgame of SALT II, the superpowers had
been playing to a draw for nearly a year. But the game itself had been
going on much longer.

2 The History and the Inheritance

Negotiations between the United States and the Soviet Union on the limitation of strategic arms predated Jimmy Carter's assumption of the presidency by a full decade. When Llewellyn Thompson, the ambassador to Moscow in the Johnson administration, began laying the ground for those negotiations in early 1967, Carter was running his family's peanut business and recovering from his defeat the year before by a segregationist restaurateur, Lester Maddox, in the Georgia Democratic gubernatorial primary. During the next ten years, while Carter was engineering his spectacular political rise, SALT was becoming an institution of Soviet-American relations. Dean Rusk, who was secretary of state in the first days of SALT, predicted irreverently but by no means disapprovingly that the negotiations would become "history's longest permanent floating crap game." Ten years later, at the outset of the debate in Washington over ratification of SALT II, the State Department issued a series of pronouncements echoing Rusk's observation in more anodyne terms: SALT, said its proponents and functionaries in Foggy Bottom, is an ongoing process. Or as Secretary of Defense Harold Brown put it in a speech in April 1979, "SALT has become part of the fabric of international relationships." The "T" in the familiar acronym* stands for "Talks," not for "Treaty." The talks

---

* The etymology of SALT, as explained by John Newhouse in his history of the first round of the negotiations (*Cold Dawn: The Story of SALT,* Holt, Rinehart & Winston, 1973), goes back to 1968, when the Central Intelligence Agency was looking for a convenient heading under which to file the sudden inundation of material on the subject. The man who coined the acronym was Robert Martin, an official in the Bureau of Politico-Military Affairs at the State Department. His own bosses did not like the term. They found it too cute. So did the Arms Control and Disarmament Agency

went on and on, producing, if they went well, agreements along the way; but even if they went badly, they provided a forum in which Soviet and American officials sat across from each other at long tables, sipped mineral water and discussed military matters that used to be the stuff that spies were paid and shot for. So in that sense, even SALT *dis*agreements were often salutary. The process was the product. There emerged SALT bureaucrats in Washington and SALT apparatchiks in Moscow. SALT became a career in the civil service. The process acquired an institutional mass that some political innovators might have considered dead weight but that served as a kind of deepwater anchor in Soviet-American relations.

The formal opening of the negotiations was delayed in 1968 by the Soviet invasion of Czechoslovakia, which coincided with a presidential campaign in the U.S. Lyndon Johnson was a lame duck, and Leonid Brezhnev was denounced as an international villain. Between them, they could not muster the political wherewithal for formal, full-scale negotiations. Johnson's successor, Richard Nixon, moved slowly at first. He circled the idea of SALT cautiously, indeed mistrustfully, before deciding to make it his own. But when he moved it was with dispatch and skill. Hoping that SALT would encourage Soviet cooperation in other areas, Nixon and his national security adviser, Henry Kissinger, initiated SALT I in a series of meetings with Ambassador Anatoly Dobrynin, the Soviet envoy in Washington with whom officials of the Johnson administration had also been trying to get the talks started. Thus SALT was born in the so-called back channel, the informal but often crucial tête-à-têtes between Dobrynin and a series of senior American officials. In November 1969, what might be called the "front channel" came into being as the two sides' permanent delegations buckled down to work. The negotiators migrated between Helsinki and Vienna, then settled down in Geneva. The American chief was Gerard Smith. Like many of the Americans who would hold key jobs in the SALT apparatus for the next decade, Smith was a lawyer. Because the enterprise was bound to draw so much from the theory and practice of the law—after all, the superpowers were to enter into a contract—attorneys soon found their place among the politicians, diplomats and academicians who made and carried out policy in SALT. Smith's Soviet counterpart, Vladimir Semyonov, was a deputy foreign

---

(ACDA). But the CIA, in one of its earliest skirmishes with State and ACDA over SALT, fought the issue up to a high-level interagency committee and won.

minister and a veteran of tough dealings with Americans: he had been a senior Soviet political adviser in Berlin during the blockade of 1949. He was known to be an advocate both of peaceful coexistence with the U.S. and of a vigorous Soviet strategic weapons program.

The business between Smith and Semyonov and their fellow delegates quickly assumed a life of its own. SALT survived the American mining of Haiphong harbor in 1972 and the Watergate crisis of 1974. Despite those and lesser traumas, the strategic arms limitation talkers kept talking. They were insulated in part by the complex and esoteric nature of their subject. In the first years, too few politicians understood what the talkers were talking about for SALT to be an inviting topic of public debate. That would change somewhat by 1976, when the policy of détente which SALT had helped spawn was in disfavor. But while the political environment became less hospitable, the institution of SALT had grown hardier, and it had produced a track record: a treaty, an interim agreement, and a framework for SALT II.

Another factor that gave SALT its staying power was the durability of the Soviet leadership. In those ten years since the dawn of SALT, there had been three changes of leadership in the White House—and none in the Kremlin. When the Carter administration inherited SALT, it found itself dealing with virtually the same collective leadership in Moscow that Lyndon Johnson had instructed Llewellyn Thompson to approach in 1967. And it was a collective leadership almost obsessed with preserving the continuity of the negotiations in the face of political change.

Defense and Offense

SALT I yielded two documents, both signed by Nixon and Brezhnev at the Moscow Summit of May 1972. The first was a treaty limiting the defensive capability of each side. The U.S. and the Soviet Union agreed to restrict their antiballistic missile (ABM) defenses to two sites —one protecting the national capital, the other protecting a single cluster, or field, of silo launchers for intercontinental ballistic missiles.* The treaty was to be of unlimited duration and reviewed at five-year intervals. At the time, some observers found the agreement a bit cockeyed: here were the superpowers solemnly undertaking not to

---

*In 1974, Richard Nixon and Leonid Brezhnev agreed to cut back to one ABM site on each side.

defend themselves. In fact, they were decreasing the chances that
they would attack each other. The ABM treaty was a momentous
achievement. It recognized that, in the games strategists play, the best
offense is a good defense. If one side is able to protect itself against the
threat of a nuclear strike, that side is emboldened to throw its
geopolitical weight around, and the other side is spurred to come up
with new and better offensive weapons while at the same time improving its own defenses. The proliferation of defensive weapons,
therefore, is just as much anathema to arms control as the proliferation
of offensive ones. In the jargon of the arms controllers, ABM was
"destabilizing" for a number of reasons: it would promote competition
in defensive arms, with each side seeking to match if not surpass the
other's ABM; it would promote competition in offensive arms, with
each seeking the capability to "beat" the other's ABM; and it could
lead to the illusion or even the fact of overall strategic superiority. And
superiority, either real or imagined, could be highly destabilizing by
itself, especially, in the American view, if it was the U.S.S.R. that
achieved superiority. One goal of arms control is an absence of superiority usually described as parity. In the psychology of the relationship
between the U.S. and the Soviet Union, parity means a delicate balance of anxiety. The reciprocal self-denial of ABM in 1972 meant, to
its American proponents, that each side was willingly exposing itself
to the retaliatory deterrent of the other. Such mutual hostageship
made it theoretically inconceivable that either side would contem-
plate a preemptive strike—a state of affairs that fit most definitions of
strategic stability. The U.S. had a significant technological lead over
the Soviet Union in the development of ABM, and the U.S. has always
been better able to get the Soviets to accept "mutual" restraints on a
weapon system or an area of technology that is an American specialty.
Much more than the Soviets, the U.S. over the years has demonstrated
a willingness to forgo a specific advantage for the sake of the general
cause of parity and stability. The partisans of SALT have considered
this self-restraint a credit to American political wisdom and far-sight-
edness. The critics have often seen it as the most egregious folly.

The second document Nixon and Brezhnev signed in Moscow was
the "Interim Agreement Between the United States of America and
the Soviet Union of Soviet Socialist Republics on Certain Measures
with Respect to the Limitation of Strategic Offensive Arms." As the
rather convoluted, circumspect heading suggests, this was a pact of
limited scope and duration. It froze for five years, until October 1977,

each side's launchers for intercontinental ballistic missiles (ICBMs) and submarine-launched ballistic missiles (SLBMs). An accompanying protocol allowed each side to deploy a limited number of additional SLBMs as long as an older ICBM or SLBM was taken out of service for every new SLBM added. "Launcher" in the context of ICBMs meant fixed-site, underground silos; for SLBMs, it meant missile-firing tubes aboard submarines. The negotiators had agreed to count launchers and submarines rather than missiles, since the aerial reconnaissance of each side can keep track of the other's silos and boats but not necessarily of its individual rockets.

The interim agreement contains no figures for the number of ICBMs to be frozen. The Soviets stubbornly refused to divulge those figures. They took the position that the U.S. must rely on its own devices and its own data for counting weapons on *both* sides. Early in SALT, the U.S. pressed the Russians to provide a "data base," or inventory of the weapons to be counted and constrained. By laying out such information, the Soviets would be building public and official confidence in the SALT process—a goal sufficiently worthy to merit its very own acronym: a data base would be a CBM, or confidence-building measure. For years the Soviets remained unimpressed. SALT obliged them, they said, to stay within certain limits—not to make it easier for the U.S. to maintain quality control on its intelligence service. Besides, continued the Russians with straight faces, they were not demanding that the U.S. officially provide them with data about American weapons. The Soviet position was almost charming in its absurdity. Not only was the U.S. routinely providing facts and figures at the negotiating table, but the American data base is practically a matter of public record. All that Russian experts had to do to monitor American military developments was read the annual posture statement by the secretary of defense, the *Congressional Record, Aviation Week and Space Technology* and a variety of other publications. There were, as the U.S. negotiators delicately pointed out in reply, "informational asymmetries" between the Soviet and American systems.

If the dearth of numbers in the interim agreement was troublesome, the missing numbers themselves proved even more so because they were unequal. The freeze on offensive weapons left the Soviets with approximately 2,400 missile launchers and the U.S. with 1,700. The Nixon administration argued that giving the Soviets a 40 percent advantage in number of launchers was justified on at least six grounds. First, the U.S.S.R. was actively deploying new missiles when the freeze went into effect, while the U.S. was not, so the freeze stopped the Soviet program without immediately affecting the American one. Second, the U.S. had more and better heavy bombers than the Soviets, and bombers were left untouched by SALT I. Third, while the Russians were allowed more ICBMs, the U.S. had more accurate and reliable ones. Fourth, American submarines and the missiles launched from them were superior in every respect to the Russian ones. Fifth, the U.S. had the benefit of its own and allied military bases around the periphery of the U.S.S.R. And sixth, the U.S. was far ahead in the technology of multiple independently targetable reentry vehicles, or MIRVs; so while the Russians had more launchers, the U.S. had more warheads to launch.

These six points made a compelling case when SALT I was presented to the U.S. Congress. The agreements were approved by a wide margin. But so was a resolution, sponsored by Senator Henry Jackson of Washington, insisting that future agreements embody the principle of numerical parity—that they contain what were often referred to as equal aggregates.

Never again would Jackson or many of his colleagues support a pact that allowed the Russians more launchers in a given category than the U.S. could have. Jackson was not entirely swayed by the argument of offsetting qualitative and quantitative advantages. He knew that it has been a chronic fallacy of American strategic policy to assume that Yankee ingenuity and free enterprise bestow upon the U.S. a permanent technological superiority over the notoriously inefficient Communist system. SALT I was negotiated, signed and ratified on the widespread assumption that the U.S. had not only a giant head start in MIRV technology but a virtual monopoly on MIRV deployment for some time to come.

Enter Heavies

That complacency was rudely shaken in the summer of 1973, barely a year after SALT I was signed. The Soviets began flight testing a new generation of ICBMs—all with payloads larger than anything the U.S. had and some with multiple warheads. In one fell swoop, the Soviets had nullified a major justification for the U.S.'s acceptance of unequal aggregates in SALT I. The MIRVing of Soviet land-based missiles threw into stark relief another inequity: not only did the interim agreement leave the U.S.S.R. with more ICBMs in general than the U.S.—it left the U.S.S.R. with an advantage in an especially threatening category of ICBMs. These were the so-called heavy or modern large ballistic missiles (MLBMs). "Heavies" have a history of their own that is worth recounting, since their monstrous bulk has cast a long shadow over SALT II.

Back in the early 1960s, the U.S. relied on a heavy missile of its own. It was called, aptly, the Titan, and it could carry a warhead of more than five megatons—the equivalent of five million tons of TNT. Then American defense planners, led by Robert McNamara, decided that Titan made no strategic sense. It was too crude. It was an objectification of the forbidding word "overkill." Titan's self-contained inertial guidance system was an improvement on the navigational equipment of earlier missiles, which had to be guided by radio commands from earth, but Titan's inertial guidance was still fairly primitive and did not provide a high degree of accuracy. Therefore, in order to be sure of destroying a target, Titan had to destroy much of the surrounding countryside and population as well. Also, Titan was propelled by liquid fuel, against which U.S. military planners have nurtured a traditional bias. Volatile, bulky and corrosive, liquid fuel can be difficult and dangerous to store, and therefore liquid-fueled rockets can be difficult and dangerous to move around the country for testing and redeployment.

McNamara decided that what America needed as the backbone of its deterrent was a smaller, cheaper, more reliable, more versatile, more accurate solid-fueled missile that could threaten the Soviet Union with pinpoint retaliatory strikes against a variety of targets, civilian and military. The result was Minuteman. It, too, was aptly named: spare, compact, quick, efficient—a sharpshooter's rifle rather than a blunderbuss. The largest version of Minuteman weighs only about one fifth as much as Titan, and its payload is only half as big. As American strategy shifted from "massive retaliation" to "flexible response," and as American technology became more sophisticated, the land-based deterrent evolved, as a matter of policy, from liquid-fueled "heavy" to solid-fueled "light" ICBMs. Hence the composition of the U.S. ICBM force: 54 obsolete, single-warhead Titans, 450 smaller but much more accurate single-warhead Minutemen, and 550 MIRVed versions, each with three warheads. These made up the land-based leg of the so-called strategic triad and were considered more than adequate in tandem with the other two legs—the B-52 heavy bombers of the Strategic Air Command and the U.S. Navy's fleet of missile-launching nuclear submarines. McNamara and his colleagues defined adequacy in terms of "assured destruction"—the damage that the American deterrent could inflict on the Soviet Union even after the U.S. had absorbed a Soviet first strike. Strategists somewhat arbitrarily determined an adequate level of assured destruction as about half the industrial capacity and a fourth of the population of the U.S.S.R. If the Soviet leaders were certain that enough of the American triad would survive a Soviet attack to retaliate with such awesome vengeance, American officials presumed the Russians would never start a war. American strategic doctrine was preeminently one of deterrence. It was a cornerstone of American policy that the U.S. would never attack first. There was, therefore, no need for American ICBMs to have the additional capability of disarming the Soviet Union in a preemptive strike. Once a thousand Minutemen were in place, the U.S. turned what additional resources it chose to expend to enhancing the other two legs of the triad—the bombers and submarines.

But the Russians, meanwhile, were developing a different sort of mix in their own triad, and it suggested a different strategic doctrine. They concentrated on their land-based missiles much more than on their airborne and sea-going forces, partly because it is easier to build and work with big machines on solid ground than in the air or under water. And in their ICBM program, they seemed to be moving in the opposite direction from the U.S.—toward heavy missiles. On the eve of SALT they deployed a liquid-fueled behemoth, the SS-9 (the prefix stands simply for surface-to-surface), which the weapons watchers of the North Atlantic Treaty Organization code-named "Scarp." This huge missile took away the breath of the assembled Western military attachés when it rolled through Red Square in a parade marking the fiftieth anniversary of the Russian Revolution in November 1967. It was nearly twice as long as Minuteman. Its single warhead was in the 25-megaton range, five times that of Titan and more than twelve times that of Minuteman.

As U.S. experts watched the SS-9 rumble into deployment, their puzzlement gave way to a deep worry. The thing seemed suited for none of the strictly deterrent assignments in the American play book. Later the U.S. observed the Soviets test the SS-9 with a primitive forerunner of MIRVs. The "triplet" of dummy warheads fell too far apart to suggest they were meant to wipe out one city but too close together to destroy three cities. The targeting pattern, or "footprint," suggested instead that the SS-9 was learning to stamp out one of the

Minuteman fields spread out over many square miles in North Dakota, South Dakota, Montana, Missouri and Wyoming. Many analysts at the Pentagon and elsewhere deduced some very bad news from this piece of evidence. The SS-9, they concluded in dismay, was a *counterforce* rather than a retaliatory weapon; its mission, in other words, may have been to knock out the American land-based ICBM force in a preemptive strike. If that was true, then it meant the Soviets did not share the American assumption that nuclear war was unwinnable; Soviet strategic thinking was not a mirror image of American faith in mutual assured destruction; the Soviets were not as preoccupied as the Americans were with deterrence; the Kremlin was pursuing, at least contingently, a *war-winning* strategy, which Russian military theorists had been propounding for years, and war winning, at least in some imaginable contingencies, could mean war starting.

Minuteman Feels Vulnerable

American defense planners began concocting worst-case scenarios with renewed urgency. A MIRVed heavy ICBM force might someday give the Soviets the hypothetical capability of wiping out the American land-based deterrent in one fell swoop and then, in effect, daring the U.S. to retaliate with its bombers, which might not be able to penetrate Soviet air defenses, and with its submarines, only some of which might be within striking distance of their targets. At that stage in the scenario, the U.S. would have suffered only a surgical nuclear strike against its Minuteman fields in the hinterlands. The civilian population would be largely unhurt—but it would be excruciatingly vulnerable to a follow-up Soviet attack, this time aimed at cities. What would an American President do in such a dilemma? Would he order the two surviving legs of the triad to kick back at the U.S.S.R. in order to vindicate Robert McNamara's calculations of a few decades before? To do so would be to commit national suicide. More likely, according to the conjurers of the nightmare, an American President would save his country by submitting to a Soviet ultimatum. There was a slightly less apocalyptic version of the scenario whereby the Kremlin, exploiting some international crisis, would threaten to knock out the Minuteman deterrent, and the U.S., knowing that there were MIRVed heavies behind the threat, would submit to blackmail rather than call the Soviets' bluff.

It should be stressed that these dark imaginings did not haunt—or at least did not seem credible to—all the American strategists who contemplated the SS-9 in the late sixties and early seventies. A putative aspiration to a war-winning capability was by no means the only explanation for the Russians' giant missiles. On the contrary, Scarp's mammoth size could be seen as a function of Soviet technological inferiority, rather than a harbinger of Soviet strategic superiority. Arguably, the U.S.S.R. was impelled toward a reliance on heavy missiles by the backwardness of its propulsion and guidance systems. The less accurate a warhead, or cluster of warheads, the bigger it has to be to destroy its target. Also, the Soviets should not necessarily be expected to believe official American protestations that the U.S. would never strike first. Soviet planners had to make sure that their own retaliatory capability would survive an American preemptive attack. Since their bombers and submarines were considerably inferior to the other side's—and since they had no "forward bases" in Mexico and Canada to match Western or pro-Western forces near their borders in Europe, Turkey and (in those days) Iran—the Soviets could argue with some logic that they needed huge payloads of nuclear explosives and huge land-based delivery systems simply to be sure that they would have something to hurl back at the U.S. after most of their launchers had been wiped out in an American first strike. Their monsters, in other words, might be creatures of deterrence that guarded the gates of the Soviet castle, not creatures of aggression that terrorized the countryside.

Nevertheless, especially as the heavies became more accurate but no less monstrous in the seventies, the Soviet ICBM program sharply focused attention on the more eschatological themes in the American strategic debate. Aside from the objective qualities of the SS-9, the supermissile acquired in the minds of many planners and commentators an almost mystical ominousness. A glowering, lumbering bully, redolent of barbarism, scornful of the refined, essentially defensive concepts that held sway in the West, choosing instead to flex raw power—the SS-9 came to symbolize Russian brutishness. It cast into doubt whether the Soviets truly accepted the twin notions of parity and mutual assured destruction that comprised much of the rationale for SALT I. The negotiations had been posited on the assumption—at least in American minds—that each side had a vested interest in the ability of the other side's deterrent to survive a first strike. The antiballistic missile treaty, the interim agreement and the entire concept of SALT were based, in American minds, on the notion that it should be impossible for either side to eliminate the retaliatory deterrent of the other. Parity was based on the equation: survivability equals stability. Conversely, vulnerability equals instability. And *perceived* vulnerability is as dangerous and destabilizing as real vulnerability, the reality of which could be tested only when a nuclear war occurred. Perceptions are all-important in strategic relations and therefore in SALT, since the weapons being deployed and controlled are meant never to be used. Credibility is the essence of both arms build-ups and arms-control measures, since one side's arms are meant to convince the other side that it cannot use its own arms without incurring catastrophic retaliation. But even in the realm of perception, credibility and other such vital abstractions, the U.S. has felt itself at a disadvantage: the long-standing American policy never to strike first has had to be coupled with the presumption that the Soviet Union *might* strike first, and that fact has always put an additional onus on SALT. The abstractions of the strategic relationship are measured in hardware, and the SS-9 was a new piece of hardware that exacerbated the American problem of reconciling a no-first-strike policy with effective deterrence while at the same time pursuing arms control; SALT would be politically viable in the U.S. only if it was perceived to be consistent with the overarching American interest in guaranteeing that a fundamentally predatory and untrustworthy Soviet Union remained in a no-win situation if it ever contemplated striking first. With the emergence of the SS-9 and the Soviet modern heavy missile program, the issue of Minuteman vulnerability—so troublesome to the negotiators and defenders of SALT II—was born.

The 1972 interim agreement did address the issue of heavy missiles, but in a way that was doubly upsetting to critics of SALT. First, the agreement banned the conversion of launchers for "light" ICBMs into ones for "modern large"—or heavy—ICBMs. That freeze left the Russians with over 300 modern heavies and the U.S. with none. "Modern" was understood by both sides to mean deployed since 1964, so the Titan was too old to qualify. Second, the agreement failed to define "light" and "heavy." This imprecision turned out to be a loophole big enough to launch an extremely powerful new Soviet missile through. The U.S. had resigned itself to the Russians' using their "heavy" allowance to replace the SS-9 with its "follow-on" or successor, the MIRVed SS-18, which carries up to ten warheads. But the Soviets were testing another, smaller but technologically more advanced and potentially more accurate, ICBM which the U.S. would dearly have liked to define as "heavy." This was the SS-19. It has six warheads—twice as many as the MIRVed version of Minuteman. The American negotiators tried to write into the agreement a definition of heavies that would have subsumed the SS-19. The Russians successfully resisted—precisely because they were protecting their SS-19 program. Later, after SALT I had been signed, the U.S. unilaterally issued its own definition, which would have categorized the SS-19 as heavy—and the Soviets simply rejected that definition.

In its handling of the heavy-ICBM issue, SALT I did its greatest political disservice to SALT II. The only unequal numerical limit carried forward from the interim agreement into the SALT II treaty would be the freeze on modern heavies, which left the Russians with about 300 and the U.S. with zero.* Recriminations over the misclassification of the SS-19 as a "light" ICBM and intramural disputes over whether the SS-19 was as big a threat as the SS-18 would haunt the deliberations in Washington until 1977. Well into 1979, Henry Jackson would cite the failure of SALT I to define "heavy" as proof that all ambiguities in SALT agreements are there for a sinister Soviet purpose, and any loophole will end up being exploited by the U.S.S.R. and regretted by the U.S.

SALT I did, however, contain a number of other features that would be important to the credibility of future SALT agreements. Article XII of the ABM treaty and Article V of the interim agreement prohibited the parties from using "deliberate concealment measures which impede verification by national technical means of compliance with the provisions." Just as each side must, in the interests of stability, willingly expose itself to the retaliatory force of the other, so, in the interests of verification, each side must also expose itself to the espionage of the other. "National technical means" refers primarily to satellite photography, remote radar and electronic eavesdropping. One reason for the cumbersome euphemism is that the signatories were, in effect, signing away a modicum of their sovereignty in order to reduce the chances that either side could cheat and get away with it. In the years to come, whenever SALT became a subject of congressional and public debate in the U.S., the critics and skeptics sounded the refrain, "No! because you can't trust the Russians." Even many supporters of SALT have worried out loud, "Yes—but remember, you

---

*The exact number of modern heavy ballistic missile launchers permitted to the Soviet Union was either 308 or 326, depending on whether eighteen launchers at the Tyuratam test facility, between the Aral Sea and Lake Balkhash, counted as operational.

can't trust the Russians." American public opinion polls revealed a profound and widespread ambivalence toward arms control agreements with the U.S.S.R.: a majority of Americans seemed to favor such pacts, but a majority also felt the Russians would cheat. SALT negotiators have therefore been under a strong political imperative to produce agreements that rely on a minimum of mutual trust and a maximum of confidence in American "national technical means" to monitor Soviet compliance. The drafters of the ABM treaty and interim agreement felt that imperative acutely.

Vladivostok: Accord and Discord

SALT II began formally in November 1972, six months after the signing of SALT I. The objective of both sides was to replace the five-year interim agreement on offensive systems with a more comprehensive treaty of indefinite duration. The American objective was to codify the concept of parity, to reduce the Soviet arsenal, and if possible to solve the problem of Minuteman vulnerability. The task proved unexpectedly difficult. During Brezhnev's visit to Washington in June 1973, he and Nixon signed an agreement setting 1974 as a target for a SALT II treaty. SALT, among many other things, is a story of missed deadlines.

The Nixon administration was negotiating under a mandate from the Congress—endorsed by the Pentagon—that SALT II must entail identical numerical limits for both sides. Henry Kissinger was reluctant to take that mandate too literally. He thought that Senator Jackson was short-sightedly preoccupied with equal aggregates and that the goal of SALT was better described as "essential equivalence." The vagueness of the phrase was its virtue, Kissinger believed, because it acknowledged that SALT entails counting apples and oranges, or Soviet heavy missiles and American heavy bombers. Kissinger wanted to explore the possibility of leaving the Soviets with a numerical advantage in total number of missiles, but forcing them to cut back their heavy missiles and slow down or, better yet, stop their MIRV program. The U.S. would have had an edge in MIRVed ICBMs to compensate for the Soviet edge in total ICBMs. Such "offsetting asymmetries," he argued, might be more advantageous for the U.S. than gross numerical equality. In 1973 and early 1974, Kissinger tried various means of limiting Soviet MIRVs—a low ceiling on MIRVed ICBMs, a ban on MIRVed heavy missiles—while he also explored the possibility of getting the Russians to accept equality in total payload or throw-weight, rather than in overall number of launchers. As it happened, Kissinger never had to defend the concept of "offsetting asymmetries" before Jackson because the Russians resisted any proposals that were specifically aimed at curtailing the potential of their precious heavies.*

Instead, by late 1974, the U.S. and the Soviet Union had agreed in principle to seek equal aggregates in a SALT II treaty that would run until 1985. (The goal of an open-ended treaty had gone by the board.) By that time, Richard Nixon had resigned the presidency. Kissinger arranged a November summit meeting between Gerald Ford and Brezhnev in Vladivostok, the Soviet seaport in northeastern Siberia. The meeting was described by American officials at the time largely as a "getting-to-know-you" session, "a stopgap fix for political reasons," "a way of breathing new life into the Soviet-American relationship at a time of perilous uncertainty." The meeting turned out to be much more than that. It yielded a communiqué on the framework for SALT II. The key features of the accord were a ceiling of 2,400 for total offensive strategic nuclear launch vehicles (SNLVs) and a subceiling of 1,320 launchers for multiple warheads. Thus, the Soviets had accepted the equal aggregates that the U.S. Congress demanded and the Pentagon desired.

Kissinger believed that Brezhnev had to "knock heads" within the Soviet leadership in order to get his comrades—particularly his military comrades—to accept equal aggregates. One reason the Russians agreed to give up the numerical advantage they had enjoyed under SALT I was that the new, equal ceiling and subceiling of SALT II were high enough to leave intact the weapons that they most cared about —and high enough to allow them to continue full tilt their program of MIRVing their ICBMs. (At the time of the Vladivostok accord, the Soviet Union was only slightly above the overall ceiling and well below the multiple-warhead subceiling, while the U.S. was well under the overall ceiling and had approximately 80 percent of the MIRVed missiles permitted by the multiple-warhead subceiling.)

---

*When Kissinger saw his first ICBM, he was moved to ponder the bugbear of Soviet heavies. It was in 1974. He was accompanying the West German foreign minister, Hans-Dietrich Genscher, from Washington to San Clemente, California, for what turned out to be Genscher's farewell call on President Nixon, then in the final throes of the Watergate crisis. En route, Kissinger and Genscher stopped at Grand Forks Air Force Base in North Dakota to tour an ICBM field and an ABM installation. Kissinger descended into one of the silos to inspect a Minuteman. One of his first comments was on the size of the silo itself: "It's big enough to contain a heavy missile," he remarked. "All this fuss about the Soviet advantage in heavies, and here's a reminder that we could have had heavies too if we'd decided to go that route ten years ago."

The Soviets made another important concession at Vladivostok. They dropped a long-standing insistence that SALT II restrict U.S. nuclear weapons in Europe, the so-called forward-based systems (FBS). But this concession, too, had its price: the U.S. had to give up, once and for all, its dogged pursuit of a cutback in Soviet heavy missiles. This Kissinger agreed to do. He also agreed that the new SALT II ceiling of 2,400 strategic launchers would include heavy bombers, a category in which the U.S. was superior—and one that had been omitted from SALT I.

But here another definitional ambiguity occurred. What was a heavy bomber? The term was understood by both sides at Vladivostok to refer to the American B-52 Stratofortress and the Soviet Mya-4 and Tu-20, which NATO designates the Bison and Bear respectively. All three are 1950s-vintage, subsonic, intercontinental workhorses. But at the time of the Vladivostok summit, there was a profound conviction in the Pentagon that a newcomer to Soviet aviation should also be treated as a strategic aircraft. It was the Tu-26, known as Backfire. First observed in 1969, the Backfire is a twin-engined, swing-wing supersonic airplane. It is smaller than the aged Bison and Bear—but bigger, faster and altogether more formidable than the Tu-22 Blinder supersonic medium bomber it was intended to replace. Backfire is also superior to the F-111, the most capable American fighter-bomber based in Europe, an aircraft not covered by SALT. At the same time, Backfire would definitely be *in*ferior to the B-1, the expensive and controversial new American penetrating bomber which was still under development, but which would, if deployed, be covered by SALT. In short, the Backfire's operational characteristics—its length, weight, wingspan, range and payload—placed it in a gray area of SALT, between medium and heavy. Backfire's initial deployment indicated that its mission was confined to a theater of operations around the U.S.S.R. rather than strikes against another continent. It seemed particularly suited for use by the Soviet Naval Air Force against enemy shipping. But the worst-case scenarists in Washington have easily imagined Backfire's playing a strategic role. If the Soviets ever decided to use their MIRVed ICBMs to knock out the American land-based systems in a preemptive strike, the Backfire might lead the charge in a mopping-up operation—sweeping in from its bases along the Arctic Ocean to hit American military targets that escaped—or were spared in—the preemptive strike. Meanwhile the Kremlin would confront the U.S. government with an ultimatum: "Surrender or we destroy your cities." With midair refueling, the Backfire could make the round trip for such a mission; without it, the plane could, according to the scenario, land in Cuba.

The Pentagon—which is, after all, a very big building populated by civilians as well as military—has never had a unanimous view on the Backfire and what to do about it. Almost since the earliest prototype was spotted on the ground outside a factory in Central Asia, the Backfire has been a point of contention between the Office of the Secretary of Defense (OSD) and the Joint Chiefs of Staff (JCS). The uniformed military has tended to the position that Backfire should be treated by SALT in terms of what it *could* do in the future. The ranking civilian authorities in the Department of Defense have tended to the position that Backfire should be treated in terms of what it seems intended to do in its actual deployment and with its present capabilities—but that the Soviets must provide verifiable assurances that the plane will not be upgraded to a strategic, intercontinental role.

The institutionalized dispute over the Backfire bomber illustrates a central feature of SALT: the process involves at least two sets of negotiations—one between the Soviet and American governments, and the other *within* the American government. The second set has, on occasion, been just as important and difficult as the first. On the issue of Backfire, for instance, there have been running disagreements not only between OSD and JCS but also between the Defense Department as a whole and the CIA; between the Defense Department and the CIA on the south bank of the Potomac and the conservative side of the argument, and the State Department and Arms Control Agency on the north bank of the river and the liberal side of the argument; between the State Department and Arms Control Agency in Foggy Bottom and the National Security Council uptown; between the executive branch as a whole and the legislators on Capitol Hill. There has almost certainly been a third set of negotiations, within the Soviet government, but evidence about those deliberations has been rare and inconclusive.

Another flying machine left undefined by the Vladivostok accord is about as different from Backfire as it could be. Small, fixed-wing, subsonic, cheap, unmanned—the more sophisticated versions existed in 1974 mostly in the minds and wind tunnels of its inventors. This is the cruise missile, the latest manifestation of American technology and therefore the object of the latest Soviet phobia. The jet-propelled drone can be launched from sea, land or air; it would sneak under enemy radar, skimming the treetops, finding its way by retracing a preprogrammed map of the terrain below, zigging and zagging to avoid known antiaircraft installations, and homing in on its target with uncanny accuracy.

Much as the U.S. had second thoughts about whether the Backfire bomber might not at least potentially be a heavy bomber, so the Soviets took the position that they had meant to include cruise missiles in the limits agreed at the Vladivostok summit. Actually, the words "cruise missile" were never even mentioned at the Ford-Brezhnev meeting or in the subsequent *aide-mémoire.* The U.S. did agree to count against the 2,400-ceiling air-to-surface missiles with a range greater than 600 kilometers, but later "clarified" that to mean *ballistic* air-to-surface missiles, rocket-propelled vehicles that flew to their targets by following high, parabolic trajectories. The Soviets insisted that the 600-kilometer-range definition applied to *all* air-to-surface missiles, regardless of locomotion and flight path, and that ground-launched and sea-launched cruise missiles with ranges over 600 kilometers should be banned.

Thus the cruise missile came to share with the Backfire bomber the gray area of Vladivostok definitions. By 1975 Kissinger often wished that neither aircraft had been invented. He regarded both as "hang-ups" of the Pentagon—the Backfire because the U.S. military was so determined to stretch SALT to cover it, and the cruise missile because the Defense Department was so determined to prevent SALT from covering it. Kissinger had originally thought of the cruise missile—and in 1973 supported its development—largely as a "bargaining chip," a fiendishly clever but rather exotic device of marginal value that could be offered as a hostage to the Soviets in exchange for concrete and meaningful concessions. However, the military men who had developed the cruise missile came to see their brainchild as too valuable to sacrifice. "Those geniuses," said Kissinger once, gesturing irritably across the Potomac River in the general direction of the Pentagon, "think the goddamn thing is a cure for cancer and the common cold."

The Compromise That Came Too Late

But Kissinger soon realized that the cruise missile, like Backfire, was here to stay and that the gray area they occupied was a swamp in which SALT was in danger of becoming hopelessly bogged down. Ford and Brezhnev had agreed in Vladivostok to the goal of concluding the new treaty by the end of 1975, thus giving it a life span of ten years, since it was due to expire in 1985. Because of the Backfire and the cruise missile, that was another in a long series of deadlines destined to be missed. Ambassador U. Alexis Johnson, who had taken over chairmanship of the U.S. SALT delegation from Gerard Smith, resumed negotiations with Vladimir Semyonov on the Joint Draft Text (JDT) of the new treaty. There was significant progress on some important definitional issues. The Soviets accepted a U.S.-proposed rule whereby once a missile of a certain type had been tested with a multiple warhead, all the missiles of that type would count under the 1,320 subceiling for MIRVed launchers. This so-called MIRVed-booster counting rule made it harder to circumvent the treaty by secretly storing rockets with multiple warheads near unMIRVed launchers for quick replacement in the event of a crisis. The rule was therefore vital for verification. The delegations worked out a ban against any storing of spare missiles—MIRVed or otherwise—and against stationing rapid-reload equipment near launch sites. The Soviets also agreed to limit the payload or throw-weight of their largest "light" missile, the SS-19, to about 7,000 pounds and their largest "heavy," the SS-18, to about 15,000 pounds. But the delegations made no progress in resolving the ambiguous status of the Backfire bomber and cruise missile.

Kissinger flew to Moscow in January 1976 in a last-ditch attempt to conclude a treaty before that year's presidential campaign made compromise and rational debate impossible. As always, Kissinger managed to keep flexible the negotiating instructions approved by the President before he left, so that he would be able to bargain and improvise on the spot. On this occasion, trading apples for oranges meant Backfires for cruise missiles. There was give-and-take on both sides. Kissinger first proposed a "set-aside" or free allowance of 120 Backfires—the number of those bombers the Soviets would have operational by the time the new agreement went into effect. If the U.S.S.R. chose to deploy additional Backfires, each one over 120 would count against the Vladivostok ceiling of 2,400 strategic launchers. The Soviets rejected that proposal, so Kissinger proposed instead to limit the Russians to 275 Backfires for a five-year period, during which the U.S. would be allowed cruise missiles on surface ships while accepting restrictions on submarine-launched cruise missiles. But the provision that most interested the Soviets was that heavy bombers armed with cruise missiles would count against the Vladivostok subceiling of 1,320

MIRVed launchers. Kissinger's opposite number, Foreign Minister Andrei Gromyko, had finally heard what he was waiting for, but he wanted more. All right, he said, but each supersonic (and still undeployed) B-1 bomber armed with cruise missiles should count as three units against the 1,320 subceiling, while a B-52 would count as one.

"Why?" asked Kissinger.

"Because," replied Gromyko, "the B-1 is faster and will arrive earlier."

"Not if it takes off later," deadpanned Kissinger.

There was befuddled silence on the Soviet side of the table. Still, Kissinger and Gromyko had agreed in principle that the U.S. would count cruise-missile-carrying bombers against the 1,320 MIRV subceiling if the Soviets accepted constraints on the Backfire. The Kremlin would self-righteously remind the U.S. for years afterward about the first half of that agreement while conveniently forgetting the second. It has always been standard Soviet procedure to select from a set of interlinked U.S. proposals the ones they like and ignore those they do not. But Kissinger's salvage mission to Moscow had come too late. Détente, SALT and Kissinger himself were already under attack from candidates in both parties—including the Democratic dark horse, Jimmy Carter. As a result, Kissinger was on a shorter leash than he realized as he negotiated with Gromyko. Tugging at the other end back in Washington were Donald Rumsfeld, the secretary of defense, and Fred Iklé, the director of the Arms Control and Disarmament Agency. At their instigation, Kissinger's proposal for a compromise that limited cruise missiles was not pursued, although it was left on the table. A month later came a new American suggestion that the Vladivostok ceilings be ratified, with the definitional ambiguities left unresolved, and that the outstanding issues of Backfire and cruise missiles be solved on a temporary basis for three years. The Soviets rejected that idea abruptly and angrily. They thought they had just made a deal on the basis of Kissinger's January proposal. To the consternation of Kissinger and the Kremlin alike, American domestic politics had obtruded on SALT.

3 The Making of a Debacle

Jimmy Carter was the newly elected President of the United States, and the Kremlin was nervous. After eight years of dealing productively with Henry Kissinger, the Soviets would have been uneasy about any change that confronted them with an unknown quantity. Even though they proclaim themselves revolutionaries, or at least guardians of a revolution, the Soviet leaders are among the most conservative on earth. They hate, and fear, change. Consistency is the hobgoblin of their bureaucratic minds, and the American political system has an annoying way of confronting them with new Presidents whose policies are often inconsistent with those of their predecessors. The Soviets are quick to interpret even capricious shifts as deliberate maneuvers directed against them. Many of them are paranoids who fancy themselves pragmatists. Idealistic rhetoric offends them and makes them suspicious—unless, of course, it is their own.

Thus, the prologue to the Carter presidency made the Kremlin especially nervous. Here was a politician who had capitalized on being an unknown quantity; he had criticized détente during the campaign; he had appointed as his national security adviser the Polish-born international relations expert Zbigniew Brzezinski, whose name itself, with its Slavic sibilants, connoted the special hostility of an East European emigré. Brzezinski's copious writings on the Communist bloc made him, in Moscow's eyes, the most dangerous sort of cold warrior. He was the author of works with titles like *The Permanent Purge: Politics in Soviet Totalitarianism* and a leading proponent of the view that the U.S. must shore up its "trilateral" relations with Western Europe and Japan, a concept that naturally seemed to the Russians like a blueprint for capitalist-imperialist encirclement of the U.S.S.R. When Jimmy Carter spoke out on foreign affairs, the Soviets tended to hear echoes of Brzezinski's anti-Sovietism. Carter's moralizing about human rights seemed, in Moscow's ears, like a blatant attempt to exploit the world-wide outrage over the repression of Soviet dissidents. His idealism about arms control was equally suspect. In his inaugural address, Carter voiced the hope that "nuclear weapons would be rid from the face of the earth." To most of his listeners around the world, it was a noble but innocuous sentiment. Indeed, the Soviets themselves had championed disarmament in their own propaganda. But coming from this particular politician during a politically imposed hiatus in SALT, Carter's long-term goal spelled short-term problems. "Already we felt Carter was maneuvering for publicity," recalled a Soviet diplomat of the inaugural address. "We felt he was weaseling out of the Vladivostok promises. We felt he was insincere."

The notion that irrevocable promises had been made at Vladivostok was firmly embedded in Leonid Brezhnev's mind. Carter had inadvertently misled the Soviet leader on that count during the campaign. W. Averell Harriman, the dean of the Democratic foreign policy establishment, had visited Moscow and met with Brezhnev in September 1976—after Carter's nomination but before his election. Carter authorized Harriman to tell Brezhnev that if elected, he would move quickly to sign a SALT II agreement based on the Vladivostok accord and incorporating a compromise on the issues left unresolved at Vladivostok. At the time of Carter's inauguration, Brezhnev gave a speech saying that the essential features of the Vladivostok accord should be ratified without renegotiation. Significant reductions in the nuclear arsenals of both sides might be possible in SALT III, said Brezhnev, but that was new business. First, there was some old business to be completed. Brezhnev made it sound as though the presidential elections had interrupted the two sides just as they had been about to sign the SALT II treaty.

In fact, however, Carter inherited from his predecessors an ill-defined commitment and a well-defined stalemate. Gerald Ford had committed the U.S. at Vladivostok to a SALT II treaty that would limit each superpower to 2,400 strategic launchers, of which 1,320 could be armed with multiple warheads. But the Ford administration was also committed to the development of cruise missiles and a new, super-sonic heavy bomber from which to launch them. Ford's final budget, submitted to Congress his last week in office, earmarked money for eight B-1 penetrating bombers and for the cruise missile program. Whether those planes, armed with cruise missiles, would eventually count merely as heavy bombers against the 2,400 ceiling or as multiple-warhead weapons against the 1,320 subceiling was a contentious piece of old business, as Brezhnev knew perfectly well. Even the Kissinger compromise of January 1976 had made clear that the U.S. would limit bombers armed with cruise missiles only if the Soviet Union accepted constraints on the Backfire bomber. And that proposal had been abandoned by the Republican administration because Donald Rumsfeld and Fred Iklé felt it gave away too much for too little.

The Carter administration reached a similar verdict even before it formally assumed office. A group of arms control and military experts assigned to supervise the post-election transition at the Defense Department produced for Harold Brown, the secretary-designate, a series of reports, including a thick loose-leaf folder on the outstanding issues in SALT. It concentrated on the question of cruise missiles and concluded that any limits on the deployment of air-launched cruise missiles must be in exchange for greater Soviet concessions than Kissinger had extracted in Moscow.

The author of a number of Pentagon transition-team reports was Walter Slocombe, Brown's principal adviser on SALT. Slocombe, then thirty-six, had been educated at Princeton, Oxford and Harvard Law School, clerked for a Supreme Court justice and worked for a Washington law firm. But lucrative private practice was merely an interlude between ventures into the thickets of national security policy. At Oxford he had studied Soviet politics. After his term at the Supreme Court he worked for Henry Kissinger as a member of the Program Analysis Office of the National Security Council, specializing on matters of strategic nuclear forces, intelligence, the fate of the modern navy and SALT. He spent a year in London at the Institute for Strategic Studies, a prestigious, privately funded think tank, where he wrote a paper on "The Political Implications of Strategic Parity." Its message was that the U.S. should learn to live without the overwhelming superiority it had so long enjoyed; a delicate balance of nuclear power might very well contribute to the safety and stability of the world and would not—as many feared—impair the "nuclear umbrella" with which the U.S. protected Western Europe. In 1972, when Nixon was basking in the afterglow of SALT I and his first Moscow summit meeting with Brezhnev, Slocombe was a campaign aide to Nixon's quixotic opponent, George McGovern. He worked on a paper that attempted to explain how a McGovern administration would implement the sweeping cuts in the defense budget that the candidate had promised. Shortly after the election of 1976, the Carter-Mondale talent scouts assigned Slocombe to the Pentagon transition team. His liberal background at first worried the admirals and generals with whom he worked, but he quickly impressed Harold Brown as disciplined, hardworking—and cured of McGovernism. Slocombe's title—Principal Deputy Assistant Secretary of Defense for International Security Affairs and Director of DoD [Department of Defense] SALT Task Force—was quintessentially bureaucratic, in that it managed to make him sound both important and subordinate. The title also made him sound very busy. Slocombe's large but windowless office in the Pentagon was a nexus where the military and civilian perspectives on SALT came together. Slocombe knew he was in for a long siege. Soon after moving in, he installed a tape deck that played, as a kind of highbrow white noise, Beethoven symphonies and other classics continuously and at low volume. One clock on the wall was set to Geneva time; once the negotiations resumed, he would be in frequent contact with the U.S. SALT delegation there. His file cabinets, decorated with crayoned drawings by his children, were soon overflowing with paper—most of it stamped TOP SECRET and SENSITIVE—generated by the negotiators of the previous administrations, the Pentagon task force Slocombe headed and the hierarchy of interagency committees that set SALT policy and supervised the negotiations.

When Slocombe crossed the Potomac, it was often to call on his opposite number at the State Department, Leslie Gelb. Gelb had worked at the Pentagon in International Security Affairs during the Johnson administration. He had been a coauthor of the *Pentagon Papers.* He had worked as a diplomatic correspondent for the *New York Times* until two weeks before the Carter inauguration, when he quit to become director of the State Department Bureau of Politico-Military Affairs. He and Slocombe met at least weekly in Gelb's office for a "brown bag" lunch.

Where SALT was concerned, Slocombe and Gelb were the alter egos of Harold Brown and Cyrus Vance respectively, the cabinet officers who would have the largest roles to play in the development of a new U.S. position. But their ultimate boss, Jimmy Carter, did not have an alter ego for SALT or anything else. He came into office determined that no one in his administration—neither Brzezinski nor Vance nor Brown—would monopolize influence on presidential thinking in the way that Henry Kissinger had managed to do with both Nixon and Ford. Carter was determined that in SALT, as in other matters, he would make decisions on the basis of "cabinet government," a collegial consensus guided by his own ideals and instincts. The trouble was, Carter came into office without a clear or consistent idea about how he wanted to proceed in SALT.

His first week on the job, Carter told the Associated Press and United Press International he wanted to resume SALT quickly. He envisioned a "two-stage evolution": the first stage would be to "put firm limits on ourselves," and the second would be "substantive [sic] reductions . . . to demonstrate to the world we are sincere." As for the cruise missile and Backfire bomber, he "wouldn't let those two items stand in the way of some agreement." These initial pronouncements from the Carter White House found their most attentive audience four blocks away, at the Soviet embassy. Ambassador Anatoly Dobrynin and his fellow Americanologists seized on any evidence that might help them anticipate what sort of SALT position this unpredictable new President would espouse. In this regard, the interview with the two wire services was tantalizing but ambiguous. When Carter spoke of two stages, did he mean SALT II and SALT III? Were "substantive reductions" a goal he was willing to postpone until after the Vladivostok accord was enshrined as a treaty? Did the Vladivostok accord represent, by his lights, "firm limits"? And when he said he would not let the issues of the cruise missile and Backfire bomber "stand in the way of some agreement," was he signaling his willingness to accept a deadlock-breaking compromise of the sort Kissinger had proposed in January 1976? Or was he floating anew the idea of deferring the two troublesome issues, the "quick fix" that the Ford administration had suggested—and the Kremlin had rejected—in February 1976?

Those questions, so much in the minds of Dobrynin and other Soviet officials, were also in the air around the Pentagon, the State Department, the Arms Control and Disarmament Agency, and in the west wing of the White House, headquarters of the National Security Council. Throughout the administration, there was uncertainty over exactly how to proceed in SALT. From the moment he began focusing on SALT during the transition, Carter had been ambivalent about whether, in effect, to get Vladivostok over with and move on—or whether to try to leapfrog over Vladivostok directly into what he had called in his wire service interview the "second phase," in which the U.S. would seek deep reductions.

In a pre-inaugural meeting at Blair House across Pennsylvania Avenue from the White House, President-elect Carter startled the Joint Chiefs of Staff by asking what would be the minimum force of strategic nuclear missiles necessary to deter war between the superpowers. He then dismayed the nation's top brass, of whom he was about to assume command, by suggesting that perhaps a mere two hundred ICBMs on each side might constitute adequate mutual deterrence. At his first meeting with his staff on SALT after taking office, Carter declared with tight-lipped intensity that he had been serious in his inaugural address about dreaming of the day when nuclear weapons could be rid from the earth and that his "most cherished hope" was to contribute to progress in that direction. But how? In one step or two?

The first week after the inauguration, Carter ordered the National Security Council to coordinate preparations for renewed high-level strategic arms talks in late March or early April. With that directive, embodied in one of the first NSC "tasking memoranda" of his presidency, Carter turned the bureaucracy loose on SALT so that he could devote his own attention to other problems, such as how to proceed with American diplomacy in the Middle East, Africa and Asia. For about six weeks, the President left the government experts to their own devices in SALT.

They were prolific. Some of the paper that began to flow, then fly, back and forth across the Potomac was recycled from previous administrations. Some of it was attached to trial balloons launched by young men and women who had just entered the government and who were confident that their fresh perspectives, brimming energies and bright ideas could dissolve the impasse in SALT. But a common denominator was soon detectable in this flurry of option papers. There was widespread agreement that the administration should, as Carter had implied in his wire service interview, take SALT one step at a time; it should use the Vladivostok accord as a starting point for the resumption of negotiations; it should find some imaginative variation of the accord on which to base a SALT II treaty and then pursue deep reductions in SALT III.

In a way, the bureaucracy was letting history be its guide, and the historian of record was a young government SALT expert who had worked for the previous administration. He was Roger Molander, then thirty-six, a member of the Policy Analysis group at the NSC. Molander was what Jimmy Carter sometimes claimed to be—a nuclear engineer. He had a Ph.D. in nuclear engineering from Berkeley and was a specialist in the technical aspects of arms control. He served as chairman of the interagency committee that drafted Presidential Review Memorandum No. 2,* a survey of the options available to the President in SALT. He was also the author of a confidential history of the negotiations commissioned by Brzezinski, classified EYES ONLY and distributed to Carter, Vance and Brown. The document stressed that until the 1976 political season intervened, the negotiations had been moving toward a refinement of the Vladivostok accord that would have included some kind of trade-off between cruise missiles and Backfire bombers. While a better deal than the one Kissinger had been working on might be possible, the momentum of the previous administration's approach should be preserved and harnessed to the diplomatic purposes of the new administration. PRM 2 and Molander's history took respectful account of Carter's declared intention of seeking reductions in the Vladivostok ceiling and subceiling as soon as possible, but the government experts canvassed for both documents seemed to agree that deep reductions would probably have to wait until the Vladivostok accord had been consummated. The reasoning was essentially Kremlinological: The Soviet leadership had staked its prestige on the Vladivostok accord as the basis for SALT II and therefore any attempt to short-circuit that understanding would blow fuses in Soviet-American relations.

One of the most influential proponents of that view was himself a Kremlinologist—and a veteran of Henry Kissinger's stewardship of SALT. This was William Hyland, a career specialist in Soviet affairs who had come up through the ranks of the Central Intelligence Agency. At the beginning of the Nixon administration he had joined Kissinger's inner circle, first at the National Security Council, subsequently at the State Department. In the last days of Gerald Ford's presidency, Hyland had been deputy director of the NSC. He agreed to stay on as an NSC senior staff member for nine months after the Carter team came into office, partly because he wanted to complete a full twenty-five years of government service, which meant better pension benefits, but also because he wanted to help complete SALT II. He was forceful and straightforward in advocating that the Carter administration follow through on the Vladivostok accord, although he

*PRM 1, initiated at about the same time, concerned another urgent matter inherited by the new administration—the renegotiation of the status of the Panama Canal.

was as interested as many of the newcomers in moving quickly to a follow-on agreement that would lower the ceiling and subceiling.

Where Soviet-American relations were concerned, Hyland embodied what little continuity existed between the upper reaches of the Republican and Democratic administrations. He knew not only the dossiers of the top Soviet officials, but was on a first-name basis with many of them. When Anatoly Dobrynin came to the White House for his introductory calls, Hyland could assure Carter and Brzezinski afterward that the ambassador's idiosyncrasies were deceptive and his skills considerable. Dobrynin's manner was somewhat nervous; he tended to jabber in his fluent but heavily accented and not always idiomatic English; and he had the disconcerting practice of almost never taking notes, nor did he bring an assistant to do so. Yet Hyland knew from numerous encounters over the years that Dobrynin was able to report home accurately, that he had a firm technical grasp of the most complex issues, and that the Soviet leadership was, as a result, usually well briefed on the nuances as well as the substance of American policy.

Along with Roger Molander, Hyland served as the NSC's institutional memory on the negotiations. The two often exercised a restraining influence during staff meetings early in the administration. What many of the incoming policy-makers lacked in experience they made up in enthusiasm, and some well-worn and discarded wheels of SALT were rediscovered at these sessions. After listening patiently as someone propounded what he thought was a brilliant innovation, Hyland or Molander would point out that the same thing had been rejected by Gerald Ford—or by the Soviets—a few years before. For example, measures to restrict antiaircraft and antisubmarine defenses were good ideas, in the abstract, because, in the terminology of their proponents, they would have increased the survivability of the bomber and submarine legs of the triad and thus enhanced strategic stability. But they would have been premature as contributions to a negotiation that left in much more immediate doubt the survivability of the crucial land-based leg of the triad, to say nothing of a negotiation that had not yet determined whether cruise missiles and Backfire bombers were strategic weapons. "A lot of us were pretty wet behind the ears," commented a colleague who came to the administration full of ambitious plans for SALT, "and Hyland and Molander had to spend quite a bit of time walking us back to reality."

The Vladivostok Options

The old-timers and newcomers soon focused on three options, all variations of the Vladivostok accord. The first option, nicknamed "Basic Vladivostok," had the strongest backing of Gelb and the State Department. It would have given the Soviets the benefit of the doubt on the Backfire by not counting the bomber against the Vladivostok ceiling of 2,400; and it would have counted U.S. bombers armed with cruise missiles against the subceiling of 1,320 multiple-warhead systems, although by a more lenient formula than the one Gromyko had suggested to Kissinger in January 1976. At the Pentagon, Slocombe and others tolerated this option, but called it, with a touch of scorn, the "As If Ford Had Won the Election Proposal."

The Pentagon favored "Vladivostok-Plus"—that is, the Vladivostok accord plus a separate but accompanying accommodation on Backfire. As to what kind of accommodation, there remained a split between the Joint Chiefs of Staff and the Office of the Secretary of Defense. The JCS took its traditional hard line, pressing for the Backfire to be counted as a strategic weapon. OSD acknowledged the ambiguous status of Backfire but wanted to make sure that the long-range ground-launched cruise missiles (GLCM), a comparably ambiguous weapon system being developed by the U.S., would be treated equally under SALT II. OSD, in short, urged a trade-off between Backfire and GLCMs.* The Vladivostok-Plus option included a trade-off between Soviet heavy intercontinental ballistic missiles, of which there were approximately 300, and U.S. heavy bombers armed with air-launched cruise missiles. This was in effect the prototype of a proposal that would find its way back onto the negotiating table in a variety of versions for many months to come. Vladivostok-Plus would also have lowered somewhat the ceiling of 2,400 total strategic systems and 1,320 multiple-warhead launchers.

The third option was "Vladivostok-Minus"—the 1974 accord minus a solution to the twin problems of Backfire and the cruise

---

*SALT acronyms tend to look bad and sound worse. GLCM is pronounced "glickum." ALCM—air-launched cruise missile—is pronounced "alcum," and SLCM—the sea-launched version—"slickum." In February 1977, while the SALT II options were taking shape, Harold Brown ordered a slowdown in the development of the antiship version of SLCMs because early tests of the drones over water had not been very successful. But at the same time, Brown recommitted the U.S. to the full-scale development of GLCMs, a weapon potentially of great use to the Western European allies.

missile. The possibility of a quick fix was still very much on Carter's mind when he gave his first formal press conference in office on February 8. The President said he "would be willing to go ahead with the Soviet Union to conclude a quick agreement, if they think it advisable, and omit the Backfire bomber and the cruise missile from the negotiations at this stage." The Soviets had made quite clear to Carter's predecessor that they did not think it one bit advisable to defer restrictions on cruise missiles to SALT III, but the Carter administration thought the idea might be worth another try, especially if the Soviets remained steadfast in their refusal to consider what the U.S. saw as improvements in the Vladivostok accord. Gelb, Slocombe, Hyland and others felt that the Soviets might now reconsider a "barebones Vladivostok" proposal. Henry Kissinger—who was out of office but by no means out of sight or out of circulation—agreed. He commented that Carter could probably get "Vladivostok plus or minus 10 percent simply because he is a new President."

Slocombe laid out these three options in a stand-up display chart which he labeled "Decision Tree for Major SALT Issues." The chart managed to impose order—albeit a complex one—on the chaos of numbers and acronyms concocted by the bureaucracy in its orgy of brainstorming. With all its arrows and boxes, its permutations and combinations, its elegantly refined and precisely defined "excursions" or options-within-options, the chart looked at a glance like parallel genealogies of three rather overbred, indeed inbred, families. It became a regular fixture at staff meetings on SALT. Government officials, on the whole, loved it. It was a perfect exhibit for them to discuss with the aid of their aluminum pointers. Many of them could find their own ideas neatly schematized somewhere amid the connecting lines of "the Slocombe triptych," as the chart came to be called.

The President, however, did not love it. Neither did Zbigniew Brzezinski. Neither did Brzezinski's deputy, David Aaron. Neither, in fact, did Slocombe's boss, Harold Brown. These four men found the chart and the options it represented too complicated. More importantly, they found the Basic Vladivostok and Vladivostok-Plus recommendations insufficiently imaginative and ambitious. To be sure, Vladivostok-Plus did contain some "excursions" into substantial reductions. Slocombe himself had drafted a deep-cuts option in late February. But Brzezinski, Aaron, Carter and Brown all felt that the good ideas in the chart were undercut by the dizzying complexity and equivocal group-think of the document as a whole. Brzezinski complained that the Vladivostok options were "pedantic," that they "counted trees rather than looked at the forest." He also felt that the option-makers were looking backward too much, at proposals that had already been aired, and not forward enough—at interesting new possibilities. "There are no sacred cows in the position of the previous administration," he admonished his staff at one point. The Soviets could have a quick-fix SALT II agreement based on the Vladivostok accord if they insisted, but the new administration was not bound to the tentative compromise on Backfire and cruise missiles that Kissinger had offered in January 1976.

Brzezinski was restless with what seemed the glacial pace and institutionalized cautiousness of the SALT process. He also nurtured a deep mistrust of the Soviet attitude toward SALT. An official who observed Brzezinski closely during that period sensed he was intrigued by the idea of SALT as a "truth test" of Soviet intentions. The next stage of the negotiations might reveal whether the Soviets were genuinely interested in arms control or whether they were using the negotiations to lull the West into complacency while they built up their already formidable war-making powers so as better to exploit political opportunities by military intimidation. Brzezinski sometimes spoke of his desire to "smoke the Russians out," to discover what they really wanted to do and were willing to do.

Brzezinski saw a connection between arms control and Soviet-American relations that was quite different from the one underlying Henry Kissinger's theory of détente. Kissinger believed that arms control was integral to a larger policy of improving Soviet-American relations. SALT was one means among others of inculcating the superpowers with a mutual interest in peace. Brzezinski was more concerned with pursuing arms control for its own sake. He wanted, insofar as possible, to insulate the talks and the treaties from the trade deals and summit conferences, as well as the tensions and crises, to which superpowers are prone. The purpose of SALT, in his view, was not so much to spur a cooperative relationship as it was to enhance the stability of an essentially competitive relationship and to blunt the military means by which the Soviets might pursue competitive advantage. He believed that the Soviet Union was aggressive by nature and far less encumbered—or perhaps less blessed—with built-in restraints on military spending and adventurism than was the U.S. Therefore he was all the more impatient with bilateral arms control agreements that froze weaponry at levels which had been arrived at unilaterally.

He reasoned that sooner or later such agreements would favor the bigger bully.

A number of Brzezinski's associates felt he had deep-rooted personal motives, as well as philosophical ones, for being reluctant merely to finish the work of the previous administration. "Why should Carter just step into Jerry Ford's shoes? Why should Zbig just accept Henry Kissinger's strait jacket?" asked a close colleague and defender of Brzezinski's at the time. Kissinger's strait jacket would be even more uncomfortable for Brzezinski than Ford's shoes for Carter. Ever since their days as fellow junior faculty members at Harvard, Brzezinski and Kissinger had been rivals. Both were immigrants—Brzezinski from Poland, Kissinger from Germany. Both had succeeded in building bases in academe—Brzezinski at Columbia, Kissinger at Harvard—for forays into government. Both had attached themselves to presidential aspirants in 1968—Brzezinski to Hubert Humphrey, Kissinger to Nelson Rockefeller. While Kissinger was exercising unprecedented power and enjoying unprecedented success in the Nixon and Ford administrations, Brzezinski tried in much of his writing, lecturing and extracurricular activity to establish himself as an advocate of an alternative world view and as a potential successor to Kissinger. From 1973 until 1976, he served as director of the Trilateral Commission, a private group that sponsored the strengthening of relations among the U.S., Japan and Western Europe. The very name of the commission was an implicit refutation of Kissinger's emphasis on bipolarity—the centrality of the Soviet-American relationship. Jimmy Carter was a member of the Trilateral Commission, and it was through that association that Brzezinski became his friend, tutor and—after the election —his special assistant for national security affairs. It was the same post Nixon had given Kissinger. In the early days after the Carter administration took office, Brzezinski displayed acute sensitivity about the comparisons he knew everyone was making between his performance and Kissinger's. He sought, sometimes defensively and gratuitously, to distinguish his style, his approach, his policies from Kissinger's. A number of high-ranking associates found Brzezinski inclined to dwell in private conversation on how determined he was to come up with a "better" SALT II treaty than Kissinger had been on the verge of concluding the year before.

Jimmy Carter shared this inclination to do more than just dot the *i*'s and cross the *t*'s on a document that would be widely perceived as Henry Kissinger's handiwork. Carter's campaign for the presidency had been largely a campaign against Kissinger's foreign policy. "We've become fearful to compete with the Soviet Union on an equal basis," Carter had proclaimed during a televised debate with Gerald Ford in 1976. "The Soviet Union knows what they want in détente, and they've been getting it. We have not known what we wanted and we've been out-traded in almost every instance. . . . As far as foreign policy goes, Mr. Kissinger has been the President of this country." Yet now Carter was confronted with advice from within his own administration to the effect that he should allow Kissinger's influence to linger a little longer—long enough to conclude the agreement that Gerald Ford would have signed with Kissinger looking proudly on, had it not been for the Backfire and cruise missile issues.

Harold Brown and David Aaron were also unhappy with that advice, but they seemed to their colleagues less preoccupied with politics and personalities and more concerned about the strategic issues at stake in SALT. They were experts on those issues. Both had, in previous jobs, tried to push the Nixon and Ford administrations in the direction of more stringent, more ambitious SALT provisions than Henry Kissinger had been willing to attempt.

Brown was a physicist, a manager and a civilian who knew how to deal with—and give orders to—the military. He had been secretary of the Air Force in the Johnson administration and a part-time member of the SALT delegation during the Nixon and Ford administrations. As President of the California Institute of Technology, he was responsible for liaison between the delegation and the academic scientific community. When Carter named him secretary of defense, Brown quickly established himself as the single most influential SALT policy-maker in the new administration aside from the President himself. Since SALT affected the programs of the Defense Department more than those of any other government agency, the secretary of defense naturally had considerable say over the manner in which this ox would be gored. But in addition to the institutional influence that came with his job, Brown had a reputation among Carter's closest advisers for combining one quality they knew they lacked—government experience—with another quality they felt abundantly endowed with—intellectual boldness. In this respect, Cyrus Vance suffered somewhat by comparison with Brown. His record of public service was every bit as distinguished—general counsel to the Defense Department, secretary of the Army, deputy secretary of defense, troubleshooter plenipotentiary for crises both domestic and foreign during the Johnson administration. But his style was very much that of the corporate board room. Between stints in the government, he had been a Wall Street lawyer, a director of large companies and foundations. Some of Carter's more free-wheeling advisers found him stiff and stuffy, cautious and methodical to a fault, the token establishmentarian in an administration that prided itself as being comprised mostly of outsiders and innovators. "No one ever accused Cy of being a good ol' boy," commented one of the Georgians on Carter's staff.* No one ever leveled that charge at Harold Brown either, but he was more compatible with the Carter White House early in the administration than Vance, and the contrast made it almost inevitable that Brown would be the preeminent cabinet officer in the formulation of SALT policy during the first months, even though Vance was to be the cabinet member responsible for the conduct of the negotiations.

David Aaron had been an associate of Brown's for some time. As an official of the Arms Control and Disarmament Agency, he had served as an adviser to the SALT delegation when Brown was a negotiator. Aaron combined liberal credentials and a background in arms control with a quality that Carter approvingly called "aggressiveness." He advocated toughness when it came—as it soon did in the Carter administration—to rhetorical and political confrontations with the Soviet Union. Aaron got the job as Brzezinski's deputy at the NSC largely because he had spent more than two years as Walter Mondale's foreign policy adviser. Aaron and the Vice-President frequently discussed SALT over lunch in the White House Mess, as the senior staff dining room is known. Sometimes Harold Brown joined them. These conversations focused on Brown's and Aaron's shared worry about the eventual vulnerability of the U.S. land-based deterrent in the face of an increasingly powerful, increasingly accurate, increasingly MIRVed Soviet ICBM force. They were concerned that SALT I had left the Soviets with too many heavy missiles and that the SALT II options generated by the bureaucracy, including the Pentagon bureaucracy, would do too little to redress that imbalance. At one of these meetings, Aaron remarked that "the options ginned up by the working level symbolize how rarefied this whole process has become and how we're in danger of losing sight of where we want to go in SALT." Where they wanted to go was further in the direction of deep cuts, further toward

---

*Nor did it count to Vance's credit among the Georgians that he had been a moving force behind Sargent Shriver's brief bid for the 1976 Democratic presidential nomination.

constraints on the Soviet MIRVed ICBM program which threatened the survivability of Minuteman, and when they wanted to get there was sooner than SALT III. Brown, Aaron and Brzezinski were all subscribers to the theory that both superpowers were still governed by the strategic doctrine of mutual assured destruction (MAD), whereby each side could deter an attack by being able to inflict unacceptable damage on the attacker. But while they were confident that MAD prevailed in 1977, they were deeply doubtful about whether some new and unpredictable Kremlin leadership in the early and mid 1980s—when SALT II would still be in force—would be adequately deterred from attempting a "cosmic roll of the dice," as Harold Brown sometimes called a preemptive Soviet first strike. It was an old worry, and these particular worriers were anything but overeager greenhorns. But they now occupied much more important jobs than they had ever held before. They now had an opportunity to make policy, not just implement it. They shared a conviction that during the postinaugural honeymoon with Congress and with the rest of the world, they had a unique opportunity to move boldly toward Carter's publicly stated goal of "real arms control" measures which reduced arsenals rather than merely limited them. Mondale once remarked that a mere resubmission of some dressed-up version of the Vladivostok accord would be a "masquerade": "Kissinger says he put a cap on the arms race at Vladivostok. Well, he did, but the cap was fifteen feet over the head. The Vladivostok agreement was basically a matter of taking the force levels of the two sides, adding fifteen percent, and stapling them together. It was certainly not real arms control."

Another influential figure in the emergence of the new U.S. approach to SALT was not even a member of the administration. This was Henry Jackson, the Senate's leading expert on—and critic of—SALT. Jackson breakfasted with the President at the White House two weeks after the inauguration. The senator rehearsed his misgivings about SALT I and the Vladivostok accord. The problem with the first, he said, was that it left Soviet forces intact and gave the U.S.S.R. a numerical advantage to boot; the problem with the Vladivostok accord was that, while it did set equal aggregates, the numbers were much too high. Nor did he like what he had heard about Kissinger's January 1976 proposal: it provided for too many restrictions on cruise missiles and too few on Backfire bombers. The President expressed interest in Jackson's views and asked him for amplification in writing. Jackson had his right-hand man for strategic affairs, Richard Perle, draft a memorandum to the President. It arrived at the White House, with a covering letter from Jackson, on February 15. The twenty-three-page, single-spaced document was a catalogue of dos and don'ts —with heavy emphasis on the latter. The message, in essence, was: don't continue in the direction in which Henry Kissinger was proceeding. The memo concluded: "If further negotiations were to begin where the Ford-Kissinger negotiations left off, you would unnecessarily assume the burden of past mistakes, and the options available to you will be few and narrow."

The Jackson-Perle memo called for reductions not only in Soviet intercontinental ballistic missiles but in intermediate-range ballistic missiles as well. It called for a reopening of the dispute over the definition of "heavy" ICBMs; Jackson did not think the U.S. should give up on categorizing the SS-19 as a heavy ICBM. And even if the definition of heavies was extended to include the SS-19, the Soviet allowance should still be reduced from the level of more than 300 established by SALT I. Moreover, the U.S. should have the option, forbidden under SALT I, of developing heavy ICBMs of its own, and the cruise missile program should continue apace, unhindered by SALT. As for Backfire, it should count as a heavy bomber, pure and simple.

Recognizing that they were placing a tall order, Jackson and Perle included their own fallback position: in the event that the Soviets balked at a U.S. proposal requiring them in effect to tear up the Vladivostok accord and dismantle a considerable portion of their existing arsenal, "it would be defensible to replace the interim agreement with a new interim accord which would at least codify the basic numerical equality and MIRV limitations of Vladivostok, as long as it were made clear that this accord would be replaced within a relatively short period of time by a more satisfactory resolution of the bomber and throw-weight issues."

The Jackson-Perle memo was circulated to Harold Brown and Cyrus Vance, who in turn gave it wide, though classified, distribution in the Defense and State Departments. Paul Warnke, whom Carter had designated to be his chief SALT negotiator and director of the Arms Control and Disarmament Agency, dismissed it as a "first-class polemic." When Hyland saw it, he noted wryly that after bitterly denouncing the interim agreement and Vladivostok accord, Jackson and Perle had ended up recommending that those heinous covenants be extended. Carter, however, ordered that the administration send

Jackson a detailed, respectful, but circumspect response. There was
some grumbling within the administration that Carter was being
excessively solicitous of Jackson's support. Dark rumors circulated
that Perle was at the White House "almost every day" and was
functioning as a kind of ex officio member of the NSC. Those rumors were occasioned by nothing more substantial than that Perle
was seen lunching with Slocombe and with Gelb, neither of whom
had offices in the White House, was attached directly to the NSC,
or was enthralled by Perle's recommendations. But while Perle's
personal influence on the administration was exaggerated, the Jackson-Perle memo unquestionably reinforced the instincts of Carter,
Brown, Brzezinski and Aaron to seek more than a mere consummation of the Vladivostok accord. The memo amounted to Jackson's preemptive rejection of any SALT II treaty based on either
the Basic Vladivostok or the Vladivostok-Plus options which were
then making their way toward the President's desk. Carter and his
closest advisers were determined, if possible, to go beyond those
options and find a SALT position that would be acceptable not
only to the Kremlin but to the junior senator from the state of
Washington as well.

By mid February the Special Coordination Committee of the NSC
was thrashing out SALT in earnest. This was a cabinet-level body that
met in the eerie privacy of the Situation Room, a windowless chamber
in the basement of the White House west wing. Brzezinski was the
chairman, although Aaron sometimes sat in for him. The secretaries
of state and defense or their deputies, along with representatives of
the Arms Control Agency, the Joint Chiefs of Staff and the intelligence
community, sat around a polished board room table in deeply cush-
ioned red chairs, with their SALT experts seated behind them along
the wall—Hyland behind Brzezinski, Slocombe behind Brown, and
Gelb behind Vance. The Slocombe triptych, with its variegated alternatives based on the Vladivostok accord, was one of the central exhib-
its. The Vladivostok-Plus option had acquired a new feature. After
hearing Harold Brown suggest that the U.S. could perhaps live without a successor to Minuteman, Roger Molander came up with the idea
of banning new ICBMs on both sides—sacrificing a successor to Minuteman in exchange for the Soviets' giving up their next generation
of big missiles. At an SCC meeting devoted to SALT on March 10,
Aaron proposed consolidating this and the other more ambitious elements of various options into a package that would entail "summary

deep reductions" in the overlapping categories of Soviet heavy ICBMs and MIRVed ICBMs. Aaron spoke of "the whole issue of Minuteman vulnerability coming up fast on the horizon" and urged a deep-cuts proposal as a way of "staving off our strategic problem."

Harold Brown seconded Aaron's suggestion and coupled it with one of his own—a limit on the number of missile tests each side could conduct in a year. Such a limit would, he said, both impede the modernization of rockets and reduce their general reliability. That would represent a net advantage to the U.S., since it was the side that most feared a first strike. Soviet missiles were still insufficiently accurate to threaten the American Minuteman deterrent, but in a few years, well before the expiration of the projected treaty in 1985, an unfettered testing program would turn those Soviet missiles into "hard-target killers." They would be able to hit Minuteman silos with such precision and explosive force that even the "superhardened" concrete covers would not protect the American rockets in the ground below. The CIA estimated that it took the Soviets at least fifteen flight tests to perfect a new missile. By that calculation, if SALT II restricted the Russians to two tests a year for each of their three MIRVed ICBMs (the SS-17, 18 and 19), it would take more than seven years to hone the performance of more accurate new versions. Seven years was nearly the duration of the treaty. Brown's suggestion had the crucial feature that it was verifiable. There was no way the U.S. could monitor improvements in accuracy per se, but by satellite reconnaissance it could monitor the flight tests by which greater accuracy was achieved.*

Also present at this meeting was Paul Warnke, whom the Senate had confirmed only the day before as director of the Arms Control Agency and chief SALT negotiator. Warnke had already established himself as by far the most controversial administration personality in the clamorous realm of SALT. He was an articulate and quick-witted lawyer who had the dual credentials—but at the same time suffered the double jeopardy—of having both worked at the Pentagon and been a vigorous advocate of arms control. Like Harold Brown, he had

---

*While the flight test limit was Brown's pet idea and he was its highest-ranking proponent, he was not the originator. More than to anyone else, that distinction belongs to Sidney Drell, a professor of physics at Stanford University. Drell had been toying with the idea since 1972. On a trip to Moscow in 1976, he found some Soviets expressing interest in the possibility of including a flight test limit in SALT. Drell then advocated the proposal with renewed vigor in a speech before a conference at the Aspen Institute in August 1976. Brzezinski and Aaron were in attendance. They found Drell's presentation intriguing.

been an official of the Defense Department during the Johnson administration. Like Walter Slocombe, he had worked for George McGovern in 1972. But unlike Brown and Slocombe, Warnke was openly impatient with many concerns of the Carter administration Pentagon. He sometimes found it hard to conceal his low regard for generals—and senators—who saw sinister purposes and apocalyptic prospects in every new piece of Soviet weaponry or doctrinal utterance. He was disdainful of the contagion of anxiety over the Soviet threat to the survivability of Minuteman. He believed that the indisputable superiority of two legs of the American strategic triad—the submarine and bomber forces—more than made up for the hypothetical vulnerability of the third, land-based leg. Not surprisingly, Warnke's confirmation hearings were extremely contentious. They presaged the difficulties that lay ahead for the ratification of SALT II. Henry Jackson accused Warnke of being "a tireless advocate of deep and, I believe, irresponsible cuts in the defense budget and of unilateral restraints in our defense programs." But Warnke's most vociferous detractor—and one of the administration's most formidable opponents on SALT—was Paul Nitze, a former colleague of Warnke's at the Pentagon, a member of the U.S. SALT delegation during the Nixon administration, and a founder, in 1976, of the Committee on the Present Danger, a private, unabashedly hawkish lobbying group. Nitze had become increasingly disillusioned with SALT and appalled at what he regarded as American complacency in the face of "a clear and present danger" from the Soviet Union. He saw Paul Warnke as the personification of that complacency, and he testified passionately against his confirmation. On March 9 the Senate confirmed Warnke 70–29 as director of the Arms Control and Disarmament Agency, but by the much narrower margin of 58–40 as chief SALT negotiator. Jackson, Nitze and other SALT skeptics considered the latter vote to be a symbolic victory for their own position—and a stern warning to the administration, since 58–40 was less than the two-thirds majority that would be required to ratify the SALT II treaty Warnke would be trying to negotiate.

By the time he was finally confirmed, Warnke was already the object of strong and divided opinion within the executive branch as well as on Capitol Hill. His dovish views, at least as characterized in the press during the debate over his confirmation, were anathema to much of the military. A number of members of Brzezinski's staff regarded Warnke with a jaundiced eye, and even before he was sworn in, he was the target of sniping from the NSC. The civilian experts at the Pentagon also tended to mistrust Warnke. Cyrus Vance, however, had immense respect for Warnke's knowledge, judgment and debating skills; and Leslie Gelb, who had worked for Warnke at the Pentagon, regarded him as a mentor and an ally.

At the SCC meeting on March 10, Warnke joined good-naturedly in the jokes about his "landslide victory" in the Senate the day before. He then made a characteristic contribution to the discussion of Brown's and Aaron's proposal for far-reaching restrictions. Warnke urged that the U.S. SALT position contain at least one provision that the Kremlin would welcome and some Pentagon planners would resist. This was to impose strict limits on the range of cruise missiles, particularly ground-launched cruise missiles. Long-range ground-launched cruise missiles could threaten the Soviet Union from Western Europe. More specifically, the Soviets had an acute fear of such latter-day buzz bombs ending up in the hands of the West Germans. Having reviewed the negotiating record of the previous administration, which was replete with evidence of Soviet nervousness about cruise missiles, Warnke could not imagine the Kremlin accepting any new U.S. proposal that left long-range ground-launched cruise missiles unconstrained. Looking further into the future, Warnke also worried about what might happen when the Soviets finally closed the cruise missile gap. It was important, he said, to "get a handle on the problem now, while we have control of the issue, before it's too late." By the time the Soviets caught up with the U.S., they would no longer be amenable to limiting ground-launched cruise missiles. By way of cautionary example, Warnke often pointed out that the U.S. might have gotten the Kremlin to accept a ban on multiple warheads at the beginning of SALT and thus prevented the ominous proliferation of Russian MIRVs in the late 1970s. Instead, the U.S. chose to "protect" its own MIRVs early in SALT, only to end up feeling terribly threatened by Soviet ones a decade later. True to his reputation, here was Warnke, his second day in office, trying to persuade his colleagues to consider the long-term, destabilizing consequences of a still undeployed American weapon system, the cruise missile, rather than concentrating—as was their wont—on the more immediate and obvious dangers posed by existing Soviet weapons. Vance supported Warnke's position. He was skeptical of Brown's and Aaron's case for presenting the Soviets with a proposal that differed radically from the Vladivostok accord. Since the beginning of the administration, the secretary of state had tended to favor what he described as a "quick agreement validating Vladivostok."

It had been a stimulating but inconclusive session. The participants at the SCC meeting came away still without a clear sense of where the administration was going in SALT. In retrospect, however, a number of them agreed that the meeting was a turning point. Brown and Aaron had given new, high-level impetus to the idea of reducing the levels and impeding the modernization of Soviet ICBMs. Those ideas had their antecedents in the three Vladivostok-based options favored by the bureaucracy, particularly in the Vladivostok-Plus option. But it was not until the SCC meeting of March 10 that those threads started to come together in a form and with a sponsorship that would make them attractive to the President. Carter read an account of the meeting afterward, and commented that it had clearly been "an especially good session."

Two days later, on Saturday, March 12, Brzezinski summoned Vance, Brown, Warnke and Aaron to the White House for a "principals only" SCC meeting (no deputies allowed). It was billed as a tour of the horizon in foreign policy, with special emphasis on SALT. Also invited were General George Brown, the chairman of the Joint Chiefs of Staff, and Director of Central Intelligence Admiral Stansfield Turner, who, like Warnke, had been sworn in only a few days before (Turner was Carter's second choice for DCI after Theodore Sorensen's nomination was withdrawn because of overwhelming political opposition). Some of the participants came anticipating a follow-up SCC meeting in the Situation Room. Instead, the meeting took place in the Cabinet Room, with Carter and Mondale present. The President, in blue jeans and a flannel shirt at the head of the table, threw out questions and comments about a variety of issues. In the course of this relaxed and wide-ranging discussion, he reiterated his long-standing hope for "real arms control" and his impatience with the notion of "merely staying within the Vladivostok framework." One participant later recalled Carter saying that he felt the bureaucracy had been "sloughing off" and that he was still interested in "a fundamentally new kind of proposal." Brown explained the idea he and Aaron had discussed at the SCC two days before. Brzezinski argued—in the paraphrase of a colleague—that Nixon, Ford and Kissinger had "gone down a blind alley on the Soviets' turf and it was time to get back on our own." Consecrating the Vladivostok accord might serve a political purpose by establishing continuity between American administrations and thus, arguably, enhancing Soviet confidence in arms control negotiations. But achieving deep reductions and constraints on missile modernization would serve a higher, strategic purpose by remedying a dangerous development in the military balance—the impending superiority of Soviet land-based ICBMs. Carter listened intently, asked a few questions, then said emphatically, "Good, let's do that." Warnke did not oppose the plan, but he cautioned that there was at least one danger in making such far-reaching proposals: "If they're shot down, and we end up with a compromise, then we'll be criticized for retreating." Whatever misgivings Vance felt, he suppressed them with relative ease. The President was obviously impatient with the notion of "validating Vladivostok" which Vance had preferred. The President plainly wanted a bold approach. And the President was the boss. Vance explained afterward that he simply became convinced an ambitious, far-reaching, albeit risky proposal was worth a try, and he made up his mind to support it "fully and enthusiastically."

For at least two years, the very occurrence of that decisive meeting remained a mystery to the many government officials who were not present but who were otherwise intimately involved in SALT. In memos to his staff, Brown deliberately avoided noting that Carter had even been present—not to mention that Carter had presided over the meeting and given the go-ahead for a major decision. Brown told his colleagues he had been at an SCC meeting, which Carter would not normally have attended. One reason for the deception was that the Saturday session in the Cabinet Room had been intended as a gathering of the Carter team—not as a formal NSC meeting. Yet the decision to go for broke with a radical deep-cuts proposal was more important than most NSC and SCC initiatives, and for months afterward there were rumors throughout the government about a "rump" or "phantom" NSC meeting sometime in early March at which the President had drastically and summarily changed the administration's policy toward SALT. The misimpression lingered for a long time that a naïve, impetuous, overambitious, overconfident Jimmy Carter had rammed the deep-cuts idea down the throat of an experienced and therefore skeptical Harold Brown. In fact, according to an official with firsthand knowledge of what happened, Brown was "the key man in presenting and selling the proposal to the President; but it was like a beautifully tied, juicy fly dropped right in front of a hungry trout's nose. The President bit and swallowed right away."

Immediately after the meeting, Brzezinski and Aaron assigned

Hyland the task of translating Carter's command—"Good, let's do that"—into a set of negotiating instructions for Cyrus Vance to take to Moscow at the end of March. For "philosophical guidance," Brzezinski referred Hyland to a Carter campaign paper on SALT. Hyland hardly needed such inspiration. Ingenious remedies to the looming problem of Minuteman vulnerability were strewn all over the historical and bureaucratic landscape. Hyland himself had helped design some and reject others in the previous administration. In 1974 he and Aaron had worked on an "equal MIRVed throw-weight" proposal that foundered in the negotiations leading up to the Vladivostok summit. There was a backlog of deep-cuts proposals that Kissinger had turned down on the grounds that they would not be negotiable with the Soviets. But now negotiability with the Russians was clearly not the criterion in which President Carter and his key advisers were most interested. Under Aaron's supervision, Hyland produced what became known as the comprehensive proposal. Its key features were reductions in the Vladivostok ceiling and subceiling so deep as to change the structure of the framework—from 2,400 total strategic launchers to a level between 2,000 and 1,800, and from 1,320 multiple-warhead launchers to a level between 1,200 and 1,100. An entirely new subceiling was added for MIRVed ICBMs. It would hold Soviet land-based multiple-warhead rockets to 550, a level equal to the number of America's MIRVed ICBMs, the Minuteman III. The comprehensive proposal would also have cut the Soviet heavy-missile force in half—from about 300 to 150. It incorporated Harold Brown's proposed limit on the flight testing of existing ICBMs and would have banned the development, testing and deployment of mobile ICBMs and any new ICBMs.

The proposal would not have counted the Backfire as a strategic bomber, as long as the Soviets adhered to a list of measures that would inhibit its range. A few provisions in the package would have impinged on American programs. The ban on mobile missiles and new ICBMs, for instance, would have brought a halt to the development of MX, the "Missile Experimental." This was to be a rocket larger than the Minuteman and capable of being moved around on trucks or tracks in order to thwart a Soviet preemptive strike. But MX was just a gleam in the Pentagon's eye, while many of the Soviet weapons slated for drastic reduction in the comprehensive proposal were already in place. They represented research and development completed, money spent and promises fulfilled. In the comprehensive proposal, the U.S. was seeking substantial reductions in existing Soviet systems in exchange for marginal cuts in future American ones. Had it been negotiable, it would have been a very good deal indeed for the U.S. As Aaron later put it, "We would be giving up future draft choices in exchange for cuts in their starting line-up."

In its treatment of cruise missiles, the comprehensive proposal seemed almost calculated to provoke the Russians. It would have limited all cruise missiles to a range of 2,500 kilometers.* Applied to ground-launched cruise missiles, that range limit would have been especially upsetting to the Soviets, since it would have allowed GLCMs based in West Germany to reach over East Germany and Poland into the Soviet Union. In that respect particularly, the comprehensive proposal outdid the Vladivostok-Plus option in the Slocombe triptych. The Office of the Secretary of Defense had proposed a 2,500-kilometer range limit for air-launched cruise missiles coupled with various combinations of stricter limits for ground- and sea-launched ones. Roger Molander at the NSC along with experts in the Arms Control and Disarmament Agency had favored a range limit of 1,500 kilometers for all cruise missiles, including ALCMs. They were assuming that the President would give a go-ahead to the supersonic B-1 bomber as a launching platform for ALCMs, and they calculated that a 1,500-kilometer range limit would be adequate for ALCMs as long as they were teamed up with the B-1. In a number of meetings, representatives of the Joint Chiefs of Staff indicated they agreed. "In fact," remarked a JCS officer, "we figured that a 1,500-kilometer limit on ALCMs was sure-fire insurance that we would get the B-1, because without the B-1 the limit made no sense." Other aspects of the comprehensive proposal—notably the prospective sacrifice of the MX and the qualified acceptance of the Soviet definition of the Backfire as a medium, nonstrategic bomber—disgruntled the JCS when they found out about them. Later, when Brzezinski was asked why the comprehensive proposal had given the military more than it had asked for on cruise missile range, he replied that it was "the only way to get the

---

*The Soviet position on cruise missile range had already shifted several times, but in a way that showed Moscow was increasingly and especially worried about GLCMs. Shortly after the 1974 Vladivostok summit, the Russians maintained that the range of GLCMs and SLCMs should be limited to 600 kilometers. Then, at the Helsinki Ford-Brezhnev summit a year later, the Russians tentatively proposed counting GLCMs of intercontinental range (5,500 kilometers) against the SALT ceiling—in other words, treating long-range GLCMs as though they were ICBMs. The U.S. countered with the suggestion of a 2,500-kilometer limit, but GLCMs covered by that limit would not count against the ceiling. The Soviets then retrenched, arguing again for a 600-kilometer limit.

Chiefs on board" the entire proposal. But the fact remains that the across-the-board limit of 2,500 kilometers on all cruise missiles exceeded the Pentagon's own recommendations during the early months of the administration, and even those military planners who were unhappy about the treatment of MX and Backfire in the comprehensive proposal had to concede that deep reductions in the Soviet heavy and land-based MIRV forces were much more important.

At the time, some of Hyland's colleagues had the impression that he thought the comprehensive proposal was unrealistic in the extreme and that he drafted the instructions knowing they were foredoomed. Months later, Hyland said he had never had any illusion that the Kremlin would accept the comprehensive proposal in the form in which the U.S. presented it. But he justified the proposal as an opening bid that might have led to a compromise. With that in view, the negotiating instructions he helped draft for Vance included fallback positions on various features of the proposal. And even if a compromise based on modifications in the comprehensive proposal proved impossible to negotiate, Hyland reasoned that the Soviets would still accept a Vladivostok quick-fix that deferred the Backfire and cruise missile issues to a future round of negotiations. He hoped that by comparison with the drastic nature of the comprehensive proposal, the idea of "closing out" Vladivostok and deferring the gray-area systems to SALT III would look good to the Russians, and they would accept it in March 1977, even though they had already rejected it in February 1976.

However, it remained for Vance himself to insist on the inclusion of such a Vladivostok-Minus alternative in the package he was taking to Moscow. At a formal NSC meeting just before his departure, Vance argued that fallback instructions for various provisions of the comprehensive proposal might not be sufficient to meet the contingencies of the negotiations. What if the Soviets were to reject the entire concept of the comprehensive proposal, which was, after all, a wrenching departure from the established course of the talks? Perhaps there should be an overall fallback, presented to the Soviets simultaneously with the comprehensive proposal. Some of Carter's advisers complained among themselves that Vance was showing his colors once again as an overly cautious lawyer, fretting over what could go wrong. But Carter approved Vance's suggestion, as long as the Soviets understood that the comprehensive proposal was the "preferred" U.S. position and the so-called Vladivostok deferral was a stopgap second choice.

Carter also ordered that the negotiating instructions be revealed to no one outside those present at the NSC meeting. Vance and Warnke were authorized to brief members of their staffs who would be accompanying them to Moscow—but only on the broad outlines of the comprehensive proposal, not on the numbers and details. The existence of fallback instructions for the various provisions in the comprehensive proposals was to be kept the strictest secret, even from Warnke's and Vance's most senior aides. Prepared fallback instructions implied a willingness to compromise, and Brzezinski—who mistrusted both the bureaucracy and the press—feared that leaks about the existence of such instructions would prompt the Soviets to try to pry loose American concessions before they made any of their own.

Gloom Sets In

While Vance was willing to suppress his misgivings and give the comprehensive proposal a try, many of his colleagues back at Foggy Bottom were less sanguine. One official directly involved in SALT—but left out of the crucial round of meetings at the White House—was "flabbergasted and dismayed" when he learned what had happened. "All the work we've done is for naught," lamented another. A third official, whose job would require him to put the best possible light on the proposal in regular contacts with the Russians, commented sardonically, "Kissinger initialed an *aide-mémoire* after Vladivostok that in effect said the Soviets could keep the heavy ICBMs they had if we kept all our forward-based systems, so I guess it won't be completely outrageous if they resist our suggestion that they throw away half of their heavies." Throughout the government the fear was expressed, in muted tones, that by asking for so much, the U.S. would get nothing —or would have to settle for so much less that it would look like a mammoth cave-in.

A week before Vance's departure for Moscow, Gelb was dispatched to Brussels to brief an assembly of North Atlantic Treaty Organization officials on SALT. He had still not seen the negotiating instructions drafted by Hyland, and he did not fully realize how sweeping and profound the proposed reductions would be. A number of the NATO officials who listened to Gelb's presentation came away with the impression that Vance would essentially be seeking to wrap up the Vladivostok accord. That indeed had been the approach Gelb earnestly favored, but it was no longer his government's position. Marshall Shulman, a Columbia University Kremlinologist who was serving as

Vance's part-time consultant on Soviet affairs, did not learn of the comprehensive proposal until the day before Vance and his party left for Moscow. Warnke's deputy negotiator, Ralph Earle, and his principal technical expert, James Timbie, were caught by surprise by the starkness and magnitude of the proposal when they learned of it. Walter Slocombe had only a few days' warning. Brown told him about the comprehensive proposal after the formal NSC meeting at which the instructions were presented, but that was nearly a week after the President had decided in favor of a proposal more ambitious even than the Vladivostok-Plus option in the Slocombe triptych.

The professional diplomats and Soviet affairs experts were especially skeptical about how the proposal would fare in Moscow. In a series of speeches Brezhnev had made clear that the Kremlin was in high dudgeon over Carter's human rights policy. Therefore the Soviet leaders would be more inclined than usual to see any new U.S. initiative as a provocation. In the very first weeks of the administration, the President had sent a letter to Andrei Sakharov, the leader of the dissident Soviet intelligentsia, and in early March Carter had received Vladimir Bukovsky, a prominent dissident in exile, in the Oval Office. Both gestures dramatized the Carter administration's determination to be bold, open and, above all, different from its predecessors in the way it handled the Russians. The Soviet leadership strongly protested what it called interference in the internal affairs of the U.S.S.R. The administration attempted to balance its criticism of repression in the Soviet Union with palliative assurances that the American concern with human rights would not harm U.S.-Soviet relations "in areas of common interest"—an often repeated phrase officially acknowledged to mean primarily SALT. Such disclaimers rang hollow. It took two to prevent the deterioration of détente from affecting SALT, and the Soviet Union clearly did not share the new American administration's desire to insulate the arms control negotiations from the sparks flying around the rest of the relationship.

When Ambassador Anatoly Dobrynin arrived at the State Department for a briefing by Vance on the comprehensive proposal, he came anticipating trouble. The last-minute timing of the meeting was itself troublesome. Kissinger had routinely given Dobrynin a few weeks' advance notice of any initiatives he was planning to present to the Soviet leadership. Kissinger knew the Kremlin hated surprises. Dobrynin's superiors back in Moscow were inclined to reject out of hand anything new and complicated that they had not had ample opportunity to heft, sniff and hold up to the light. Yet now Dobrynin was summoned to the State Department shortly before Vance was to make the first high-level contact between the Carter administration and the Politburo. After listening with arched brows to Vance's presentation, Dobrynin responded pointedly that the proposal seemed to have little to do with the Vladivostok accord, which, he reminded the secretary of state, the Soviet leaders considered sacrosanct. Vance stressed that while the comprehensive proposal was the preferred American position, he would submit the Vladivostok deferral at the same time. He would also be prepared, he added, to discuss ways of making the comprehensive proposal a basis for further negotiation. Vance intended this rather oblique statement as a broad hint to Dobrynin that his negotiating instructions contained fallbacks and that the Soviet leaders would find him authorized to compromise on various features of the comprehensive proposal. Vance's briefing of Dobrynin, while thorough, was entirely oral. That the Soviet ambassador was given nothing in writing, combined with his habit of taking few if any notes, led to speculation later that Dobrynin may not have fully understood the magnitude of the proposed American reductions and that his misunderstanding may have contributed to the unpleasantness of the surprise awaiting his superiors in Moscow. Vance himself, however, was convinced that Dobrynin both absorbed what Vance told him and transmitted it accurately to the Kremlin.*

As a result of the White House's insistence on keeping SALT paper work within the most restricted circle possible, the comprehensive proposal was not "staffed out" to government specialists in the usual fashion. The CIA, for example, was asked to provide predictions of the likely Soviet responses to various earlier options—but not to the final position. Carter had campaigned against the secret diplomacy of Henry Kissinger, and the new administration had, from the moment of Carter's famous inaugural walk down Pennsylvania Avenue, advertised its openness. Yet here was the Carter inner circle—and more specifically, Kissinger's old power base now under new management, the National Security Council—engaging in secrecy of Kissingerian dimensions.

The irony was compounded on the very eve of Vance's takeoff for

---

*Henry Kissinger also received an oral briefing, although how thorough is in dispute. Kissinger, Vance, Brzezinski and their wives dined with the Carters at the White House just before Vance's departure. The President summarized the comprehensive proposal for Kissinger. The former secretary of state turned his eyes skyward, thought for a moment, and said, "Yes, I think they might accept it." Asked about the conversation two years later, Kissinger said he had no recollection of being briefed in great detail or of venturing a concrete prediction of what the Soviets might accept.

Moscow. The administration, having virtually hidden the comprehensive proposal from itself, was seized by a spasm of openness. Carter revealed to the world both the main features of the comprehensive proposal and the second-choice, "deferral" option. The President lifted up the corner of the veil in an address before the United Nations General Assembly in mid March, his first major foreign policy speech in office. The U.S. would pursue "strict controls or even a freeze on new types and new generations of weaponry," he said, and "a deep reduction in the strategic arms of both sides." If such an agreement could not be concluded quickly, then he would settle for "a limited agreement based on those elements of the Vladivostok accord on which we can find a complete consensus."

Harold Brown had misgivings about the tactical wisdom of such sneak previews. Having negotiated with the Russians himself in Geneva, he knew that the Soviet Union would interpret the publicity as a propaganda ploy; the Kremlin would see the U.S. attempting to establish itself as the most vigorous proponent of disarmament and to put the Soviet Union on the defensive before Vance even reached the negotiating table. But Carter continued to go public with the proposals in even greater detail. One reason for doing so he spelled out in a press conference the day before Vance left: "I believe that it's very important for the American people to know the framework within which the discussions might take place and to give me, through their own approval, strength as a party to some of the resolutions of disputes and also to make sure that when I do speak, I don't speak with a hollow voice." Carter the populist was in effect going over the head of his own government to seek a mandate from the people. By floating the proposal before national television cameras, Carter was also seeking support from Congress, particularly from Senator Henry Jackson, who had been informed about the comprehensive proposal in advance of Carter's public statements. Once Carter had unveiled the proposal, Jackson issued a statement to the press praising it as a step in the right direction—away from what he saw as the folly of the "Kissinger-Nixon-Ford approach." Finally, Carter was trying to go over the head of most of the Soviet bureaucracy as well. He had a notion, encouraged by Brzezinski, that he might be able to shock the highest level of the civilian leadership in Moscow into paying close attention to his initiative before the rigidly conservative Soviet military and diplomatic establishments had a chance to pick the proposal apart and lobby against it.

In the question-and-answer portion of his press conference, Carter said, "We will be taking new proposals to the Soviet Union. We're not abandoning the agreements made in the Vladivostok agreement. As you know, all previous SALT agreements have been in effect limitations that were so high that they were in effect just ground rules for intensified competition and a continued massive growth in nuclear weapons." It was a telling non sequitur. The second sentence—"We're not abandoning the agreements made" at Vladivostok—was a sop to the Soviets and to the Sovietologists in the U.S. government, but it was a meager one, coming between a frank declaration that the U.S. was sending "new proposals" and an equally frank dismissal of "all previous SALT agreements." At the end of the press conference, Carter made an extemporaneous statement that caused even his most loyal and obedient supporters to wince: "If we're disappointed—which is a possibility—then we'll try to modify our stance." Now the President was *inviting* the Soviets to reject both proposals out of hand and simply to wait for the U.S. to come back with something more to their liking. Not that the Soviets needed any more inducement than they already had. Disappointment in Moscow was not only possible—it was inevitable.

4 The Making of a Compromise

Just before he flew off to Moscow, Cyrus Vance sounded a characteristically cautious note about his mission. The talks would be "exploratory," he told the press. The meeting would probably not produce a new agreement right away. He hoped it would provide the foundation for further negotiations, both in follow-up meetings between Gromyko and himself and in the resumption of work by the permanent SALT delegations in Geneva. En route to Moscow, Vance stopped in Brussels to brief NATO. Contrary to the impression left by Leslie Gelb in his own consultations with alliance officials a few days before, the Vladivostok accord was no longer the order of the day. Instead, President Carter had decided to find out if the Soviets were interested in deep reductions right away. Gelb himself—who had now been informed about the main provisions in the comprehensive proposal—prepared the "talking paper" that Vance used in Brussels. Often in such circumstances, the secretary would distribute his prepared text so that the assembled West European diplomats and military officers could send copies to their governments. On this occasion, however, Vance read the paper aloud, then put it in his pocket. Vance was under orders not to discuss the numerical levels of the proposed new ceiling and subceiling. The secrecy seemed excessive, given all the publicity that had preceded Vance's departure. Carter's press conference—with all its candor about what Vance would be proposing and about the U.S.'s willingness to modify its position—was still ringing in everyone's ears. Moreover, the widespread pessimism of Vance's staff was infectious.

On arrival in Moscow, however, the American delegation's mood began to change. The cameras, the lights, the array of dignitaries at the foot of the steps to the Air Force plane, the limousines, the motorcade, the VIP guesthouses in Lenin Hills—all this was heady stuff, even for Vance. The skepticism began to dissipate. Maybe something would come of these talks after all—the Soviets almost certainly would not accept the whole proposal, but maybe they would accept something. But what exactly *was* the whole proposal? That question still disturbed the members of Vance's entourage who had been briefed generally on the plane but had not been permitted to see the formal negotiating instructions drafted by William Hyland. Walter Slocombe, Lieutenant General Edward Rowny, the SALT representative of the Joint Chiefs of Staff, and others went to Hyland and complained that it was ridiculous for them to accompany the secretary to Moscow without being allowed to see the centerpiece of their mission. Hyland went to Vance and said, "We've got a morale problem. Can I show them the proposal?"

"All right," replied Vance, "but only up to a point." That point did not extend to the fallback instructions within the comprehensive proposal. Those remained the most closely held secret. The President had made clear at the National Security Council meeting that he did not want the Soviets even to know that the U.S. was prepared to compromise on the comprehensive proposal until they demonstrated their own willingness to engage in genuine negotiations. Even if Carter had seriously undercut the appearance of take-it-or-leave-it resolve at his press conference, the NSC secrecy order still stood.

Hyland went to the U.S. embassy, where an office had been set up for the delegation in the "vault," the inner sanctum which was specially insulated against Soviet electronic eavesdropping. Hyland began clipping out of the negotiating instructions those passages that Vance did not want the entire delegation to know about. While he was in the midst of this hasty cut-and-paste job, a number of members of the delegation arrived early for their first look at the text. They surprised Hyland in the act. That evening there were sour jokes at the guesthouses about how Hyland had been "caught shredding our marching orders."

Brezhnev presided at the opening session in the Kremlin. It was a chilly welcome. Echoing a speech he had given at a trade union congress in Moscow a few days before, Brezhnev railed against the Carter human rights campaign. The constructive development of relations was impossible, he said, if the U.S. did not respect "the principles of equality, noninterference in each other's internal affairs and mutual benefit." SALT had become "stagnant," continued Brezhnev. He launched into a lecture on the Vladivostok accord, hailing it both as a momentous diplomatic achievement in its own right and as the only acceptable basis for further progress. Andrei Gromyko picked up the same theme at the beginning of the first working session. He stressed that there was a long and complex history to the negotiations, that both sides must respect the history, and that any attempt to depart from the continuum would jeopardize what had already been accomplished. Even by Soviet standards, the message was not subtle. A number of Americans listening to the foreign minister had the distinct impression that he was rejecting the comprehensive proposal before it was formally presented. After Gromyko finished his statement, he declared a recess and left the Americans sitting at the table to mull over what he had said. Gelb turned to Vance and said, "I think we just heard their answer." The secretary was incredulous. "You mean they're not going to come back with a counterproposal?" "That's right," said Gelb, and he bet one dollar on his prediction.

Warnke, too, could tell that the Soviets were anything but receptive. He was especially struck by Dobrynin's demeanor. Normally so ebullient back in Washington, the ambassador was strangely subdued at the opening of the talks in the Kremlin. Warnke wondered if the transformation was because he was cowed by his bosses. But that hypothesis did not adequately explain Dobrynin's moroseness. It was as though he knew the meeting was already a failure. Still, Warnke guessed that however unhappy Dobrynin's comrades were with the comprehensive proposal, they would at least respond with a counterproposal, if only to keep alive those few American provisions they welcomed—the offers to sacrifice the MX and to leave the Backfire uncounted by SALT. Vance figured that Gromyko was setting the stage for tough bargaining—not for outright rejection.

Vance formally presented the U.S. position by passing out a stark, one-page version of the comprehensive proposal, in English and Russian, that he, Warnke, Hyland and Gelb had drafted on the airplane. The Soviets were at first noncommittal. For almost two days Gromyko and his colleagues picked and probed and sparred. In the process they suggested they might be willing to lower the Vladivostok ceiling from 2,400 total strategic launchers to 2,200 if the U.S. was willing to include the cruise missile and exclude the Backfire. A reduction of 200 was hardly cause for jubilation among the Americans, who were under instructions to seek a maximum reduction of 600 in the Vladivostok ceiling (from 2,400 to as low as 1,800). Nor could the Soviet suggestion be interpreted as a hint of willingness to accept the Vladivostok deferral, since that backup American position would have excluded both the cruise missile and the Backfire from SALT II.

Gromyko's talking points contained another gesture intended to demonstrate that even in the face of what he considered to be extreme American unreasonableness, the Soviet government was determined to be as magnanimous as possible. At issue were two Soviet rockets, the SS-16 and the SS-20. The SS-16 was unique among the new generation of Soviet ICBMs in that it was propelled by solid fuel. That feature made it theoretically more advanced than the SS-17, SS-18 and SS-19, since many American military analysts believe that solid-fuel propulsion, when it works properly, is more efficient and reliable. But unlike its three liquid-fueled, MIRVed siblings, the SS-16 was armed with a single warhead. Moreover, its testing history had been a series of blowups and fizzles. The Soviet breakthrough into solid-fuel technology for ICBMs had been something less than a stunning success. In the files of the Pentagon and the Arms Control Agency, this accident-prone rocket bore the designation "SS-X-16." The "X" stood for "experimental." The U.S. wanted that particular experiment stopped in its tracks, before the SS-16 could be made to work properly and deployed, for the SS-16 had a much more proficient junior partner, the SS-20. The SS-20 is an intermediate-range ballistic missile (IRBM), not an intercontinental ballistic missile (ICBM). IRBMs were not to be covered by SALT II. The SS-20 is a two-stage version of the three-stage SS-16. While the SS-16 was a single-warhead weapon, the SS-20 is MIRVed, and while the SS-16 was still in an experimental phase, the SS-20 was ready to be deployed. Moreover, it was to be deployed "in a mobile mode," on trucks. Mobile missiles enhance unilateral security but undercut bilateral arms control agreements, because they are harder to find, harder to count, harder to hit as targets of retaliation. Mobiles are more survivable but less verifiable than fixed-site rockets. If the Soviets ever perfected the SS-16, they would be able to stockpile the third stage and, in an international crisis, rapidly convert mobile IRBM launchers in mobile ICBM ones. That danger had a name in the lexicon of SALT. It was called "breakout": the Soviets might be in a position to break out of the agreement—to abrogate it abruptly in a way that gave them an immediate, potentially decisive strategic advantage. One of the goals in SALT II has been reducing the danger of breakout. That was the purpose of the long-sought ban on ICBM launchers that could be rapidly reloaded and the ban on the storage of excess missiles. The SS-16 represented a particularly threatening sort of breakout because of its similarity to—and therefore interchangeability with—the SS-20. Seeming to confirm the worst suspicions of the U.S., the Soviets had begun testing the intercontinental SS-16 from a mobile launcher virtually identical to the one on which the SS-20 was already deployed. As the Soviet delegation circled around the comprehensive proposal, Gromyko took note of the U.S.-proposed ban on mobile ICBMs and said the Soviet Union might be willing to promise not to deploy the SS-16 "in a mobile mode." That was, as an American negotiator grumbled afterward, a "nonoffer," for it left wide open the possibility that the Soviets could at any time transform the SS-20 into a mobile SS-16 simply by adding the third stage. As long as the SS-16 program continued, the U.S. anxiety would remain, and Gromyko indicated no willingness to abort the program altogether.

On the third day Brezhnev rejoined the talks. His manner was grim and his rejection of both the comprehensive proposal and the Vladivostok deferral was categorical. He said that his government especially objected to the proposition that the Soviet Union should destroy half of its land-based heavy missiles while the U.S. would only postpone some technological innovations. All this talk about a triad was in a way deceptive; the U.S. had a fourth threat to use against the Soviet Union—its forces based in Western Europe. As another Russian official paraphrased Brezhnev shortly afterward, Soviet intermediate-range weapons, such as the controversial SS-20, "can't hit you from anywhere. But you can drop thousands of missiles on us from Europe. The words strategic and tactical don't mean anything. It is my people who will be killed." Brezhnev was reminding the Carter administration that he had agreed to omit American forward-based systems from SALT II in exchange for Kissinger's agreement at Vladivostok to leave intact the Soviet heavy ICBM force.

Brezhnev did not close the door on dealing with some aspects of the comprehensive proposal in SALT III, but he made clear that there would never be a SALT III unless first there was a SALT II based on the Vladivostok accord. As for the deferral of an accommodation on cruise missiles to SALT III, the Soviets were just as adamant in their refusal now as they had been a year earlier, when the Ford administration proposed the same thing. The Soviets chose, in effect, to pretend

that a third American option—Kissinger's January 1976 compromise
—had the endorsement of the Carter administration, and they made
clear they were willing to engage in further negotiations on that. But
the American delegation was under orders to bargain on the basis of
the Carter proposals, not a left-over Kissinger one. Vance's mandate
made it impossible for him to resort to his fallback instructions, since
the Soviets were clearly unwilling to negotiate on the basis of the
comprehensive proposal. Instead, he moved quickly to try to salvage
the appearance of progress on some ancillary issues. He and Gromyko
agreed to set up eight working groups to negotiate a comprehensive
test ban, prior notification of missile tests, the demilitarization of the
Indian Ocean, and curbs on civil defense as well as chemical, radiologi-
cal, conventional and antisatellite weapons. They also deputized aides
to conduct regular meetings on the proliferation of nuclear weapons.
Vance and Gromyko themselves would meet again on SALT. It was
a hastily improvised grab bag of consolation prizes, and no one was
really consoled. "What are you trying to do—kill SALT?" asked one
Soviet official in private conversation with his American counterpart.
Gromyko's deputy Georgy Kornienko took Paul Warnke aside and
admonished him, "You shouldn't have disregarded the fact that
Brezhnev had to spill political blood to get the Vladivostok accords."
Kornienko said that the Soviet leader had been especially incensed by
the American attempt to cut the heavy-missile force and by the across-
the-board 2,500-kilometer range limit on cruise missiles.

The Soviets were willing, indeed eager, to downplay the failure
and to muffle their accusations in public. TASS issued a terse statement
saying, "The two sides agreed to continue their exchange of views on
SALT and other subjects." Vance, however, was determined to adhere
to the spirit of openness to which the Carter administration had committed itself with enthusiasm if not with total consistency. The two
men in his entourage who were most doubtful about the wisdom of
advertising the failure of the mission were Under Secretary of State
for Political Affairs Philip Habib and William Hyland. A professional
diplomat and a professional Kremlinologist, they knew that a public
airing of the disagreement would be bad diplomacy and a psychological mistake in the handling of the Soviet leadership. The Russians
would conclude that the U.S. was yet again trying to put them on the
defensive, just as Carter had done on the eve of Vance's departure.
But when Vance returned to Spasso House, the residence of Ambassador Malcolm Toon, after the last negotiating session, Hyland and

Habib remained in the Kremlin to draft a communiqué aimed at downplaying the failure and keeping SALT alive. They missed Vance's press conference and thus missed a chance to talk Vance out of going public with the failure.

"Good evening," said Vance to the chamberful of newsmen, microphones and cameras. "We met this afternoon with General Secretary Brezhnev and Foreign Minister Gromyko and other officials. At that meeting the Soviets told us they had examined our two proposals and did not find either acceptable. They proposed nothing new on their side." Vance went on to spell out in even greater detail than had Carter the week before the main features of the comprehensive proposal—although he still did not reveal the numbers. Vance pronounced himself "disappointed," but said the talks had been "useful" and that "U.S.-Soviet relations will continue to be good." He was confident, he said, that a SALT II agreement could be reached before the expiration of the five-year SALT I interim agreement on October 3.

Back in Washington, Jimmy Carter struck a less conciliatory note. He said it was "very encouraging" that the Soviets had agreed to keep talking, but he vowed that the U.S. would not give up in its pursuit of its goals. Then came a threat: "Obviously, if we feel at the conclusion of the discussions that the Soviets are not acting in good faith," he said darkly, "then I would be forced to consider a much more deep commitment to the development and deployment of additional weapons." That statement, coupled with the President's indication that the U.S. intended to stand pat on its main proposals, infuriated the Soviet leadership more than ever. As Dobrynin later explained: "President Carter seemed to be saying, 'Either you accept our position or we start the arms race and the cold war again.' His statement was taken as a *diktat* or ultimatum."

No sooner was Vance heading westward than Gromyko gave a rare press conference of his own. He denounced the comprehensive proposal as a "cheap and shady maneuver," aimed at achieving for the U.S. "unilateral advantages." Gromyko made public the Soviets' own threat which Brezhnev had hinted at in his rejection of the American position: if the U.S. persisted in seeking deep reductions in Soviet force levels, especially heavy missiles, the U.S.S.R. would "have the right to raise the question of liquidating" U.S. bases in Western Europe, submarines belonging to NATO, medium bombers and "other vehicles capable of carrying nuclear arms" but so far excluded from SALT.

Then Gromyko did something entirely unprecedented on either side: he revealed for the record the numbers in the U.S. comprehensive proposal. He was going Vance one better, showing that two could play the game of mixing diplomacy with propaganda. Gromyko apparently calculated that telling the world how drastically the U.S. had proposed to cut the Vladivostok ceiling and subceiling would dramatize his charge that the Americans were being grossly unreasonable. Jody Powell, the presidential press secretary, defended the comprehensive proposal as "extremely fair and equitable." Zbigniew Brzezinski appeared in the White House press room to deliver a lengthy rationale for the controversial provisions.

As Vance headed home, the strategic arms limitation talks were degenerating into an intercontinental shouting match. Morale and discipline in Vance's party were in shambles. A spate of news stories appeared reporting the dismay of anonymous officials on Vance's plane over the Powell statement and the Brzezinski press briefing. Tempers were frayed back in Washington, too. When he saw the newspaper accounts of the angry and embittered mood aboard the plane, Brzezinski demanded, "Who is the leaker? We must find the leaker!" The fact was that virtually every official aboard the secretary's plane, with the possible exception of the secretary himself, was making no secret of his shock and discouragement to the accompanying reporters; and while Vance's upper lip may have remained stiff, his eyes had a glazed, traumatized look.

Unhappy Homecoming

Even before Vance's return, the Carter administration divided into factions over whom to blame for the diplomatic disaster. The intelligence community was ordered to produce an analysis of what had gone wrong. "We'd been left out of the huddle and then cut out of the play," bitterly remarked a high CIA official, "and now they were coming to us and demanding to know in this accusatory tone of voice why they'd dropped the ball." With the acuity of hindsight, most of the experts agreed on at least six reasons why the meeting had been a debacle: the old boys in the Kremlin were testing the mettle of the new boys in the White House; the Soviets resented the American attempt to conduct diplomacy out in the open; they resented the new administration's trying to change the rules in a game that had been going on for eight years; they resented the effort to put them on the defensive; they resented the administration's assumption that it could keep SALT on an even keel while rocking the boat of Soviet-American relations with propaganda about human rights; but most of all they resented what they saw, with justification, as the one-sided nature of the comprehensive proposal itself.

Only those who had been involved in the concoction of the comprehensive proposal doubted that the proposal itself was the biggest of the booby traps that had blown up in Vance's face. Hyland, for instance, argued for more than a year afterward that the Soviets were so annoyed by the way the proposal was sprung on them that they never considered it on its own merits. Carter said the Soviets had rejected his initiative because "it [was] so substantive and such a radical change from the past." Even Warnke, who had nurtured—and expressed—strong misgivings about the political wisdom of seeking drastic cuts, felt afterward that the primary problem was an American misjudgment about the workings of the Soviet system: "The military and political bureaucracy [in the U.S.S.R.] turned out to be too constipated to digest the proposal." David Aaron made no apologies for the substance of the initiative. "If we'd taken the same position in 1972," he said, "we'd be better off today." It became the party line at the NSC that the proposal had been "mishandled politically" in Moscow—that Vance should never have gone public with the Soviet rejection, that he should have left the Soviets to ponder it quietly—perhaps to come back later with a counterproposal of their own. Henry Kissinger, commenting from the sidelines, seemed to agree. He had gone to Moscow and been rebuffed many times, he said, but he had never held a press conference about it afterward.

Vance's aides and partisans within the administration responded with the charge that the comprehensive proposal had been made up out of whole cloth within the NSC and foisted on Vance; under orders but against his better instincts, Vance had done his best to sell the NSC's shabby goods to the Russians, and in holding a press conference at the end of the visit he had only been following the President's example of diplomacy in the sunshine. Vance himself made no excuses, nor did he join in the game of pin the tail on the NSC that suddenly became the number one sport in Foggy Bottom. But he still managed to stumble into a fresh controversy with the White House. Vance's inherent cautiousness in those days was exceeded only by his candor. At yet another news conference shortly after his return to Washington, Vance was asked if the whole venture had been a mistake. "No one can say that one never makes any miscalculation," he replied. It was a double negative that translated loosely into an affirmative—and indisputable—admission. The next day Jody Powell felt obliged to "clarify" what the secretary of state had said. Powell denied that Vance's statement had contained "any implication" of a "significant miscalculation." The Soviets' "initial rejection," continued Powell, simply meant that the Kremlin needed more time to consider the proposal.

While considerable energy was expended in self-justification, obfuscation and recrimination, some officials were engaged in the more constructive, though not necessarily more convincing, exercise of trying to find a silver lining in the thunderhead Vance had encountered in Moscow. Some middle-level Pentagon and NSC officials concluded that there were a few useful if discouraging lessons to be learned from the rejection of the comprehensive proposal. The U.S. was fooling itself if it thought the Soviets shared the belief that in the age of arms control, less is better. The Soviets had now revealed their own fundamental conviction that more is better. By so abruptly and reflexively refusing to consider substantial reductions in force levels, the Soviets had betrayed the basic primitiveness—and dangerousness—of their own strategic doctrine. They still put their faith in brute power and had no use for elegant theories about parity and crisis stability. American concerns that the vulnerability of Minuteman might have a destabilizing effect on the strategic balance simply did not impress the Russians. The protection of Minuteman was a problem for the U.S. to solve, and the U.S. could not count on Soviet cooperation. Or so it seemed. "Vance's experience in Moscow," concluded one official philosophically, "was good for us in that it made us less naïve about the Russians. It gave us a clearer-headed idea of what we were dealing with."

Some optimists in the government argued an almost diametrically opposite point: however feckless the American handling of the comprehensive proposal may have been and however rude the Russian rebuff, at least the proposal had established the U.S.'s determination to impose upon the Soviet-American relationship a more sophisticated concept of strategic stability than the Russians had traditionally accepted. The Carter administration was going to make the Russians address the problem of Minuteman vulnerability whether they liked it or not. Carter had shown he was committed to reducing force levels rather than merely limiting them—that he was bent on reining in the technology that had always run away with arms control agreements in the past. Said one proponent of this view: "The comprehensive proposal put the Kremlin on notice that we were serious about a more meaningful sort of arms control than previous administrations had attempted, and it forced the Soviets to pay attention to some problems they'd managed to ignore when SALT was pursued much more timidly by Kissinger."

But even the most Panglossian analysis could not conceal that the comprehensive proposal had done damage, and the damage outweighed whatever didactic or cathartic good may have been accomplished. The proposal led the Soviet leadership to conclude that the new administration did not really know what it was doing—and to the extent that it did know, it was up to no good. The episode damaged institutional and personal relations within the Carter administration, especially between the State Department and the National Security Council. But most important, the comprehensive proposal established a yardstick against which the critics of SALT could evaluate subsequent compromises. By such a measure, any reasonable, negotiable agreement would seem to be an ignominious retreat. Thus, the yardstick of the ill-conceived, ill-fated comprehensive proposal was destined to become, in the jaundiced eyes of the skeptics, a bench mark of failure—and in the hands of the opponents of the SALT II treaty a bludgeon with which to beat the Carter administration over the head in years to come.

Trying Again

The administration threw itself into the task of preparing to compromise while minimizing the appearance of retreat. Having been baptized by fire in Moscow, Vance became a more assertive adviser to the President. In a number of private conversations and written memoranda, the secretary of state urged a fundamental change in the handling of SALT. The negotiations could no longer take place in an atmosphere of high drama and intense publicity. In such conditions, the Soviets' natural suspiciousness became raving paranoia, and their reluctance became intractability. As Vance later recalled his advice to the President: "In dealing with the Soviets, we couldn't be as open as we had hoped we could. Out in the open is just not the way that they are prepared to negotiate. Informal, exploratory discussions are an essential part of the process. Without those kinds of discussions, it was going to be impossible to make the kind of progress we wanted to make. You have to be able to sit down and talk very directly, with essentially nobody else around. Then they will open up and tell you, 'Well, now, this is what our problem is. . . .' So you understand their problem and can see if there are ways to take it into account while still achieving your own objective. They [the Soviets] can't possibly do that in an open session, with all their colleagues around. Those kinds of discussion are critical."

There had to be, in short, a return to secret diplomacy in the "back channel"—regular, informal, unpublicized contacts in Washington, away from the klieg lights of press conferences, full-dress ministerial meetings and summits. In essence, Vance was telling the President that the Carter approach to SALT had not worked and that they must do it Henry Kissinger's way instead. This was easier advice for Vance to give than for Carter and Zbigniew Brzezinski to accept. Vance had immense respect for Kissinger, and that respect seemed almost completely undiluted by envy. Washington, especially early in the administration, reverberated with comparisons between Kissinger and Vance, many of them unfavorable to Vance. By contrast with Kissinger, Vance was dull, and dullness was close to a mortal sin in the eyes of the capital's arbiters of favor. But Vance was also a profoundly secure individual. He knew his strengths. They were experience, judiciousness, integrity, an ability to absorb and argue a brief, and a quality that he sometimes referred to with a characteristically inelegant but utilitarian phrase—"stick-to-itiveness." He had no hope or aspiration to compete with Kissinger as a charmer, an intriguer, an explicator or a grand master of the global concept. Therefore Vance had no deep psychological aversion to adapting his and the administration's style of operation to Kissinger's when it seemed to make sense. Also, by background and temperament he was more at home and more effective in confidential deliberations behind closed doors than on the hustings or at the podium. Thus, back-channel diplomacy more naturally suited him than the open, confrontational style favored by Carter and Brzezinski.

The President and his national security adviser were driven much more by a sense of competition with Kissinger than was Vance, and it was to the White House, not the State Department, that Kissinger was obviously speaking early in April, in his first public address since leaving office. He warned against "self-imposed deadlines or rhetorical battles that publicly stake the prestige of both sides." Gerald Ford, lecturing at the University of Michigan, said, "There was too much public rhetoric before the negotiations" in Moscow. Even Henry Jackson engaged in some after-the-fact kibitzing about how best to handle the Russians: "Frankly I would not have gone public," he said. "You never want to push them into a corner." This counsel, however sound, had a ring of unintended irony, coming from the author of the Jackson Amendment which had linked U.S. trade concessions to Soviet emigration policy and pushed the Russians so far into the corner that they lashed out at Kissinger when he came to Moscow to negotiate SALT in 1974. It was also ironic coming from the senator whom Carter had been most eager to impress with his bold and very public March initiative.

Vance argued forcefully that lowering the volume and visibility of the talks would make SALT less subject to the ups and downs of the Soviet-American relationship. He was particularly concerned about the downs, since almost from the first day of the Carter administration, the relationship had been in decline. The primary irritant had been the human rights policy, but the Kremlin's adventurist activity in Africa, the conflicting interests and tactics of the superpowers in the Middle East, and a range of other quarrels had exacerbated mistrust and misunderstanding. As part of his own post-mortem of the Moscow debacle, Vance's adviser on Soviet affairs, Marshall Shulman, now upgraded to a full-time special consultant with ambassadorial rank, prepared what he called a "tabular account of related events." It was a device he had often used as a teaching aid in his course on Soviet foreign policy at Columbia—a diagram showing the coincidence of developments in different areas. It was a handwritten, fold-out, chronological chart illustrating that the Kremlin's mounting complaints over the new administration's emerging arms control policy had closely paralleled the escalation of tensions on other issues, particularly human rights. Vance and Shulman felt that by reducing the public drama associated with SALT, the administration might be able to diminish the "negative linkage" between the negotiations and the rest of the Soviet-American relationship. Here, too, Vance was following a course on which Kissinger had embarked at the end of his term. Kissinger, too, used to complain that SALT was difficult enough without having to negotiate under the additional burden of being "held responsible for the peace of the world." Of course, it was partly because of Kissinger's own earlier overselling of SALT in the heyday of détente that public opinion and the press tended to identify the negotiations as the "cornerstone," "touchstone," "bellwether," "linch-pin" and "acid test" of détente. But as that fancy French word fell out of favor in 1975 and 1976, Kissinger attempted as much as possible to separate the pursuit of a treaty from the more elusive and politically controversial pursuit of Soviet-American friendship. Vance shared that objective.

Reactivating the back channel meant reengaging Anatoly Dobrynin as a central figure in SALT. Dobrynin had been Kissinger's principal negotiating partner on SALT. Throughout SALT I and at the beginning of SALT II as well, Kissinger had found Dobrynin more intellectually versatile, more self-confident, more conversant with the strategic ramifications and technical complexities of SALT, more capable of give-and-take, and altogether a better negotiating partner than Gromyko. Largely because Dobrynin had been so closely associated with Kissinger, the Soviet ambassador was suspect at the Carter White House. He and Brzezinski were particularly wary of each other, and each found it difficult to resist the temptation to play mischievously on the other's sensitivities. Dobrynin made a point of keeping in close touch with what he once called "the shadow foreign ministry," Kissinger's office at the Georgetown Center for Strategic and International Studies. For his part, Brzezinski seemed to enjoy Dobrynin's discomfiture whenever his principal rival for influence and prestige, Georgy Arbatov, came to town. Arbatov was the director of an institute for America-watchers in Moscow, and he was for a while rumored to be destined to succeed Dobrynin.

Aside from mistrusting Dobrynin as a holdover from the Kissinger era, Brzezinski, Aaron and others in the administration had another, less personal reason for wanting to "cut Dobrynin down a peg or two," as one of them put it in the early spring of 1977. During his sixteen years in Washington, but especially in the Nixon and Ford years, Dobrynin had enjoyed far more access to the upper echelons of the host government than had his various American counterparts in Moscow. The Carter administration wanted to restore a degree of reciprocity in the treatment of envoys. At the very least, they wanted to open a second back channel through Malcolm Toon in Moscow. But it was not to be. Toon was a career diplomat with considerable experience in Soviet affairs, whom Gerald Ford had nominated for the Moscow post. Carter had decided to keep him on because he had a reputation for toughness, even gruffness, in dealing with the Soviets, and the new team in the White House was eager to cultivate a bit of that reputation for itself. The Kremlin tolerated Toon but never granted him anything like the special position that Dobrynin had carved out for himself in Washington. Eventually, reluctantly, the Carter White House came to accept Dobrynin not only as the indispensable Russian but as a much more vital link than Toon.

Within a week after Vance's return from Moscow, Dobrynin began shuttling back and forth between his embassy and the White House and State Department. He held a series of unpublicized meetings with Carter, Brzezinski, Vance and Warnke. In order to avoid the reporters who regularly staked out the diplomatic entrance to the State Department, Dobrynin's limousine took him into an underground garage. From there he ascended by private elevator to Vance's office on the seventh floor. The first meetings were devoted to an assessment of why Vance's mission to Moscow had gone so badly and to assurances that both sides were determined to put that episode behind them. Dobrynin recalled how much importance the U.S. had attached to the principle of equality in the aggregates negotiated at Vladivostok. The Soviet Union, too, was interested in equality, he said. Moscow was no less committed than the U.S. to the goal of reductions, but they must be "fair and equal." The comprehensive proposal would have required the U.S.S.R. to make drastic cuts in existing systems, "while you would give up nothing." At one point he asked almost woefully, "Don't you realize that for us, too, this is an insecure world, an unstable world?" The American officials told Dobrynin that the U.S. was prepared to work hard to find some compromise that took account of the Soviet objections to the comprehensive proposal but at the same time was consistent with the goals of the proposal.

Brezhnev and Carter traded encouraging words in public early in April. The Soviet leader said "a reasonable accommodation is possible"—if the U.S. abandoned its "one-sided position." Carter replied three days later that while the comprehensive proposal as a whole was fair, he would be "very eager to change" any provisions that Moscow could prove were inequitable. It was a somewhat puzzling statement, but it was clearly meant as a signal of flexibility, and Moscow took it that way.

The primary questions that Vance and Gromyko would have to address at their next meeting, scheduled for May in Geneva, were two: what could and should SALT II accomplish? What form should the agreement take? Before the Carter administration could hammer out mutually acceptable answers with the Soviets, it had to agree, within its own ranks, what answers were desirable and feasible. The President told his aides that while he was willing to change the style of his approach to a SALT II treaty, he wanted to preserve as much of the substance as possible. The administration must find an imaginative way of accomplishing the main goals of the comprehensive proposal —slowing down the modernization of Soviet missilry and postponing if not eliminating the threat to the survivability of Minuteman. David Aaron and Leslie Gelb both saw it as their task to "repackage" the provisions of the comprehensive proposal. Warnke described the objective as a "synthesis" of the preferred comprehensive proposal, the Vladivostok deferral second choice, and the Soviet proposal then on the table—i.e., the Kremlin version of the compromise Henry Kissinger had suggested in January 1976. Hyland spoke of the need "to get the Soviets' attention this time in a way that we didn't before because our come-on was too stark." Brzezinski described the new objective as a "staged fusing" of the short-term and long-term goals contained in the comprehensive proposal.

The administration set about to divide and conquer that tangle of problems. The most important of many informal but intensive brainstorming sessions turned out to be a two-and-a-half-hour luncheon between Gelb and Hyland in the executive dining room on the eighth floor of the State Department. Hyland marked off three columns on his paper napkin. The two men then sifted through the wreckage of the Vance mission to Moscow and sorted SALT into three categories: (1) those elements necessary to satisfy the Russians that the Vladivostok accord would be enshrined in the SALT II treaty; (2) interim measures to cover the weapons that had proved most contentious in Moscow—cruise missile, mobile missiles and new types of Soviet ICBMs; and (3) long-term goals for the period after the expiration of SALT II. Column 1 on Hyland's napkin became the outline for the treaty to run until 1985,* column 2 a three-year protocol to the treaty,

---

*Within the administration, the main document was almost always referred to as a treaty. The assumption was that it would be submitted to the Senate in that form, thus requiring ratification by a two thirds majority. However, the precedents were mixed, and the future was uncertain, so Carter did not want to rule out altogether the possibility of submitting the main document as an agreement to be approved by a simple majority of both the Senate and the House. SALT I included the antiballistic missile treaty of indefinite duration, which was ratified by two thirds of the Senate, and the five-year interim accord on offensive weapons, which was an agreement. The prospective SALT II accord had already evolved—or in the view of some, degenerated—from an agreement of indefinite duration to one that would expire in 1985. But almost everyone in the administration assumed SALT II could be concluded before the October 1977 expiration of SALT I. That would give the new accord a life span of eight years

and column 3 a statement of principles to govern SALT III.

As conceived at the time, the SALT II treaty and the SALT III statement of principles were fairly straightforward devices to accommodate, first, the Kremlin's fixation with the Vladivostok accord and, second, Jimmy Carter's devotion to "real arms control." The protocol was more ingenious and more problematic. The Soviets had complained in Moscow that the comprehensive proposal unfairly demanded they make sacrifices in their one area of strength, land-based ICBMs, without comparable concessions on the American side. In the newly conceived protocol, the Soviets would be asked to accept temporary constraints on the modernization of their ICBMs in exchange for temporary constraints on the American weapon system they most feared, the cruise missile. But here the brainstormers had to be careful to distinguish between ground- and sea-launched cruise missiles on the one hand and air-launched cruise missiles on the other. The U.S. had no plans to deploy SLCMs and GLCMs within the period of the protocol and it would therefore be relatively painless to accept a ban on such deployment. But air-launched cruise missiles—ALCMs—figured crucially in a decision already facing the President. Carter was still trying to make up his mind whether to proceed with the development of the B-1 supersonic penetrating bomber. He was tantalized by the idea that cheap cruise missiles aboard reliable old B-52s might be just as effective at penetrating Soviet air defenses as the crushingly expensive B-1. Therefore the designers of what became known as the three-tier proposal had to be sure that they protected the option of deploying long-range ALCMs against any constraints on cruise missiles in the second tier. Dobrynin said in April that Moscow could live with a SALT II agreement that permitted the U.S. to have long-range ALCMs as long as there were no ground-launched cruise missiles "within striking distance" of Soviet targets from American forward-based systems. The proposed protocol, therefore, would ban the deployment of long-range GLCMs and SLCMs. Any cruise missile with a range greater than 600 kilometers would be considered long-range. While air-launched cruise missiles with a range greater than 600 kilometers would be permitted under the new American proposal, it was tentatively decided that SALT II would permit ALCMs a maximum

---

and hence make it worthy of submission as a treaty. Not until 1978, when time was running out for SALT II and opposition to ratification was mounting, did the White House actively—and abortively—press to keep open the possibility of submitting it as an agreement.

range of 2,500 kilometers—the same limit that the March comprehensive proposal would have imposed on all varieties of cruise missile.

Like the comprehensive proposal, the three-tier proposal that Vance would take to Gromyko in May came about with a minimum of involvement by the bureaucracy. The circle of those who knew about, and contributed to, the refinement of the plan was widened somewhat to include Marshall Shulman, one of Gelb's assistants, Charles Henkin, James Timbie at the Arms Control and Disarmament Agency, and a handful of others. But many experts at the Pentagon, the CIA and even the NSC were, once again, left mostly in the dark. There was some feeling around the State Department and the Arms Control Agency that since Harold Brown had been largely responsible for the disastrous comprehensive proposal, Brown's "boys," if not Brown himself, deserved to be frozen out of the rescue operation. Brown's principal "boy" on SALT was Walter Slocombe, and he was for the most part bypassed during the preparation of the three-tier proposal.

If the Pentagon felt left out of the flurry of repackaging in April and early May, it could commiserate with the U.S. SALT delegation in Geneva, which was just resuming work. The permanent negotiators learned of the existence of the new proposal less than forty-eight hours before Vance arrived to meet with Gromyko. But an important difference from the comprehensive proposal in March was that this time Gromyko himself had ample time to ponder the new U.S. position. Vance, Brzezinski and Warnke had held another round of unpublicized, intensive meetings with Dobrynin in Washington to go over the proposal well in advance and in great detail.

Picking Up the Pieces on Neutral Ground

Gromyko came to Geneva authorized to accept the general contours of the three-tier proposal—but instructed to fight the Americans every inch of the way over which weapons would be covered in each tier. He was also under instructions to deliver yet another stern lecture on how obnoxious his government had found the March comprehensive proposal, in particular its provisions for a MIRVed ICBM subceiling of 550, a reduction in Soviet heavy missiles and a 2,500-kilometer range limit for all cruise missiles. Those provisions epitomized, said Gromyko, the American "attempt to achieve unilateral advantages." Vance and Warnke both replied that the U.S. had only been attempting to prevent the Soviets' emerging advantage in large, land-based MIRVs from undermining the stability of the relationship and the utility—indeed, the political acceptability—of the agreement. To that same end, the U.S. proposed that the three-tier proposal halt the headlong MIRVing of Soviet heavy missiles. The SALT I interim agreement had frozen Soviet heavies at about 300; the U.S. was now suggesting that SALT II contain a freeze-within-the-freeze of 190 MIRVed heavies. It was what Warnke called an "offer to marry" the MIRVed ICBM subceiling and the reduction of heavy missiles proposed in March. Gromyko rejected it. Refinements in the Vladivostok accord might be in order, he said; modest reductions in the Vladivostok ceiling and subceiling might be further discussed, although the magic numbers 2,400 and 1,320 must appear in the treaty as starting points to be lowered later on. But the Soviet side would steadfastly reject efforts to "tamper with the spirit" of Vladivostok or to "disregard" the accord. Any new proposal aimed at Soviet heavy missiles —whether it concerned all heavies or just MIRVed ones, whether it would reduce them or just freeze them—was completely out of order. Moreover, American persistence on this point could jeopardize the negotiations.

The revised U.S. position on cruise missiles—that the three-year protocol should ban deployment of long-range ground-launched and sea-launched cruise missiles, but not air-launched ones—prompted Gromyko to reiterate, with new vigor, another of the Soviets' well-worn demands: there must be no "special privileges" for air-launched cruise missiles. Heavy bombers had been designated at Vladivostok as strategic nuclear launch vehicles, and by logical extension of the Vladivostok understanding, a heavy bomber armed with cruise missiles was a multiple-warhead vehicle and therefore should be covered by the 1,320 subceiling.

In their initial presentation of the three-tier proposal, the Americans had envisioned the three-year protocol as an executive agreement, which the U.S. Congress could consider separately from the longer-term treaty. Gromyko objected to any such arrangement, for it might allow the Congress to approve the treaty but reject the protocol. Since the protocol contained the cruise missile limits in which the Soviets were most interested, the protocol must be integral to the treaty in whatever legislative form the final agreement took. Vance agreed: the administration would submit the treaty and protocol to the Congress as a single package.

After his final session with Gromyko, Vance held a news conference. He unveiled the three-tier proposal and announced that "the
differences between the two sides have been narrowed." While Vance
was striking an upbeat note in the press center at the Intercontinental
Hotel, Gromyko was doing just the opposite at Geneva Airport before
boarding his plane to fly back to Moscow. "Major, serious difficulties
remain," intoned Gromyko, looking more dour than usual. The U.S.
was continuing its "attempts to achieve unilateral advantages." Newsmen who had covered the Gromyko departure rushed back to the
hotel downtown to find out whether the Soviet foreign minister and
the American secretary of state had indeed been at the same meeting
for the past three days. U.S. officials were genuinely puzzled by
Gromyko's dyspeptic remarks. Subsequently, a Soviet diplomat explained that Gromyko had decided to grumble over his shoulder at
Vance for three reasons: (1) he objected to Vance's going public with
the three-tier framework and stressing only what had been accomplished—it all smacked of the new American administration's apparently incorrigible penchant for blabbermouth diplomacy, and it
looked as though the U.S. was taking credit for the breakthrough; (2)
he wanted to underscore that whatever progress had been made, the
Soviet Union was not going to be stampeded into an agreement; and
(3) he deeply resented the U.S.'s seeking a moratorium on MIRVed
heavy missiles—a proposal that Vance had left on the table despite
Gromyko's summary rejection.

Gromyko's parting shot notwithstanding, Vance returned to Washington confident that the Carter administration's pursuit of SALT II,
after a giant misstep in March, was now back on track.

5 Words and Numbers in Geneva

Until the end of September 1977, SALT was in a state of dynamic uncertainty. At their meeting in May, Vance and Gromyko had come together on a three-tier framework for the final agreement, but they remained far apart on the contents of each tier. The Carter administration was still committed to imposing restraints on the modernization and MIRVing of Soviet missiles, although it now realized that the Soviet concessions would have to be more modest and gradual than those sought by Vance in Moscow—and the American concessions would have to be more significant and immediate than the ones Vance had offered. The administration had not figured out exactly how to repackage the March initiative in a way that would make its ingredients negotiable with the Russians. How the final agreement should cope with Soviet heavy missiles and MIRVed ICBMs as well as American cruise missiles was a question still open within the U.S. government.

The complexity of the challenge was compounded by the pressure of the impending expiration of SALT I on October 3. Since April, Harold Brown had been saying he was "by no means confident" there would be an agreement by then. Paul Warnke, during a visit to Moscow in June, cautioned that October 3 should not be seen as an "absolute deadline." Nonetheless, it was obviously a psychological deadline of political importance. If the two sides failed to reach a SALT II treaty by then, the whole process would be in jeopardy. The U.S. and the Soviet Union would no longer be formally bound to honor the 1972 interim agreement. Whatever stopgap device Washington and Moscow invented to tide them over, the political volatility of SALT in the

U.S. would increase, to the detriment of diplomacy. Proponents of arms control would accuse the administration of having pressed unreasonable demands and dragged its feet; they would clamor for a quick agreement as proof of good faith. The administration was much more concerned about the opponents of SALT. They would cite the expiration of SALT I as proof of Soviet bad faith and be more inclined than ever to condemn American concessions as a desperate attempt to "save" SALT.

The sheer volume of the unfinished business facing them and their shared sense of urgency made both sides anxious to accomplish as much as possible through back-channel contacts in Washington and Moscow and between the permanent delegations in Geneva before Vance and Gromyko met again at the end of the summer. The full-time negotiators in Geneva were given a larger role to play in SALT than they had ever had before. In the Kissinger period, they had been confined mostly to ritualistic exchanges of prepared statements on established positions and the drafting of agreements reached at the "political level"—i.e., between Kissinger and the Soviet officials with whom he dealt. Genuine negotiating by the Geneva negotiators was not encouraged. When Kissinger flew into Geneva for talks with Gromyko on SALT, he bypassed the delegation headquarters and frequently kept its resident chief, Ambassador U. Alexis Johnson, only cursorily informed of what was going on. It was Kissinger's style to monopolize authority. Vance preferred to delegate it.

At the end of their first meeting in March, Vance and Gromyko authorized the Geneva delegations to tackle four issues. Three were U.S.-proposed measures that would help guarantee the American ability to monitor Soviet compliance with the new treaty. The fourth was a Soviet effort to prohibit the U.S. from sharing with its NATO allies the technical secrets of the cruise missile. Officially, all four items were considered secondary, although they were destined to become increasingly important and contentious as the talks progressed. After their second meeting, in May, Vance and Gromyko extended the agenda of the delegations to cover all the outstanding issues except one—the Backfire bomber. Brezhnev considered it a matter of personal honor that Backfire not be negotiated as part of SALT. He had given his word to two American administrations that the plane was not a heavy bomber and therefore not within the jurisdiction of SALT. If the U.S. was so brazenly mistrustful as to doubt his word and to demand collateral restraints on the production and deployment of the bomber, then those restraints would have to be negotiated outside regular SALT channels. For that reason, throughout the long summer of 1977, Backfire was exclusively a topic for Vance to discuss with Anatoly Dobrynin in Washington and occasionally for Malcolm Toon to raise with Gromyko and his deputy Kornienko in Moscow.

The U.S. negotiators in Geneva were just as glad to be spared the task of arguing with their Soviet counterparts about Backfire. They had enough to do when Washington assigned them the task of negotiating a 10 percent reduction in the Vladivostok ceiling—from 2,400 to 2,160—and a declaration of principles to govern SALT III. From a strategic, military standpoint, the proposed reduction was hardly of great significance. It was certainly a far cry from the deep cut the U.S. had proposed in March—from 2,400 to between 2,000 and 1,800 total strategic weapons. But politically, any reduction at all was difficult for the Soviets to accept. One reason they had agreed to the Vladivostok equal aggregate of 2,400 was precisely because it did not require them to cut back much in operational systems; and in the nearly three years since the Vladivostok summit, the Soviet leadership had become more and more stubbornly devoted to the 2,400 figure. Nevertheless, by the end of the Ford administration, the Kremlin had indicated it might undertake modest reductions once SALT II was in force. At the disastrous March meeting in Moscow, the Soviet side had said it might be willing to go down to 2,200—if the U.S. agreed to count cruise missiles and exempt Backfire from that limit. And at his meeting with Vance in Geneva in May, Gromyko had reiterated a willingness to lower the ceiling—slightly. Since the Soviet military was already bumping its head against that ceiling, lowering the number would mean dismantling some Soviet weapons. The Soviet air force had about 150 older heavy bombers it could easily afford to scrap. But the prospect of having to dismantle any weaponry at all still stuck in the Russian craw. Soviet officials in Geneva confided privately that that was the case. After all, the sacrifice would be mandated by an agreement with the U.S.S.R.'s principal rival and potential enemy. The U.S., for its own part, would not have to build similar bomber bonfires. This was because U.S. strategic forces were well below the Vladivostok level of 2,400 total systems. If the Soviets were going to agree to any such "unilateral" reduction in their existing arsenal, they were determined to make the U.S. pay a price in the coin of its investment in the future of the cruise missile. Both delegations in Geneva knew that they were in for a marathon of the most tedious horse-trading. They quickly settled into a routine intended to make the long haul as painless and productive as possible.

As a rule, the full delegations met biweekly. They took turns hosting each other. The American delegation was headquartered in the top floors of a nondescript modern office complex called the Botanic Building because it overlooked Geneva's botanical gardens. It had been built by the financier and playboy Bernie Cornfeld to house his International Overseas Services before the company collapsed. The delegation's conference room was in an eighth-floor penthouse with a panoramic view of Lake Geneva and the Alps. The Russians used as their headquarters a cluster of apartments, offices and meeting rooms in the walled compound of the Soviet mission to the various United Nations organizations based in Geneva. The main building was a nineteenth-century, neoclassical mansion that had once served as the Lithuanian mission to the League of Nations.

Since Paul Warnke served as both chief negotiator in Geneva and director of the Arms Control and Disarmament Agency in Washington, he was a transatlantic commuter. In his frequent absences from Geneva, he left the leadership of the delegation in the hands of Ralph Earle, a lawyer who had labored on SALT since 1972, first for the Pentagon, then for the Arms Control Agency. Working with him were representatives of the State Department, the Joint Chiefs of Staff and the Office of the Secretary of Defense. In September 1977, the delegation acquired an at-large member, George Seignious, a retired Army general. The Russians evinced some puzzlement about, and deference toward, Seignious. He was a courtly Southerner and a professional soldier, which led the Soviets to guess he was a close associate of Jimmy Carter's, and Seignious did nothing to disabuse them of that notion.* The member of the U.S. delegation with the most seniority was the JCS representative, Lieutenant General Edward Rowny, who had been in Geneva since early 1973 and whose assignment had been renewed by the Carter administration largely because he was a protégé of Henry Jackson's. Rowny's four years of service would, however, have made him the most junior negotiator on the other side of the table. The Soviet SALT delegation—like the Soviet leadership itself—was marked by almost sclerotic continuity. The chief, Vladimir

---

*Seignious's background was in the Army and South Carolina, while Carter's was in the Navy and Georgia. Nevertheless, the Soviets probably felt vindicated in their earlier assessment when Seignious was named to succeed Warnke as director of ACDA in late 1978.

Semyonov, had been in his post since the dawn of SALT in 1969. He was nearing his seventieth birthday and his fortieth anniversary in the Soviet foreign service. The highest-ranking Soviet scientist, Alexander Shchukin, was nearly eighty. He had joined the Red Army the year of the Revolution. He had been Paul Nitze's and Harold Brown's interlocutor when they were on the U.S. delegation in the Republican administrations. The Foreign Ministry representative, Victor Karpov, had also been on the delegation since 1969. Rowny's opposite number, General Ivan Beletsky, who represented the Defense Ministry, had come relatively late to Geneva—in 1972, the year SALT II began. To assist the full members each side had between fifteen and twenty advisers and a half-dozen translators and interpreters. The CIA and KGB were both represented, and their principal agents were well known to—indeed, on congenial terms with—each other.

The negotiators met in a variety of settings and combinations governed by an elaborate protocol. After each of the biweekly plenary sessions, the delegations would divide into smaller working groups for what they called postplenaries. Warnke and Earle would go into a separate room with Semyonov, while Rowny would pair off with Beletsky in one corner, Shchukin with the American scientist in another, the two intelligence agents in a third, and so on. Over coffee, tea, juice and cookies, in lowered voices, with their heads together, the negotiators would sit around in informal but intense clusters. The atmosphere was that of a genteel bazaar where very exotic goods were bartered. Warnke's predecessor, Alexis Johnson, had in 1973 introduced a "dry rule" prohibiting alcoholic beverages at postplenaries. He reasoned that SALT was parlous enough without the additional danger of a slightly loosened tongue producing an unauthorized breakthrough or breakdown in the negotiations. At the social events that frequently brought the delegates together in the evening, liquor was allowed— a number of the Americans drank vodka, the Soviets preferred bourbon—but other rules were still in force. One of the strictest was that the Soviets assiduously avoided echoing their government's complaints over Carter's human rights crusade, and the Americans reciprocated by avoiding mention of the persecutions of dissidents in the U.S.S.R. Unaware of this rule, a recent American arrival in Geneva once brought up the case of Anatoly Shcharansky in a private conversation with his assigned Soviet contact. He dutifully reported the exchange afterward in a "memcon" that was circulated among his colleagues and sent back to Washington. He was told sternly never again to mix the business of SALT with displeasure over human rights.

There were moments of genuine informality, even light-heartedness. The Soviets would occasionally—quite mischievously—slip in a question based on a press leak about some supposedly secret American military development. Both sides knew they could afford to laugh, because leaks almost always originated from Washington, rarely from Geneva. The Soviets had to rely on old-fashioned carbon paper to duplicate their documents. Sometimes they would somewhat sheepishly ask the U.S. delegation to run off extra copies on its Xerox machine. An American once chided his counterpart about this "technological asymmetry." The Russian replied with a grin, "Yes, and it proves you should stop all this worrying about the threat of Soviet superiority."

In his dealings with Warnke, Semyonov had relaxed somewhat from the days of Gerard Smith and Alexis Johnson. Away from the negotiating table, Semyonov was more inclined to lapse into stories about World War II and to discuss history and modern art. Semyonov was at first chilly toward Ralph Earle, the alternate chairman of the U.S. delegation; it seemed to offend Semyonov's highly developed self-esteem to have to deal so often with the number two man on the other side. But that relationship warmed, and soon Semyonov and Earle were exchanging classical records and comparing notes on their shared experience of bringing up teen-age daughters. Still, whenever conversation turned to SALT, the mood as well as the substance of contacts at every level and in every setting remained, in the antiseptic phrase of the terse biweekly press releases, "serious and businesslike." The Soviet side was often almost paralytic in obedience to orders from home. Whenever Semyonov had the slightest new ground to break, he would reach into his pocket and produce a prepared text which he would carefully recite. Even the most routine Soviet statements tended to be far more verbose and formal than American ones, and the civilians on the Soviet delegation were more loath to discuss military hardware than their American counterparts. Secrecy on the Soviet side was more stringent, and the Soviets took their own rules more literally.

The focus of the delegations' labors was the Joint Draft Text (JDT) of the SALT II agreement—one of the most complicated and important pieces of paper in the world. The JDT had been a work in progress since early 1975, and it was already more than ten times as long as the SALT I agreement. The many passages still in dispute were set apart by brackets from the agreed text. In the English version, the bracketed U.S.-preferred language preceded the Soviet-preferred wording. In the Russian version, it was the other way around. The State Department and Soviet Foreign Ministry representatives were cochairmen of a biweekly drafting group—or "editorial commission," as the Russians called it—which painstakingly put agreements reached at the negotiating table and approved by the capitals into treaty language. In 1977 the drafters were still slogging away at the legalistic formulation of matters that had been resolved in principle for years. Sometimes punctuation was in dispute—whether to use a comma or a semicolon. They haggled over semantic distinctions between English and Russian, sometimes because of genuine linguistic anomalies but often to score political points or as a matter of negotiating tactics. The biggest problem was defining, with a mutually agreeable combination of precision and flexibility, the weapons and properties of weapons to be governed by SALT. The definition of a MIRV alone, for instance, went on for four pages in the JDT. Moreover, each of the nineteen articles in the treaty was glossed by a mass of footnote-like agreed statements ("The parties agree that . . .") and common understandings ("The parties agree that the negotiating record reflects that . . ."). One of Leslie Gelb's deputies, Jerome Kahan, once remarked, "It would take seven Talmudic scholars three weeks just to get through the JDT."

The Home Office

While the U.S. delegation had more authority during the Carter administration than previously and much more latitude than did the Soviet team, the American negotiators in the Botanic Building still took regular, detailed orders from the SALT policy-makers in Washington. Three or four coded messages a day flashed back and forth along a State Department communications line. Washington dictated the pace and subject of the negotiations. The exactitude of the instructions and the level at which they originated depended on the importance of the issue at hand. New departures on primary problems, such as the decision to proceed with bargaining on reductions in the Vladivostok aggregate, came from the National Security Council by way of the Special Coordination Committee (SCC). The principal members of the SCC were of cabinet rank. Their deputies also met occasionally to chart SALT policy. They called themselves the "Mini-SCC." Their chairman was David Aaron, and the other regular participants were Walter Slocombe, Leslie Gelb, Spurgeon Keeny (Warnke's deputy at ACDA), General William Smith (a JCS representative) and Robert Bowie (a right-hand man to Director of Central Intelligence, Stansfield Turner). For more routine matters, such as the clarification and amplification of earlier instructions, the delegation in Geneva relied on a SALT Backstopping Committee, chaired by Spurgeon Keeny and made up usually of Roger Molander from the NSC, James Timbie from ACDA; Charles Henkin or Jerome Kahan from the State Department; Slocombe or his deputy, George Schneiter; a JCS colonel, James Granger; and Ray McCrory, a CIA expert. There was considerable flexibility and overlap in both the agendas and the memberships of these various groups. Slocombe, for example, had a way of showing up everywhere—"from the gerbil level to the elephant level," as one of his colleagues once put it.

The delegation in Geneva usually drafted statements for presentation at the plenaries and passages of treaty language for inclusion in the Joint Draft Text, but it cleared these in advance with Washington. In addition to the cables, there were also members of Congress flying back and forth between Washington and Geneva. The Vice-President designated a group of senators and the Speaker of the House designated some representatives to serve as advisers to the U.S. delegation. These legislators had access to much of the paper work and were invited to sit in on the plenary sessions with the Soviets. Vladimir Semyonov and his colleagues were less than delighted with this arrangement. There were no reciprocal privileges for members of their own, considerably less assertive legislature, the Supreme Soviet of the U.S.S.R. Also, it rankled to have strangers showing up at closed-door meetings where matters of the greatest secrecy were discussed. Moreover, these congressional invasions meant extra work for the Soviets, since they were obliged to brief and entertain the American politicians. But the Soviets swallowed their complaints, for they knew that, sooner or later, the U.S. Congress would decide the fate of SALT II. If the visiting senators and representatives could be advisers on SALT, then the Soviet negotiators could be lobbyists of Congress.

In general, the congressional advisers had little substantive impact on the course of the negotiations. One exception early on concerned the matter of an "agreed data base," the inventory of information that the U.S. had been pressing the Soviets to provide about their arsenal so that the U.S. could double-check its own data gleaned by remote radar, long-distance electronic intercepts, satellite reconnaissance and other "national technical means of verification." The Congress had insisted on a data base as part of SALT II when it debated SALT I, but for years the Russians had stubbornly maintained that such information was for them to know and for the U.S. to find out. The idea of voluntarily and routinely giving out military secrets ran against the Soviet grain. These were secrets that Russian officials often kept from each other, not to mention from the Americans. When Gerard Smith headed the U.S. delegation, he had found that the Soviet negotiators became extremely nervous when the American side referred to facts and figures about Russian weaponry that the Soviets themselves were not formally cleared to know. When Alexis Johnson put forward an example of what a data base would look like, Semyonov had replied irritably, "Who needs it? You've got national technical means, so you already know all that. You don't need us to tell you."

The visiting senators and congressmen were adamant on the subject of a data base. It was, after all, an issue relating to the verifiability of the treaty—and that was the single biggest concern of the Congress. Among the senators who appeared in Geneva during the summer of 1977 was Charles Mathias, the liberal Republican from Maryland and a leading supporter of SALT. Over cocktails, he told Semyonov very bluntly that there was "no way we could vote for this treaty without a data base." He underscored his point with a homily about how "the folks back home" outwit fruit and vegetable vendors who put the ripest strawberries at the top of a carton; Baltimore housewives always turn the carton over to look at the ones on the bottom. Just before leaving Geneva, Mathias stopped in to introduce Semyonov to his teen-age son, who was traveling with him—and to give the Soviet diplomat a pint of strawberries as a friendly reminder of their conversation. Mathias made a point of putting the largest, juiciest fruit in the top layer. He also gave Semyonov a bottle of bourbon.

Not long afterward, Semyonov announced at a plenary that the Soviets might provide data on certain weapon systems in exchange for American concessions on "other important issues, including cruise missiles." The U.S. replied that it welcomed this new sign of forthcomingness on an old problem, but an agreed data base was an absolute necessity, not a bargaining chip, for SALT II. A short time later, Semyonov quite suddenly volunteered figures on the Soviet heavy bomber force. This information came out of the blue; it was free, in that it was not traded for an American concession; and it was accurate, in that it squared with what the U.S. knew from its own intelligence. Later Semyonov and his colleagues surrendered information about the number of Soviet silos for intercontinental ballistic missiles and tubes for submarine-launched ballistic missiles. After that, they told the U.S. what it already knew about Soviet heavy bombers armed with cruise missiles and air-to-surface ballistic missiles (ASBMs). These were the "zero categories"—the U.S.S.R. had no such weapons, but it was the first time the Russians had formally acknowledged the fact.

Not surprisingly, the Soviets held out longest on data for their perennially most troublesome weapons, MIRVed missiles, and they refused to provide a data base on heavy missiles. They were especially reluctant to yield figures on MIRVed missiles because they were still in the process of converting single-warhead rockets to MIRVs. Once they started giving out numbers they would have to keep revising them upward. As for heavies, the Soviets refused to recognize modern large ballistic missiles (MLBMs) as a separate category within the data base, since SALT II did not contain any numerical limitation on MLBMs per se. Rather, there was merely an obligation, carried over from SALT I, not to construct or convert additional fixed ICBM launchers or convert light ones into heavies. The U.S. conceded that point, but argued that providing MLBM data would be a useful confidence-building measure (CBM). The Soviets had never been impressed by talk about CBMs. One Soviet diplomat, who knew his SALT acronyms backward and forward, once cracked disdainfully, "A CBM? What's that? Some new ballistic missile you're threatening us with? Or is it one you think *we're* threatening *you* with?"

The Russians also dragged their feet on accepting the American-preferred phrase "agreed data base." The words were redundant, insisted the Soviet negotiators: *data* is a matter of objective fact, so what need was there for the adjective "agreed"? As usual when the Soviets seemed to be splitting hairs, they were carving out a deliberate ambiguity. They knew perfectly well that the Americans wanted to make it explicit that the data base must be mutually agreed so that the U.S. could challenge any information it could not independently confirm. The Soviets played a similar semantic game with the word "base." They said it did not conform exactly to the phrase in the Russian text, which is literally translated "initial data" or "point-of-departure data." The Americans replied that the Soviets were welcome to that Russian phrase, but the English text of the treaty must contain the word "base" because a base is something that is *built upon*

—and a data base is something that must be regularly and accurately updated. The U.S. ultimately got its way on both points.

Providing the U.S. with information it already had may not seem a great concession, and progress on the data base was glacial—continuing until early in 1979—and the negotiations on the problem were sometimes excruciating. Nevertheless, the U.S.S.R. was overcoming, albeit in small measure and in mostly symbolic ways, its basic secretiveness. "You realize," Vladimir Semyonov remarked to Paul Warnke, "you have just repealed four hundred years of Russian history. But on reflection, maybe that's not a bad thing."

6 Waiting for Gromyko

While the delegations in Geneva were negotiating a data base and other secondary issues, the SALT policy-makers back in Washington spent the summer of 1977 asking themselves elementary but difficult questions about what the Carter administration had been doing in SALT up until then and what it ought to do in preparation for Vance's next meeting with Gromyko in September. This fundamental reevaluation was occasioned in part by the conundrum of Minuteman vulnerability, the nagging but unanswerable question of whether the Soviets might be able to wipe out the U.S. ICBM force in one fell swoop sometime before 1985. This hypothetical military problem had become a very immediate political problem. It was therefore also an arms control problem. The climate of public and congressional opinion about SALT was charged with worries over whether the U.S. was becoming the number two superpower and must therefore try harder —not to conclude a SALT agreement but to counteract the Soviet threat with more ICBMs, bigger ICBMs, mobile ICBMs, and an unfettered cruise missile program. In such a climate, "arms control" itself had become an unfashionable term. Paul Warnke and other inveterate believers in the concept of arms control talked less and less about SALT as an exercise in controlling arms. Instead, they talked about it as the enhancement of national security by means other than a massive military build-up. The survival of SALT in peacetime had begun to depend on how convincingly the arms controllers could address the speculative issue of the survival of Minuteman in a nuclear war. The negotiators had been asking themselves for some time how SALT could postpone the day when Soviet ICBMs would achieve the theoretical ability to destroy virtually all of America's ICBMs. They had found one answer in the March comprehensive proposal and its drastic, summary reduction of Soviet land-based missiles. That had not worked, so the question had arisen: should the U.S. continue to seek limitations on what were commonly believed to be the most formidable Soviet ICBMs, the heavy rockets?

The strategy of protecting Minuteman had become a political imperative in SALT, but in the early summer of 1977, the policy-makers and analysts began rethinking the wisdom of their previous tactics, especially the tactic of constraining heavies. Since the beginning of the new administration, the U.S. had already twice proposed, and the Kremlin had twice rejected, SALT II provisions that specifically addressed the problem of Soviet heavy missiles. The comprehensive proposal would have cut the number of modern large ballistic missiles in half, and the May three-tier proposal would have frozen the number of MIRVed MLBMs at 190. On both occasions the Soviets had gone to histrionic lengths to make clear that they were never going to consider *any* proposal intended to roll back their allowance for heavies granted by SALT I and reaffirmed at Vladivostok. They regarded their 300 or so heavies as a kind of birthright of Vladivostok, the sanctity of which Gerald Ford and Henry Kissinger had blessed. In the Soviets' stubborn and resentful view, each new Carter administration attempt to reopen the issue and deprive them of heavies was more perfidious than the last.

Still, the idea of a moratorium on multiple-warhead heavies if not a reduction in all heavies was not about to go away altogether. For one thing, the idea had the vigilant backing of Senator Jackson, and Carter had not entirely given up hope for a SALT II treaty that Jackson would support. For another thing, Carter's own advisers and the bureaucracy on which they sometimes relied had not completely given up the notion that the Soviets might still relent on heavies in exchange for a sufficiently attractive American concession on cruise missiles. A SALT Working Group of the National Security Council, chaired by David Aaron, came up with a plan for a "heavy systems" limit of 250: the Russians could have 250 heavy missiles, a reduction of about 50, and the Americans could have 250 heavy bombers armed with cruise missiles—the maximum number the Pentagon then calculated it might need by 1985. That option had the virtue of simplicity. It established a straightforward, explicit, one-for-one trade-off between two categories of weapons that Moscow and Washington cared about with comparable passion—weapons that also, conveniently, were both described by the adjective "heavy." But the plan had at least three severe drawbacks. First, there was the near certainty of Soviet rejection—and the very real possibility that SALT might grind to a halt if the U.S. made a last stand on the issue of heavies. Second, even if the plan proved negotiable, some members of the SALT Working Group, notably Walter Slocombe, felt that a reduction of merely 50 in the Soviet heavy force—from 300 to 250—would make barely a dent in the perceived superiority of Soviet land-based missiles; it would have no effect, for instance, on the number of SS-19 "light" ICBMs. And finally, the "heavy systems" limit would not placate Senator Jackson and his confreres. "The idea was regarded by its proponents," said Jackson's expert on strategic affairs, Richard Perle, "as a neat, cosmetic solution to the fact that we were letting the Soviets keep something we didn't have—namely, heavy missiles—while 'giving' the U.S. something that both sides are entitled to—cruise missile bombers. It was a phony trade."

Nonetheless, the 250 heavy systems limit took its place in the package of alternative proposals awaiting Gromyko, along with the 190 MIRVed-heavy freeze that Vance had offered but Gromyko had already rejected in May. Meanwhile the administration kept looking for another option that would do more to avert Minuteman vulnerability and less to provoke a Russian temper tantrum. As it searched, the Carter administration backed away from its single-minded contemplation of Soviet heavies and began to ponder instead the problem of MIRVed ICBMs in general—and the SS-19 in particular. The SS-19 was not the biggest MIRVed missile in the Soviet arsenal. That distinction belonged to the SS-18. But the SS-19 was, arguably, the best, and it was getting better all the time. Its MIRVed version carried six warheads—four less than the MIRVed SS-18, but three more than the Minuteman; and each SS-19 warhead was twice as big as Minuteman's. Thanks to a vigorous and quite successful testing program, the SS-19 was well on its way to becoming a "silo-buster," a "hard-target killer," a "counterforce" weapon—a missile with such a lethal combination of accuracy and explosive power that a barrage of them might be able to destroy more than 90 percent of America's one thousand Minutemen in their underground silos. Since the SS-19 was technically defined by SALT as a *light* ICBM, the question arose at the highest level of the Carter administration: what was the use of reducing Soviet heavies if the SS-19 could run rampant? Didn't the SS-19 render meaningless the distinction between light and heavy missiles, and therefore wasn't it pointless to pursue so doggedly a limit just on heavies? "It dawned on us," said a high-ranking newcomer to the National Security Council, "that maybe we had been wasting negotiating capital by going after the SS-18 when we should have been focusing on the SS-19 instead."

The Pentagon's chief analyst of Soviet forces, Andrew Marshall, opened the eyes of Vance's Soviet affairs adviser, Marshall Shulman, to the ominousness of the SS-19. Shulman began to see the pursuit of a reduction in Soviet heavies as not just hopeless from a negotiating standpoint, but misguided from a technical and strategic standpoint as well. Paul Nitze, who was increasingly outspoken as one of the most knowledgeable and influential critics of the administration's SALT policies, began telling officials and private groups alike that the emphasis on the SS-18 had been misplaced and that the SS-19 represented an equal, possibly greater threat to the survivability of Minuteman. The most persuasive voice within the government was, as usual, Harold Brown's. He had been instrumental in the President's decision to seek a reduction of Soviet heavies in March, but now he was in favor of a new tack. A ceiling on MIRVed ICBMs, heavy and light, was more important than a reduction of heavies. At a meeting of the NSC Special Coordination Committee in mid August, Brown argued, according to the recollection of a participant, "We've probably got to fall off a limit on heavies per se anyway, since the Russians refuse to negotiate such a limit, and we might be able to make a virtue out of that necessity. We could do as well, conceivably better, with a MIRVed ICBM limit."

For months afterward, the decision to give up on a reduction in Soviet heavies and try for a MIRVed ICBM subceiling instead was widely advertised—and justified—within the government as having been spurred by new intelligence information about the SS-19's overall potency. While it is true that during the spring and summer of 1977, the intelligence community did revise upward its estimates of the missile's power, throw-weight and accuracy, the experts had known for a long time, certainly since the Ford administration, that in the long term the SS-19 posed a greater threat to Minuteman than the SS-18. There had been a consensus among many analysts for years that the Jackson forces on Capitol Hill and the Joint Chiefs of Staff were short-sighted in their obsession with heavy missiles. In its eagerness to have Jackson and his allies "on board" in SALT II, the Carter administration had incorporated that short-sightedness into the emphasis in the comprehensive proposal on cutting the Soviet heavy force in half. The issue of heavy missiles had a powerful political symbolism but not much strategic significance. In the summer of 1977, the political desirability of limiting heavies finally gave way to negotiating considerations in favor of leaving heavies alone and limiting all MIRVed ICBMs instead—and those negotiating considerations were reinforced by long-standing analytical conclusions.

When Is an ALCM a MIRV?

Not that a MIRVed ICBM subceiling was a brand-new idea. The Republican administration had proposed one in 1974. The Carter administration had tried the same thing in March 1977. In addition to cutting the Soviet heavy force in half, the comprehensive proposal would have also established a subceiling of 550 for MIRVed ICBMs on each side. The figure 550 had been chosen in March because that was the number of MIRVed Minutemen in the American ICBM force. If the Soviets had accepted it, there would have been a new equal aggregate in SALT—without the U.S. having to add or subtract a single MIRVed ICBM. But the Soviets were not about to accept a MIRVed ICBM subceiling of 550—not in March, not in May, not in September. Their all-out MIRVing program was to build up their land-based MIRV force to well over 900 launchers. They were no sooner going to accept a cut of 40 percent in their projected total MIRVed ICBM force than a cut of 50 percent in their existing heavy force, as the comprehensive proposal would have also required. But they might accept a smaller reduction in MIRVed ICBMs if it was part of a package that contained a significant American concession. The most obvious and logical American concession would be to count heavy bombers armed with cruise missiles against the Vladivostok subceiling of 1,320 MIRVed launchers. Henry Kissinger had been on the brink of achieving a SALT II agreement when he agreed in principle to count cruise-missile-carrying bombers as MIRVed launchers in January 1976. Gromyko and Dobrynin had put great Soviet stock in treating air-launched cruise missiles as multiple warheads during the months after the collapse of Vance's mission to Moscow.

While counting ALCM bombers under the MIRV subceiling might have been logical, it was by no means easy or attractive in the summer of 1977. For one thing, the administration would be criticized for having resorted to a compromise lifted straight out of Henry Kissinger's bag of tricks. For another, since January 1976, the air-launched cruise missile had begun to prove itself in testing and establish itself in the programs of the Air Force and the budgets of the Congress. Jimmy Carter was much enamored of the ALCM. The wizardry of its guidance system appealed to the engineer in him. Its nature as an exclusively retaliatory device—it was much too slow to be a first-strike weapon—appealed to the arms controller in him. And its relatively low cost appealed to the cost-cutter and budget-balancer in him.

Carter's infatuation with the air-launched cruise missile was one factor that led him, in June 1977, to make a decision that greatly complicated the development of both a sensible SALT position and a sensible strategic weapons program. He canceled the B-1 bomber. He made the decision on the basis of cost effectiveness. For him, it seemed to come down to an either/or choice between the B-1 and the cruise missile. The U.S. needed a dependable means of penetrating Soviet air defenses. Carter saw the B-1 as the expensive alternative, the ALCM as the cheap one. Carter decided that the virtues of the ALCM made the B-1 unnecessary. B-52s would make perfectly adequate platforms from which to launch ALCMs at the Soviet Union.*

Carter's decision to cancel the B-1 struck many officials inside the executive branch, to say nothing of the growing vigilance lobby, as simplistic and short-sighted. By casting the decision in narrow budgetary terms, Carter opened himself to the charge that he had committed the logical fallacy of thinking of the B-1 and the ALCM as mutually exclusive. He did not give sufficient consideration to the possibility of teaming up the two weapons. Instead of relying on a slow, sitting-duck "stand-off platform" like the B-52, the U.S. could have greatly enhanced the penetrability of the cruise missile by launching it from a plane that was itself a penetrating aircraft. Few of Carter's own advisers claimed to understand the timing of his decision, and few found it comfortable to support or easy to defend. Even many of those who agreed that the B-1 was too expensive wished he had waited until after

---

*Back in the early seventies, many Pentagon officials had anticipated presidential accountancy like Carter's. They feared the air-launched cruise missile would be in competition with the B-1 for Air Force funds, and many tended to favor canceling the ALCM program in order to protect the B-1. Henry Kissinger was among those who intervened to save the cruise missile, at least partly because he wanted it for the bargaining leverage it gave him on other issues, notably Backfire. Subsequent events are ironic in a number of respects: Kissinger came to regret his defense of cruise missiles; the Pentagon came to embrace the cruise missile as too important to bargain away; and the ALCM came to compete—successfully—with the B-1.

SALT II. The decision was sure to anger proponents of a stronger military program and make Carter seem, in their eyes, a President inclined to "give aways"; the cancellation of the B-1 seemed premature, impolitic, and sure to complicate both the negotiation and the ratification of SALT.

There was another view, equally critical of the President. A number of officials closely involved in SALT felt that Carter had made the decision five months too late. Conceivably, if he had abandoned the B-1 at the very beginning of his administration, as part of the March comprehensive proposal, the Soviets might have seen the entire proposal as more balanced and accepted it as a basis for further negotiation. As it was, the White House announcement in June scrapping the B-1 elicited nothing but skepticism and suspicion from Moscow. *Pravda* called the decision "ambiguous" because the U.S. would continue testing a penetrating bomber. The Soviets were filled with more foreboding than ever about cruise missiles, now that Carter had committed himself to the ALCM as the miniaturized, unmanned flagship of the U.S. airborne deterrent. "The speedy development of cruise missiles and the bombers for these missiles is only part of a vast program for the production of new weapons and systems," proclaimed a *Pravda* commentary on the B-1 decision. "Cruise missiles pose a grave threat to peace and put additional obstacles in the way of [SALT]."

At the Pentagon, many military officers and civilian experts were just as unhappy with the B-1 decision as the Soviets. Even those who stopped short of questioning Carter's leadership thought the cancellation of the B-1 made it all the more crucial that air-launched cruise missiles be given sanctuary from the long arm of SALT. Harold Brown did a yeomanly job of defending the B-1 decision in public, but in private he raised new questions about the wisdom of a 2,500-kilometer range limit on ALCMs. At a meeting in the summer of 1977, the Defense Science Board, a commission of outside experts who advise the Pentagon, warned Brown that the 2,500-kilometer limit might not be adequate for assuring coverage of all targets in the Soviet Union, especially if the B-52 was to be the principal launching platform. Brown relayed this concern to Brzezinski in a letter, suggesting that the range limit for ALCMs be no less than 3,000 kilometers. Vance and Warnke vigorously opposed upping the ante on cruise missile range in the negotiations with the Russians. "Are we really going to go back to them and say, 'Well, if you didn't like 2,500, how would you feel about 3,000?' " asked Warnke sarcastically in a White House meeting.

Brown said at one point he and the Pentagon could live with a 2,500-kilometer range limit for ALCMs as part of the three-year protocol, but not as part of the treaty that would run until 1985. Said one official close to both Vance and Warnke: "In the Alice-in-Wonderland world of SALT, the B-1 cancellation put additional pressure on us to treat the cruise missile as some sort of holy thing. The decision sent the Pentagon brass up the wall and endowed the cruise missile issue with a political hysteria that was not helpful. Altogether, whatever the merits of abandoning the B-1 might have been in the long run, in the short run it just increased the intensity of the debate within the administration over how to deal with ALCM bombers in the package we were preparing to present to the Russians."

Henry Jackson's and Richard Perle's lengthy memorandum to Carter back in February had admonished him sternly on the subject of cruise-missile-carrying bombers: "There must be no constraints on our ability to modernize our bomber and missile forces in the face of unconstrained Soviet threats to those forces. In particular there must be no limitation on the deployment of ALCMs on U.S. heavy bombers as a means of penetrating unconstrained Soviet air defenses." If the administration decided—despite Jackson's warning, despite the President's controversial abandonment of the B-1—still to count ALCM-carrying bombers as multiple-warhead launchers under the 1,320 Vladivostok subceiling, there would be some hell to pay on Capitol Hill. Partly for that reason, the administration kept alive old options and churned out new ones that avoided counting ALCM carriers as MIRVs.

Lunching with the Russians

Aaron remained for some time disposed to the "heavy systems" subceiling of 250—the one-for-one trade-off between MIRVed Soviet heavy missiles and American heavy bombers armed with cruise missiles. One of Leslie Gelb's assistants, Charles Henkin, suggested a new subceiling of between 700 and 800 that would cover any combination of ALCM-carrying bombers and MIRVed ICBMs. That idea had three attractions: (1) since there were only 550 MIRVed Minutemen, the subceiling would have left the U.S. free to deploy between 150 and 250 ALCM carriers—more than enough to meet the Pentagon's anticipated needs; (2) Henkin's subceiling would have been well below the projected Soviet land-based MIRV level of 900-plus, so even if the

Soviets decided not to arm any heavy bombers with cruise missiles, they still would have had to pull back in their MIRV program; and (3) the new subceiling would have been separate from the Vladivostok subceiling of 1,320 total MIRVed launchers, so critics would have found it harder to accuse the administration of "caving in" to the Soviet demand that cruise-missile-carrying bombers be counted against the 1,320 Vladivostok subceiling. "We pretty well worked ourselves into a lather of righteous determination not to give in to the Russians on that score," recalled an official of the National Security Council. "We knew Gromyko was going to come and beat us about the head and shoulders on the need to count CMCs [cruise missile carriers] as MIRVs, and I think some of us probably knew in our hearts-of-hearts that it made sense for us to concede on that in order to get him to move on a MIRVed ICBM subceiling. But as I say, we'd worked ourselves into a pretty stubborn frame of mind." Right up until shortly before Gromyko's arrival in Washington, David Aaron and others steadfastly insisted that whatever compromise came out of the meeting, it would not include an American concession to treat ALCM carriers as MIRVs or, more precisely, as "force multipliers" to be counted like MIRVs.

But there were hints in advance of the meeting that a compromise might include the abandonment of separate limits on MIRVed heavy missiles and agreement instead on a new subceiling covering all MIRVed ICBMs. Finding an optimum level for that subceiling was an exercise in fairly simple arithmetic combined with complex bureaucratic politics and Kremlinology. Once again, columns of figures proliferated on paper napkins during working lunches in the White House Mess, in the State Department executive dining room, and at the conference table in Walter Slocombe's office, where he and his colleagues frequently lunched off trays from the Pentagon cafeteria. The members of the interagency SALT Working Group considered a dizzying array of permutations and combinations. Some were brand new, others were cannibalized from other options, such as Charles Henkin's 700–800 subceiling. Their calculations had to take account of current Soviet force levels, projected improvements in the U.S. deterrent, predictions about future Soviet programs and—trickiest of all—guesswork about what sort of limits in their future programs the Soviets might be willing to consider.

The scratch pads and the pocket calculators, the brainstorming lunches and the formal meetings, finally came up with the number 800 for the MIRVed ICBM subceiling to be proposed to Gromyko. If the Soviets accepted it, they would be able to MIRV about 100 fewer ICBMs than they might have MIRVed otherwise by 1985.* It was a relatively modest constraint. It was certainly modest compared to the provision in the comprehensive proposal that would have held the U.S.S.R. to only 550 land-based MIRVs until 1985. No one was under any illusion that by depriving the Soviets of a mere 100 MIRVed ICBMs, the U.S. would solve the problem of Minuteman vulnerability. Still, it was a step in the right direction. Unlike the existing SALT ceilings, the new limit would involve programmatic reductions—that is, cutbacks in future programs—and the reductions would be mandated in the most threatening, destabilizing Soviet program of all—land-based MIRVs. Moreover, its designers hoped the proposal would be realistic, in that it would give impetus to the negotiations and perhaps break the impasse.

In late August, Aaron and Hyland first sounded out the Russians on a MIRVed ICBM subceiling over lunch at the Soviet embassy. They met with Dobrynin's two minister counselors, Alexander Bessmertnykh and Vladillen Vasev. "We've got to keep SALT from staying at a stalemate," Hyland told the Soviets. "We've got to find a new approach." Added Aaron: "We're at a dead end, and we've got to turn the corner." The two Americans explained that the U.S. might be willing to give up on reductions in the Soviet heavy missile force if the Soviets accepted a new subceiling for MIRVed ICBMs. They did not reveal a number for the new limit; in fact, 800 was then still just one alternative under consideration. The conversation was strictly exploratory and hypothetical, but the Soviets listened carefully and signaled a positive interest. Returning to the White House afterward, Aaron remarked to Hyland, "I think we may have made some money today."

The MIRVed ICBM subceiling was still a backup option to the 250 "heavy systems" subceiling. No single idea had yet galvanized the

---

*The calculations can be summarized as follows: If the Soviets had accepted Vance's proposal in May to freeze MIRVed heavy missiles at 190, they would still have been allowed 1,130 additional MIRVed ballistic missiles, including "light" land-based and submarine-launched ones, under the 1,320 subceiling for total MIRVs. The U.S. figured the Russians wanted at least 400 MIRVed submarine-launched missiles (SLBMs). That left them with the freedom to have another 730 "light" land-based MIRVs—specifically SS-17s and SS-19s. Thus, if left to their own devices under the original Vladivostok subceiling and the proposed 190 MIRVed heavy freeze, they could have had altogether 920 MIRVed ICBMs—190 heavy SS-18s plus 730 light SS-17s and SS-19s. The newly formed consensus within the U.S. government that the SS-19 was at least as threatening as the heavy SS-18 made it desirable to limit the Russians to a total of 800 MIRVed ICBMs, which would be 120 fewer than the projected level of 920 they could be expected to deploy otherwise.

support of either the working-level experts or the policy-makers. That began to change around Labor Day, when the MIRVed ICBM subceiling caught the interest of Aaron's mentor, Vice-President Walter Mondale. Mondale was starting to do homework on SALT in preparation for Gromyko's visit to Washington in September. He asked his personal assistant for national security affairs, Denis Clift, to fly out to International Falls, Minnesota, where Mondale was fishing and relaxing over the weekend before Labor Day. Clift brought with him a thick briefing book that contained papers on the 190 MIRVed heavy freeze left over from May, the 250 "heavy systems" option generated by the SALT Working Group, the 700–800 trade-off between ALCM carriers and MIRVed ICBMs that Charles Henkin had devised, and the latest idea, the MIRVed ICBM subceiling. (Aaron and Hyland had already reported to Mondale the week before on their lunch with the Soviets.) Immediately after his return to Washington, Mondale summoned Brzezinski, Aaron, Hyland and Clift to the vice-presidential residence on the grounds of the Naval Observatory. As they discussed the gamut of alternatives, Mondale kept coming back to the MIRVed ICBM subceiling. He was especially sensitive to congressional concerns on SALT, and he liked the idea of a new limit in SALT that would constrain the most dangerous part of the Soviet arsenal without preventing the U.S. from beefing up its own land-based deterrent. At the end of the session, Mondale said, according to the recollection of a participant, "Let's be sure to include that one in our package of options." Shortly afterward, Mondale went to the President and argued that a MIRVed ICBM subceiling "made more sense from both a strategic and a negotiating point of view" than a limit on heavies.

Two Small Towns in the Ukraine

Once the Carter administration began shifting its focus from a reduction in Soviet heavies to a new subceiling on MIRVed ICBMs, it became all the more important to guarantee that the U.S. could keep accurate count of Soviet land-based MIRVs. American policy-making in SALT has always been driven by a determination to make sure that the treaty could be verified—and that an increasingly skeptical Congress would see the treaty as verifiable. The issue of MIRV verification had been a point of contention since early in SALT II. The Soviets had maintained that there was already, in Article V of the SALT I interim agreement, a rule prohibiting either side from using "deliberate concealment measures which impede verification by national technical means of compliance with the provisions." This "nonconcealment" clause in SALT I, the Soviets claimed, was adequate to ensure the verifiability of SALT II as well. As applied to MIRV verification, "nonconcealment" meant that neither side could build, say, a giant tent over a silo housing a single-warhead rocket, truck in the components of a multiple warhead, and convert the rocket into a MIRV undetected by the other side's spy satellites overhead. The U.S. argued that the prohibition against concealment—an essentially negative provision in SALT I contained in one verbose but vague clause of the agreement —must be supplemented by a variety of affirmative "counting rules" for MIRVs in SALT II. Once a missile booster of a certain type had been tested with a multiple warhead, the U.S. insisted, then all missiles of that type must count as MIRVs. The U.S. argued that without such a rule, the vigorous Soviet MIRVing program put too heavy an onus on American surveillance and monitoring techniques. Once a particular Soviet booster had been used to launch multiple warheads, the U.S. simply could not be expected to keep an accurate, up-to-date count of which rockets of that type were armed with multiple warheads and which ones were armed with single warheads. Therefore all must be "deemed" to be MIRVed.

The Soviets balked. They did not reject the principle of the MIRV counting rule, but they resisted making it explicit in the treaty. It was their position that the MIRV counting rule was implicit in the SALT I provision whereby all elements of the agreement must be verifiable by national technical means. However, since their fourth-generation MIRVed ICBMs, the SS-17, SS-18 and SS-19, contained both multiple-warhead and single-warhead versions, the Soviets wanted to construe an unMIRVed individual rocket and a MIRVed one as sufficiently different to avoid counting in the same category. To accept the American counting rule would mean that all individuals of the SS-17/18/19 series would count against the 1,320 subceiling—and against the new MIRVed ICBM subceiling as well. The fully tested, already deployed single-warhead versions of the SS-17 and SS-18 would have to be abandoned or they would count as though they were MIRVed. To compound the Soviet discomfiture, the U.S. faced no comparable dilemma. The Americans' MIRVed ICBM program was static and simple compared to the Soviets'. The U.S. had only two types of modern ICBMs, the Minuteman II and the Minuteman III. Only the Minuteman III had been tested with multiple warheads, and all 550 individuals of that class had been deployed with MIRVs. Finally, the Soviets accepted the fact that there was a price to pay in SALT for the proliferation of warheads on their land-based rockets. During U. Alexis Johnson's tenure as chief SALT negotiator, the Kremlin accepted the principle "once tested, always counted" with regard to the MIRVing of missiles. This was called the "booster-type counting rule," and it was written into the Joint Draft Text of the treaty in Geneva.

But the U.S. demanded a higher price. It wanted a "launcher-type counting rule," whereby once a launcher, or silo, of a certain type had been used to launch a MIRVed missile, then all launchers of that type counted as though they contained MIRVed missiles. The American concern was not abstract. It arose largely because the Soviets had begun to deploy a mixture of MIRVed and unMIRVed rockets in nearly identical launchers at two sites in the Ukraine. These were the ICBM fields near the small towns of Derazhnya, not far from the Rumanian border, and Pervomaisk, some 500 miles south of Moscow. Even with his fabled verbal facility, Paul Warnke found, soon after taking up his post in Geneva, that he had difficulty saying Derazhnya and Pervomaisk in one breath. The towns—and the critical issue of SALT verification they represented—became known to all but the most fluent Slavists on the American side as "D-and-P."

D-and-P was an exceedingly knotty and ambiguous problem, a paradigm of what can be most fascinating and maddening about SALT. Well before the signing of SALT I in 1972, there had been 60 silos at each site—120 in all. They were built to contain the SS-11, an older (third-generation), single-warhead ICBM, somewhat more powerful than the unMIRVed version of Minuteman but considerably less accurate. Then, just prior to SALT I, the Russians starting building 30 new silos at each site. D-and-P now consisted of 180 holes in the ground, of which 120 were believed to house SS-11s and the other 60 awaited new occupants. Meanwhile the Soviets were testing the SS-19, their modern, potentially most lethal MIRVed ICBM. The American spy-in-the-sky monitors and weapons analysts watched what happened next very, very carefully. The Soviets began to lower SS-19s into the 60 new holes at D-and-P and then remodeled the 120 older silos, but left the SS-11s in those 120 holes. There was a problem, however: once the concrete caps were in place, the SS-19 launchers looked just like the remodeled SS-11 launchers. The only difference was not in the missile silos themselves but in the nearby manned underground command-and-control silos. The ones for the SS-19s

were marked by a domed antenna that some officials at the State
Department and Arms Control Agency dubbed "the midget."

Even after they had accepted the booster-type MIRV counting
rule, the Soviets contended that only the 60 SS-19s at D-and-P should
count as MIRVs, since SS-11s and SS-19s were, everyone agreed, different types of rockets. The U.S. acknowledged that the SS-11 had never
been tested with a multiple independently targetable warhead, and
the U.S. was quite sure, on the basis of the most vigilant monitoring,
that the Soviets had not secretly replaced any of the SS-11s with
SS-19s. But many American officials, particularly in the intelligence
community and at the Pentagon, argued strenuously that it undermined the verifiability of SALT II for the Soviets to deploy MIRVed
and unMIRVed missiles together and in fields made up of a single type
of launcher. "We had no confidence," explained a high Defense Department official, "in our ability to verify in the future the Soviet claim
that those 120 launchers weren't MIRVed. Therefore it was our position that all 180 launchers at D-and-P must count as MIRVed."

The Soviets reacted as though the Americans had sunk to new
depths of obstreperousness and illogic. The U.S. knew perfectly well,
said the Russians, that there were actually two types of launchers as
well as two types of missiles at D-and-P; the SS-19 holes were distinguishable by virtue of the domed antennae on the neighboring command-and-control silos. In a series of meetings in Geneva, Ralph Earle
and Vladimir Semyonov wrestled over the issue. Semyonov would cite
the domed antennae as proof that there were "visible differences"
between the launchers, and Earle, who had been living with the issue
of D-and-P since his days at the Pentagon, would reply, "You're
wrong; the antenna doesn't prove anything because we know a silo
without one could still handle a MIRVed missile." Semyonov, who
once professed to be flattered when he heard that some of his American interlocutors had nicknamed him "Old Iron Pants," simply kept
repeating the Soviet position. Finally, in some exasperation, Earle said,
"Look, the existence of the antenna is irrelevant to the capability of
launching a MIRV; we know you can launch one without it because
we've seen you do it." What Earle was saying was that U.S. intelligence
had observed the Soviets fire a MIRVed missile from a launcher complex *without a domed antenna* at one of their test sites in another part
of the Soviet Union. That shut Semyonov up for a moment, but it also
caused acute heartburn back in Washington. When some military
officers at the Pentagon saw a memorandum of the exchange, they

worried that Earle had "compromised national technical means" by revealing to the Soviets more than they had previously known about the extent and precision of American surveillance.*

During the summer of 1977, D-and-P was almost as controversial in the deliberations of the Special Coordination Committee at the White House as it was in the negotiations with the Russians in Geneva. The Pentagon and the CIA, in the persons of Harold Brown and Director of Central Intelligence Stansfield Turner, stuck to the hard line that the 120 unMIRVed launchers at D-and-P were so similar to the 60 MIRVed ones that they must all count as MIRVed. Turner referred in a number of meetings to the danger that the Soviets might someday secretly substitute SS-19s for the SS-11s when U.S. spy satellites were "blinded" by cloud cover. Cyrus Vance and Paul Warnke saw the matter more in terms of a principle than the specific case. The important thing, they said, was to get the Soviets to accept what Warnke called "an essential verification rule," whereby MIRV launchers must be visibly distinguishable from unMIRVed ones. It was more important, continued Vance and Warnke, that the Soviets accept such a rule for the future than it was for them to accept the application of the rule retroactively in the case of D-and-P. D-and-P was, after all, a potential problem, not an actual one. Regardless of what American intelligence may have seen the Soviets do with the SS-19 elsewhere, the SS-19 MIRVed launchers at D-and-P were distinguished by the domed antenna. Why delay agreement on an essential verification rule with a long and fractious debate over whether the domed antenna constituted a *sufficiently* distinguishing feature?

During one of many heated arguments on the subject of D-and-P, Warnke was accused of being "willing to give the Soviets the benefit of the doubt, and that is not only unsound—it is terribly unwise politically, since this treaty won't be acceptable to the Congress if it gives the Soviets *any* benefit of *any* doubt." According to the recollection of participants in the conversation, Warnke snapped back: "That is nonsense. There is no doubt in this case. No one is saying that there are MIRVs in those 120 holes. What you're asking us to do is force the Soviets to join us in *pretending* that there are MIRVs in those holes.

---

*On this occasion, as in others, the sensitivity of the U.S. military about "compromising" intelligence information in the negotiations considerably exceeded the sensitivity of the intelligence community itself. At one point, the office of the Joint Chiefs of Staff objected when a U.S. negotiator in Geneva gave his Soviet opposite number an *un*classified Air Force document about the deployment of MIRVed and unMIRVed Minutemen.

And you know what? If we succeed in getting them to do that, they're not just going to continue pretending that single-warhead rockets are MIRVed—they're actually going to MIRV those 120 holes. If we classify every animal we've got to count as a lion rather than a pussycat, the Soviets will end up with more lions."

At an SCC meeting, Warnke said the Pentagon was "overreacting" on D-and-P. No, replied Harold Brown, the Pentagon was prudently anticipating. The Soviets were probably going to put MIRVed SS-19s in the holes at D-and-P sooner or later, so the U.S. might as well count them now. And if the Soviets "got off scot-free" on the 120 SS-11 holes at D-and-P, they would have the option of putting 120 MIRVed SS-19s somewhere else; therefore the U.S. might as well force them to put the SS-19s at D-and-P, which was already subjected to the closest American scrutiny, and thus deprive the Soviets of the choice of deploying them elsewhere. Turner and the CIA analysts agreed. Their projections showed the Soviets might take full advantage of whatever MIRVed ICBM allowance they had under SALT; it was critical for verification and ratification of the agreement that there be no ambiguities—at D-and-P or anywhere else—about exactly how many MIRVs the Russians had and exactly where they were. Warnke remained skeptical of Pentagon and CIA projections about future Soviet deployments; the military and the intelligence communities were in the business of being prepared for the worst and therefore had the habit of predicting the worst.

The Snows of Montana

Vance and Warnke had another reason for being chary about pressing the Soviets too hard to accept a MIRVed-launcher counting rule retroactively in the case of the Derazhnya and Pervomaisk missile fields: the U.S. had its own D-and-P. This was the Minuteman installation at Malmstrom Air Force Base in Montana, where MIRVed Minuteman IIIs were deployed together with unMIRVed Minuteman IIs. Not only were the two types of launchers proximate—they were virtually indistinguishable. Indeed, they were harder to tell apart than the MIRVed SS-19 and unMIRVed SS-11 launchers at D-and-P. Also, while the only SS-11 launchers that looked like SS-19 launchers were the controversial 120 holes at D-and-P, *all* 450 Minuteman II and 550 Minuteman III launchers—deployed in missile fields throughout the American Northwest—looked alike. Part of the Soviet defense of

D-and-P had always been that the SS-11 and SS-19 holes there looked no less different from each other than the Minuteman II and Minuteman III holes that were intermixed at Malmstrom. The Russians maintained that if they could distinguish between the MIRVed and unMIRVed Malmstrom silos by their national technical means, then surely the U.S. could distinguish between MIRVs and non-MIRVs at D-and-P. The U.S. negotiators were somewhat uncomfortable dealing with that particular Soviet argument, for American intelligence had good reason to believe that regardless of what Semyonov and his colleagues claimed, Soviet photoreconnaissance was actually *not* able to distinguish between the silos at Malmstrom. The Russians could keep track of the ratio of unMIRVed to MIRVed Minutemen there and elsewhere not so much by analyzing satellite photography as merely by reading the *Congressional Record, Aviation Week and Space Technology,* U.S. Air Force handouts and small-town Montana newspapers —by taking advantage, in other words, of the "informational asymmetries" between the Soviet and American systems. Thus it was the inescapable essence of the American position on D-and-P that the Soviets should submit to a double standard with regard to MIRV-launcher counting rules; the closed nature of Soviet society, combined with the vigorousness and therefore the unpredictability of the Soviet MIRVing program, meant that the Russians would have to accept a stricter rule than the one that applied to American Minutemen.

To make the whole matter even trickier, the United States Air Force, in something less than perfect coordination with the SALT process, had for some years been engaged at Malmstrom in practices that the Soviets considered to be in violation of SALT I. Since 1973 the Air Force had been hardening the covers on the silos so that as the accuracy and throw-weight of Soviet missiles increased, the U.S. deterrent would stand a better chance of surviving near-direct hits in a preemptive strike. In order to protect the workmen who were hardening the silos against harsh winter conditions, the Air Force installed prefabricated shelters over the launchers for days or even weeks at a time, depending on the severity of the weather.

In 1973, the same year that the Malmstrom shelters went up, the U.S. observed what it regarded as suspicious behavior on the Soviet side. At their new MIRV complexes the Russians were building silos of a different design than had ever been seen before. If these were intended to contain ICBM launchers, they would have constituted a violation of Article I of the interim agreement ("the parties undertake not to start construction of additional fixed land-based intercontinental ballistic missile launchers after July 1, 1972"). The U.S. brought the question to the Standing Consultative Commission in Geneva, a bilateral review panel set up by SALT I to adjudicate charges of cheating. The Soviets responded that the new silos were not launchers but hardened facilities for launch command and control; they were meant to house men rather than missiles. But as has often happened in SALT, an American challenge led to a Soviet counterchallenge. As a matter of pride, principle and negotiating tactics, the Russian SALT monitors made a point of matching their American counterparts in what they considered fastidious vigilance against any peccadillos. So once they had dispensed with American questions about the command-and-control silos, the Soviets tabled an objection of their own. They officially —and repeatedly—protested that the Malmstrom shelters violated Article V of the interim agreement ("each party undertakes not to use deliberate concealment measures which impede verification by national technical means"). The U.S. defended itself by explaining that the shelters were there for "environmental" rather than "deliberate concealment" purposes. ("Environmental" in this context refers to protection of the silo and the workmen from the elements; it has nothing to do with the protection of natural resources.) The Soviets were not satisfied. They claimed that the shelters blinded their photoreconnaissance satellites, and therefore constituted concealment. As for the question of whether the concealment was deliberate, the Russians pointed out that the shelters erected at Malmstrom in 1973 were about four times larger than the ones the Air Force used during the construction and modernization of Minuteman silos from 1962 until 1972. The dramatic increase in the size of the Malmstrom shelters was obviously deliberate; hence, the Soviets contended, the suspicious American activity was inconsistent with the spirit if not the letter of SALT I.

The issue of the Malmstrom shelters was almost as contentious within the U.S. government as it was between the two sides at the Standing Consultative Commission. Some civilian SALT experts at the State Department, the National Security Council and the Arms Control and Disarmament Agency felt that the Soviets, perhaps unwittingly, were asking to establish a principle that would ultimately be beneficial to the U.S.: namely, that regardless of whether a concealment measure was deliberate, if it had the effect of impeding verification then it should be banned. To put it differently, the Russians were suggesting that there should be an onus on the side engaging in a questionable practice to make sure it did not conceal and impede, rather than an onus on the other side to prove that the concealment was deliberate. "When the Russians started giving us a hard time on Malmstrom," said an NSC official, "we should have let them throw us right into that brier patch." Certainly it would have been useful to have the principle firmly established when, in 1978 and 1979, the U.S. found itself in the thicket of negotiating with the Russians the question of whether their use of codes in missile tests constituted a "deliberate concealment measure which impedes verification."

The top officers of the Air Force and the Joint Chiefs of Staff saw the issue very differently. They regarded the Soviet complaint about Malmstrom as absurd and insulting. "Goddamn it," said one missile man at the Pentagon, "the Soviets knew perfectly well we weren't using those shelters to conceal the substitution of Minuteman IIIs for Minuteman IIs, and by harping on their phony line, they were accusing us of being liars." The principle that the Air Force and JCS were interested in preserving was simply that the Soviets should not be allowed to raise false issues and force the U.S. to alter practices it was engaged in for legitimate purposes. Finally, however, at Kissinger's instigation, the Ford administration agreed to modify the controversial shelters but procrastinated in doing so. In 1977 the Carter administration, with the grumbling of the military ringing in its ears, reduced the size of the shelters by about half. But that left the Soviets with an opportunity to point out, whenever it suited their negotiating purposes, that the structures were still twice as large as the ones used in the 1962–72 period. Malmstrom remained an issue of contention in Geneva, in the back channel and within the U.S. government until the final days of the negotiations in mid 1979.

The virtual indistinguishability of Minuteman II launchers from Minuteman III launchers under any circumstances, compounded by the problem of the shelters, made Malmstrom an ideal counterpoint for the Soviets to raise every time the U.S. pressed the point of D-and-P. Since Vance, Warnke and Earle were in the position of having to negotiate regularly and directly with the Russians, they were naturally more sensitive to the weaknesses and liabilities in the American position than their Pentagon, CIA and NSC colleagues, who had the luxury of simply reading cables about the negotiations and scrawling derisive comments in the margin every time a Soviet official was quoted as scoring a debating point on Malmstrom.

The dispute flickered, and sometimes flared, through the summer. Officials at the State Department and Arms Control Agency groaned and rolled their eyes whenever the subject of D-and-P came up. It was, they said, the "latest Pentagon fixation." Across the Potomac, at the Defense Department and CIA, there was grumbling that Vance and Warnke were being soft on the Russians by offering to make D-and-P an exception to the MIRVed-launcher counting rule. As one Pentagon official put it, "Paul's position boiled down to saying that the Russians had gotten away with something at D-and-P and we should settle for their promise never to do it again." Warnke was said to be willing to "grandfather" D-and-P in exchange for the Soviets' granting a similar exemption to Malmstrom. Brown stuck to his position that conceding on the issue of D-and-P would be to punch a loophole into SALT II, and the Soviets would take advantage of that loophole as surely as they had exploited the failure of SALT I to define heavy missiles.

The issue came to a head at a Special Coordination Committee meeting in late August. Gromyko and Vance were scheduled to meet in Vienna in early September. Vance and Warnke were willing to persist for a while longer in trying to get a Soviet concession on D-and-P, but they argued that it was basically a "technical, definitional" problem that should be negotiated at the level of the permanent delegations in Geneva, not at the "political level" between Vance and Gromyko. William Hyland spoke up from his chair along the wall, behind the principal members of the SCC, who were seated around the table. D-and-P should not be regarded as a technical, definitional problem to be remanded to the delegations, he said. "This could turn out to be a critical bargaining point, not just a token of good faith but vital to the viability of our overall proposal." Hyland had in mind the formula he had helped design for a proposed MIRVed ICBM subceiling of 800. He had settled on that figure by adding the 300 MIRVed "heavy" SS-18s allowed under SALT I to a projected force of 320 MIRVed "light" SS-17s and SS-19s to be deployed at fields other than D-and-P, plus all 180 launchers at D-and-P. The sum of those figures was 800. Thus, the number of MIRVed ICBMs that was going to be proposed to the Soviets at the next Vance-Gromyko meeting depended upon counting D-and-P as entirely MIRVed.

The disagreement over how hard to press the Soviets on D-and-P, and at what level, contributed to the postponement of Vance's meeting with Gromyko from early September in Vienna until late September in Washington. That way Gromyko could see Carter as well as

Vance. Carter sided with Brown on the importance of D-and-P. The President himself would raise the issue with the foreign minister. He would make D-and-P a crucial test of Soviet flexibility—indeed, a test of whether SALT would continue.

7

The September Breakthrough

While the apparatus was grinding out options for a compromise in SALT, misunderstandings and recriminations persisted between Washington and Moscow on a whole range of international issues involving Africa, the Middle East, the repression of Soviet dissidents, and American diplomacy toward China. These disagreements had no bearing on how many MIRVed ICBMs the Soviets would deploy by 1985 or whether air-launched cruise missiles would be constrained in the protocol. Nonetheless, despite the best efforts of the negotiators, the fortunes of SALT had come to depend increasingly on the outlook for the overall Soviet-American relationship, and that outlook was bleak and getting bleaker. Marshall Shulman's "tabular account of related events"—the fever chart of the relationship—showed the summer of 1977 to be yet another season of discord between the superpowers. Insofar as SALT was linked to the fluctuations of Soviet-American relations, there was little reason to expect much good from Andrei Gromyko's visit to Washington in September.

The Soviets continued to complain bitterly that the Carter administration's human rights policy constituted interference in the internal affairs of the U.S.S.R. and was incompatible with the negotiation of an arms control agreement. The administration tried, rather lamely, to dismiss the Soviet complaints as empty propaganda in which the Kremlin leaders themselves did not believe. At a press conference at the end of June, Jimmy Carter was asked if his outspokenness on behalf of Soviet dissidents might not endanger SALT. The President said he doubted "there is any connection between the two in the minds of the Soviets." Carter also sought to "unlink" SALT and summitry. He suggested that he and Leonid Brezhnev should meet later in the year regardless of whether there would be a treaty to sign. The Soviet-American relationship "should be one of continuing consultations, not just to ratify a final agreement but to get to know one another." The U.S. ambassador in Moscow, Malcolm Toon, delivered a letter from Carter to Brezhnev underscoring that suggestion. A few days later, in early July, Brezhnev summoned Toon to the Kremlin and told him firmly that if there was to be a summit meeting with Carter, the principal item of business must be the signing of a new SALT treaty. Washington press accounts at the time, based on so-called background interviews with the most authoritative senior official on the staff of the National Security Council, made clear that it had largely been Brzezinski's idea to have a "purely consultative, low-key," getting-to-know-you summit. Such sponsorship made the idea even less attractive to the Kremlin. More than ever, the Soviets saw Brzezinski as the bad cop to Cyrus Vance's good cop in the administration, and they were perplexed—as were many American pundits and even some government officials—about who was in charge of policy toward the Soviet Union and who had the upper hand in the reworking of the U.S. SALT position. Carter's speeches on Soviet-American relations seemed sometimes to have been drafted by Vance and Shulman, sometimes by Brzezinski and his aides. The America-watchers on Dobrynin's staff parsed the texts and scratched their heads—as one put it, "jotting 'ZB' in the margin next to one paragraph, 'CV' next to another." According to one Soviet, when David Aaron and William Hyland came to lunch at the embassy in late August with their tentative proposition that SALT II should contain a new subceiling for MIRVed ICBMs, there was considerable discussion afterward among the Russians over whether Aaron and Hyland, as NSC staff members, were bringing a "Brzezinski proposal," which, almost by definition, must contain a trick or trap.

On the American side, the approach of the October 3 expiration of SALT I was reason enough for pessimism. In Foggy Bottom, the prospect of failing to meet that psychological deadline caused demoralization and, in some officers, near panic. The policy planning staff and the legal adviser of the State Department as well as the general counsel of the Arms Control Agency were directed to prepare contingency plans on how to keep the 1972 interim agreement alive in the absence of a SALT II follow-on accord. The diplomats and lawyers considered the possibility of an *aide-mémoire,* to be initialed by Vance

and Gromyko, but administration political advisers warned that any
such formal document might have to be submitted to the Congress,
where it could become a hook on which Henry Jackson could hang
meddlesome amendments. Instead, it was decided that the U.S. and
the Soviet Union should issue simultaneous but unilateral statements,
each declaring its intention not to violate the terms of the interim
agreement so long as the other side exercised similar restraint. These
statements were prepared for release at the time of Gromyko's arrival.

As Gromyko's September visit to Washington drew near, there
were portents from Moscow that the life of SALT I might have to be
artificially prolonged for a long time. The Soviets mounted what
looked like a concerted psychological-warfare offensive. The principal
theme was that it was up to the U.S. to make all the concessions
necessary for an agreement. Brezhnev met with Kurt Waldheim, the
secretary general of the United Nations, and wanted to talk about little
else but SALT. The Soviet leader said he was terribly worried that the
impasse in the negotiations, for which he blamed the Americans,
might not be broken. When Warren Burger, the Chief Justice of the
Supreme Court, visited Moscow, Brezhnev lectured him on the "stagnation and recession" in Soviet-American relations. George McGovern saw Gromyko in Moscow, and the foreign minister said the outcome of his next meeting with Vance would depend on what Vance
was "carrying in his briefcase." Malcolm Toon interpreted that to be
bad news. This remark, too, suggested that the Russians were expect-
ing the U.S. to do all the compromising at the upcoming meeting. On
the very eve of Gromyko's arrival in the U.S., *Pravda* and *Za Rubyezhom (The World Abroad)*, a foreign affairs journal, echoed a favorite
Gromyko complaint from earlier meetings. "The blame for the slowdown lies entirely with the U.S.," said *Za Rubyezhom*, "for it was the
Carter administration which deviated from the agreements reached
in Vladivostok, trying under the guise of a new initiative to gain
unilateral advantages."

"Oh, boy," moaned a diplomat on the Soviet desk in Washington,
"here comes Gromyko with that 'unilateral advantages' line again. I'm
not sure we can keep this thing going if we have to listen to that all
over again. I sure hope they don't think we're bluffing this time when
we tell them that they've used up all their rejections."

"Up until now, the Soviets have just sat there like a giant sponge,
absorbing all our proposals," commented another official at the time.
"They either don't say anything or they give us the big *Nyet*. I don't

think this process can stand another *Nyet.*" But Gromyko arrived in Washington looking like a man whose vocabulary consisted of nothing but variations on that word. Even after a night to catch up on his sleep at the Soviet embassy, he scowled and glowered, radiating rejection. Vance, for his part, was under extraordinary strain. Just before Gromyko's arrival, he had been tied up in tortuous consultations with the Egyptian and Israeli foreign ministers. He had to switch gears mentally from trying to mediate the Middle East dispute to the very different challenge of negotiating SALT with the Russians.

The Stone Wall Cracks

Vance's first encounter with Gromyko was almost completely unproductive. The secretary resubmitted the U.S. plan for a freeze on Soviet MIRVed heavy missiles that he had proposed in Geneva in May. Gromyko brusquely repeated his earlier refusal to consider that or any other proposal that "discriminated against" Soviet systems. More discouraging to the Americans, Gromyko offered no counterproposal of his own. Only later did the U.S. side come to realize that it was standard Soviet procedure always to stonewall in the first session. The principle was pure poker: never show what's in your own hand until you've had a look at your opponent's cards; don't make a bid until he's tipped his hand. Therefore, no matter what proposals Gromyko and his colleagues were authorized to consider, they always spent the first session of every round repeating old positions and old rejections. That way, they hoped they would seem less eager for an agreement than the Americans—and that their daunting display of inflexibility would frustrate the Americans into showing some new flexibility of their own. Gromyko gave no hint that his intransigence was primarily tactical, that he was merely following orders to probe the Americans first and concede to them later. He stonewalled convincingly and with a certain perverse relish. As one participant put it, "He was being a son of a bitch, and he really had his heart in it." Vance and a number of his colleagues thought they were watching SALT die before their very eyes.

The atmosphere improved somewhat during lunch in the James Madison Room on the top floor of the State Department Building. Surrounded by masterpieces from the government's collection of early-nineteenth-century American antique furniture, the negotiators put aside for the moment their wrangles over nuclear hardware.

Gromyko slipped into the role of ranconteur. He held the table spell-bound with stories about World War II, and he delivered a graceful panegyric to W. Averell Harriman, the Democratic elder statesman who had served as ambassador to Moscow during World War II, when Gromyko was Soviet envoy to the U.S., and with whom Vance had worked during the Vietnam peace talks in Paris in 1968. "That was the only time I ever saw the sour curl disappear from Gromyko's lip—and the only time Cy seemed utterly relaxed in Gromyko's presence," said an American official who sat through numerous meetings between the secretary and the foreign minister before and since.

The sour curl reappeared after lunch. Gromyko reverted to his more familiar, less charming role. He was just as peremptory in reject-ing the U.S. suggestion of a 250 "heavy systems" limit as he had been with the 190 MIRVed heavy freeze. William Hyland took Georgy Kornienko aside and told him that Gromyko's meeting with President Carter, scheduled for the next day, would be a disaster if the Soviet side continued to stonewall. Vance delivered the same message to Gromyko during a private talk in Vance's spacious office. Only their interpreters were present. With unaccustomed bluntness, the secre-tary of state said that if Carter was subjected to the same spectacle of recalcitrance that Vance and his colleagues had endured all day, SALT would probably collapse, then and there. Gromyko yielded. He hinted he was authorized to negotiate a compromise based on the American alternative suggestion of a MIRVed ICBM subceiling: the Soviet gov-ernment might consider such a thing if the U.S. agreed, once and for all, to count cruise-missile-carrying heavy bombers under the Vladi-vostok subceiling for multiple-warhead launchers. Gromyko also re-vealed that he had brought with him a letter containing measures that the Soviets would undertake in order to assure the U.S. that the Backfire bomber would not be used for intercontinental missions. It was all Vance could do not to lean back and give a huge sigh of relief. After four months of suspense since his last meeting with Gromyko in May, and after seven hours of grueling negotiations that day, the Soviet sponge had finally been squeezed enough to produce a drop of flexibility. The stone wall had cracked. SALT was finally showing the promise of a breakthrough.

Shortly after Gromyko returned to the Soviet embassy, Dobrynin called Vance to confirm that the meeting with the President the next day would almost certainly be productive if the U.S. coupled its pro-posal of a MIRVed ICBM subceiling with a willingness to count ALCM bombers under the Vladivostok 1,320 limit. Vance telephoned Harold

Brown on a secure line that connected the State Department with the Pentagon. Vance told Brown that Gromyko had given him an encouraging signal: the Kremlin might accept new limits on land-based MIRVs—but only on the condition that the Carter administration give up its earlier refusal to count ALCM bombers as MIRVed missiles. Vance and Brown then met with Carter and Brzezinski to plan for the next day's meeting. The first problem was whether to accept Gromyko's predictable but painful condition. The second was how to incorporate it into the U.S. package. Clearly, the Soviets were going to accept a subceiling on MIRVed ICBMs only as part of a new American proposal that contained a big "sweetener," and Gromyko had made it clearer than ever that the only sweetener that would entice the Soviets would be a somewhat bitter pill for the administration to swallow: Carter and his advisers must take a deep breath and agree to count ALCM carriers under the 1,320 subceiling—something Henry Kissinger had been willing to do nearly two years before. Brzezinski took up the matter with David Aaron and William Hyland. How could they accept the principle of counting ALCM carriers under the 1,320 subceiling while at the same time preserving maximum flexibility in the American arsenal and maximum constraint on the Soviet MIRVs?

In a frenzy of last-minute brainstorming, Brzezinski and his NSC colleagues settled on what they called an "allowance," or "set-aside" for cruise-missile-carrying bombers. As the idea developed, it took on a feature that made it more advantageous to the U.S. than merely counting ALCM-armed bombers as though they were slow-flying, low-flying, manned MIRVed missiles—which was what the Soviets wanted. An ALCM carrier set-aside would permit each side a certain number of bombers armed with cruise missiles "free." Once that allowance had been used up, additional ones would count as though they were MIRVed missiles. It was Aaron's and Hyland's idea to have an allowance that permitted the U.S. as many ALCM carriers as it wanted within the 1,320 subceiling, as long as it was willing to give up one MIRVed missile for every extra bomber over and above the allowance. There would be, in other words, complete "freedom to mix" within the 1,320 aggregate between ALCM carriers and MIRVed missiles, just as the original Vladivostok subceiling had allowed both sides "freedom to mix" between land-based and submarine-launched MIRVs. Aaron described the ALCM carrier allowance as "fungible," a lawyers' term meaning that one item may be used in place of another to satisfy an obligation or to fill out a quota.

But the designers of the formula wanted to limit the Soviets' free-dom to mix between ALCM carriers (of which they were likely to have none for some time to come) and MIRVed rockets (of which they were likely—if given a chance—to have too many). So the NSC brainstorm-ers set out, quite deliberately and unabashedly, to seek what Soviet propagandists liked to call a "unilateral advantage." The fungibility of the formula would work in one direction only—in favor of extra ALCM carriers, but not in favor of extra MIRVed missiles. True to his reputation as the archvillain in Soviet eyes, it was Zbigniew Brzezinski who came up with the necessary gimmick: the allowance for ALCM carriers would be downwardly flexible, but the allowance for MIRVed ballistic missiles would *not* be upwardly flexible. The U.S. could "buy" extra ALCM carriers by paying a price in MIRVed missiles, but the Soviets could not do the reverse. There would be an inflexible maxi-mum on total MIRVs, covering both submarine-launched ballistic mis-siles and intercontinental ballistic missiles. Brzezinski did not concoct this idea out of thin air. It had surfaced from time to time in memos from the SALT specialists on his staff—William Hyland, Roger Mo-lander and another NSC expert, Victor Utgoff—ever since June. But it was very much at Brzezinski's initiative that the MIRV maximum was inserted at the last minute between the MIRVed ICBM limit and the 1,320 subceiling on the eve of the Gromyko-Carter meeting. Brze-zinski favored a figure between 1,100 and 1,150. The Joint Chiefs of Staff wanted to go as high as 1,250, in order to give themselves more "freedom to mix" between ALCM bombers and submarine-launched MIRVs. The President settled on 1,200 as the new aggregate for MIRVed missiles. That meant a set-aside of 120 "free" ALCM carriers (1,320 minus 1,200). The new MIRVed missile aggregate fitted into the emerging American package like this:

• Each side could initially deploy a total of 2,400 strategic nuclear launch vehicles of all kinds, but that ceiling would be lowered to 2,160 during the life of the treaty.

• Each side could deploy 1,320 multiple-warhead strategic nuclear launch vehicles or "force multiptiers," including cruise-missile-carry-ing bombers and MIRVed ballistic missiles.

• Each side could deploy a maximum of 1,200 MIRVed missiles, including land-based ICBMs and submarine-launched ballistic mis-siles.

• Each side could deploy a maximum of 800 MIRVed ICBMs.

Even its inventors admitted the formula was not designed to pacify those who complained that SALT was a dizzyingly complicated affair. But while it lacked the virtue of simplicity, the plan left the 1,320 subceiling in place and therefore had the advantage that the Soviets might see it as falling within the Vladivostok framework, in contrast to other American proposals, which appeared to disregard or even defy the 1974 accord. Nor was the concept of ceilings within ceilings unprecedented in SALT or alien to the Russians. The Vladivostok accord itself was based on a simple, two-in-one version of that concept. Here was a four-in-one modification that might appeal to Russians— who as children had played with *matryoshkas,* hollow wooden dolls that nest inside each other.

Once Carter had approved the 1,200 MIRV missile maximum, Brzezinski went home, exhausted but exhilarated. Aaron and Hyland stayed on in the west wing of the White House, putting finishing touches on the proposal for the next day's meeting. As they worked into the night, they began to have second thoughts about the wisdom of the 1,200 limit. Instead of the 1,320/1,200/800 formula Brzezinski favored, why not drop the 1,200 figure and make the formula not only simpler but more attractive to both the Pentagon and the Kremlin? The U.S. Navy at that time had plans for a Trident submarine-launched missile program that would have given the U.S. a total MIRV force, on land and at sea, of 1,238 by 1985, so the 1,200 MIRV missile maximum would have cramped the Defense Department, possibly squeezing out 38 multiple-warhead rockets. The Soviets were likely to balk at the 1,200 figure for precisely the reason that Brzezinski wanted it: the limit would prevent them from compensating for the relative backwardness of their air-launched cruise missiles by deploying extra MIRVed missiles on submarines—missiles that could be used to knock out American airfields where cruise-missile-carrying bombers would be based. The U.S. was not nearly as concerned about constraining submarine-launched missiles as land-based ones. So why not make the package a bit more enticing to the Soviets and save a few American MIRVs in the bargain? Aaron and Hyland phoned Brzezinski at home, waking him up, to get his permission to drop the 1,200 limit. Absolutely not, said Brzezinski. It was crucial as a matter of principle that the Soviets not be able to trade MIRVed missiles, of which they had too many, for cruise missile carriers, of which they had none. So the formula remained 1,320/1,200/800.

At his meeting with Gromyko the next day, Carter formally proposed for the first time that the U.S. would count ALCM carriers under the 1,320 subceiling as long as land-based MIRVs were held to 800. Gromyko mostly listened, but in the way he asked for amplification and clarification on certain points, he seemed to be indicating a positive interest. Carter made clear that the U.S. proposal was contingent on Soviet acceptance of the MIRVed-launcher counting rule at Derazhnya and Pervomaisk; if there was to be a MIRVed ICBM subceiling of 800, all 180 silos at D-and-P must count as though they contained MIRVed ICBMs. On that point, Gromyko's response was anything but positive. According to one participant in the meeting, "he hit the ceiling, accusing the U.S. of illogic that bordered on bad faith." Carter was firm. For the sake of ensuring the verifiability of the proposed MIRVed subceiling, D-and-P must be deemed entirely MIRVed. The three-hour meeting dealt with other contentious subjects, including the administration's human rights policy. Since this was Gromyko's first meeting with Carter, he used the occasion to object in the strongest terms to Carter's reception of Vladimir Bukovsky at the White House the previous March. Either because he actually forgot Bukovsky's name or because he wanted to dramatize his contempt for someone he dismissed as a "common criminal," Gromyko stumbled over the name, saying something like "Stupovsky-spukovsky-putovsky." Carter told the Soviet foreign minister that the U.S. government would continue to speak out on behalf of persecuted dissidents, and that he was particularly concerned about the case of Anatoly Shcharansky, the young Jewish computer scientist who was awaiting trial on trumped-up charges of spying for the U.S.

But despite these altercations, the meeting went well enough for Carter to say he would like to get to know Brezhnev personally before too long. Gromyko replied, in his heavily accented English, "I think there are chances." Gromyko told the White House press corps as he left the meeting that a SALT II agreement was "within our field of vision." Vance then took the Soviet visitors back to the State Department for more negotiations on SALT as well as other subjects, particularly the Middle East. They agreed to assign Leslie Gelb and Dobrynin's deputy, Alexander Bessmertnykh, to continue negotiations in the months ahead on the Backfire issue, using the letter Gromyko had brought from Moscow as a starting point. Bessmertnykh's name is derived from the Russian word for "immortal," leading Harold Brown to comment that the Soviets must have been underscoring their determination to drag out the Backfire issue forever. On the central issues of new limits for MIRVs and how to count D-and-P, Gromyko made it clear he would have to transmit the President's proposals to Moscow and await further instructions.

The Americans expected it would take at least five or six days for the Politburo to digest the latest U.S. position and respond. Vance and Gromyko were due to spend the next week in New York attending the United Nations General Assembly. They arranged to meet again about SALT on Friday at the end of that week. Tuesday, much to the surprise of the administration, Gromyko requested a meeting that very evening not just with the secretary of state but with the President as well. There was some suspense on the American side about exactly what Gromyko's new instructions from Moscow were, but there was little doubt that they must be positive. If he were to be the bearer of bad news, Gromyko would have delivered it to Vance in New York, not to Carter in Washington.

William Hyland was then in his last week on the federal payroll. He had now completed his twenty-five years in the government and was about to go to work for his old boss, Henry Kissinger, at the Georgetown University Center for Strategic and International Studies. Brzezinski asked Hyland, as a kind of swan song, to write a briefing paper for the President anticipating Gromyko's counterproposals and recommending how the President should respond. A colleague of Hyland's remembers him joking that it must have been Brzezinski's way of punishing him for leaving the NSC to make him commit himself in writing to a guess about what cards the world's best poker player would have in his hand. Hyland wrote a paper predicting that Gromyko would accept the MIRVed ICBM subceiling and agree to count all the D-and-P silos as MIRVed, but that he would seek somewhat higher numbers than the U.S. wanted for the MIRVed ICBM subceiling, the MIRVed missile aggregate and the overall aggregate. Hyland recommended that if the Soviet-preferred numbers were only slightly higher than the American ones, the President should accept them on the spot and thereby give the negotiations an additional fillip.

Gromyko played to a full house. Carter, Mondale, Vance, Brown, Brzezinski, Warnke, Aaron, Hyland and Carter's chief staff aide, Hamilton Jordan, were all there as the foreign minister delivered the Kremlin's response. He began with a peevish litany of all the unreasonable demands the U.S. had made in the past. He then launched into a peroration about the patience and magnanimity of his own government. David Aaron, who had listened to similar harangues from Vladi-

mir Semyonov in Geneva, knew that this was the *pro forma* Soviet
overture to a concession. But while Semyonov was a skilled performer,
Gromyko was a true virtuoso. Aaron waited for the magic Russian
word meaning "but"—as in, "You've made all these outrageous demands, *but* for the sake of peace, we've decided to agree . . ." Brown
and Brzezinski were sitting next to each other. During his own tour
of duty as a negotiator in Geneva, Brown had picked up a smattering
of Russian, and Brzezinski's Russian is nearly fluent. The two of them
realized almost simultaneously—before Gromyko's interpreter, Victor
Sukhodryev, began to translate—that the message from Moscow was,
for a change, a big *Da*. Hamilton Jordan could tell from Brown's and
Brzezinski's expressions that he was missing something; he tugged at
Hyland's arm and whispered for him to translate. While Gromyko
droned on, Mondale busied himself by reading over Hyland's briefing
memo. It was as though the Vice-President were preparing to grade
the paper against what Gromyko actually said.

The grade would have been an "A." Gromyko conceded on D-and-
P; he accepted a MIRVed ICBM subceiling; and he agreed to lower
the overall ceiling from 2,400. In exchange for the American willingness to count cruise-missile-carrying heavy bombers against the 1,320
MIRV subceiling, he accepted a lower limit on total MIRVed missiles.
But also, as Hyland had predicted, Gromyko countered with numbers
higher than the Americans wanted. Instead of 2,160, 1,200 and 800 for
the overall ceiling, the MIRV aggregate and the MIRVed ICBM subceiling respectively, the Soviets wanted a hierarchy of multiples of 50
—2,250, 1,250 and 850. Contrary to Hyland's advice, Carter chose not
to accept the Soviet numbers on the spot. He felt it important that the
U.S. play a bit of poker too, especially since the U.S. had already, at
Soviet insistence, reshuffled the deck, dealt itself a new hand, and
given away a number of cards since March. Also, Brzezinski had ad-
vised the President before the meeting not to give an inch upward on
the 1,200 MIRVed missile aggregate that he had designed and fought
so hard to preserve. Carter told Gromyko that the U.S. welcomed the
progress that had been made at the meeting; he was hopeful the talks
could be brought to a successful conclusion in the near future. It
remained for the negotiators in subsequent rounds to work out a
compromise on the three key numbers: the Soviets eventually got
their way on 2,250 for the overall ceiling; the U.S. got its way on 1,200
for the MIRVed missile aggregate, and the two sides split the difference on the MIRVed ICBM subceiling, settling on 820.

Vance later recalled his own sense of relief and accomplishment: "We'd made a major breakthrough. I was convinced we'd broken the back of the problem. Now I knew we would get where we were going. It was still going to be a tough road to walk, but we'd get there." (Walter Slocombe, however, encountered some skepticism when he reported on the meeting to his young daughter, who was then more interested in ecology and saving the whales than in arms control and banning the bomb. "We made some important progress with the Russian foreign minister," Slocombe told the seven-year-old. "That's good," she replied, "but when are you going to do something about the whales? The Russians are very bad about whales, you know.")

It had indeed been a highly productive and promising encounter —certainly the best SALT meeting since Vladivostok. The Carter administration had made two significant concessions. It had given up, once and for all, on reductions in the Soviet heavy missile force; and it had agreed to a modified version of the January 1976 compromise whereby heavy bombers armed with air-launched cruise missiles would be counted against the 1,320 subceiling. The Soviets had made five significant concessions. They had agreed to lower the Vladivostok ceiling during the life of SALT II. They had agreed to accept a new subceiling in the Vladivostok framework—a special limitation on land-based MIRVs, the strongest and most destabilizing component of their military might. They had agreed to deploy fewer total MIRVs, land-based and submarine-launched, than they had been permitted by the Vladivostok subceiling of 1,320. They had agreed to an ALCM bomber counting formula that allowed the U.S. 120 of the aircraft free before they must count as though they were MIRVed missiles. And finally, the Russians had budged on D-and-P after years of intractability. Moreover, at D-and-P they had agreed to treat as indistinguishable MIRVed and unMIRVed launchers that were actually at least as distinguishable as the MIRVed and unMIRVed Minuteman silos at Malmstrom. Thus, implicitly, the Soviets had accepted the reality that the closed nature of their society put a somewhat greater burden on them than on the U.S. to conform to the strictest possible verification rules. All these concessions were important in and of themselves. They were potentially even more important as precedents on which to build in future agreements.

Toward the end of the meeting, Carter showed Gromyko a plastic scale model of U.S. and Soviet ICBMs lined up side by side. The Russian behemoths, painted black, both outnumbered and dwarfed the graceful white figure of Minuteman. "Now you see why it's so important to limit these things," said the President to the foreign minister. The meeting had gone well enough for the two sides to initiate preliminary discussion of a Carter-Brezhnev summit. Lower-level Soviet and American officials talked tentatively about timing for the meeting—possibly before the end of the year—and even a site. Since Nixon had been to Moscow in 1974 and Ford to Vladivostok later that same year, it was Brezhnev's turn to visit the U.S. The Soviets suggested holding the summit at some rather exotic location, as far from Washington as Vladivostok was from Moscow. Alaska, perhaps. "Brezhnev might get there and demand it back," cracked one U.S. official. Hawaii seemed altogether a more appealing site, especially if the summit was held during the upcoming winter. Publicly, however, the President and his aides tried at first to prevent a build-up of expectations that a SALT agreement and a summit were at hand. "Reasonable progress" had been made, said Carter immediately after Gromyko left. "We've narrowed down the differences to a relatively small number." But the remaining differences, he warned, "could take quite a long time to resolve." Right after Gromyko's Tuesday-evening visit to the White House, David Aaron told the press that the negotiations had reached a "delicate and hopeful stage." But privately, he was less qualified in his optimism. He went home and told his wife that night, "I think we've got a deal."

8 The Long, Cold Winter

Once Gromyko was safely out of town, the administration found its optimism increasingly difficult to contain. At the State Department, where many officials had anticipated the October 3 expiration of SALT I with deep foreboding, dejection quickly gave way first to relief, then to near euphoria. That psychological deadline had passed without disaster befalling the negotiations. As expected, when the Carter administration and the Kremlin exchanged statements of intent to abide by SALT I, Senator Henry Jackson complained that the stopgap device was in violation of the spirit, if not the letter, of the 1961 statute establishing the Arms Control and Disarmament Agency; that law subjected to congressional review any action by the executive branch that "obligated the U.S. to limit its military capabilities." On the Senate floor, Jackson said he regarded the administration's tactic as "contrary to established statutory and constitutional procedures for concluding" arms control agreements. In order to demonstrate his "insistence that the Congress retains the authority to approve agreements that have the effect of limiting the armaments of the U.S.," Jackson sponsored—and the Senate passed—a resolution bestowing on the administration the congressional approval that the administration had chosen not to seek. While Jackson sought to interpret the resolution as a rebuke and warning to the executive branch, the White House and State Department welcomed the unsolicited congressional approval as an indication that the Senate as a whole was willing to let SALT live, for a while anyway, on borrowed time.

The September breakthrough in Washington was followed in October by an important Soviet concession in Geneva. Vladimir Semyonov read a statement saying that the Soviet Union would undertake not to produce, test or deploy its solid-fuel ICBM, the SS-16, or any component unique to it—i.e., the third stage which distinguished it from the SS-20, the mobile intermediate-range ballistic missile (IRBM) that had just been deployed to the acute distress of the West Europeans. It should be recalled that during the calamitous March meeting in Moscow, one of the Soviets' few gestures of flexibility was an offer not to deploy the SS-16 in a mobile mode. But they had reserved the right to continue the development of a fixed-site SS-16. That meant that simply by building and storing large numbers of SS-16 third stages, the Soviets would be able rapidly to convert mobile IRBMs into mobile ICBMs in a moment of international crisis, thus making it easier to subject the U.S. to nuclear blackmail. The Carter administration had dismissed as a nonoffer the Soviets' March proposal to cancel only the mobile portion of the SS-16 program and had continued to press the Russians to abandon the program altogether. The principal argument, as with D-and-P, concerned verification: SALT II would meet neither the administration's nor the Congress's standards of verifiability if all SS-20 launchers, which were to be unconstrained by the treaty, were readily convertible into SS-16 launchers. In October, the Soviets conceded that point. On purely technical grounds, it was an easy enough concession to make. The SS-16 had been, in the words of a Pentagon expert who followed its undistinguished career closely, "a dog of a missile—it was just no good, and it wasn't getting much better." But on political grounds, the abandonment of the SS-16 was highly significant. Not only did it make verification easier and thus enhance the prospects for ratification of the treaty in the Senate, but the concession also indicated a softening of Soviet policy. Just as providing an agreed data base on the number of weapons in various SALT-related categories meant overcoming a deeply inbred secretiveness, so it went against the Soviet grain to halt any military program for the sake of SALT. Once the Kremlin had promised the Soviet military establishment a new missile, and especially once the development of that new missile was under way, the program usually acquired a kind of inviolability. Kissinger's initial willingness to treat cruise missiles as bargaining chips, Carter's offer to sacrifice the MX as part of the comprehensive proposal and later his decision to cancel the B-1 bomber program after prototypes had already been built—this American behavior was almost totally alien to the Soviets. It was an article of faith among critics like Paul Nitze and Henry Jackson that the

Russians never let arms control get in the way of the testing and deployment of new arms, especially once testing had begun. So it was especially heartening for the U.S. negotiators in Geneva to hear Semyonov formally commit his government to renouncing the SS-16.

That concession did not eliminate entirely the worries back in Washington about the SS-16. Henry Jackson and Richard Perle were concerned that the Soviets might have already sufficiently tested the SS-16 for them still to manufacture—secretly and in violation of the treaty—third stages for stockpiling. The Pentagon and the CIA were more sanguine, for two reasons: first, they calculated that without a flight-testing program, the reliability of the missiles, which had never been perfected, would be further degraded; and second, intelligence experts were confident that they would know if the Soviets tried secretly to start up those assembly lines again.

The SS-16 concession was one reason for Jimmy Carter's own burst of optimism about SALT in October. He had been deeply worried that the Soviets might end up with an ICBM that was readily convertible into a mobile missile. In a meeting with a group of advisers, he exulted in "the great, great significance that the Soviets would unilaterally agree not to build something they've already tested." At the end of October, Carter was speaking to a dinner meeting in Des Moines, Iowa. In the midst of a discussion primarily about farm and energy policies, he blurted out that a SALT agreement would be consummated "within a few weeks." It was the sort of effervescent imprecision that caused him trouble so many times before and since. Iowa Senator John Culver, an outspoken supporter of SALT, was with Carter in Des Moines; he joked afterwards that the President was simply using the subject of SALT to tell his audience how glad he was to be back in Iowa, the site of his first major victory during the presidential primaries of 1976. But to the press it sounded as though the President was announcing that an agreement would be ready for his own signature in a matter of weeks. In addition to local farmers and Democratic politicians, Carter's audience included Soviet officials back in Washington and far away in Moscow. They were flabbergasted by the President's wildly unrealistic prediction. Their shock, as usual, quickly turned to suspicion, especially when Carter said a week later, at a press conference back in Washington, that there was "a fairly good prospect within the next few weeks for a general agreement with the Soviet Union" on SALT II. Actually, Carter was now choosing his words more carefully and climbing off the limb on which he found himself as a result of the Des Moines statement: he and Gromyko had already reached a "general agreement" on SALT II the month before. But that subtlety escaped the Russians. Besides, even some of Carter's more cautious advisers were hoping aloud for "SALT by Christmas" —a phrase that would have a melancholy ring when it was echoed a full year later. "It sounded to us," said a Soviet diplomat later, "that your President was up to his old trick of trying to put propaganda pressure on us by generating a lot of false expectations."

Anger on the Hill

Meanwhile Senator Jackson and other likely opponents of SALT were beginning to close ranks around an issue more politically potent than whether the administration had honored the 1961 Arms Control and Disarmament Act with its unilateral statement of continued compliance with SALT I and more vital than whether SS-16 third stages could be secretly stockpiled. Jackson and others were disturbed about revelations in the press that the administration had, once and for all, given up on new limits for Soviet heavy missiles and settled instead on a subceiling for MIRVed ICBMs. Jackson and like-minded senators were especially annoyed because the administration had abandoned a limit on heavies without soliciting the Congress's views. Moreover, the proposed MIRVed ICBM subceiling was, according to the press accounts, in the range of 800—some 250 more than the level of MIRVed ICBMs the administration had sought in March as part of the comprehensive proposal. Jackson said the negotiators were guilty of a "double—and therefore doubly disastrous—cave-in: they've surrendered on their own earlier efforts both to reduce heavies and to put a meaningful cap on land-based MIRVs." In Richard Perle's view, the administration had "given away the store."

A Senate committee summoned Vance to explain in executive session why the administration had backed away from limits on Soviet heavies and gone after a MIRVed ICBM subceiling instead. Vance glossed over the political reason—namely, that the Soviets had repeatedly refused to negotiate a limit on heavies, and the U.S. had finally decided there was no point in continuing to butt its head into that particular stone wall. Instead, he justified the shift in negotiating tactics on technical and strategic grounds. He cited, rather vaguely, evidence that the "light" SS-19 was potentially every bit as formidable as the heavy SS-18 because of its steadily improving accuracy. In so doing, he inadvertently led some senators to infer that the administration was relying on a single, formal, exhaustive and rather recent study rather than a loose and long-standing consensus among Pentagon and intelligence-community analysts. A number of senators naturally wanted to see the phantom report, so Harold Brown had to bail out Vance by providing one. Walter Slocombe drafted a brief memorandum stating that it was the judgment of the Defense Department that the SS-19 was potentially a greater danger than the SS-18 and therefore that a MIRVed ICBM subceiling was "at least as advantageous and could be more so" than a reduction of Soviet heavies. Brown backed up that contention in secret testimony before the Senate Armed Services Committee in early November.

Jackson and Perle were angrier than ever. They denounced the Vance-Brown maneuver in terms like "fabrication," "attempt to deceive the Congress," "not just tendentious—but an outright lie!" Said Perle, "The reason they dropped off on heavies was simply that they believed the Russians weren't going to yield; yet here they were trying to persuade us that the U.S. had just gotten around to having its eyes opened to the fact that the SS-19 was a formidable counterforce weapon. Hell, Scoop himself [Senator Jackson] had been warning the arms controllers about the SS-19 ever since SALT I failed to define the SS-19 as a heavy!"

The congressional opponents also felt that the administration was making unscrupulous use of the press, planting news stories that cast the September breakthrough in a light most favorable to the administration. As a result, there was a series of counterleaks from the Congress, news stories with a much more critical slant, revealing information that the administration had shared with the legislators in closed session. Paul Nitze released a report charging that the prospective SALT II agreement would give the Soviets such an overwhelming advantage in throw-weight that well before the expiration of the treaty in 1985, the U.S.S.R. would be able to destroy 90 percent of the U.S. Minuteman force in a preemptive strike. The Nitze document included details about the state of the negotiations that the administration had revealed in secret testimony before Congress. The syndicated columnists Rowland Evans and Robert Novak carried a column ridiculing Vance's defense of the treaty in closed session before a subcommittee chaired by Henry Jackson. Senator John Culver accused Jackson of instigating breaches of security that had "the effect, if not the intent, of sabotaging SALT." Jackson denied responsibility. But with this spate of leaks and counterleaks, charges and countercharges, a new and fractious phase in the history of SALT had begun in earnest. The battle lines were drawn. In the period leading up to the Vance mission to Moscow in March, the administration had sought an alliance with the Jackson forces. In the period from April to September, the White House had hoped for the neutrality of those vigilant skeptics. But in the wake of Gromyko's September visit, Jackson and other critics of SALT declared war on the treaty to which the Carter administration had now committed itself.

Intramural Tension

Nor was there complete harmony within the administration after the September breakthrough. By November, recalls one of the principal policy-makers, "a kind of postcoital depression had set in. We began to understand that not only did we still have lots of old problems to resolve with the Russians, but we had lots of new problems to resolve with the Congress and some new headaches among ourselves as well. That's one of the frustrating things about SALT: you agree on something, and some people are mad at you for reaching that particular agreement, while other people start pointing to a whole new set of troubles that the agreement either causes or highlights."

A case in point was the issue of D-and-P, a problem that simply would not go away. Gromyko had agreed that the 120 unMIRVed SS-11 launchers at Derazhnya and Pervomaisk would count as though they were MIRVed. Just as Warnke had predicted, the Soviets almost immediately began converting those 120 launchers to MIRVed SS-19 silos. But that is what Harold Brown had predicted the Soviets planned to do anyway, so whether the Soviets would have MIRVed the 120 holes if they had not been forced to do so remained moot. D-and-P presented another, less academic problem: there was a lingering ambiguity about whether the Soviets had indeed accepted a strict, affirmative MIRVed-launcher counting rule—"if it looks the same, it counts the same"—or whether they had simply made a tactical concession at D-and-P while reserving the right to deploy a mixture of MIRVed and unMIRVed rockets at some other ICBM field in the future. In its interpretation of the September proceedings, the Pentagon came down squarely on the latter conclusion and put forward a firm recommendation: Gromyko had left the Soviets another loophole, which the U.S. must close in the treaty. Paul Warnke argued that it was more than sufficient to have gotten the Russians to "pretend" that 120 single-warhead launchers were MIRVed; it was hardly necessary, as he put it, "to come back at them and say, 'Now we want you to promise never to do anything like D-and-P again.'" But that is exactly what Harold Brown and Walter Slocombe wanted. They insisted that the launcher-type counting rule should be written into the treaty. Warnke felt that the rule was adequately established by the precedent of D-and-P's counting as fully MIRVed. He and Vance pointed out again, as they had during the summer, that the righteousness of the U.S. position on D-and-P was undermined by the uncomfortably similar situation at Malmstrom Air Force Base in Montana, where MIRVed Minuteman IIIs and unMIRVed Minuteman IIs were deployed together and where their hardened silos were, in effect, disguised by "environmental shelters." Vance and Warnke were concerned that if the U.S. was too fastidious in seeking treaty language on a launcher-type counting rule, that clause could boomerang: the U.S. was trying to have its cake at D-and-P and eat it at Malmstrom. But the Pentagon persisted. The Soviets had accepted the principle that D-and-P and Malmstrom were different cases, and now that principle must be turned into an explicit provision of the treaty, albeit one that left the definition of a launcher somewhat vague because of the Malmstrom problem.

The Pentagon won the point within the administration, and the Soviets conceded at the ongoing negotiations in Geneva. In January 1978 they submitted to a "common understanding" on a launcher counting rule that satisfied the Pentagon. In Warnke's view, the resulting clause was innocuous gobbledygook. But the Pentagon pressed for still more. It wanted the common understanding to include a phrase spelling out a "launcher distinguishability rule," whereby the treaty would state explicitly that in order to avoid being counted as a MIRV launcher, any new launcher for a single-warhead rocket must look substantially different from any existing launcher that had been tested with a MIRV. The Pentagon wanted to minimize the danger that the Soviets would build new silos which would ostensibly be for an advanced single-warhead ICBM they were planning to develop but which could also be rapidly converted into launchers for multiple-warhead ICBMs. Warnke and many of his colleagues were having some difficulty suppressing their annoyance with the Pentagon's unrelenting proliferation of new rules and new negotiating instructions spun off from D-and-P. But the President sided, once again, with

Brown, so Warnke and Earle dutifully argued the case in Geneva. The Soviets, who were even more impatient with the American fixation over D-and-P, balked at the launcher distinguishability rule. That passage remained in brackets in the Joint Draft Text until the very end of SALT II. The Soviets reminded the Americans from time to time that as long as the U.S. wanted to talk about D-and-P in all its aspects, the U.S.S.R. would keep reopening discussion of ambiguities and questionable activities at Malmstrom. Winter was a particularly good time to do so, since the Air Force's "environmental shelters" were in place in the snowy wastes of Montana.

Tensions between the Pentagon and Foggy Bottom were reflected within the American delegation in Geneva. The Joint Chiefs of Staff representative, Lieutenant General Edward Rowny, was increasingly unhappy with Warnke's and Earle's leadership of the delegation. He felt they were much too inclined to advocate a position because it promised to be negotiable rather than one that was, in his view, in the national interest, and he considered them much too susceptible to Soviet pressure tactics and bluffing at the negotiating table. In a word, Rowny thought that the leadership of the delegation was soft. Indeed, he believed that charge applied to the Carter administration as a whole. He had been appointed to the delegation in 1973, and he longed for the days when Paul Nitze had been a member of the team rather than a critic on the sidelines. Rowny's civilian colleagues, not surprisingly, regarded him less than collegially. He was sometimes called "our house spoiler" and "Jackson's man here." The latter epithet referred to the by now widely regretted and even resented fact that Harold Brown had renewed Rowny's appointment at the outset of the Carter administration largely because Rowny had Senator Jackson's confidence and because the administration had hopes of winning Jackson's backing for SALT II. Many on the delegation now worried that Rowny would stay on until the treaty was concluded, accumulating ammunition, then resign in protest and join the Jackson-Nitze forces, who were expected to oppose ratification. "That man is a time bomb," said one official in the Botanic Building. Sparks from the fuse flew publicly in December. Walter Pincus, a correspondent of the *Washington Post*, visited Geneva and wrote an article headlined: "Discord Surfaces in U.S. SALT Team." It reported in considerable detail the backbiting and bad blood between Rowny and the other negotiators.

Transatlantic Tension

The winter of 1977–78 also saw SALT become, to a new and worrisome degree, a matter of contention between the U.S. and its West European allies. In Bonn, Brussels, Paris and London there was a growing fear of an imbalance in "Euro-strategic" forces. Many Europeans quite rightly saw a Soviet effort to use SALT as a means of limiting American weapons, particularly cruise missiles, that might help counter the twin threats of the Backfire bomber and the SS-20 mobile, MIRVed, intermediate-range ballistic missile. In SALT II, the Carter administration was determined to extract collateral restraints on the Backfire, assuring that it would not be used against the U.S.; and the negotiators had already gotten the Russians to cancel the SS-16 program, so that the SS-20 could not easily be converted into an intercontinental missile. But those provisions of SALT II were little comfort to the West Europeans, who, along with the Chinese, were obvious potential targets of both the Backfire and the SS-20. NATO planners had been putting considerable stock in long-range ground-launched and sea-launched cruise missiles as means of at least partially redressing the Euro-strategic balance. But it was now clear, from press reports and official briefings, that the three-year protocol of SALT II would ban the deployment of long-range GLCMs and SLCMs. Moreover, while the protocol permitted the U.S. to test and develop GLCMs and SLCMs, it was well known, again from leaks and consultations, that the Soviets were vigorously trying to shoehorn into the treaty a prohibition against the "transfer" of cruise missile technology from a signatory, i.e., the U.S., to a third party, i.e., NATO. In October 1977, the NATO Nuclear Planning Group held a two-day closed meeting at which the West European representatives spent hours quizzing their American colleagues, with undisguised apprehension, about the prospective fate of cruise missiles and allied access to technology in SALT II. The same subject loomed large at the semiannual NATO defense and foreign ministers' meetings in December. Cyrus Vance sought to assure his counterparts that the treaty—and its even more controversial protocol—would serve Western Europe's interests as well as those of the U.S. Concluding a world tour in January with a stop at the alliance headquarters in Brussels, Jimmy Carter promised that the U.S. would "increasingly draw the NATO allies into its counsels" on SALT. Ralph Earle flew from Geneva to Brussels to brief NATO officials almost once a month on the progress of the negotiations.

But West European anxieties remained at a high pitch—and a high level. West German Chancellor Helmut Schmidt, a former defense minister and a formidable defense intellectual in his own right, delivered an address in October 1977 at the International Institute of Strategic Studies in London accusing the U.S. of shoring up its own, narrowly defined security at the expense of its allies' interests. "We in Europe must be particularly careful to ensure that these negotiations do not neglect the components of NATO's deterrence strategy," said Schmidt. "We are not unaware that both the United States and the Soviet Union must be anxious to remove threatening strategic developments from their relationship. But strategic arms limitations confined to the United States and the Soviet Union will inevitably impair the security of the West European members of the alliance vis-à-vis Soviet military superiority in Europe if we do not succeed in removing the disparities of military power in Europe parallel to the SALT negotiations." Edward Luttwak, a private consultant on defense matters and a close adviser to Richard Perle and Henry Jackson, argued that among its many perfidious ulterior motives in SALT, the Soviet Union was seeking to use the negotiations "as a way of dividing us from our allies," particularly on the issue of cruise missiles. Regardless of whether the Soviets had any such deliberate design, they seemed, during the winter of 1977–78, to be reaping precisely that benefit. In a far from harmonious way, the negotiations had become a multilateral affair.

Going Public with Compliance

As the winter wore on, the administration looked more and more like a beleaguered fire department. While one team was off in Brussels reassuring the allies that their interests would be protected in SALT II, another was on Capitol Hill reassuring the legislators that the shift from a reduced heavy limit to a MIRVed ICBM subceiling was a tactical adjustment rather than a strategic concession. Just as that brush fire was dying down, Melvin Laird, the former congressman and secretary of defense in the Nixon administration, tossed a match into the most flammable issue of all—the verifiability of the prospective treaty. Laird was an executive of *Reader's Digest,* and the December 1977 issue carried an article by him accusing the Soviets of "repeatedly, flagrantly and indeed contemptuously" cheating on the 1972 antiballistic missile treaty and interim agreement. The Laird article put the administration in the awkward position of having to defend Soviet compliance with the ABM treaty and interim agreement, while at the same time affirming the ability of the U.S. to detect Soviet violations of the new treaty. Senators and representatives cited the Laird article repeatedly in their cross-examination of executive branch witnesses. The administration's answer to the Congress had to be: no, the Soviets had not cheated on SALT I; and yes, the U.S. could catch them if they cheated on SALT II.

After much bickering among the Defense and State Departments, the National Security Council and the Arms Control Agency, the administration decided to release to the Senate two reports, one on compliance with SALT I and the other on verification of SALT II. In order to refute the headline of Melvin Laird's article—"Arms Control: The Russians Are Cheating!"—Cyrus Vance and Paul Warnke felt they must go public with declassified versions of the secrecy-shrouded proceedings of the Standing Consultative Commission, the Geneva-based joint panel at which either side could confront the other with evidence of questionable activity. Among the issues that had come before the commission were a number that Laird had alluded to in his article. For example, in 1973 the U.S. spy satellites had spotted what looked like newly constructed missile silos. The 1972 interim agreement banned the building of new ICBM launchers. Challenged, the Russians replied that the holes were actually "hardened facilities built for launch-control purposes"—to house men rather than missiles. Subsequently, U.S. intelligence confirmed that explanation. The U.S. had also monitored the Soviets' use of an antiaircraft radar station to track one of their own rockets during a test flight. The ABM treaty prohibited the conversion of antiaircraft installations into antimissile defenses. The Soviets said they intended nothing of the sort; they had merely been using the radar to check the navigation system of the rocket. The purpose of the exercise was to test the missile, not to upgrade the radar.* Nevertheless, a short time after the U.S. raised the matter before the Standing Consultative Commission, the Soviets stopped using the radar for missile tests. Melvin Laird's interpretation was that these and other instances were deliberate violations, which the Ford administration had hushed up in order to avoid jeopardizing détente. The very different

---

*In SALT I, it was the U.S. itself that had insisted on explicitly exempting such "range instrumentation radars" from the limits imposed by the agreement.

conclusion of the Carter administration was best articulated by James
Timbie, the principal technical expert on Warnke's staff at the Arms
Control Agency: "The Soviets certainly take full advantage of loop-
holes and ambiguities in the interim agreement. They certainly oper-
ate at the limits of the ABM treaty. But there is nothing that can be
called a clear-cut violation. We've had five years' experience monitoring Soviet compliance with SALT, and the record to date has been
generally good. Moreover, in the Standing Consultative Commission
we have a proven mechanism for assuring ourselves of compliance."

The decision to share those assurances with the Congress was controversial within the Carter administration for three reasons. There
was some concern at the State Department that the Soviets might feel
it was out of order for the U.S. to go public, albeit in sanitized form,
with the top-secret business of the Standing Consultative Commission.
The Russians were obsessed with secrecy and their own prestige, and
they might feel that American propaganda was trifling with both. But
if the steady parade of senators and representatives through the Botanic Building and the Soviet mission in Geneva had accomplished
nothing else, it had persuaded the Russians of the importance of verification as a political issue. So when Marshall Shulman notified Ambassador Dobrynin that the administration intended to make a fairly specific report on compliance and verification to the Congress, Dobrynin
gave his tacit approval. Another reason for controversy was that some
officials, particularly at the Pentagon, felt that the record of the Standing Consultative Commission did not constitute proof of Soviet compliance with SALT I. "Some of that stuff was pretty ambiguous," said
a Pentagon expert on SALT, "and a lot of us didn't think it would shut
up the critics to lay out the record, especially since we'd have to keep
secret some important details." But the biggest problem concerned
ambiguities on the American side of the record. If questions raised by
the U.S. about Soviet activities were to be aired in a report to the
Congress, then Soviet challenges had to be reported too. That meant
publicizing Malmstrom, where unMIRVed and MIRVed Minutemen
were mixed. Both because of the long and troubled history of the U.S.
position on D-and-P and because of the American foot-dragging in
accommodating Soviet objections to the "environmental" shelters
over the Minuteman silos, the Malmstrom issue was one of the rawest
Pentagon nerves. There was much lobbying from across the Potomac
to "keep Malmstrom out of that goddamn report," as one Defense
Department representative put it at the time. Vance and Warnke

stood firm: there was no need to reveal the geographical site, but the problem had to be reported—and so it was, in a paragraph headed in boldface, "Questions Raised by the U.S.S.R.: Shelters over Minuteman Silos."

Vance finally sent the compliance report to the Senate Foreign Relations Committee in late February, and Warnke followed a few days later with a verification report, asserting that "national technical means" had grown in sophistication to keep pace both with advances in Soviet technology and with the increased complexity of the agreements. The response on Capitol Hill was predictable. Supporters of SALT hailed the documents. "The compliance report is a welcome development," said Senator Gary Hart of Colorado. "The U.S. has been vigilant." His close political ally, John Culver of Iowa, said both reports "should lay to rest attempts to undermine arms limitation efforts by making ill-founded and mistaken assertions about violations of the accords." Henry Jackson and his camp maintained a stony silence in public, but Richard Perle said at the time, "Those papers prove nothing. This is still an unverifiable agreement in important aspects." The aspects he stressed were the ability of the Soviets to modernize their ICBMs, to convert intermediate-range ballistic missiles (SS-20s) into intercontinental ones (SS-16s), and to upgrade the Backfire into a strategic bomber. All, of course, were new issues, beyond the scope of the interim agreement. All were based on the presumption that the Soviets would violate the agreement if they thought they could get away with it. The negotiators of SALT II were much more ambitious in their objectives than they had been in SALT I, but it was already apparent that the critics of arms control were going to be even more skeptical, rigorous and demanding in 1978 and 1979 than they had been in 1972.

9   The Slow Thaw

The coming of spring in 1978 did little to warm the climate for SALT. Marshall Shulman's "tabular account of related events" showed yet another deep trough in Soviet-American relations. The Carter administration still seemed unable to make up its mind whether it believed in linkage. In the world view propagated by the White House, linkage existed when it served American political or rhetorical purposes, but not when it was inconvenient. On human rights, for example, the administration continued to claim that its championship of dissident intellectuals in the U.S.S.R. was not incompatible with negotiating SALT. At the same time, however, the administration warned the Kremlin repeatedly that Soviet policies in Africa could jeopardize SALT. The Ethiopian army, with the help of massive Soviet and Cuban support, was in the final stages of crushing a Somali-backed secessionist movement in the Ogaden desert. U.S. officials were concerned that if the Soviets' Ethiopian "proxies," as they were seen to be, chased their fleeing enemies across the border into Somalia—if the Soviet defense of Ethiopia became, in effect, a Soviet-backed invasion of Somalia—SALT would be finished. Some officials feared that Congress would make this linkage. Others toyed with the idea that the administration should take the initiative by explicitly holding up the negotiations until the Soviets and Cubans withdrew from Africa—or at least threatening to do so.

In February Leonid Brezhnev complained publicly about the stagnation of SALT. In response, the State Department noted that Soviet policy in the Horn of Africa could not help but affect "other issues." Zbigniew Brzezinski was more direct. Soviet behavior in the Horn, he said, could affect both "the negotiating process" and "any ratification that would follow the successful conclusion of the SALT negotiations." Then came the loaded noun, artfully used in the passive voice: "Linkages may be imposed by unwarranted exploitation of local conflicts for larger international purposes." Brzezinski was deliberately imprecise about who would do the imposing, but the Soviets wasted no time puzzling over the grammatical subtleties of Brzezinski's threat. In a remarkably quick reaction, only a day later, *Pravda* called Brzezinski's statement "unsavory and dangerous"; he was "playing with the main problems of international security and détente"; his warning "smacks of crude blackmail which is impermissible in international relations." Jimmy Carter stepped into the fray at a press conference the very day of the *Pravda* article, saying that the administration was primarily concerned about Soviet policy in the Horn jeopardizing the chances for congressional approval of SALT. "We [the administration] don't initiate the linkage," declared the President. The President's disclaimer did little to allay Soviet anger and apprehension. Carter's principal foreign policy speech of that period, an address at Wake Forest University in Winston-Salem, North Carolina, echoed what was becoming a leitmotif of Brzezinski's own statements at that time: that the Kremlin faced a stark choice between competition—even confrontation—and cooperation. It was the all-or-nothing, take-it-or-leave-it version of détente. "Unfortunately," commented TASS, "James Carter's speech is testimony to a departure from the solution of these real and vital problems"—notably SALT. In early April, Brezhnev gave a tough speech of his own. Dressed in full military regalia, he told an assembly of sailors and navy officers in Vladivostok that the Carter administration had been guilty of "indecision and inconsistency" on SALT, that the U.S. had "repeatedly made attempts . . . to annul in its favor or to call into question what was agreed earlier." It was a familiar refrain—the U.S. had strayed too far from the Vladivostok covenant and was still seeking those same old unilateral advantages. The Soviets almost always managed to sound that half-plaintive, half-outraged note loudly and at a high level just before Vance and Gromyko were to negotiate SALT face to face.

The secretary of state and the foreign minister met in Moscow in late April. Once again, Vance had to shift from one exhausting and frustrating assignment to another. He had just been jetting around southern Africa—from Dar es Salaam to Pretoria to Salisbury—in a strenuous but futile effort to play midwife to the peaceful birth of

Zimbabwe. With barely twenty-four hours to rest and review his SALT homework in London, he flew to Moscow for another slogging round of talks with Gromyko. Vance later reminisced about how he was able to cope with such strenuous, back-to-back assignments: "Before going off on a trip like that, I would start to zero in again on SALT, so that by the time I was ready to go from Africa back into negotiations with the Soviets, SALT would still be fresh enough in my mind. I found I needed twenty-four hours to sit down and reabsorb the necessary detail. My six and a half years in the Defense Department was a real help because it gave me some background in the technical details. It wasn't as difficult as if I had to start from scratch. My experience as a trial lawyer was also helpful in that I was trained to absorb a heavy dose of facts and retain them under considerable pressure and in a limited amount of time."

Vance was also feeling increasingly comfortable with Gromyko as a negotiating partner. While acknowledging that Gromyko was "a very tough cookie," Vance respected the foreign minister as "a fellow professional." Gromyko seemed to reciprocate, or so Vance sensed. He felt they shared a duty to protect ongoing matters of transcendent importance like SALT from being sullied by politicians and polemicists. Still, the absence of an established terminology for the constantly evolving substance of SALT sometimes complicated Vance's and Gromyko's discussions, causing tangled misunderstandings about which of the many subceilings they were talking about. For example, among themselves the Americans referred to the MIRVed missile maximum simply as "the 1,200," since that was the U.S.-proposed figure. But the provision could not go by that shorthand name at the negotiating table, since the Soviets wanted a figure of 1,250. In the end, after hours of haggling over several days, the Soviets agreed to accept the figure of 1,200 for the MIRV aggregate in exchange for U.S. acceptance of 2,250, rather than 2,160, for the overall ceiling on total strategic launchers. The Soviets wanted the higher figure of 2,250 for three reasons: it was closer to the cherished Vladivostok ceiling of 2,400; it would require the dismantling of fewer of their own intercontinental bombers; and finally, they claimed that a total strategic force level lower than 2,250 would make the Soviet Union vulnerable to U.S. "forward-based systems" in Western Europe. The U.S. agreed to yield on the overall ceiling in exchange for the Soviets' accepting a MIRV limit of 1,200 largely because President Carter, at the instigation of Brzezinski, had made an issue of principle out of the 1,200 figure at the September meeting in Washington. "The 1,200," in other words, had a political importance for the Americans comparable to what the 2,250 figure had for the Soviets. With this straightforward swap of a Soviet-preferred number in one category for an American-preferred number in another, SALT had moved toward what the negotiators called the "trade-off phase." From now on, SALT would increasingly become an exercise in horse trading.

Fallout from the Neutron Bomb

Another important issue on the table in Moscow in April 1978 concerned the Soviet effort to prohibit the U.S. from giving cruise missile technology to its NATO allies. The Soviets tried to invoke a precedent from SALT I. Article IX of the 1972 antiballistic missile treaty stated: "To assure the viability and effectiveness of this Treaty, each Party undertakes not to transfer to other States, and not to deploy outside its national territory, ABM systems or their components limited by this Treaty." The Russians wanted an almost identical passage in SALT II, forbidding the U.S. from "transferring" to NATO the blueprints or components of cruise missiles, particularly ground-launched and sea-launched ones. The three-year protocol already contained a ban on the deployment of long-range GLCMs and SLCMs, but not on their development and testing. The Russians wanted to prevent the U.S. from sharing the fruits of that development with the West Germans, who were especially interested in GLCMs, and with the British, who were interested in SLCMs. As recently as February, the Soviets had declared publicly, in the pages of *Pravda,* that an explicit "nontransfer" clause must appear in the new agreement. The Carter administration was determined to resist such pressure. Keeping open options in general had become a kind of battle cry on the American side in SALT, and keeping open the option of transferring the plans and parts of cruise missiles to Western Europe had acquired compelling political force. The West Europeans wanted access to that technology, and the congressional watchdogs of SALT insisted they have it.

Vance went to Moscow in April knowing he would have to stand firm on the issue of cruise missile transfer if only to help repair the damage done by President Carter's decision, announced earlier that same month, to "defer" production of the enhanced-radiation weapon (ERW), popularly known as the neutron bomb. The weapon was designed to kill attacking soldiers with a concentrated burst of intense radiation while destroying fewer buildings and raining down less fallout on the countryside for miles around than other nuclear weapons. The device was intended for use against a blitzkrieg by the armored divisions of the Warsaw Pact. The ERW was extremely controversial in Europe. Many politicians denounced it as a diabolical refinement of nuclear weaponry because it might make the use of such weaponry less unthinkable. It was seen as somehow more inhumane than nuclear weapons that did not discriminate between living creatures and property. Military strategists debated its effectiveness on technical grounds, and East Bloc propagandists fanned the controversy with a campaign to ban this latest satanic invention of the capitalist warmongers. The Carter administration did not want the full and lonely responsibility of deploying the neutron bomb in Europe. It hoped the West German government in particular would share that onus. Washington wished Bonn in effect to ask the U.S. to proceed with the bomb, or at least to commit itself in advance to accepting its deployment on German territory. Chancellor Helmut Schmidt felt that Carter was showing something less than courageous and inspired leadership of the alliance. A war of nerves developed between Washington and Bonn. At one point, Zbigniew Brzezinski turned a framed, autographed photograph of Schmidt to face the wall in his office as a sign of his annoyance with the chancellor.

Carter's threat to cancel production of the bomb, followed by his decision to defer production, was explained by administration officials as a pressure tactic aimed at the West German government. But to the rest of the world it did not seem to be a decision at all; it appeared to be a fiasco, the pettiest of charades, and it had the effect of severely undermining Carter's prestige throughout Europe. The episode did him no good in Washington either. Carter was seen to be inconsistent and indecisive—just as Brezhnev had told the sailors in Vladivostok— and prone to "giveaways" and unilateral cuts in the "arsenal of freedom." Much as Carter's cancellation of the B-1 the year before had attached new and troublesome political importance to the "protection" of air-launched cruise missiles in the treaty, so his deferral of the neutron bomb intensified allied and congressional anxieties about the fate of ground-launched cruise missiles in the protocol, since GLCMs were an alternative means of deterring a tank attack.

Some of the toughest negotiating in Moscow was over the issue of whether the treaty would contain an outright ban on cruise missile transfer. Paul Warnke and Leslie Gelb had warned Anatoly Dobrynin and Alexander Bessmertnykh in advance of the meeting that the Carter administration was bound and determined to resist such a ban. The Vance-Gromyko talks were marked by lengthy wrangles and moments of considerable tension, although there was at least one moment of general hilarity. At the beginning of a session, before the two sides had settled down to business, Reginald Bartholomew, who had taken William Hyland's place on the National Security Council staff the previous fall, noticed a curious malachite box on the conference table. He reached over to pick it up and inspect it. Pressing the top of the box set off a loud, clanging bell. The device, it turned out, was an ornamental electronic gavel. The Americans—particularly Bartholomew—were taken aback by the sudden din. Gromyko's normally humorless deputy, Georgy Kornienko, burst into a broad smile and said in English, "Well, there goes Washington!" Dobrynin threw his hands in the air in mock terror and cried, "Quick! Quick! Call Zbig and tell him it was a mistake!"

The meeting produced a hard-won victory for the Americans on the issue of cruise missile transfer. Finally, the Soviet side agreed to a provision on "noncircumvention": neither side could engage in any practice that had the effect of circumventing the treaty. It was the sort of deliberately vague language that the American negotiators would have assiduously resisted if the Russians had sought it for some political or military purpose of their own. Partly for that reason, Vance was careful not to gloat over his hard-won victory on the transfer issue. While in Moscow, he was even more cautious than usual in all his public statements, lest he appear to be making propaganda out of the progress that had been achieved. He limited his characterization of the talks to words like "useful" and "serious." He delivered a brief but gracious encomium to Gromyko's professionalism as a diplomat. Gromyko reciprocated, with only the slightest touch of sarcasm, by calling his guest "Cicero" (whatever Gromyko or anyone else may have respected in the secretary of state, it was surely not his brilliance as an orator). Vance said it was his philosophy that SALT must be built "brick by brick"; the negotiations must be allowed to develop a steady momentum of their own, and they must be guarded from the buffeting of political forces. It was his way of refuting, ever so obliquely, Brzezinski's recent dark hints of linkage.

But for all Vance's efforts to be discreet in Moscow, his visit was marred by yet another instance of what the Soviets felt was untoward publicity. It arose because Vance tried to accommodate the special needs of the two American newsmagazines *Time* and *Newsweek*. The secretary concluded his meetings with Gromyko and Brezhnev on a Saturday. He was not due to leave Moscow until Sunday. Normally, he would have briefed the reporters accompanying him aboard his plane en route to London, in the guise of a "senior American official." But that would have been too late for the two magazine correspondents. Their deadline was Saturday. In response to their joint request, Vance authorized one of his aides to give them "readout" on the talks so that they would have something for the issues of their magazines then going to press. The readout was intended as a sneak preview of the full briefing the rest of the reporters would be getting from Vance the next day on the plane. The information provided was extremely sketchy, but it gave the two magazine correspondents enough to satisfy their editors in New York. When they sent their dispatches by telex from the press center in the Intourist Hotel, the Soviet authorities as a matter of course intercepted copies—and concluded that the American official party had already begun to leak. Georgy Kornienko was ensconced with Marshall Shulman drafting a communiqué. Kornienko was called out of the meeting and told of the breach. He complained to Shulman, who told Vance that the Soviets were furious. As a result, the senior official on the plane the next day was singularly uninformative—the meeting had been "useful" and "serious," he revealed—and the two newsmagazine reporters ended up, quite inadvertently, having scooped most of their colleagues.

Back in Washington, Vance continued to try to prevent leaks from the State Department. "The secretary," said an associate at the time, "is paralyzed by a combination of his own rectitude and his fear of further annoying the Russians." But that left the press with no shortage of talkative—and critical—sources. Vance and other administration officials briefed congressmen and staff aides, who in turn briefed reporters, often tendentiously. Articles appeared playing up the American concession to the Soviets on the 2,250 ceiling and playing down the reciprocal Soviet acceptance of the 1,200 MIRV subceiling. Other stories reported that the U.S. had "given in" to a "deliberately ambiguous" noncircumvention clause—as though the ambiguity were a Soviet gimmick rather than an American one. Indeed, that was the prevailing interpretation in Western Europe, especially in Bonn. In the wake of the row over the neutron bomb, transatlantic relations were at a low ebb. So were relations between the executive and legislative branches of the government. So, indeed, were relations between Jimmy Carter and the American people. The public opinion polls showed his presidency suffering from a generalized political weakness, and that malaise threatened to contaminate SALT. The deftly drafted provisions of the treaty would be seen as no stronger, no more purposeful, no more enlightened and vigilant than the administration that negotiated them. Any ambiguities, no matter how well-intentioned, would be seen as in the interests of the Soviet Union if the strategic wisdom and the political resolve of the U.S. administration were themselves in question.

China Linkage Begins

Gromyko came to Washington at the end of May. Once again, the prologue to the meeting was inauspicious. Each side had a major, and growing, complaint against the other. The U.S. was more angered and frustrated than ever over what it saw as Soviet adventurism in Africa. In early May, during remarks at a town meeting in Spokane, Washington, Carter said that the Soviets were doomed to fail in Africa because of their "innate racism." For their part, the Soviets were angry at being frozen out of diplomacy in the Middle East. The Geneva Peace Conference on the Middle East, of which the Soviet Union was co-chairman, was moribund now that Anwar Sadat and Menachem Begin were negotiating with each other directly, under American auspices. The Soviets were deeply suspicious and resentful of renewed American initiatives in the direction of Russia's archenemy, China. Russian racism, innate or otherwise, is directed against the Yellow Peril more than against Black Africa, and the Carter administration—mostly in the person of Zbigniew Brzezinski—was reviving the long-stalled effort to normalize relations with the People's Republic of China. In May, Brzezinski journeyed to Peking, where he used a banquet toast and a much publicized visit to the Great Wall to make a number of unabashedly anti-Soviet remarks. He called the Russians "international marauders" for their policy in Africa and exuded receptivity to his hosts' suggestions that the U.S. and China make common cause against the "polar bear." Articles in the press also reported that Brzezinski briefed the Chinese leaders in detail on SALT.

Gromyko arrived in Washington looking more dyspeptic than usual. He spent much of a private session with Cyrus Vance protesting that the Chinese had "no legitimate interest" in SALT and therefore "no right" to an official briefing. The foreign minister did not mention Brzezinski by name. He did not need to. For the first time—but not for the last—the Carter administration's China policy had complicated SALT.

In his session with Carter, Gromyko delivered a lengthy diatribe of wounded innocence, denying Soviet intervention in Africa. Brzezinski, who was sitting in on the meeting, made a point of audibly and visibly snickering at what he felt was the bold-faced absurdity of Gromyko's denial. Afterward, Carter—who had campaigned on a promise always to tell the truth—told his aides he was shocked that Gromyko would lie to him. The series of meetings yielded little progress on SALT. Many in the U.S. government were disappointed. They had hoped that direct presidential involvement in the negotiations would stimulate a major advance toward an agreement, just as it had the previous September.

Trials and Tribulations

Vance and Gromyko were to meet again in July, this time on neutral ground in Geneva. Once again a controversy extraneous to SALT intervened and nearly scuttled the meeting. Less than a week before Vance was to leave, TASS announced that Anatoly Shcharansky, the Jewish dissident who had been arrested sixteen months before, and other imprisoned dissenters, would finally go on trial. The next day Vance delivered a statement deploring the persecution of Shcharansky and announcing that as a sign of its displeasure, the administration would cancel the visit of an official U.S. scientific delegation to Moscow. However, continued Vance, he would hold his own meeting with Gromyko in Geneva as scheduled because the continuation of SALT was in the national interest and in the interests of international peace.

That decision elicited an outpouring of bipartisan criticism from Capitol Hill. Henry Jackson asserted that to carry on with business as usual would be to send "the wrong signal at the wrong time." Senator Robert Dole called on the administration to suspend SALT. Privately, Ambassador to Moscow Malcolm Toon sided with the senators. He argued that there was no point in going through with the Geneva meeting, since the ill will and public recriminations generated by the Shcharansky affair virtually precluded progress. Leslie Gelb strongly disagreed. "It's absolutely essential that we hold this meeting," he said.

"Postponing it guarantees we'll be at a total standstill. Even if there's no concrete agreement this time, there will at least be some wrinkles for us to work on and that will give the delegations something to work on." It was important to preserve, in a word, the momentum of SALT. Vance held the same view. At a press conference just before leaving, he cited the "unique nature" of SALT; the negotiations were a matter affecting " the peace of the world and the possibility of mutual annihilation." Therefore "this issue must be treated differently from others and should be addressed on a continuing basis with the highest priority." However, the secretary was anything but sanguine. At his press conference he was tense and testy. His hands trembled.

On the eve of his departure, Vance held a full-day skull session in the White House Cabinet Room with Harold Brown, Zbigniew Brzezinski, Paul Warnke, Ralph Earle, Marshall Shulman, Leslie Gelb and Walter Slocombe. Also present were Stansfield Turner, the director of Central Intelligence, and Reginald Bartholomew. They considered many theories that might explain the Soviets' provocative behavior. One possibility was that the Kremlin had decided, in effect, to get the Shcharansky trial over with—to clear the docket of unpleasant business in order to assure a more favorable political ambience for SALT the following spring, when, both sides hoped, a SALT treaty would be before the Senate. Perhaps the Soviet authorities were preparing eventually to exchange Shcharansky for an East Bloc spy or a leftist hero imprisoned in the West. It was a slim hope, but a welcome contribution to an otherwise rather gloomy meeting. The gloom pursued Vance across the Atlantic. The reporters aboard his plane found him unusually tight-lipped and inaccessible. Vance spent most of the flight huddled with Warnke and Shulman around the kidney-shaped table in the middle of the fuselage, poring over papers and looking worried. The secretary did not follow his normal practice of bringing a cocktail to the rear of the plane to chat off the record with the newsmen.

In order to avoid commenting on the Shcharansky affair, Vance intended to make no statement to the press on his arrival in Geneva. But Gromyko, who had arrived earlier, had made a few bland remarks, so protocol required Vance to do the same. He stepped up to the waiting microphones and expressed the hope that the discussions would be "useful and constructive." The reporters barraged him with questions about the trials. Vance turned on his heel and strode quickly to his limousine. Later the newsmen had an opportunity to question

Gromyko. "Trials? What trials?" said the foreign minister, cupping his ear as if he had not heard the question. Then he abruptly snapped, "I don't want to talk of these things."

At the American SALT headquarters in the Botanic Building, Gromyko pointed across the street and wondered aloud whether the U.S. had stationed armed guards on the roof of the International Labor Organization to cover him with their rifles. "He's an absolute master of the bad joke," remarked one American negotiator. "Listening to him for an hour is like listening to anyone else for three." There was less informal contact than usual. After negotiating in the morning, Vance and the Americans went back to the Intercontinental Hotel for lunch, and Gromyko's armored ZIL limousine took him to the Soviet mission for a nap. Neither side wanted to make small talk or clink glasses. At the end of one lengthy session on SALT, Vance and Gromyko met privately for fifteen minutes with just their interpreters present to talk about the issue that had so clouded their meeting. The secretary of state gave the foreign minister a message of protest on the Shcharansky affair from Carter to Brezhnev.

Braking the Juggernaut

When the round of meetings was over, Vance and Gromyko said publicly their encounter had been "useful," but they declined to use the word "progress." Thus, the semantics and atmospherics of the meeting suggested that Malcolm Toon had been right in predicting that nothing could be accomplished and that it had been a mistake to meet at all. In fact, however, the Geneva meeting had yielded significant progress on one of the most vital and complex issues facing the negotiators—restrictions on the modernization of ballistic missiles. This was to be one of the paramount achievements of SALT II and one of the most important advances over earlier agreements. The 1972 SALT I interim agreement had frozen some of the forces of both sides at existing numerical levels. It had established gross quantitative controls that were relatively easy to verify with confidence. Kissinger got nowhere, during the early days of SALT II, in his efforts to bring under the control of the agreement the qualitative improvements that increased the throw-weight, megatonnage, fractionation (number of warheads) and accuracy of Soviet ICBMs. The 1974 Vladivostok accord, while it equalized the gross quantitative controls, did nothing to lay the groundwork for constraints on the modernization of weapons.

One of the banes of SALT has been that new technologies render arms control measures obsolete or inadequate, sometimes before the ink is dry on a treaty or an agreement. MIRVs and cruise missiles are the two most obvious examples.

To its credit, but also to its frustration and political peril, the Carter administration came into office determined to include in SALT II provisions that would apply the brakes to the juggernaut of technology. One of the key features of the March 1977 comprehensive proposal was Harold Brown's idea of a limit on the flight testing of missiles, a provision that would have eroded the reliability of existing missiles and considerably impeded the development of new ones. But Vance came back from his disastrous meeting in Moscow convinced that the flight test limit was simply nonnegotiable; Gromyko had been especially vociferous in his rejection of the idea. Furthermore, during the two-month period when the Carter administration was repackaging its position as the three-tier proposal, U.S. intelligence concluded from its analysis of data on recent Soviet ICBM tests that the Russians had honed the accuracy and improved the overall performance of their most modern missiles much more quickly than had been expected. They had already very nearly attained the degree of accuracy that the flight test limit had been designed to prevent. Many in the administration felt it was too late to stop the Soviets from perfecting their existing rockets. The designers of the three-tier proposal therefore proposed a ban on the testing of "new types" of missiles as an interim measure in the three-year protocol.

At the May 1977 meeting between Vance and Gromyko in Geneva, the Soviets countered with a proposal to ban the testing of any new MIRVed missiles. Later they refined their counterproposal; the ban in the protocol on new ICBMs would include an exemption for each side to develop a new ICBM with a single warhead. In an era of MIRVs, it might seem strange that the Soviets would, as it were, "waste" their sole exemption on a single-warhead ICBM. The reason probably lay in the simple fact that the collective leadership had already promised such a thing to the military establishment. But why did the military want such a thing? In the emerging structure of SALT II, the Soviets would have to keep some of their land-based rockets unMIRVed. The mainstay of the single-warhead ICBM force was the SS-11 of D-and-P fame. The SS-11 was growing obsolete, and the Russians wanted a modern replacement. Paul Warnke and Ralph Earle argued with Vladimir Semyonov, Alexander Shchukin and the other Soviet negotiators in Geneva that it was a function of SALT to let old missiles age gracefully. Semyonov and Shchukin were adamant that the Soviet deterrent required a more reliable replacement for the SS-11. Back in Washington, Anatoly Dobrynin amplified somewhat in private conversation with Warnke and Vance: the liquid-fuel propulsion of the SS-11 was a crucial and unacceptable shortcoming; the Strategic Rocket Forces of the U.S.S.R. must have a solid-fueled successor to the SS-11. There was some speculation in Washington that Soviet military planners wanted a more compact, sure-fire delivery system for a gargantuan, high-yield single warhead—a "city-killer" as opposed to "silo-busting" MIRVs. In a nuclear war with China, the Russians would have more interest in knocking out cities than crippling launchers, since Chinese ballistic missiles were few in number and poor in quality. Some of the SS-11s at D-and-P were believed to be targeted against Chinese cities.

Whatever the rationale for a single-warhead exemption to the new-types ban, the U.S. was not willing to consider such a provision. For one thing, the exemption would have been "asymmetrical," since the U.S. had no need for a new single-warhead rocket of its own to replace the Minuteman II and had no intention of developing one just because the Russians were doing it. For another, the exemption would present serious problems of verification. The Soviets might develop a new rocket ostensibly for a single warhead but in fact compatible with existing multiple warheads. Thus, they would end up with a better delivery system for MIRVs.

But the biggest American objection to the Soviet proposal was that by establishing an exemption only for a single-warhead new type, the ban would have prevented the U.S. from proceeding with its MX, or "Missile Experimental." In the wake of the collapse of the March 1977 comprehensive proposal (which would have sacrificed the MX in exchange for massive Soviet cutbacks in their land-based strategic forces) and in the wake of Carter's controversial cancellation of the B-1 bomber, the Pentagon was more committed than ever to the MX as a bigger, more powerful, more heavily MIRVed replacement for the Minuteman III. The MX was the American answer to the SS-18 and SS-19. Armed with six to ten warheads, each with a yield of between one and two megatons, it might give the U.S. the theoretical capacity to wipe out the entire Soviet ICBM force in a preemptive strike. That is, the MX would allow the U.S. to do to the Russians what the American strategists were so worried the Russians might do to the U.S. The

Soviets feared and campaigned against the MX accordingly. The missile, said the journal *Novoye Vremya (New Times)*, is an "instrument of destabilization . . . its deployment may give the U.S. the dangerous illusion that its strategic might is invulnerable and may be used with impunity." The Soviet Army newspaper, *Krasnaya Zvezda (Red Star)*, charged that the MX represented an American attempt to build up a "first-strike knockout punch": "The Soviet Union has a right not to believe the Pentagon's allegations concerning a 'retaliatory' blow; by ensuring the high accuracy of its missiles, the U.S. gains the ability to use them for a first strike." Here were the Soviets displaying anxieties and suspicions that mirrored American fears about the vulnerability of Minuteman and the survivability of the land leg of the U.S. deterrent. For the Soviets to be expressing such worries came as music to many ears at the Pentagon. More than ever, the MX seemed to represent a possible solution to the problem of an impending strategic imbalance.

From early 1977 until mid 1978, Washington and Moscow churned out a dizzying array of proposals to limit new types of ICBMs, all with the same common denominator: the Soviets maneuvered to protect their single-warhead new type of ICBM (the medium-solid follow-on to the SS-11, as it was technically known) while seeking to prevent the MX from ever getting off the drawing board onto the launching pad; the U.S., for its part, was determined to protect the MX, even if it meant letting the Russians have their medium-solid follow-on. This minuet continued until the April 1978 meeting in Moscow. There the U.S. tabled two new alternative proposals: (1) a ban on new types, with no exemption, as part of the three-year protocol; and (2) a ban with one exemption—either MIRVed or unMIRVed—but *as part of the treaty that would run until 1985.* On this issue, SALT had again assumed the aspect of poker, and the U.S. had now upped the ante by proposing to constrain the modernization of missiles under the treaty rather than the protocol. The Soviets countered with a treaty ban that would contain an exemption for a single-warhead new type of ICBM. They were keeping up with the betting but still trying to get the U.S. to discard the MX. The U.S. refused.

At the May 1978 meeting in Washington, Gromyko played his boldest hand to date. He told Carter that the Soviet Union would be willing to accept a total ban—with no exemptions—for the entire treaty period. The Soviets would live without their solid-fuel, single-warhead follow-on to the SS-11 if the U.S. would give up the MX. The foreign minister made much of the claim that in this magnanimous and far-sighted initiative, the Soviet Union was taking a page out of Carter's own comprehensive proposal of March 1977. Gromyko said he was suggesting a "real arms control" measure. His American listeners were not impressed. One senior official called Gromyko's offer "a goddamn joke." Another dismissed it as "a real step backward." They were upset because they knew that the MX had become much more important to American military planning than a solid-fueled replacement for the SS-11 could possibly be to the Russians. Gromyko was suggesting, in short, another "asymmetrical" trade.

Be that as it may, the Soviet proposal was significant for at least three reasons: it would have done away with exemptions in the new-types ban; it firmly established the elevation of the ban from the protocol to the treaty; and finally, it was extremely rare for the Soviets even to hint at giving up a weapon system that the Kremlin had already promised to the military. They had done so once before with the SS-16. Now they were doing it again—albeit conditionally—with the medium-solid follow-on. While many officials at the State Department, Arms Control Agency and National Security were shaking their heads over what they saw as Gromyko's attempt to trick the U.S. out of the MX, Harold Brown—normally among the most uncharitable skeptics where Soviet motives were concerned—found himself wondering hopefully if SALT had perhaps taught the Russians a lesson on the political flexibility of military programs. Brown's point, however, was academic. More than anyone at the top of the administration, he, as defense secretary, knew that there could no longer be any thought of sacrificing the MX. Carter was already being heavily criticized by Congress for his "surrender" of the B-1 and the neutron bomb and for allegedly "negotiating from weakness" in SALT.

While the Americans refused to consider any provision that barred the MX altogether, Vance told Gromyko in Geneva in July that the U.S. might be willing to hold off deployment—but not development and testing—of the MX until 1985 if the Soviets would refrain from deploying their single-warhead new type for the same period. *Nyet*, said the Russians. They knew that the administration had already decided to postpone deployment of the MX from 1983 until 1986 anyway. Furthermore, the Soviets were close to being able to deploy their medium-solid follow-on. Why should they hold back their own deployment while the Americans proceeded to develop the MX at a leisurely pace for deployment eight years in the future? Now it was the U.S. that was proposing an "asymmetrical" trade.

But Gromyko did not simply reject the U.S. offer to test but not deploy the MX. The foreign minister said that the Soviet Union might, under certain conditions, be willing to accept an option that the U.S. had proposed earlier, in April in Moscow. It might consider, as part of the treaty, a ban on new types with one exemption—either MIRVed or unMIRVed. Gromyko made clear that if the Soviet Union accepted such a provision—which would allow the Russians to have their medium-solid follow-on and Americans to have their MX—the U.S. would have to concede on a number of other issues. As one participant in the Geneva meeting put it, "Gromyko cast his very conditional acceptance of our new-types ban in terms of a question. He said, in effect, 'If we bought your proposal on this issue, would you agree to our terms on the other outstanding matters?' " Vance was not about to say yes. He was neither inclined nor authorized to make the prescribed concessions. But the secretary and his colleagues flew home encouraged. The left-over problems of SALT could—indeed would have to —be dealt with as a package. As Paul Warnke put it, "By saying we'll do it your way on this if you do it our way on that, the Soviets were giving us the first clear signal that we were down to the point of trading the remaining issues on a one-for-one basis. They were prepared to go into the endgame."

The Juggernaut at Sea

In reaching that point, the negotiators had made a series of moves involving how—and whether—the new-types ban should apply to submarine-launched ballistic missiles. SALT entails issues within issues, negotiations within negotiations. The treatment of SLBMs was a complicated, and ultimately not very productive or edifying, exercise that proceeded in parallel with the more important and conclusive bargaining over ICBMs. As they moved toward the endgame, the players treated SLBMs as minor pieces, to be moved around the board in feints and probes, but ultimately to be left on their original squares.

Just as the Russians had sought to use the U.S.-proposed prohibition on modernization of missiles to nip the MX program in the bud, so they tried for a long time to define the ban in a way that would constrain the American Trident submarine missile program. The larger, more advanced version of Trident would someday give the U.S. a submarine-based "hard-target killer," a missile of such range, power and accuracy that it could destroy hardened ICBM silos deep inside the Soviet Union. The editorialists of *Krasnaya Zvezda* saw the Trident and the MX as a dangerous and destabilizing one-two punch of counterforce weapons. Submarines represent an overwhelming American advantage. They are virtually invulnerable because the enemy does not know where they are. U.S. boats are far quieter than Russian ones. A much larger portion of the U.S. fleet is on patrol at any one time; and Soviet antisubmarine warfare is backward compared to American ASW. While the Russians had tried since early 1977 to use the new-types ban against the Trident program, they also wanted to upgrade their own submarine-launched rockets. Therefore they sought an exemption in the ban for a new Soviet SLBM. The U.S. at first resisted an SLBM exemption under the new-types ban, then accepted the idea. That agreement led the negotiators straight into a prolonged wrangle over "phasing"—which Soviet SLBMs should be deemed comparable to which American ones; which SLBM should be considered "new" and therefore would count as the one permissible exemption under the ban. The Soviets argued that their advanced SS-NX-18 was operational and therefore should be classified as an "existing type," comparable to the American Poseidon. (The NATO designation NX meant "Naval/Experimental," indicating that Western experts believed it was still in its testing phase.) The SS-NX-18 was long-ranged and MIRVed. For all intents and purposes, it was a submarine-launched ICBM. From launching tubes aboard the Soviet navy's largest boats, the Delta-class submarines, the SS-NX-18 could cover U.S. targets from the Arctic and North Pacific. Moscow's candidate for its one allotted new type of SLBM was the even more advanced Typhoon, which the Russians maintained was a counterpart to the U.S Trident-I, scheduled for deployment in 1979. The American negotiators did not accept the Soviet match-up. They argued that in fact the SS-NX-18 was analogous to the Trident-I, and if the Soviets proceeded with the Typhoon, the U.S. would feel free to press ahead with the development of the Trident-II, far and away the most formidable submarine-launched missile on either side.

Finally, Washington and Moscow realized that they were getting nowhere in their dispute over the phasing of U.S. and Soviet SLBMs, and Gromyko offered to restrict the new-types ban in the treaty just to ICBMs. The ban would not apply to SLBMs at all, except insofar as they would be covered by a freeze on multiple warheads: during the treaty period no SLBM could be deployed with more than 14 MIRVs, the maximum demonstrated capacity on either side.

The U.S. was just as glad to exempt SLBMs from the new-types ban. By now American strategists welcomed any feature in SALT that would deflect Soviet research and development away from land-based missiles, where the Russians were strong, into submarine-launched ones. It had become an American objective in SALT to "move the Russians out to sea." Moreover, U.S. defense planners were, in mid 1978, eager to have as few constraints as possible on their own submarine programs. The looming vulnerability of Minuteman, the postponement of the MX, the cancellation of the B-1 and the limitations in SALT on cruise missiles—all these developments impelled the U.S. toward a heavier reliance on the seagoing, underwater, most elusive, least vulnerable, therefore most survivable leg of its strategic triad.

10 Keeping the Options Open

Cyrus Vance's meeting with Andrei Gromyko in Geneva in July 1978 included some significant diplomatic byplay over the future of mobile ICBMs. Mobility is a concept that SALT was for a long time unable to deal with adequately. SALT depends on each side counting how many missile launchers the other side has. In order to do so, each side must know where the other side's launchers are. But if one side has achieved—or is about to achieve—a first-strike counterforce, i.e., the capability of destroying all the other side's ICBMs in a preemptive attack, then it behooves the side that is vulnerable to think about hiding its ICBM launchers, or at least making them moving targets. The more dedicated proponents of arms control have tended, over the years, to argue that even though it might enhance the survivability of one's deterrent, mobility is destabilizing and therefore undesirable because it hinders the verification of agreements. Also, mobility on one side begets mobility on the other. Finally, mobility on one side is an incentive for the other to proliferate warheads; as with an antiballistic missile system, defense provokes offense. But vulnerability is destabilizing too, and in recent years the U.S. has worried most about the vulnerability of its Minuteman deterrent.

Even the comprehensive proposal of March 1977 would have only put off further into the future the threshold of Minuteman vulnerability. Sooner or later, if the American ICBM force continued to sit in its 1,000-odd fixed sites, the Soviets would achieve the accuracy to threaten the ability of those 1,000 rockets to survive a first strike. The Russians would attain that point someday, even if they were limited to the levels set by the comprehensive proposal: 150 heavy ICBMs and

550 MIRVed ones. The September 1977 breakthrough established a considerably higher MIRVed ICBM subceiling of 820. While that level restrained the Soviet MIRV program by 100 or so missiles, many believed it allowed the Russians to achieve the theoretical capability to knock out Minuteman before the expiration of SALT II in 1985. That was the principal message Paul Nitze sought to impress upon the Congress, the press and anyone in the administration who would listen. It was a message echoed, quietly and guardedly, by Harold Brown himself. In his congressional testimony behind closed doors during the fall and winter of 1977–78, Brown told the senators, in effect, that neither this nor any other imaginable—which was to say, negotiable —SALT treaty would permanently solve the problem of Minuteman vulnerability.

If the U.S. and the Soviet Union had been able to conclude SALT II by the end of 1977, that problem might have been kept at bay; it might have been prevented from directly complicating the negotiations. Certainly the Carter administration would have much preferred to get SALT II out of the way quickly, then proceed, as an overture to SALT III, with a great debate about how to protect Minuteman in the mid 1980s. But when it became clear that the negotiation of SALT II was going to drag on into 1978 and possibly beyond, the administration—largely at the instigation of Harold Brown—realized it would have to address the problem of Minuteman vulnerability and answer Paul Nitze's challenges in the context of SALT II. That meant the administration would have to assert in the negotiations with the Russians the right to base Minuteman, or its successor the MX, "in a mobile mode."

The mobility issue has a checkered history in the negotiations. Minuteman itself was originally designed for deployment both in silos and in a rail-mobile system. In the end it was based just in hardened holes, largely because a fixed-site missile was, and still is, more accurate and reliable than a mobile one. To hit a target on the far side of the globe, the guidance system of a rocket has needed to know its starting point with maximum precision. For more than a decade there has been a running argument within the U.S. government between, on the one hand, those who favored "going mobile" as guidance systems learned to orient themselves by taking a fix on satellites or remote ground stations and, on the other, those who favored protecting missiles by superhardening their fixed sites—pouring ever thicker layers of concrete over the caps of their silos. In SALT I, the U.S. sought to ban mobile ICBMs. Back in those days, the U.S. was ahead in MIRVs, and it was the Soviets who were feeling vulnerable. Therefore Moscow resisted the ban. By the time of the Vladivostok summit between Leonid Brezhnev and Gerald Ford in late 1974, the tables were turned. The Soviets were well along in the MIRVing of their ICBMs and might have welcomed a ban on mobiles. The U.S. insisted that the Vladivostok *aide-mémoire* leave both sides free to move toward the deployment of mobile ICBMs. The SALT II negotiators were able to work out a treaty ban on some exotic species of seagoing mobile missiles—rockets fired from surface ships and "bottom crawlers" or "creepy crawlies" which would slither evasively along the ocean floor —and later a protocol ban on long-range air-to-surface ballistic missiles (ASBMs—pronounced "Asbums"), which some called "air-mobile" missiles. But land-based mobiles presented a much more serious problem in the negotiations, for it was the land leg, not the sea or air leg, of the strategic triad that the U.S. was most concerned about protecting, and however destabilizing they may have been in the eyes of arms controllers, land-mobiles made much more military sense than those that operated underwater or overhead.

In their lengthy memorandum to Carter of February 1977, Henry Jackson and Richard Perle wrote: "There must be freedom to deploy mobile missiles." Disregarding Jackson on that as well as almost every other point, the designers of the three-tier March 1977 proposal included in the three-year protocol a ban on all mobiles as a sweetener to get the Soviets to accept the protocol's constraints on "new types" of ICBMs. But when the negotiators elevated the new-types ban from the protocol to the treaty in 1978, Lieutenant General Edward Rowny and other in-house critics of SALT argued that the protocol had now become one-sided in favor of the Soviets because it constrained only cruise missiles and mobile ICBMs, which were of use primarily to the U.S. The protocol, said Rowny, cast a shadow over the future of mobiles. The Soviets would try to treat the temporary ban on mobiles as a permanent fixture in SALT when the protocol expired. They would contend that the U.S. had accepted the "principle" that SALT prohibited mobile ICBMs. They would try to use the precedent contained in the protocol against the U.S. mobile-missile program just as they had tried to carry over the SALT I "nontransfer" clause into SALT II with regard to cruise missiles. To allay this recurring anxiety over the danger of the protocol as precedent, the State Department put out a booklet on SALT stressing that "the limitations in the protocol in no way prejudice the manner in which these systems will be dealt with in SALT III. Any future limits on the issues covered in the protocol for the period after 1980 would require U.S. agreement and congressional approval."

But as Vance's July 1978 meeting with Gromyko in Geneva drew near, the administration faced a tactical choice. Should the U.S. rely simply on reiterations of the legal fact that the protocol would last for only three years and its restrictions on mobile ICBMs would be null and void when it expired? Or should the U.S. confront the Soviets with an explicit statement of American intent to consider deployment of mobile missiles after the protocol period? The latter course was attractive from a domestic political standpoint. Such a statement would give the administration ammunition with which to counter the charge that the protocol was a trap and that the Soviets were setting the U.S. up for a permanent ban on mobiles. However, the idea of a unilateral statement was not at all appealing to the negotiators themselves, notably Paul Warnke. It struck them as gratuitous and provocative. The protocol, according to its own provisions, would self-destruct after three years. Why not let its duration speak for itself? Why put the Soviets on formal notice that the U.S. refused to accept something that was not even hinted at in the agreement—i.e., a permanent extension of a temporary ban? But the domestic political consideration won out. At a meeting of the Special Coordination Committee a week before Vance left for Geneva, it was decided that the secretary would inform Gromyko that the U.S. reserved the option to deploy mobilely its ICBMs after the expiration of the protocol but during the life of the SALT II treaty.

Mapping the Alps

In parallel with the issue of mobility evolved the issue of "basing mode." The Ford administration's response to the problem of ICBM vulnerability was a plan to move the MX around on a track in an underground tunnel. This idea, the so-called trench option, began to fade when studies showed that the blast from an incoming Soviet missile anywhere along the trench would send shock waves through the tunnel, collapsing the roof, buckling the track and wrecking the missile. One refinement called for protective baffles that would automatically fall into place when there was a hit up the track from the missile. But further experiments showed that the baffle, too, would be destroyed by the shock waves. Another plan was to mount the MX on flatbed trucks that would drive around the interstate highways of Wisconsin and Minnesota or the back roads of military reservations. The defects of such a system were numerous and readily apparent. If the trucks were rolling around public highways loaded with their cargo for Armageddon, they would represent more than the usual traffic hazard. A drunk driver who swerved from the oncoming lane could have the same effect as a Soviet warhead: he could put a component of the U.S. deterrent out of commission. And if the missile-bearing trucks were confined to military reservations, the Soviets might be tempted to try to knock them out either with a barrage of MIRVs or with a single, high-yield warhead. The Russians would no longer need to worry about pinpoint accuracy. A groundburst anywhere near one of the trucks would obliterate it with the pressure of the blast. At the Pentagon, the "Metro" and "Beltway" options were topics of serious conversation. At the State Department and the Arms Control and Disarmament Agency, they were the object of almost giddy derision. Paul Warnke, Leslie Gelb and others regarded Minuteman vulnerability as a bugbear, the goal of protecting Minuteman as a chimera, and schemes to do so as ingenious absurdities worthy of Rube Goldberg. Warnke and Gelb believed that the U.S. should learn to live with the purely hypothetical vulnerability of its land-based deterrent. Instead of protecting its ICBMs against a fanciful danger of total, preemptive destruction, the U.S. should concentrate its ingenuity and resources on improving the other two legs of the strategic triad, bombers and submarines. Even with its existing deterrent, said Warnke in the summer of 1978, "U.S. forces could absorb a Soviet strike and, in retaliation, could destroy more of the Soviet Union than the Soviet Union had destroyed of the U.S. by striking first." Warnke, Gelb and others felt that that state of affairs—which they believed would prevail through SALT II—met Paul Nitze's definition of crisis stability: "It isn't in the interests of either side to initiate a strike."

The White House, however, was less sanguine. Partly for domestic political reasons, Jimmy Carter and Zbigniew Brzezinski felt that they must have a convincing response to the critics of SALT who were concerned about ICBM vulnerability. When the trench and truck options began to fall of their own weights, the Pentagon started to focus on an idea that had been under consideration, off and on, for more than a decade. It was to build many more holes than missiles, then move the missiles at random from hole to hole, thus confounding the Soviets about which holes were live targets and which were decoys. The notion had originally been floated in the defense community in the mid 1960s, when Cyrus Vance, Paul Warnke, Leslie Gelb and Paul Nitze were all at the Pentagon in earlier incarnations. The idea acquired new force in early 1978 when Nitze proposed what he first called a fixed alternate launch point ICBM system (FALPIS), then renamed an alternate launch point system (ALPS). He wrote a paper on the subject and circulated it widely among fellow skeptics on the sidelines, congressional leaders and officials of the Carter administration. Nitze conceived of ALPS as a quick fix to the problem of Minuteman vulnerability, a problem that he believed was looming up too fast to be addressed by the MX. His scheme would have meant digging between eight and twenty-four holes for each of the one thousand Minutemen, both MIRVed and unMIRVed. Since the system would involve only one live missile in each complex of holes, transported at intervals from hole to hole in a canister much like the one the Soviets used to load their silos, Nitze believed that ALPS would be permissible under SALT right away, despite the protocol ban on mobile ICBMs. He maintained that if deployed in an ALPS basing mode, Minuteman would become "neither mobile nor fixed—but transportable." That distinction was a bit too fine even for the most skillful hair-splitters at the Pentagon, but they liked the basic elements of the scheme. The Defense Science Board and the Pentagon hierarchy expropriated the main features of ALPS, defined it as a mobile basing mode, tailored it to MX rather than Minuteman, and rechristened it MAPS—for Multiple Aim Points System. One widely contemplated version would have moved 300 MXs around among 6,000 silos—20 holes for each missile. MAPS had three attractions—strategic, economic and political. Its proponents believed it would genuinely protect the U.S. land-based deterrent against a Soviet first strike; it was estimated to cost about half as much as the trench option; and it might induce Paul Nitze to support SALT II.

As the military strategists at the Pentagon and the political strategists at the White House closed ranks around the desirability of MAPS, there were anguished groans from the State Department, the Arms Control Agency and even from some presidential advisers within the White House. Paul Warnke had thought MAPS was madness when, as general counsel of the Defense Department, he had heard an earlier version of the plan discussed—and dismissed—by the Pentagon in 1967. He thought it was just as crazy now. One of the fundamental flaws of MAPS, in the view of its critics, was that it multiplied the number of targets for the Soviets to shoot at. Therefore it would induce them to throw more warheads at the U.S. If the Soviets were to attempt a strike against MAPS, they would have to fire 6,000 warheads—virtually their entire arsenal—at 6,000 silos in order to be sure of hitting the 300 live missiles in the system. Defenders of the plan responded that that was just the point: the Soviets would be deterred from striking against a system that required them to shoot their bolt in order to knock it out, leaving them with little or nothing left over with which to blackmail the U.S. government into surrendering. General Lew Allen, chief of staff of the Air Force, argued—very much in favor of the scheme—that MAPS would constitute "a great sponge to absorb" all the Soviet land-based MIRVs. Critics turned that image around and used it against the idea. Did the U.S. really want to use the great American heartland, where MAPS would be deployed, to attract a saturation attack? How would the senators from those states feel about the prospect? After all, General Allen and Paul Nitze, as two of the most influential enthusiasts of MAPS, would not have to go home and sell the idea to a constituency of farmers and small-town citizens whose counties would become the sponge for Soviet MIRVs.

The other devastating argument against MAPS concerned verification. In order to fool the Russians about which holes contained missiles, the U.S. would have to engage in deliberately deceptive practices, such as moving rocket-bearing canisters from hole to hole, pretending to load some and actually loading others, and perhaps even installing radioactive boxes in all silos so that remote Soviet sensors would not be able to detect which holes housed nuclear warheads. Such practices would have to be permissible under SALT. That meant the Soviets would be allowed to play the same elaborate shell game with a MAPS system of their own. And if the U.S. were able to stretch the rules to the point where it could successfully hide its missiles and still comply with SALT, then the Soviets would be able to do the same thing—only cheat and get away with it. Instead of putting dummy missiles and radioactive boxes in their decoy holes, they could load those silos with extra, illegal ICBMs. They could play the shell game with a pea under every shell.

The problem of verification convinced President Carter's science adviser, Dr. Frank Press, that MAPS was a bad idea. He tentatively concluded that instead of MAPS, the U.S. should invest in an "air-mobile" system, utilizing ICBMs launched from airplanes. Air-to-surface ballistic missiles were, like other mobiles, to be banned under the protocol but permitted in the treaty. In a nuclear crisis, the planes would take to the skies and fly around until they received an order from the President's own airborne command post to release their missiles. They would have enough fuel to stay aloft for eight hours or more. That is longer than most war-gamers expect the holocaust to last, so an air-mobile system, according to its proponents at the White House and State Department, had the dual advantages of survivability and a degree of "endurance" (although not enough to satisfy Nitze, who felt that a system must survive for a minimum of twenty-four hours). The Defense Department office of Research and Engineering came up with another alternative to MAPS. It was an "air-transportable" system, built around a fleet of short-takeoff-and-landing transport planes that would, in a crisis, fly off to preassigned fields where their missiles would be unloaded and launched.

These and other schemes initially met a hostile reception at the Pentagon. A bureaucratic consensus had solidified around MAPS. Besides, the alternatives had problems of their own. The air-mobile ICBM was not really a solution to the vulnerability of the American land-based deterrent. Rather, it enhanced the airborne leg of the triad. Nor would an air-launched ICBM be anywhere near as accurate as a fixed-site one. As for the air-transportable mobile, it lacked endurance. Once the missile was delivered to its launch site, it would become vulnerable to a Soviet strike. Therefore the air-transportable missile could not be kept on alert for hours. As Paul Nitze explained in arguing against the air-transportable mobile, "You'd have to use it or lose it."

Telling—Not Asking—the Russians

In the summer of 1978 MAPS looked to the Pentagon like the closest the U.S. could come to a panacea for Minuteman vulnerability before 1985. The President was persuaded that, once again, an option should be kept open. Cyrus Vance and Paul Warnke were willing to indulge the Pentagon in what they saw as its latest cockeyed idea. They did not mind the Pentagon pondering the possibility of MAPS, as long as the Air Force was not about to start digging new holes and pouring concrete right away. ("MAPS is the Maginot Line of the nuclear age," said one State Department official, shaking his head wearily.) Vance and Warnke were also content to have the President reserve the right to make up his mind about MAPS sometime in the future, after SALT II had entered into force. But they emphatically did not believe that the issue should be allowed to complicate the negotiations then under way.

Zbigniew Brzezinski and Harold Brown did not agree. They felt the Soviets must assent in advance to the permissibility of MAPS under the terms of the treaty. Were the legality of MAPS left moot, they feared, both the Soviets and congressional critics of the system would later raise a storm of protest if and when the U.S. government tried to deploy ICBMs in multiple aim points. Brzezinski and Brown knew that MAPS was open to the double-barreled charge that it violated the SALT prohibitions against deliberate concealment of missile launchers and against the construction of new fixed-site launchers. Also, the launcher counting rule that the U.S. had pressed upon the Russians at D-and-P could not help but discomfit the advocates of MAPS. Here was a system that depended for its efficacy on the *in*ability of the other side to distinguish live holes from decoys. Brzezinski and Brown felt that to leave these questions about MAPS unanswered now would be to guarantee a potentially paralyzing dispute later on. Postponing the issue of whether the U.S. had a right to MAPS would only mean allowing the opponents to reserve their right to object. Better to "face the issue head-on," said Brzezinski in one meeting. Once again, the political consideration was crucial in the President's decision to side with Brzezinski and Brown. The administration's straightforward claim of a right to MAPS at the negotiating table, it was hoped, would increase the chances of Paul Nitze's eventual support during the fight over ratification in the Senate.

The question of exactly how to raise MAPS with the Russians occasioned another round of lively, sometimes heated debate at the Special Coordination Committee. The result was a compromise, but it was closer to the Brown-Brzezinski position than to the Vance-Warnke one. The U.S. would tell the Soviets that it considered MAPS permissible under SALT, but the negotiators would seek only tacit Soviet acquiescence. The Russians would assent by their silence. That way they would have been served formal notice and could not claim later on that the U.S. was changing the rules. At the same time, they would be spared having to affirm the American position. It had become a mutually accepted practice in SALT that if one side confronted the other with an explicit, unilateral interpretation and the second side did not object, then the interpretation was considered agreed and became enshrined in the negotiating record.

The trouble was, the Russians were not willing simply to sit still and listen quietly while the U.S. representatives delivered their statement. Warnke raised the matter with Anatoly Dobrynin in Washington and Malcolm Toon did the same thing with Georgy Kornienko in Moscow. Warnke and Toon dutifully informed the Russians that the U.S. considered it permissible under SALT for a missile to move from launcher to launcher and that while no decision on basing mode had been made, the U.S. reserved the right to proceed with such a deployment in the future. Moreover, Warnke and Toon continued, they were "under instructions" to make clear that this was a unilateral American position and no official Soviet response was invited or welcomed. When Vance flew to Geneva in July, it was decided that while he would discuss mobile ICBMs in general with Gromyko, he would not say anything about MAPS in specific. The U.S. did not want MAPS to become an issue of high-level bargaining. However, during a break in the Vance-Gromyko talks, Vladimir Semyonov came to Paul Warnke's office at the Botanic Building and said that regardless of whether the U.S. invited or welcomed Soviet comment on MAPS, he was "under instructions" to express "grave reservations" about whether the system would be "valid and permissible." Semyonov contended that since all the holes in a MAPS-like system would be hardened, it was at least arguable that all of them should count as launchers according to the Joint Draft Text as it was then written. He also suggested that MAPS would constitute deliberate concealment. Warnke—ever the good lawyer advocating as persuasively as possible even the weakest case of his client—said that deceptive basing itself was not a violation of SALT; SALT does not stipulate that each side must know where the other side's launchers are. To wit, submarines are a deliberately deceptive basing mode for ballistic missiles that is thoroughly permissible under SALT. Warnke suppressed his own skepticism about the position he was arguing. Semyonov did not suppress his. But the Soviet response—while skeptical in the extreme—stopped short of being a categorical assertion that MAPS should be forbidden.

After the unsettling exchange in Geneva, the Carter administration regrouped and decided to make its unilateral statement on MAPS again—this time in a way that would make it harder for the Soviets to reply. Harold Brown was designated as the spokesman. In a speech to an American Legion convention in New Orleans in August 1978,

Brown said: "A number of mobile ICBM basing concepts are being evaluated, including some involving alternate launch points for each missile. This concept envisions moving missiles and their launchers among multiple sites which might themselves be hardened, thus substantially complicating Soviet targeting of our deterrent. . . . The parts of the Joint Draft Text of the SALT II agreement that have already been agreed allow deployment of mobile ICBM systems of the types we are considering."

It was one of the most fussed-over passages in the history of U.S. government declarations. The key sentences were drafted at a Special Coordination Committee meeting at which every agency involved in SALT was represented. The context made clear that the U.S. had not yet decided definitely to proceed with MAPS or any other mobile system—only that it reserved the right to do so. There was also a convoluted disclaimer on verification: "The U.S. will not deploy a mobile ICBM system that would not permit adequate verification of the number of launchers deployed," said Brown, "and we will insist that any Soviet system meet the same verification standards."

Brown seemed to have had the last word on the subject—at least in the Soviet-American dialogue. For a long time after his speech, the Soviets stayed quiet about MAPS.* Whether their silence was tantamount to assent could not be determined with certainty. Administration officials chose to stress the equivocal nature of Semyonov's "reservations" in July and the absence of any Soviet reaction since the Brown speech in August. Nitze, however, attached ominous significance to the fact that Semyonov had raised reservations at all.

Within the U.S. government, MAPS was anything but a closed issue. A high State Department official commented bitterly: "We've really shot ourselves in the foot on this one. We've ended up with the worst of all possible worlds. We've injected the MAPS issue into the negotiations, and we haven't gotten a clear-cut answer. It's an outcome that serves nobody's purposes." A member of the White House staff said that for once he sympathized with the Soviet position in SALT: "This whole MAPS episode is another example of our changing signals on the Russians. It must be confusing and infuriating as hell to

---

*Months later, another spate of American news stories about MAPS and the Pentagon's attachment to the idea caused the Soviets to allude to their earlier reservations. The U.S. replied by reiterating Brown's position. This replay of the exchange, which took place in diplomatic channels, was kept a closely guarded secret even within the administration.

them. Frankly, if the Soviets ever came to us and tried this sort of nonsense, we'd never accept it. We'd scream bloody murder." Even at the Pentagon, there were hints of misgiving. Said one senior official there: "Whether I try to persuade you that MAPS is a terrific idea will depend on whether it ends up being U.S. policy that we really want the thing."

At a press conference in September, Carter himself conceded that MAPS had "some very serious defects." In the Winter 1978/1979 issue of *Foreign Affairs*, Jan Lodal, a former Pentagon analyst and assistant to Henry Kissinger, wrote what was widely regarded at the time as the most authoritative and judicious assessment of SALT II to date. He found little to criticize in the prospective treaty. The handling of the MAPS issue was one exception: "While the new agreement is by and large extremely comprehensive in its verification provisions, one notable absence is a rigorous definition of a missile launcher. In order to eliminate any possible ambiguity about the meaning of other provisions, such a definition should be agreed upon by the two sides. However, the U.S. has resisted the inclusion of such a definition, apparently because it would be difficult to write one that drew any distinction between the unMIRVed Minuteman II missile silos and the MIRVed Minuteman III silos, and because such a definition might stand in the way of an American multiple aim point ICBM-basing system. . . . The lack of a precise definition of a launcher . . . is one of several examples in the new agreement where the U.S. has sacrificed its principles in order to avoid a constraint on its programs." The principle of precision was sacrificed in order to keep open options—one of the most stubborn and problematic features of the American conduct of SALT— and also to keep open the possibility that Paul Nitze might eventually swallow his skepticism and support the agreement.

The intramural debate over a mobile basing mode continued well into 1979. New and ever fancier alternatives were considered, including the possibility of deploying missiles aboard offshore submersible barges. MAPS itself became known by a new, less pronounceable acronym—MVPS, for multiple vertical protective structures—and then simply MPS, for multiple protective structures. The purpose of this terminological refinement was to make more credible the contention of those who wanted to play the shell game that each hole in the system would not necessarily be a launcher. ("You always know an idea is in trouble," remarked a State Department official, "when its proponents start changing its name.") In an effort to meet the objection that MAPS by that or any other name was unverifiable, the Pentagon concocted an ingenious scheme designed to ensure that the Soviets would be able to count the missiles as they were moved into a grid of multiple holes while at the same time preventing the Soviets from knowing into which holes the missiles were actually inserted. The plan involved a missile assembly plant connected to the grid by a railway track. After the requisite number of missiles had been transported by specially designed freight car into the grid, the tracks would be dismantled. All this would take place under the scrutiny—and for the benefit—of Soviet satellites. But once the missiles were in the grid, they would be moved from hole to hole with an elaborate accompaniment of deceptions to prevent the Russians from being able to tell which holes were live. While this and other variations on the theme of MAPS did little to quell the distaste of the arms controllers, they noted with some satisfaction an ironic aspect of the plan: even if one assumed that MAPS was politically viable and that it could be verified, the system would make sense only in a world governed by SALT. To be effective, a multiple/mobile system depended upon a limit on the number of land-based Soviet warheads. The version of MAPS that called for 6,000 holes, for example, was based on the assumption that Soviets would not be allowed more than 6,000 warheads. A limit on "fractionation," or number of warheads per missile, was a goal of SALT. In the absence of a new agreement, the Soviets might deploy, say, 300 SS-18 heavy missiles with 40 MIRVs each, for a total of 12,000 warheads, plus many thousands more atop SS-17s and SS-19s. In the face of such a staggering proliferation, MAPS or ALPS or MVPS or any other scheme to protect the American deterrent would be all but meaningless. Thus, whether there was a MAPS in America's future or not, the debate over the system within the U.S. government heightened the priority of negotiating a limit on the fractionation of Soviet missiles.

General David Jones, the new chairman of the Joint Chiefs of Staff, acknowledged the interdependence of MAPS and SALT when he testified in favor of "holding firm" on the MAPS option in the summer of 1978: "To the Soviets I say, 'You have caused this problem [of Minuteman vulnerability] with your large number of reentry vehicles and increased accuracy. We can solve it in one of two ways: either you reduce the number of your RVs or we will take steps to enhance the safety of our missiles.' " The negotiators had no illusion that they could get the Soviets to accept a reduction in their current number of warheads, but goaded by General Jones, Paul Nitze and others, they were more determined than ever to achieve in SALT II a freeze on warheads. That freeze, in turn, would amount to a reduction in the number of warheads the Soviets might otherwise deploy in the future.*

---

*One week before he was due to meet with Brezhnev in Vienna in June 1979, Carter formally announced his decision to proceed with the development of the MX for eventual deployment in a mobile mode. But the debate within the government over the most secure, economical and verifiable basing mode seemed destined to continue well into the summer after the summit, thus overlapping with the debate in the Senate over ratification. In 1978 the Air Force developed and tested an improved version of the closed trench, or tunnel, that seemed better able to withstand a direct hit. Therefore at the time of the Vienna summit and the signing of SALT II, the military considered both the closed trench and multiple aim points to be viable options available to the President. Carter himself, however, seemed to be leaning more toward a newer alternative, an open trench with hardened protective covers along the way.

11

Solutions
Beget Problems

When Cyrus Vance and Andrei Gromyko concluded their meeting in Geneva in July 1978, they left their permanent negotiators faced with a few major issues and a host of minor ones. In varying degrees, all the important issues and many of the secondary ones were interrelated. They were different manifestations of fundamental problems of SALT, notably problems of definition and verification, and the resolution of one depended in large measure upon the resolution of another. For the Americans, the single most important outstanding issue in mid 1978 was "fractionation," the technical term for the number of warheads on a missile. Part of the maddening dynamic of SALT has been that the resolution of a general problem often confronts the negotiators with a MIRV-like cluster of specific problems of definition and detail. The ban on new types of ICBMs was a case in point. The tentative agreement on such a ban in July intensified the disagreement over what constituted a new type. The U.S. wanted to define as a new type any existing type of rocket tested with more warheads than before. That definition would have forced the Soviets to freeze the number of warheads on their three big MIRVed rockets. The SS-17 would remain at a maximum of four warheads, the SS-19 at six and the "heavy" SS-18 at ten. Under a provision freezing each type of ICBM at the maximum number of warheads with which it had been tested, the U.S. would—unless a loophole was closed—technically have the right to add four warheads to the Minuteman, since during the Ford administration the Air Force had carried out a test, code-named Pave Pepper, of a Minuteman III with seven reentry vehicles. The purpose, explained a high official of the Ford White House, was simply "to see how many eggs you could squeeze out of that kind of bird." But the Carter administration had no plans to put more than three warheads on the Minuteman. It was the freeze on the MIRVing of Soviet existing types that the U.S. most cared about. If that objective could be achieved, SALT would have crossed a strategic and political threshold, from the limitation of missile launchers toward the limitation of missile warheads.

With the advent of MIRVs, a single missile had itself become a launcher for a number of independently targetable weapons of mass destruction. It struck many as absurd that an individual SS-18 silo should count as one launcher when it had the proved capacity to carry ten warheads and thus possibly knock out ten Minuteman launchers. To make matters worse, Pentagon weapons analysts believed that the SS-18 might, in future tests, be upgraded to carry between twenty-five and forty reentry vehicles. For years, critics had disparaged the SALT I interim agreement as obsolete and inadequate because it addressed only the problem of launchers.* The Vladivostok accord, too, set ceilings for launchers. Granted, it included a subceiling for MIRV launchers, but the subceiling was high, and it did not distinguish between a Minuteman III with three warheads and an SS-18 with ten. As Paul Nitze put it: "Launchers are the wrong currency for SALT. Whatever the right currency is, it should include number of warheads, hard-target kill capability and megatonnage." In numerous private conversations with administration officials, including a number of luncheon meetings with Vance, Nitze pressed for what he called a "meaningful fractionation ban."

By seeking a freeze on Soviet warheads, the Carter administration hoped not only to convert SALT II into a currency acceptable to critics like Nitze but also to answer the concern of military leaders like General Jones, the chairman of the Chiefs, who identified the proliferation of Soviet warheads as the most dangerous element in the strategic balance, requiring the most drastic remedy. As Jones made clear in his testimony on the multiple aim points system, the unchecked addition of warheads to Soviet ICBMs would make something like MAPS unavoidable—whatever the practical and political problems in deploying such a system, whatever the technical problems in verifying

---

*SALT I established the practice of counting launchers rather than missiles essentially because the number of launchers is far easier to verify by national technical means. In American minds, the issue of counting—and limiting—the number of warheads did not loom large in 1972 because the U.S. had MIRVs, while the U.S.S.R. did not.

it. To the civilian arms controllers, the digging of extra holes on the American side was almost as disagreeable and destabilizing a prospect as the adding of extra warheads on the Soviet side. The danger of a MIRV-MAPS spiral made them all the more determined to freeze the SS-17 at four, the SS-19 at six, and the SS-18 at ten reentry vehicles each.

But as was so often the case in SALT, the pursuit of a constraint on Soviet systems was complicated by the need to protect an American system at the same time—that is, to keep an option open. Just as the Carter administration had sought—and finally achieved—a new-types ban that left it free to proceed with the development of the MX, so it sought a fractionation freeze that left the U.S. free to arm the MX with ten warheads. The motivation here was largely political. Pentagon studies concluded that the MX might be most efficient with six to eight warheads. Some Pentagon officials even proposed at one point that the U.S. accept a six-warhead limit on the MX so that the Russians would be bound by the same limit on their new type of ICBM in case they decided to go with a MIRVed new type. But the administration decided that it would help the cause of ratification if the U.S. could reserve the right to put as many warheads on its new ICBM, the MX, as the Soviets had on their largest existing ICBM, the SS-18. As 1978 wore on and the battle in the Senate loomed closer, the policy-makers gave increasing weight to considerations of political appearance. How would the final treaty *look* with or without a particular provision? On the issue of MX fractionation, there was little interagency dispute. Leslie Gelb's Bureau of Politico-Military Affairs at the State Department, Walter Slocombe's SALT Task Force at the Pentagon, Paul Warnke and his colleagues in ACDA, David Aaron and Roger Molander at the National Security Council, all agreed that the treaty would look more equitable and would be easier to ratify if the U.S. could have ten MIRVs on the MX. The ability to match the SS-18 warhead for warhead was seen as a way of redressing the most blatant inequity in SALT—the holdover provision from the interim agreement that allowed the U.S.S.R. some 300 heavy missiles and the U.S. none. Thus, the American proposal on fractionation was to freeze the number of warheads on each side's existing types of ICBM but to allow as many warheads on the one allotted new type as on the largest existing type—i.e., ten.

The Soviets took the position that the U.S. was trying to have it both ways—minimum fractionation on Soviet existing types but maximum fractionation on the American new type—and they did not want the U.S. to have it either way. The Russians spun out an array of counterproposals, the purpose of which was to permit them to put additional warheads on their existing types of ICBMs while preventing the U.S. from putting ten on the MX. For a while they claimed the right to upgrade the SS-17 and the SS-19 to ten warheads each from four and six respectively. Then they fell back to wanting six for the SS-17—while holding the MX to six as well. The Soviets argued that the fractionation freeze should make no distinction between new and existing types, nor should there be any distinction among different existing types. The only disparity that should remain would be the one the U.S. most wanted to do away with—between "light" and "heavy" ICBMs. The Russians' largest "light" ICBM was the SS-19, which had six warheads. Therefore six should be the fractionation limit for light ICBMs in general. Since the U.S. new type must also be classified as a light ICBM, it, too, should stay within that limit. The Soviets' exclusive right to heavy missiles gave them, they maintained, an exclusive right to a rocket with ten warheads. As Paul Warnke and Ralph Earle pointed out to them repeatedly, the Russians were saying in effect that the one-sidedness of SALT's treatment of heavy missile launchers should be carried over into warhead fractionation; the Soviets were seeking not only to preserve a unilateral advantage granted them by SALT I but to make it even more advantageous.

MIRVed Bombers

At the July 1978 Vance-Gromyko meeting in Geneva, the Soviets budged—partially, tentatively and conditionally. They indicated they might freeze the SS-17 at four warheads and the SS-19 at six in exchange for an American concession on what the Russians considered a related issue. The Russians wanted a strict limit on the number of air-launched cruise missiles to be allowed on heavy bombers. They called this issue "bomber fractionation"—a term intended to underscore their long-standing contention that bombers armed with ALCMs should be treated in the same way as missiles armed with multiple warheads. By the same logic that the U.S. pressed for a freeze on warheads per missile, the Soviet Union pressed for a freeze on ALCMs per bomber.

The background here is worth reviewing: at the deadlock-breaking meeting between Carter and Gromyko in September 1977, the U.S.

had agreed to count ALCM-carrying bombers under the 1,320 subceiling. For months afterward, the Soviets tried to get the U.S. to accept a prohibition against using airplanes bigger than B-52s as ALCM bombers. Had they succeeded in negotiating such a ban, the Russians would have effectively limited ALCMs to about twenty per plane, since the maximum capacity of a B-52 is twelve cruise missiles hung from the wings plus another eight or so stowed in its converted bomb bays. The Pentagon, however, was not willing to foreclose the possibility of wide-bodied ALCM carriers. During the summer of 1977, the Air Force had set 250 as the optimum size of its prospective cruise-missile-carrying fleet. In the September breakthrough, the U.S. had agreed to a "set-aside" or "free allowance" of only 120 ALCM carriers. Should it decide it needed more ALCM bombers than 120, the U.S. would have to reduce the number of its MIRVed missiles on a one-for-one basis as each cruise missile carrier over 120 is deployed. Thus, while there was no rigid limit on the size of the airborne cruise-missile-carrying fleet, such an arrangement was bound to have a limiting effect on the ALCM bomber program. If the Air Force was going to have to settle for fewer cruise missile carriers, then it was all the more interested in eventually having bigger ones. The Pentagon studied the possibility of loading as many as eighty air-launched cruise missiles aboard a modified version of a long-range commercial jumbo jet, such as the Boeing 747SP (for special performance)—the plane that is used for nonstop flights from New York to Tokyo. The Russians fought hard for a ban on deploying cruise missiles aboard such "transport-type" aircraft. In February 1978, *Pravda* editorialized that U.S. intransigence on this issue was a principal cause of delay in the signing of a treaty. But the U.S. remained firm, and at the April meeting between Vance and Gromyko in Moscow, the Soviets gave up on a ban against wide-bodied ALCM carriers. They shifted immediately to an insistence that SALT limit cruise missiles at twenty per plane. Thus, the Russians were pursuing the same end by different means. They were trying to restrict even a modified 747SP to a payload of cruise missiles no larger than a B-52's.

At the July Vance-Gromyko meeting in Geneva, the Soviets made their acceptance of a missile fractionation freeze conditional on American acceptance of their position on "bomber fractionation": the U.S.S.R. would hold the SS-17 and SS-19 to four and six warheads respectively if the U.S. would restrict its bombers to twenty ALCMs each. If the U.S. was determined to deploy cruise missiles aboard wide-bodied planes that carried additional ALCMs, continued the Russians, then each plane would count against the 1,320 subceiling by multiples of 20: a 747 armed with 80 cruise missiles would count as four launchers against the 1,320. The U.S. countered with an "averaging approach" pegged to the number 35. By this formula, a B-52 with 20 cruise missiles and a 747 with 50 would count as two launchers, since 20 and 50 average out to 35 per plane. For months the two sides remained at loggerheads over whether to limit cruise missiles by a formula that multiplied or divided; Soviet willingness to freeze missile fractionation the U.S.'s way remained explicitly linked to an American concession to count cruise missiles the Russians' way. It was a concession the U.S. had no intention of making. Even though the U.S. had no plans to deploy bombers with more than twenty cruise missiles before 1985, the Pentagon did not want to be explicitly forbidden from doing so, and—once again—it did not want the SALT II treaty to set a precedent that the Soviets might try to extend into SALT III.

As the Crow Flies

The Soviet phobia about cruise missiles and the American love affair with them were evident on another issue: how to define the range of a cruise missile. Gross numbers had long since been agreed for limits on range. Ground-launched and sea-launched cruise missiles with ranges greater than 600 kilometers were prohibited from deployment during the protocol period, and air-launched cruise missiles were to be limited to a range of 2,500 kilometers. But did range mean the distance between the launch point and the target? Or did it mean the total distance covered as the cruise missile followed the sometimes serpentine itinerary prescribed for it by its terrain contour matching (TERCOM) guidance system? The former, said the Americans. The latter, said the Soviets.

The U.S. wanted range defined in a way that allowed for what the technicians called a "delta overage," or a "differential for operational considerations." More informally known as a "wiggle factor," this compensation for the propensity of the cruise missile to zigzag as it homed in on its target might be written into the agreement either with a vague phrase, such as "when in operational use," or with a precise formula and a set percentage. Some Pentagon experts calculated that to be sure of evading Soviet air defenses, the air-launched cruise missile would need a delta overage of 50 percent. Hence, an

ALCM with an "effective operational" range of 2,500 kilometers
would actually cover 3,750 kilometers. (Sea-launched antiship cruise
missiles needed even more room to maneuver, since they must orient
themselves over water and must search for a moving target.) As the
U.S. land-based deterrent became more vulnerable to Soviet attack,
it became more important for the Air Force to be confident of penetrating Soviet air defenses with long-range ALCMs. Because they are
relatively slow, ALCMs are strictly retaliatory weapons. They are of
little use against "time-urgent" targets, such as Ukrainian missile
launchers that might be used in a Soviet first strike. Yet because they
are so uncannily accurate, ALCMs are still hard-target killers. They
can be used against the reinforced-concrete silos of missiles that are
being held in reserve, just as they can be used against "soft" targets,
like bridges or airfields. But in order that the cruise missiles maintain
their ability to penetrate Soviet air space and reach targets deep inside
the U.S.S.R., their capacity to dodge, duck and weave must keep pace
with improvements in Soviet air defenses. In 1978 the Soviets had
thousands of modern interceptors and surface-to-air missiles, the be-
ginnings of a "look-down/shoot-down" airborne radar network and, in
the words of John Collins, a congressional staff expert on military
affairs, "the equivalent of a Manhattan Project in the area of air defenses."

Harold Brown had never been happy with the SALT II provisions
limiting the range of cruise missiles. He once said that his biggest
regret was having acceded early on, during the packaging of the May
1977 three-tier proposal, to cruise missile range limits, particularly for
ALCMs. The 600-kilometer limit on the ground-launched version essentially meant—as the Russians intended it to mean—that a GLCM
fired eastward from West Germany could not hit the Soviet Union. A
Soviet GLCM of the same range, however, fired westward from Poland could hit West Germany. As for air-launched cruise missiles,
Brown felt that any fixed range limit would, sooner or later, restrict
the ALCM's ability to penetrate and therefore to retaliate, given the
relentless upgrading of Soviet air defenses. Once the President had
canceled the B-1 supersonic bomber, the U.S. would have to rely on
lumbering, subsonic launching platforms that must fire their cruise
missiles from farther and farther outside Soviet air space. Cyrus Vance
and Paul Warnke had persuaded Brown in 1977 against trying to raise
the range limit for ALCMs from 2,500 kilometers to 3,000 kilometers
or higher, but Brown's acquiescence on that point made him all the

stauncher an advocate of holding out in the negotiations for a flexible definition of cruise missile range that allowed maximum evasiveness and maximum penetrability. In his view, the wiggle factor was a hedge against the inevitable restrictiveness of any fixed range limit. In early 1978, Brown wrote a lengthy, detailed, tightly reasoned letter to Henry Jackson on the subject. For years, Jackson had been resisting cruise missile range limits. Brown argued that the U.S. could live with a 2,500-kilometer range limit as long as it was operationally defined.

At the negotiating table, the issue of cruise missile range was predictably contentious. The Russians saw, or claimed to see, all this talk about "delta overages" and "wiggle factors" as just so much hocus-pocus intended to obscure the fact that the Americans were trying to stretch the range of their sinister little drones. At one point, a Soviet negotiator tried to use a quaint American idiom to persuade his U.S. interlocutor that the only verifiable range for a cruise missile would be "as the crow flies." Exactly, riposted the U.S. official; surely Soviet science had discovered that crows fly in a manner very much like cruise missiles, with nature's own TERCOM guiding them along an elaborate grid of landmarks and other territorial reference points.

The issue of verification, however, could not be dismissed so easily. Cruise missile range was bound to be one of the hardest aspects of SALT to verify, no matter how range was defined—with or without delta overages. If its flight profile (i.e., the altitude and speed), its fuel or the payload is changed, a cruise missile that had been tested at 600 kilometers could fly much farther. For example, one type of cruise missile with a relatively heavy payload of conventional explosives, flying at sea level has a range of about 500 miles. The same machine, armed with a lighter nuclear warhead and flying at a higher altitude, has a range of some 3,000 miles. If any or all of these variables—notably, preprogrammed flight profile and payload—are adjusted, the range can be extended without any change in the external appearance of the cruise missile. The adjustments cannot be monitored by the other side's national technical means, and the range cannot always be verified with certainty.

The Silver Bullet

One variable in particular—the payload—became a knotty issue unto itself in the negotiations. The extraordinary adaptability of cruise missiles made the nature of their warheads, like their range, a problem of both definition and verification. SALT had to answer the question: Should the agreement govern all cruise missiles, regardless of whether they are armed with nuclear or conventional explosives? Once again, since cruise missiles were an American strength and a Soviet weakness, the Russians pressed for a comprehensive, restrictive definition, while the U.S. wanted a more equivocal, permissive provision—one that might be harder to verify but that would impinge as little as possible on future refinements of the cruise missile program. The Soviets wanted SALT II to refer simply to "armed" cruise missiles, a blanket definition that would make no distinction between nuclear and conventional warheads. It was well nigh impossible for photoreconnaissance or any other "national technical means of verification" to distinguish between a nuclear-armed cruise missile and one tipped with a conventional warhead. Therefore—on the same principle that the U.S. had made stick in the case of Derazhnya and Pervomaisk, where unMIRVed launchers were deemed to be MIRVed for purposes of counting under SALT—all cruise missiles should be deemed to be nuclear armed.

For once, the logic of the Soviet position was difficult to refute. The politics, however, were more complicated. Pentagon planners were uneasy with the prospect that SALT II—which was supposed to restrain strategic nuclear arms—might end up, willy-nilly, restricting the development and deployment of some conventionally armed tactical weapons as well. "SALT should not limit conventional weapons," said Walter Slocombe. "There might well be a case for conventional-weapons-type arms control, but not in SALT." Harold Brown once asked, "Why should we put a limit on a conventionally armed ALCM with a range of 601 kilometers when the Soviets are not accepting any limit on Backfire?" The issue was not entirely abstract. The Navy was mulling over the possibility of using conventionally armed ALCMs as antiship weapons. These missiles would be deployed on tactical fighters operating from aircraft carriers. "The concept of antiship cruise missiles on maritime-control aircraft might give a new lease on life to the aircraft carrier itself," said one Defense Department official. "One advantage of the concept is that it would allow you to apply naval air power very broadly. Wherever the carrier is, you'd have command of the air and sea around it for a large area. It would give you a longer, stronger air power arm off of aircraft carriers."

Such schemes struck even some Pentagon experts as fanciful. A senior Air Force officer dismissed the idea of a conventionally armed cruise missile as "a bunch of nonsense—a silver bullet. It would be a

million-dollar wonder. There wouldn't be enough bang for the buck."
But in Europe, conventionally armed cruise missiles were taken more
seriously. After all, the U.S. and the Soviet Union were in a state of
rough equivalence on a strategic nuclear index, but the Warsaw Pact
enjoyed an indisputable advantage over NATO in so-called theater
forces and conventional fire power. Therefore West European strategists and politicians were especially concerned that SALT—a bilateral
negotiation going on over their heads between the superpowers—not
deprive them of the means to redress that imbalance. The West Germans had a special interest. Banned by international agreement from
having nuclear weapons of their own, they were anxious to have access
someday to conventionally armed ground-launched cruise missiles.
The Schmidt government's confidence in Carter had been so badly
shaken by the neutron bomb fiasco that months later Bonn was still
taking a jaundiced view of SALT. There was particular concern about
the three-year protocol as it then appeared. It contained three features that disturbed the West Germans—a prohibition on the deployment of long-range ground-launched cruise missiles, an ambiguous
and therefore ominous "noncircumvention" clause, and definition of
cruise missiles that seemed to lump conventional warheads together
with nuclear ones. The West Germans and other members of NATO
were not so much worried about the three years of the protocol itself
as they were about what happened when the protocol expired. As the
three years came to an end, the Soviets would exert considerable
pressure on the U.S. to extend those provisions of the protocol that
would prevent NATO from acquiring conventionally armed cruise
missiles, particularly ground-launched ones. The West Europeans had
little faith that the U.S. would be able to resist such pressure.

Throughout SALT II, NATO has had a vigilant, knowledgeable and
highly influential spokesman in the U.S. Senate. Georgia Democrat
Sam Nunn made himself an expert on Euro-strategic affairs. Along
with Henry Jackson, Nunn lobbied both Jimmy Carter and Harold
Brown to take special and explicit measures to protect conventionally
armed cruise missiles and thus reassure the allies. In 1977 the interagency SALT Working Group came up with a complicated device for
doing so. It was a proposal for a joint statement whereby the two sides
would agree that once the protocol expired, either side would have
the right to deploy conventionally armed cruise missiles on airplanes
other than heavy bombers without those planes counting against the
1,320 subceiling.

This device was intended to address what was usually called the issue of "cruise missile definition," but it did so only indirectly. It actually concerned the definition of heavy bombers. Under the U.S. proposal, during the three years of the protocol any airplane carrying long-range cruise missiles would be treated as an ALCM-armed heavy bomber. The plane might be a B-52, a Boeing 747 or a Piper Cub. If there was so much as a single long-range ALCM hung under its wing, it would count as a heavy bomber against the 1,320 subceiling for as long as the protocol was in force. During the protocol period, there would be no special treatment of—or exemption for—conventionally armed cruise missiles. But the moment the protocol expired, the rule, as set down in advance, would change significantly: then planes other than heavy bombers—such as F-4 Phantom fighters or FB-111 medium bombers—would be free to carry cruise missiles without counting under SALT so long as they were conventionally armed. Thus the precedent would be established that the SALT II treaty had no jurisdiction over conventional weapons, and the West Germans' conventional GLCM would be protected by implication.

Its advocates—primarily in the Defense Department—thought the idea was ingenious. Most officials in the State Department and Arms Control Agency thought it was convoluted, nonnegotiable, unverifiable and—if by some fluke the Soviets accepted it—bound to backfire against the U.S. someday. Walter Slocombe argued that almost all characteristics of cruise missiles were unverifiable, so why should the difficulty of verifying one additional characteristic prevent the U.S. from seeking a provision that was in its own and its allies' interests? How far could a cruise missile really fly, and what kind of warheads were they really equipped with—granted, these were both questions that national technical means of verification could not answer with much confidence. The point was, continued Slocombe, these were problems for the other side, not for the U.S. The CIA estimated that cruise missiles would pose problems primarily for Soviet verification at least until 1985, when the SALT II treaty would expire.

The Pentagon position, in essence, was that the verifiability of provisions in the treaty should be the cardinal principle of SALT when the U.S. was worried about the Soviets cheating—but not necessarily when it was the other way around. Slocombe could see that implication of his department's position, although he did his lawyerly best to defend it. In one meeting he tried to refute the charge that U.S. cruise missile definition represented a double standard by saying: "We will not only accept—we will insist upon—a distinguishability provision analogous to the launcher distinguishability rule for missiles. Any cruise missile that wants to be the beneficiary of the post-protocol exclusion for conventional cruise missiles must look different from a nuclear one."

"Oh, yes?" said a State Department official from across the table. "And how are you going to do that? Are you going to color code the things? Or are you going to paint conventional warheads green and nuclear ones red?"

Ignoring the sarcasm, Slocombe explained that conventionally armed ALCMs would be distinguished by "externally observable design features," but he conceded, "It's true that the distinguishability rule would not be foolproof."

Cyrus Vance, Paul Warnke and Ralph Earle were all attorneys too, but unlike Slocombe, they did not work for Harold Brown, and they vigorously opposed the Pentagon's cruise missile definition inside the government. However, Brown won—at least in the first round. He persuaded the President and Zbigniew Brzezinski that the definition had three merits: it would be helpful for a number of projected American military programs and would particularly please those Navy planners who were counting on conventionally armed cruise missiles to enhance the utility of aircraft carriers; it would reassure the jittery allies; and it might well clinch Sam Nunn's vote for ratification of the treaty. Carter ordered that the definition be included in the American position. Once that decision was made, Vance, Warnke and Earle kept their misgivings away from the negotiating table. They argued the case of their White House and Pentagon clients as best they could. That was not good enough.

"We see this as a pretext to gain unilateral advantage," said Vladimir Semyonov. "It makes a mockery of the principle that all provisions of the agreement must be verifiable by national technical means." He delivered that curt rejection repeatedly and with mounting irritation. The Soviets made clear that if the U.S. persisted in its attempt to use SALT to bolster NATO's theater forces, the Kremlin would dredge up the old question—laid aside at Vladivostok—of forward-based systems and whether they should perhaps be limited by SALT after all.

In the face of Soviet obduracy and their own discomfort with the American position, the U.S. negotiators considered the possibility of abandoning the pursuit of an agreed statement on conventional cruise missiles and resorting to the device, already used in the case of MAPS, of a unilateral American statement. The Soviets would be confronted with an American interpretation that once the protocol expired, either side had the right to deploy conventionally armed cruise missiles on aircraft other than heavy bombers. The negotiators tried to get White House approval for such an alternative. At one meeting on the subject, Brzezinski's temper flashed. "The President has already come down with a decision on this," said the national security adviser. "He wants an agreed statement, not a unilateral one. I don't understand why, in view of a firm presidential order, you insist on raising this matter again."

And there, for most of 1978, the matter remained. The Pentagon and the White House were determined to get an explicit exemption for conventionally armed cruise missiles. The negotiators, rather unhappily, tried to bargain for such a thing, while Senators Nunn, Jackson and others watched warily over the administration's shoulder. The Russians, for their part, made clear that this was one matter on which their obstinacy was more than just a negotiating tactic: either the U.S. would have to give up on the exemption, or it would have to pay a huge price on a range of other issues.

Parameters and Percentages

Another problem that was to dominate the endgame of SALT was the definition of new types of ICBMs. Fractionation, or the number of warheads per missile, was an important characteristic that could be used to define a new type, but it was not, by any means, the only criterion. Once the Soviets—tentatively, conditionally—accepted a fractionation freeze in mid 1978, the negotiators stepped up their attempt to agree on other features of existing rockets that could be frozen in order to make meaningful and verifiable the SALT II ban on more than one new type of ICBM.

It should be noted that the drafters of the comprehensive proposal of March 1977 were careful to avoid the phrase "new types." The proposal referred instead to limits on the flight testing of missiles and a ban on the modernization of missiles. The point is more than just one of semantics. The phrase "new types," which slipped into the American official argot during the repackaging of the U.S. position between March and May 1977, is somewhat misleading and therefore politically troublesome because it suggests that if the Soviets accepted a ban on new types, they would be prohibited from developing their so-called fifth generation of ICBMs, a family of successors to the SS-17,

SS-18 and SS-19. Actually, the classification of Soviet missiles is an imprecise, arbitrary and often controversial art. Even among themselves, American experts often have difficulty drawing the line where a modified version of an existing ICBM becomes a new type or where one generation ends and another begins. The CIA, for example, for a while had difficulty making up its collective mind over whether one particular Soviet heavy missile should be called a sophisticated SS-9 or a primitive SS-18. The experts could not decide whether the ICBM in question was an advanced member of the third generation of Soviet rocketry or a single-warhead member of the fourth.

That problem is compounded when it reaches the negotiating table. To wit, the Soviets might maintain that an improved ICBM is merely an improved existing type and should therefore be classified, say, as an SS-19 mod (for modification) 5. The same rocket might look to CIA and Pentagon analysts like a new type that should be tagged the SS-30 mod 1—a fifth-generation ICBM. In short, what Cyrus Vance proposed to Andrei Gromyko in May 1977 as a ban on the "new types" of missiles was actually a ban on the testing of missiles that differed in significant, observable, though still to be defined ways from missiles already tested. As Walter Slocombe once put it: "We shouldn't kid ourselves into thinking we're going to stop the entire fifth generation. What we are going to do is to allow the Soviets to make endless, elegant modifications within a strict set of parameters." In conversations with Vladimir Semyonov and Alexander Shchukin in Geneva, Paul Warnke was fond of illustrating the goal—and limits—of SALT with a homily about his grandfather's ax. The ax had been in the family for one hundred years. It had had ten new handles and five new heads. But it was still considered his grandfather's ax—and a relic of his grandfather's generation.

Once the U.S. had committed itself to a "new types" ban in early 1977, the Carter administration needed a definition of new types that would genuinely constrain the modernization of Soviet missiles. The Special Coordination Committee assigned the task to a SALT working group chaired by Roger Molander. Along with Charles Henkin of Leslie Gelb's staff, Slocombe's deputy George Schneiter, James Timbie from the Arms Control Agency and Ray McCrory from CIA, Molander drew up a lengthy "wish list" of characteristics to be frozen. In the spirit of those times, it was exceedingly ambitious. It was also largely unverifiable. For instance, it included a prohibition on "new" guidance systems. In Geneva, Alexander Shchukin arched his brow and asked with mock incredulity, "What do you mean by no new guidance system? If we change a steel screw to a brass screw, does that make an old guidance system into a new one?" The Soviets proposed their own definition of new types. It was as brief and vague as the American one was long and precise.

For months, the U.S. persisted in an effort to negotiate the most comprehensive, stringent definition of new types possible—one that would include a flat freeze on guidance hardware and thereby would, it was hoped, stop the SS-18 and SS-19 from achieving accuracies sufficient to threaten Minuteman. But it quickly became apparent that the administration would be wasting energy if it continued too stubbornly on that course. For one thing, the Soviets were bound to resist SALT provisions that constrained the modernization of ICBMs, which are their strong suit, without constraining submarine-launched missiles and bombers, which are American specialties. For another, the monitoring of Soviet ICBM tests made clear that it was already too late to prevent the SS-18 and SS-19 from threatening Minuteman. As one proponent of constraints on accuracy acknowledged ruefully, "Those horses—particularly an accurate SS-19—were already out of the barn." Furthermore, congressional advisers to the SALT delegation warned that they would oppose any provision of the treaty, no matter how well intentioned, unless it could be verified with confidence. And finally, the Pentagon began to worry that in their eagerness to constrain Soviet modernization, the designers of the American SALT position might inadvertently be making proposals that would impinge on U.S. programs as well.

That concern was highlighted by an incident in the summer of 1977. Among the criteria for defining new types then under discussion was a prohibition against altering various properties of reentry vehicles. At a meeting of the Special Coordination Committee, Harold Brown approved the inclusion of that measure in the U.S. position. The negotiators in Geneva were duly instructed to seek such a clause in the agreement. The Defense Department's technical experts belatedly realized that the restriction might boomerang and impede the U.S. in one of its own most secret, technologically advanced research and development programs—MARVs, or maneuverable reentry vehicles. These were in effect "smart" MIRVs which not only could home in on their individual targets but could take evasive action as they did so, penetrating an antiballistic missile system. Slocombe went to Brown and explained the problem. Unfazed, Brown went back to the

Special Coordination Committee and announced that the provision would have to be retracted. Paul Warnke still favored the stiffest possible definition of new types. "By proposing something and then un-proposing it," he argued, "we'll be giving the impression that we don't know what we're doing, and we'll be opening the way for more modernization of Soviet missiles." Modernization is antithetical to arms control. Warnke also noted the irony that in this case he was arguing for a "tougher" negotiating position while the Pentagon was pushing for a "softer" one.

But even when he was reversing himself, Harold Brown's position determined the outcome of the debate. Not only was he the President's single most trusted adviser on SALT, but he had both the civilian and the military experts of the Defense Department solidly behind him. Moreover, on this particular issue, Brown's position was, for once, consonant with the Soviets', since they, for their own reasons, opposed the more restrictive new-types definition (it would impinge on their vigorous MIRV testing program). Commented one of Warnke's aides, "The Joint Chiefs of Staff, the Office of the Secretary of Defense and the entire Soviet Union—it was pretty hard to buck a gang-up like that."

Warnke's frustration was sometimes visible and vocal. At another SCC meeting, Brown questioned a similarly problematic feature of the U.S. position, and Warnke asked, "Are you now going to take that one out too, Harold?" Vance, who sometimes played the peace-maker between Brown and Warnke, shook his head wearily and laughed. Despite moments of intense disagreement, Warnke and Brown tried hard to keep personal animosity out of their relationship and to minimize backbiting between their staffs. They would make a point of calling each other after a particularly quarrelsome meeting in order to smooth over ruffled feelings.

Disagreements over how stringent to make the new-types definition continued into 1978. The Arms Control and Disarmament Agency would advocate constraining measures, only to be undercut by the intelligence community, which would produce a study concluding that the measure in question could not be adequately verified by national technical means. After a Special Coordination Committee meeting in March, Molander's working group was ordered to revise its list of parameters, pruning out those that could not be verified with confidence.

By 1978, the list had been reduced to six items: (1) length of the booster, (2) maximum diameter, (3) number of stages, (4) fuel type of the booster, (5) payload or throw-weight, and (6) total weight of the missile at launch. Those were considered the essential features of an acceptable definition of new types. The U.S. wanted, if possible, to add to that list restrictions on the initial weight and power* of each stage and on the initial weight, power and fuel type of the post-boost vehicle (PBV), or "bus," the top stage which drops off the warheads that reenter the atmosphere. At first, the U.S. wanted the treaty simply to stipulate "no change" in any of the agreed parameters. The Russians replied with their old wisecrack: if they replaced a steel screw with a brass screw, would that constitute a violation? After much dickering, the two sides settled on the idea of quantitative boundaries within which either side could make adjustments without an existing missile being reclassified as a new type. The CIA decided that any alteration of less than 5 percent would be difficult to detect by aerial photography and remote monitoring, so in April 1978 the U.S. proposed plus or minus 5 percent as the permissible bounds for modification of an existing type of ICBM. A month later, at a plenary in Geneva, the Soviets responded that the U.S. was still seeking too long a list of parameters, but they indicated that once a shorter, less restrictive list had been agreed, plus or minus 5 percent would be an acceptable limit. There the issue remained through the summer and into the fall. Cyrus Vance had high hopes for the new-types definition as a "technological breakthrough" in SALT. "By limiting the parameters," he said, "and by getting plus or minus 5 percent [as the bounds for change within those parameters], we will be able to verify the rule, and we'll be able to assure ourselves that a modification will not constitute a new individual type of ICBM."

Scrambling and Spying

As they moved slowly toward an agreement on the definition of a new ICBM, the two sides found themselves confronted with a related and extremely sensitive issue: the encryption of telemetry during the flight testing of missiles. Telemetry is the electronic means by which a rocket, or a stage of a rocket, or a warhead sends back to earth data about its performance during a test flight. One way the U.S. polices Soviet compliance with SALT is to intercept and analyze Soviet

---

*Power as defined by the term from physics "total impulse."

telemetry. But the U.S. listens in on Soviet telemetry for purposes of espionage as well as arms control. It monitors Soviet tests to collect information that is valuable as military intelligence but irrelevant to the verification of agreements. The Soviets have never learned to live comfortably with the proficiency and what must seem to them like the near omniscience of American surveillance. As the most secretive and paranoid sectors of a secretive and paranoid society, the Soviet military and intelligence establishments have, by all indications, found American prying well nigh intolerable, regardless of whether monitoring is carried out in the name of arms control. Therefore the Soviets have, from time to time, scrambled or otherwise put into code their missile telemetry in order to inhibit remote eavesdropping by the U.S. It should be added that encryption also makes it harder for the Russians to read their own telemetry. The data is contained on lengthy computer printouts that look like a chaos of myriad broken lines on scores of channels, each line representing a fuel valve or a component of the guidance instrumentation as it switches on or off. Even when telemetry is transmitted in the clear, deciphering requires the most painstaking analysis by the technicians running the test as well as those spying on it. Every time the Russians have used code, officials in the U.S. government, particularly those in the intelligence community, have tended to give a nervous jump and worry about the long-term implications for SALT.

How could the U.S. be confident that the Soviet Union is abiding by SALT if the Russians encrypt their telemetry? It was a question that sparked heated debate within the government, but officials have traditionally been reluctant to raise the issue at the negotiating table with the Russians for a number of reasons. For one, the more the U.S. remonstrates with the Soviets about their encryption practices, the more the Soviets will know about the American capability to intercept and decode their transmissions. And the more the Soviets know, the easier it will be for them to take countermeasures. To make encryption a topic of negotiation, in short, is to run the risk of "compromising intelligence sources and methods." Also, American officials knew that if they remonstrated about encryption with the Russians, the ensuing conversation might not be entirely one-sided. The U.S., too, has used encryption and other methods of depriving foreign intelligence services of telemetric information about the testing of American systems, and the Pentagon has wanted to be able to do so in the future.

Said one member of the U.S. SALT delegation in Geneva, "Our

side has never encrypted anything that is SALT-related." A senior Pentagon official put it this way: "Our record is as pure as the driven snow where ICBM tests and encryption are concerned." Both men were choosing their words very carefully. But the Defense Department has, with the explicit approval of the Secretary of Defense in each case, used encryption in testing some shorter-range missiles and an antiballistic missile radar; on at least one occasion, the U.S. encrypted signals back to earth from a single-warhead ICBM, but the coded information concerned the performance of an ABM system "watching" the missile—not the performance of the missile itself. The U.S. has also transmitted telemetry at very low levels of power to highly directional antennas. Such a technique permits the use of a lighter-than-normal power pack aboard the top stage of the rocket. That means a lighter payload, which can be important in testing small ICBMs of the sort in which the U.S. specializes. But while the purpose of low-power telemetry transmission may simply be to save weight, its effect can be to make it more difficult for the other side to monitor the transmission. Thus, it can be a form of "telemetry denial." Also, the U.S. has used capsules—like the black-box flight recorders aboard airliners—to retrieve information about the performance of ICBM components during reentry into the atmosphere, when the extreme temperatures generated by friction make telemetric transmission impossible. Any comprehensive discussion of, or ban on, encryption would probably have to extend to low levels of power and encapsulation too, since capsules are even more effective than codes if one side wishes to "black out" a test. Codes, after all, can be—and often are—broken. Capsules must be—and almost never are—captured.

Because of the extreme complexity and sensitivity of the issue, encryption was, for a long time, not only never discussed in Geneva; the very word was taboo.* Under instructions from Washington, Paul Warnke and Ralph Earle sought Soviet assent in the U.S. position that the SALT prohibition against "deliberate concealment measures which impede verification by national technical means" covered what Warnke and Earle referred to only as "methods of transmitting tele-

---

*Until July 1976, even the word "telemetry" had been taboo in the negotiations. Henry Kissinger and two defense secretaries, James Schlesinger and Donald Rumsfeld, had all signed off on orders to the U.S. delegation in Geneva that telemetry was not to be mentioned in discussion of the ban on deliberate concealment measures. It was the Soviets who, for reasons that are still obscure, first introduced the word "telemetry" into the negotiations. The Carter administration then allowed the American negotiators to follow suit.

metric information." Alexander Shchukin, who was a specialist in radio wave theory and therefore the most knowledgeable Soviet negotiator on the subject of telemetry, sometimes teased the Americans: "Why are you delivering your message in code—encrypted, as it were?" But the Soviets talked in code too, and their message was quite different. They contended that the prohibition on "deliberate concealment measures which impede verification by national technical means" should not apply to "current test practices." Without uttering the taboo word, they were taking the position that telemetry used in missile tests is not relevant to SALT and that encryption of test telemetry should therefore be treated as an exemption to the ban against concealment measures.

Warnke and Earle argued that in testing, as in any other practices, the Soviets should be forbidden in SALT from doing anything that "impeded" verification. Warnke once asked one of the U.S. interpreters if "impede" meant the same thing in Russian that it means in English. It means "to make more difficult," the interpreter replied. "There," said Warnke to Semyonov. "We are simply asking you to undertake not to do anything in your testing practices that would make verification more difficult." By September 1977, Semyonov had finally conceded that point as a general principle, although without explicit reference to encryption. Warnke and Earle felt that the issue had been laid to rest—without either's ever having uttered the word. The Soviets would be allowed to use encryption to protect genuine intelligence secrets, such as matters relating to the guidance system of a missile, while the U.S. would be free to raise before the Standing Consultative Commission in Geneva any case in which there was a suspicion that the Soviets might be using encryption to camouflage information necessary for verification, such as the number of warheads and the throw-weight of the missile. Warnke, Earle and others were confident that the U.S. would know if encryption was being used to deprive American intelligence of information it needed for purposes of verification as opposed to espionage. The principal reason for their confidence was that the monitoring of telemetry is only one of a number of "national technical means" used to verify SALT, and there is considerable overlap—or "redundancy," as it is known—among those various means. Even if the Soviets successfully disguised a SALT-related feature of a missile test by encryption, that feature would likely show up on a radar screen or a satellite photograph or in some other piece of evidence available to the American monitors.

Also, the memory banks of the computers used by U.S. intelligence had already accumulated masses of telemetric data from the Soviet ICBM testing program. If a channel of telemetry regularly used to transmit SALT-related information in the past were suddenly scrambled or otherwise blacked out in a new test, the U.S. experts would be alerted to look even more closely at the evidence extracted by other national technical means, and if their suspicions were sustained, to ask the American representatives on the Standing Consultative Commission to challenge the Soviets. Most American officials were quite satisfied with the way the commission had worked throughout the life of SALT I. Each side had questioned suspicious or ambiguous activities of the other, and—with the notable exception of the environmental shelters at Malmstrom—the activity in question had been adequately explained, altered or halted. Warnke, Earle and like-minded officials back in Washington, including Vance, were certain that the consultative process could be extended to SALT II in a way that would guarantee American access to the Soviet telemetry necessary for verification of the new-types ban and the fractionation freeze.

But that sanguine view was not unanimous within the Carter administration, and in late 1977 the administration changed the signals it was sending to Geneva. CIA officials said they were increasingly concerned about their ability to verify a SALT II agreement that was explicit and restrictive in its definition of new types of missiles but circumspect and therefore seemingly permissive in the way it addressed the problem of encryption. Stansfield Turner, the director of Central Intelligence, and Robert Bowie, his principal deputy for National Intelligence Estimates, argued that they would not only have difficulty verifying the prospective treaty, they would have difficulty defending its ratification before the Senate, if encryption was dealt with obliquely. Ratification was increasingly on the minds of the policy-makers, and encryption went to the heart of the American grand obsession with verification. Ohio Senator John Glenn, the former astronaut, staked out encryption as "his" issue. As a congressional adviser to the SALT delegation, Glenn had visited Geneva in August 1977 and stressed to Semyonov and Shchukin that his vote for or against ratification would depend largely on how encryption was handled in the treaty. He also told the American negotiators that by avoiding mention of encryption, they were "obfuscating" the issue.

Over a period of months, the CIA changed its position a number of times. At one point, Turner and Bowie argued for an across-the-board ban on encryption—an idea that John Glenn and Paul Nitze advocated too. President Carter at one point said he could support an outright ban. But Cyrus Vance and Paul Warnke took the view that there was no way the Soviets would ever, under any circumstances, agree to a ban. Not only was it nonnegotiable; it was unnecessary. While SALT in general should strive for rigor and precision, encryption was one area where a little "creative imprecision" was in order. The Soviets had accepted the proposition that SALT entitles the U.S. to some but not all information about Soviet missile tests and therefore that test practices should not impede verification. Better to leave well enough alone, they felt. Harold Brown, Walter Slocombe and their Pentagon colleagues came down somewhere between the intelligence community and the State Department/Arms Control Agency position. They were uneasy about an outright ban on all encryption because it might complicate American practices, but they felt that the Soviets' acceptance of a proposition expressed in euphemisms was not enough, that imprecision was to be avoided, and that in pursuit of precision the negotiators should not allow themselves to be paralyzed by their presumption of what would be negotiable. In general, the Pentagon harbored the recurring criticism that Vance, Warnke, Earle and the others who had to deal with the Russians on a regular basis were too willing to let Soviet sensitivities and stubbornness set bounds for the American negotiating position. This criticism came sharply into focus on the issue of encryption. It was the Pentagon view that SALT II should include an explicit reference to encryption as something to be banned when it constituted deliberate concealment. Zbigniew Brzezinski sided with Brown, but he sometimes pretended to go even further and side with Turner in order to put pressure on Vance to come closer to Brown's middle-of-the-road position. At a series of meetings on the subject, according to a participant, "Zbig played Vance and Turner off against each other in a masterfully manipulative way. He was using Turner's hard line, which he didn't really agree with, to try to toughen up Vance's position, which he essentially sympathized with."

In December 1977, Warnke was ordered to bring up the matter of encryption explicitly with Vladimir Semyonov. Warnke did so over lunch in Geneva. He reviewed their earlier understanding that the ban on "deliberate concealment measures which impede verification" would extend to the testing of missiles. Then Warnke said, "I assume you agree this applies to encryption." The next day, after Warnke had returned to Washington, Earle repeated to Semyonov both orally and in writing the American interpretation that the ban on deliberate concealment "applies to encryption." Semyonov did not dispute the interpretation, but he did not endorse it either. "The agreed text," he said, "contains everything necessary" to provide the Standing Consultative Commission with a basis for resolving any problem that might come up. In subsequent discussions, Semyonov and his colleagues adopted a tactic that tended to confirm the feeling of Warnke, Earle and others directly involved in the negotiations that raising encryption explicitly was a mistake—and at the same time tended to confirm the feeling of Turner, Brown and others back in Washington that the Soviets were up to no good and had better be faced down on the issue sooner rather than later. The Soviet negotiators took the position that since the U.S. had other sources besides telemetry for data necessary to verify compliance, telemetry was not really relevant. They did not deny that *if* telemetry was, in some hypothetical case, relevant, then its encryption would constitute deliberate concealment and should not be allowed. But they seemed to be saying that they could not imagine such a case. Occasionally they would go on to say, in effect, "If you insist that you need telemetry and that our methods of transmitting it [i.e., in code] impede legitimate monitoring, for purposes of verification, then give us some examples." The Russians knew perfectly well that such a suggestion put the U.S. in a bind: how could U.S. officials in Geneva give their Soviet interlocutors cases in point of encryption that impeded without also giving Moscow new insight into U.S. "sources and methods" of intelligence gathering, thus making it easier for the Russians to thwart American detection and deciphering in the future?

Not that there was any shortage of examples to cite. On July 29, 1978, the Soviets fired a new version of a single-warhead SS-18 down one of their test ranges and encrypted its telemetry to an unprecedented extent. Telemetry from the booster had been coded before, but for the first time, encryption was used on those channels of telemetry that relayed back to earth information about the performance of the warhead, or reentry vehicle (RV). It was information that would help American analysts determine the weight of the warhead and therefore the payload or throw-weight of the missile. Thus it was information to which the U.S. would feel entitled under SALT II, since throw-weight was one of the parameters to be used in differentiating between a modified old type and a new type of ICBM. Even though the missile tested on July 29 was unMIRVed, the U.S. was concerned that the encryption of the same RV channels of telemetry, if extended to a multiple-warhead rocket, could complicate verification not just of the throw-weight constraints but of the fractionation freeze as well. The Russians' purpose in encrypting the RV channels in the July 29 test may have been threefold: they could well have been trying to hide some new improvement in their technology before SALT II came into force, but they were probably also seeking to lay down a base line of what they considered permissible encryption and at the same time probing the American ability to monitor such tests. "They were smoking us out," said one U.S. intelligence official. "They wanted to see how quickly we responded, how much we revealed about knowledge of their transmissions, and how upset we were."

Stansfield Turner was very upset indeed. At a series of meetings, he took a harder line than ever on encryption. Turner and the CIA, after all, were in the business of monitoring Soviet military activity, and no one could dispute that encryption made their task more difficult. By the same token, an outright ban on encryption would have made their job easier. It was a case in point of the Washington adage: "Where you stand is where you sit." Turner sat in a job that required him both to verify SALT and to defend its verifiability to the Senate, so it was not surprising that he stood for a ban on encryption.

On few issues in SALT have the national interests and negotiating strategies of the two sides been so clearly at odds as they were on encryption. The U.S. pursued a comprehensive definition of new types that would genuinely curtail the modernization of Soviet missiles. The more meaningful the definition, the more it required explicit restrictions on encryption in order to be verified. The Soviets, for their part, sought to minimize the number of parameters in the new-types definition in order to maintain the freedom to upgrade their missiles but also, some analysts have speculated, to maintain maximum freedom to encrypt. The encryption issue had brought the CIA into the center of SALT policy-making in Washington. No doubt the issue had a mirror-image effect in Moscow. The KGB and the other Soviet intelligence services almost certainly bridled at what they considered an American attempt to use an arms control agreement to pry deeper into Soviet military secrets. This complicating factor was only hinted at in Geneva, where Semyonov and his colleagues began making statements like, "National technical means does not legitimate overhead espionage." As one American official put it, "All of a sudden, the Soviets started taking the lofty and offended position that gentlemen do not read each other's telemetry." The U.S. negotiators persisted in arguing that for the new-types rule to be enforceable—indeed, for the overall prohibition against deliberate concealment to be meaningful —there had to be a "common understanding" which explicitly identified encryption as a testing practice that would be forbidden if it impeded verification. The pursuit of treaty language on that point was made more difficult by the fact that on this critical and delicate issue, the intelligence services of the two sides now had their backs up. They were taking a more active and mistrustful part in the home-office supervision of the Geneva negotiators than ever before.

12 Two Steps Forward, One Step Back

By the fall of 1978, there was a spreading and deepening sense within the Carter administration that SALT was in trouble if for no other reason than that it had gone on too long. It had already been six and a half years since the signing of SALT I, four years since the framework for SALT II had been agreed at Vladivostok, two years since Carter's election, one year since the expiration of SALT I—and almost that long since the President had first declared an agreement only a few weeks away. In meetings with his closest advisers, Carter expressed intense frustration. "I'm getting no credit for tough negotiating," he said. "I'm just getting beaten up on for failing to finish the thing." The process of SALT was in danger of bogging down, perhaps grinding to a halt. Proponents of SALT have always liked to talk about the "momentum" of the process. Now they were worried about its inertia. External forces were, as always, buffeting SALT, but now the negotiations seemed more vulnerable to derailment than they ever had in the past. Nineteen seventy-eight was a political year in the U.S. Criticism of the Soviet Union for its military build-up and its intervention in Africa was a theme in the congressional election campaigns around the country. So was criticism of the Carter administration for failing to do more to counteract the Russians. SALT was often mentioned in lists of the problems that Carter had so far failed to master and promises he had not yet been able to keep. The elusiveness of an agreement seemed to symbolize what was widely perceived as a basic problem of the Carter presidency: an inability to deliver. In the White House and at the State Department there was a feeling of urgency, sometimes bordering on desperation. There was also a sense that the enterprise was losing its dignity; the saga of SALT II was becoming a shaggy dog story. Breakthroughs on individual issues were no longer enough. "Serious and businesslike" meetings at which "progress" was made were no longer enough. To have entered the "trade-off phase" —to have begun the endgame—was no longer enough. There had to be a final deal, an end to the game, if the administration was effectively to refute the charges of its critics. As long as confidential negotiations were still under way and key provisions of the treaty were not yet agreed, the administration was at a considerable disadvantage in the debate that was already raging. Paul Nitze's Committee on the Present Danger had been in existence—and on the attack—for more than a year, arguing that the U.S. was falling dangerously behind the Soviet Union in military might and that SALT was part of the problem. The administration's self-defense would be severely hamstrung until it could go public with the negotiating record and the full text of the agreement itself.

"One of my real frustrations has been that it has taken us so long to get this far," said Cyrus Vance. "And the fact that the negotiations have dragged on and on has inhibited us from laying out the strengths of our position and from answering misleading or false statements that are being made by those who oppose SALT. This has given an impetus to the anti-SALT movement that it's going to take us a while to push back. If we'd been free to lay it all out to our critics as we went along, it would have been a lot better, but you have to deal with the realities of your negotiating parameters. God knows, it's been frustrating to read some of these stories and not be able to say, 'That's untrue! Here's what the actual facts are. . . .' It's just been frustrating the hell out of me."

If SALT in general was to survive as a permanent institution, SALT II had to be concluded soon. That meant there had to be an exertion of political will on both sides at the highest level. In the decade of SALT, the Soviet leaders had, on important occasions, showed themselves better able to close ranks behind the necessary compromises than the Americans. While the men in the Kremlin must worry a great deal about their personal prestige and bureaucratic power bases, they are unencumbered by concern about their reelection, about skeptical editorials in *Pravda,* and about unfriendly private lobbying groups made up of distinguished former Soviet government officials and military officers. That basic difference between the political systems of the two countries made it possible for Leonid Brezhnev in 1972 to take a position of linkage be damned and push through an agreement on the antiballistic missiles treaty and the interim agreement on offensive strategic weapons despite the American mining and bombing of North Vietnam a few weeks before. Brezhnev took another big step at Vladivostok in 1974, when he accepted equal aggregates and exempted U.S. forward-based systems from SALT II. But by 1978 Brezhnev's own energies were clearly flagging. Reports of illness and temporary incapacity were increasingly frequent and taken increasingly seriously. It was widely assumed that his ability to have his way within the Soviet leadership must be at least somewhat diminished. American Kremlinology had become partly an exercise in remote, speculative diagnosis of the Soviet president's physical condition. Uncertainty over Brezhnev's future made U.S. policy-makers feel that it was all the more important to wrap up SALT quickly, while the Soviet leader believed to be most committed to the success of the negotiations was still in office.

Already the pace of high-level talks was quickening. Andrei Gromyko was due to come to the U.S. for the United Nations General Assembly in September, and he would use the occasion to meet with Cyrus Vance on SALT. It would be the fourth such encounter in five months. Gromyko would meet with Carter too, and by then the politically beleaguered President would have reaped a windfall; he would be in his strongest position yet to exercise leadership of the sort necessary to deliver a SALT treaty. After nearly two weeks of intensive, secret talks at Camp David, he emerged on September 17 with Menachem Begin and Anwar Sadat at his side to announce an agreement on the contours of an Israeli-Egyptian peace treaty. Even though it was only a tentative and incomplete agreement and its consummation would prove difficult, the outcome of the Camp David summit was the single greatest triumph of Carter's foreign policy to date. The President felt a surge of confidence in his own statesmanship. So did many of his countrymen, according to the public opinion polls. The administration was determined to harness some of the uplift from Camp David and apply it to SALT. One of Carter's closest advisers later recalled the President's saying in the first days after Camp David that he hoped to "convert the force for peace-making we've unleashed here into something that will finally give us SALT." Carter the nuclear engineer was hoping for a chain reaction.

Depressed Trajectory

Paul Warnke had been dispatched to Moscow in early September to give the Soviet leadership an advance look at the American position awaiting Gromyko. It was the first time that the U.S. had chosen to prepare the ground for a Vance-Gromyko meeting in this way. In the past, the administration had relied on the two ambassadors, primarily Anatoly Dobrynin in Washington and occasionally Malcolm Toon in Moscow. But the National Security Council, notably Zbigniew Brzezinski and David Aaron, felt a lingering dissatisfaction with the ambassadorial "back channel." After two years at his post, Toon had still not been given anything like the official access in Moscow that Dobrynin enjoyed in Washington, and that fact continued to rankle in Brzezinski and Aaron. It offended their sense of reciprocity. Also, they continued to nurture doubts from time to time about Dobrynin's reliability as an intermediary and his grasp of the technical issues in SALT. They were still somewhat disconcerted by his habit of taking few if any notes during discussions of the most sensitive and complex details. The State Department and Arms Control Agency did not share the NSC's misgivings about Dobrynin, but they had no objection to sending Warnke to Moscow as an emissary in preparation for the September Vance-Gromyko meeting. Doing so would foster the impression that the occasional but well publicized tensions between the White House and Foggy Bottom had been brought under control and that the administration was solidly united behind the position that Warnke was taking to Moscow. Moreover, there was little danger of seeming to bypass Dobrynin, since he was on home leave in the U.S.S.R.

Warnke's mission was primarily to clarify and amplify the U.S. position that was already on the table between the permanent delegations in Geneva. His task, as he put it at the time, was to "review the bidding." The U.S. wanted a definition of cruise missiles that would allow the unfettered deployment of conventionally armed ALCMs on aircraft other than heavy bombers after the expiration of the protocol; it wanted a definition of cruise missile range that included "delta overages"; and while insisting that the MIRVing of existing types of ICBMs should be frozen at the number of warheads already tested, the U.S. wanted the treaty to permit the MX as many as ten warheads. Warnke was also authorized to hint some flexibility on the average number of cruise missiles per bomber—the U.S. was then asking for

35—if the Soviets would accept a missile fractionation freeze in accordance with the American proposal.

But Warnke's package included at least one new item—a proposed ban on testing ballistic missiles that would follow a so-called depressed trajectory, a flattened flight path which would allow them to cover the distance between launch point and target in much less time than a conventional high-arching parabolic trajectory. A depressed-trajectory missile, particularly if fired from a submarine in a staging area off the coast of the target country, would be an effective instrument of surprise attack. It would increase the capability of one side to destroy the other's bombers before they could take off from their runways and its submarines before they could leave their ports. A depressed-trajectory missile, therefore, would be a highly destabilizing addition to the arsenals of the superpowers. However, no such thing existed in 1978, nor were there any known plans for such a thing on either side. Nor had the issue of depressed trajectory come up at a high level in SALT before Warnke raised the matter with the Soviets in Moscow. It arose now, very much at the eleventh hour, because of SALT's increasing susceptibility—and Jimmy Carter's increasing receptivity—to the efforts of members of Congress to influence the substance of the U.S. position and the course of the negotiations.

SALT was such a copious grab bag of political and military problems that there was something for almost every senator and representative who wanted to play a part. Sam Nunn carved out Eurostrategic affairs in general and cruise missile definition in specific as his specialties. John Glenn did much the same thing with verification by national technical means and the problem of telemetry encryption. Depressed trajectory was the hobby-horse of two young, liberal Democratic representatives with an interest in defense policy and a strong belief that SALT should anticipate and prevent destabilizing technological advances. Robert Carr of Michigan and Thomas Downey of New York were both among the original fourteen congressmen appointed by the Speaker of the House as advisers to the SALT delegation in 1977. In early 1978 they attended a briefing at the Arms Control and Disarmament Agency at which they were told that one of the U.S. objectives in SALT was to "drive the Soviets out to sea"— that is, to induce the Russians to divert resources from their land-based missiles to their submarine force. Intercontinental ballistic missiles were considered much more threatening than submarine-launched ballistic missiles because of their superior range, power and accuracy.

Soviet ICBMs were counterforce weapons—hard-target killers that threatened Minuteman; Soviet SLBMs were not. It was partly for that reason that the U.S. sought a new-types ban on Soviet ICBMs much more doggedly than on SLBMs. But Carr and Downey began to worry that the strategy of "driving the Soviets out to sea" might prove short-sighted if the Russians were ever able to use their seagoing launchers to strike preemptively against the American airborne and submarine deterrents. As Carr explained later: "The whole purpose of SALT was to try to get a handle on the Soviet threat to our land-based deterrent while beefing up the other two legs of our triad. Well, if we ended up by putting the Soviets in a position where they not only still had a considerable ability to threaten our land-based deterrent but were better able to threaten our bombers and subs as well, then we'd have cut off our noses to spite our faces."

The congressmen raised the issue of depressed trajectory with Ralph Earle during a visit to Geneva. He pointed out that defining depressed trajectory would be a problem in itself, since "every time you launch an SLBM that fails, its trajectory would be 'depressed' and you may have technically violated the treaty," but he told the congressmen that the Soviets might consider a ban. Carr and Downey then took their case to President Carter himself in early August. Carter was interested in the notion of a ban on the testing of de-pressed-trajectory missiles as a "crisis-stabilizing element" for possible inclusion in SALT. Through the Special Coordination Committee, he ordered up an addition to the negotiating package that Warnke carried with him to Moscow in September. The Soviet reaction was predictable—raised eyebrows and stiffened backs. The Russians tended to regard all surprises as unpleasant. Ever since the comprehensive proposal of March 1977, the Soviets had been especially suspicious and resentful of the American penchant for improvisation. Now here were the Americans changing their position again. But after considerable haggling, the Soviets said they might consider a ban on depressed-trajectory missiles—if it was part of a comprehensive treatment of the problem of sneak attack, including severe limits on antisubmarine warfare (ASW). At one point the Russians floated the idea of "ASW-free zones," a sort of underwater version of the ABM treaty, and perhaps a submarine-free zone too. The U.S. Navy was far ahead of the Soviet Union in both ASW and submarine technology and was determined to hold that edge, so the Carter administration eventually withdrew the depressed-trajectory ban from its SALT II position, and it was agreed instead to deal with the problem of sneak attack in SALT III. The whole episode had demonstrated that Jimmy Carter was more eager than ever to accommodate congressional concerns about SALT. It also demonstrated that he still prided himself on being interested in bold, innovative steps in the direction of "real arms control," even if those steps risked complicating the negotiations. Certainly the last-minute addition of depressed trajectory to the agenda did nothing to improve the chances for a final breakthrough at the Vance-Gromyko meetings in New York and Washington at the end of September.

The Eleventh-Hour Squeeze

While the U.S. generally took care to give the Soviets an advance look at the American negotiating position before a high-level meeting, the Russians almost never reciprocated. U.S. officials justified this procedural inequity on the grounds that the preview was not a courtesy to the Russians—it was a negotiating tactic: the Soviets were more likely to show flexibility at a meeting if they knew exactly what to expect and had a chance to prepare their concessions ahead of time. The American governmental process was more adaptable than the Russians'. The Soviets moved purposefully but slowly. The Americans were more willing to improvise. The American SALT team could adjust to a change in the Soviet position much more quickly than the other way round, and the President of the U.S. could make a decision more quickly than the Politburo. Therefore giving the Soviets an advance look at the U.S. position before each meeting was justified in Washington as making an allowance for Soviet weakness rather than granting the Russians an advantage. Still, in the weeks between Warnke's return from Moscow and Gromyko's arrival in the U.S., the suspense on the American side was mixed with annoyance that the Russians, as usual, said little to indicate whether they were prepared to move on any of the outstanding issues. Once again, they just absorbed Warnke's presentation noncommittally.

They said much, however, to bolster the impression that SALT was approaching a moment of truth. The Soviet press referred to SALT as a "task of supreme urgency." Gromyko called it a "grim truth" that the negotiators might soon face the last chance to reach an agreement. Many American officials also sensed that SALT was approaching a point of make-or-break, but they expressed their intimations more optimistically than the Russians. Paul Warnke said he expected that

the upcoming round would be the last Vance-Gromyko meeting before an agreement was concluded. He suggested that the trade-offs
necessary to produce an agreement were relatively few and readily
negotiable: "It's like a Chinese menu. You can have one choice from
column A and three from column B, or you can take some other
combination—as long as you end up with a balanced mix and as long
as you stay within the fixed price."

The day before Vance and Gromyko were to begin their talks, both
sides had a brief scare. Gromyko was delivering an address to the
United Nations General Assembly. He was denouncing the Camp
David summit on the Middle East as "a new anti-Arab step that makes
it difficult to achieve a just solution." Suddenly he slumped forward
onto the podium. Aides rushed forward to help him out of the hall.
Fifty-five minutes later he returned to the rostrum and finished his
speech, explaining that he had collapsed because of the "very, very
hot lights." News of the incident was flashed immediately to the White
House Situation Room, where it caused intense concern. No longer
was Gromyko regarded, as he had been by Kissinger, as a mere mouth-
piece for the Kremlin on SALT. Since his elevation to the Politburo
in 1973, he had gained influence, confidence and a greater knowledge
of the subject. By 1978 he was considered a key figure in the making
of Soviet policy on SALT. His death or incapacitation would almost
unquestionably have set back the negotiations, especially since Brezhnev's own health was so much in doubt. "For a long hour there,"
recalled an American official, "we thought Gromyko had had a heart
attack. We were ready to kiss SALT good-bye for another six months
at least."

The next day, however, Vance arrived at the Soviet U.N. mission
in New York and found Gromyko looking fit and joking about his
fainting spell. Vance himself was still feeling the effects of a politically
frustrating and physically exhausting whirlwind tour of Jordan, Saudi
Arabia and Syria which had ended only a few days before. After the
meeting he reported to Zbigniew Brzezinski that Gromyko "seemed
at least as chipper as me—maybe a bit more so."

Vance and Gromyko negotiated intensively in New York, then flew
to Washington for a session with Carter. The most important development at that round of meetings was a Soviet concession on cruise
missile ranges. But it was a concession with an important condition
attached and an obvious ulterior motive. Gromyko said that his government would be willing to do away with the 2,500-kilometer range

limit for air-launched cruise missiles altogether in exchange for American acceptance of a strict definition of the 600-kilometer range limit for the deployment of ground-launched and sea-launched cruise missiles in the protocol.* Six hundred kilometers was also the base-line figure used to define long-range ALCMs aboard bombers that would count against the 1,320 subceiling. A strict definition of 600 kilometers would mean no allowance for delta overages or wiggle factor. The Soviets wanted cruise missile range defined as the maximum distance the missile can fly measured by projecting its flight path onto the earth's surface. As long as range was strictly defined, Gromyko told Carter with a magnanimous sweep of his hand, "You can fly your air-launched cruise missiles around the world if you like."

By proposing to eliminate the 2,500-kilometer range limit in exchange for a rigorous 600-kilometer limit, Gromyko was signaling a number of Soviet concerns. First, the Russians were clearly more worried about preventing West Germany from having a ground-launched cruise missile that could reach into the U.S.S.R. than they were about inhibiting the ability of American air-launched cruise missiles to penetrate Soviet air defenses and reach targets deep inside the Soviet Union. However it was defined, cruise missile range was difficult to verify by national technical means, but delta overages compounded that difficulty. So by insisting on a strict definition of the 600-kilometer range limit, the Soviets were using against the U.S. the Americans' own long-standing insistence that all provisions of SALT must be verifiable—or as verifiable as possible. The Russians were shoring up their contention that the U.S. position on cruise missile definition—with its exemption for conventionally armed ALCMs after the expiration of the protocol—was unverifiable and therefore unacceptable. Also, the Kremlin knew that Harold Brown and the Pentagon were uncomfortable with the 2,500-kilometer range limit on ALCMs because they feared it might eventually hamper the effectiveness of the Air Force's cruise missile carriers. So by giving up that upper range limit on ALCMs, the Soviets hoped to induce the Pentagon to be more flexible on a gamut of other issues. Said a Soviet afterward: "We knew how much importance the Defense Department attached to its long-range cruise missiles on bombers, and we

---

*Just as Warnke had given Gromyko a sneak preview of American flexibility in Moscow earlier that month, Semyonov and Shchukin had, in their conversations in Geneva with Warnke and Earle, hinted that Gromyko might be bringing a partial concession on cruise missile range.

were doing everything we could to make it easier for the Pentagon to be reasonable on matters that we considered to be of equally great importance."

Specifically, the Soviets were hoping that if they threw the Pentagon a bone on ALCM range, the U.S. would then agree to the Soviet position that the definition of cruise missiles should not distinguish between nuclear and conventional armaments. The immediate effect of Gromyko's proposal, however, was the opposite. The American side feared that many NATO planners and their friends on Capitol Hill would see a stringent definition of the protocol range limits on ground-launched and sea-launched cruise missiles as impinging even further on the West European interest in long-range GLCMs and SLCMs. That would seem to put a greater onus than ever on the U.S. to protect that other West European interest—in conventionally armed cruise missiles. Hence the initial American response to Gromyko's proposal was that the U.S. would accept a strict lower limit on cruise missile range only if the Soviets agreed with the long-standing U.S. proposal to exempt from SALT conventionally armed ALCMs on other than heavy bombers after the expiration of the protocol. As was often the case during the endgame of SALT, the interlocking quality of the outstanding issues hindered, rather than helped, the two sides in their efforts to find compromises.

In the course of his visit to the U.S., Gromyko explained his own view of the interrelationship among the remaining problems. "The talks have now reached a stage where the solution to the questions depends on the sum total of other open issues, and they must all be considered and resolved in one context," he said. "If you were to isolate one of these questions and take it out of the general context, it might lend itself to a fairly easy solution. Only you cannot isolate these questions. . . . If I had a ball of twine at my disposal, I could show you that graphically."

Gromyko's ball of twine would have illustrated that the remaining issues of SALT were all tied together. The piece of string representing the definition of cruise missile range was tightly knotted at the end to another piece representing the definition of an air-launched cruise missile warhead. That in turn, because it concerned the definition of aircraft armed with ALCMs, would be attached to the string representing "bomber fractionation," or the number of ALCMs per heavy bomber. And that would be connected with the string representing missile warhead fractionation, which was connected with the definition of new types of ICBMs, which was connected with missile telemetry and its encryption, and so on.

But there had been, ever since shortly after the Vladivostok summit of 1974, one loose piece of string in SALT. That was the issue of the Backfire bomber. The Carter administration had resigned itself to securing collateral restraints on the bomber outside the formal SALT agreement. At the meeting in Washington in September 1977, Gromyko had offered a list of specifications on the aircraft and some measures that the Soviets said they would undertake in order to ensure that the plane did not become an intercontinental heavy bomber. The specifications were questionable ("if they were true," said an American official, "then you had to wonder why they ever built the plane in the first place") and the assurances were far from adequate. The issue was relegated to parallel negotiating channels between Vance and Dobrynin and between Leslie Gelb and Alexander Bessmertnykh. For a long time the U.S., largely at the instigation of the Joint Chiefs of Staff, sought, among other things, restrictions on where Backfire could be deployed. These proposed basing restraints, along with limits on the number that could be produced each year and restrictions of the number and size of tankers that could offer midair refueling to the bomber, were meant to keep Backfire from threatening the U.S. The Soviets categorically refused to consider basing restrictions. Bessmertnykh said on a number of occasions that it was impermissible for the U.S. to try to "dictate" to the Soviet government where on its own territory it could deploy a weapon.

"It is one thing for us to accept certain reasonable limits on refueling so that you can be sure it won't reach the U.S.," said Dobrynin. "But we will not be told where it can be based. Within our own country, we will base it wherever we want." Vance, Warnke and Gelb also felt that basing restraints were a bad idea, both for the reason Dobrynin and Bessmertnykh stressed—it was an affront to national sovereignty—and because it would afford little extra security to the U.S.; even if the Russians accepted the "dictates" of SALT on where they could base the Backfire, in a moment of crisis they could quickly redeploy the planes forward, to bases closer to the U.S. By mid 1978 the Joint Chiefs had second thoughts of their own. They began to question whether there might not be a dangerous precedent if the Soviets were to accept basing restraints on Backfire. What reciprocal restrictions might the Soviets demand on the deployment of American systems inside the U.S.? General David Jones, the chairman of the Joint Chiefs, came up with a new idea for dealing with the Backfire problems. The U.S. should confront the Russians with an American intention to "count or counter" the Backfire: either the bomber would count against the SALT ceiling—as the JCS still preferred—or the U.S. would dramatically upgrade its air defenses, with squadrons of interceptors, improved radar and antiaircraft missiles. It was a hugely expensive proposition. Instead, David Aaron suggested "countering" the controversial Soviet bomber with what he called "our own Backfire," which would not count as a strategic weapon but might be subject to restraints on production and refueling. Aaron made his suggestion at a Special Coordination Committee meeting. Brzezinski brought the President into the meeting, and Carter seized on the idea as a good one. The Air Force's candidate for the "counter-Backfire" was an advanced version of the swing-wing, supersonic FB-111 medium bomber. At the September 1978 meeting in Washington, almost exactly a year after Gromyko had brought the first list of Soviet assurances on Backfire, Carter told Gromyko that the U.S. reserved the right to deploy a "comparable aircraft." Disagreements remained over exactly how many Backfires a year the Soviets would be allowed to produce and what additional assurances they must provide, but the "count or counter" solution went a long way toward removing the issue of the Backfire as an obstacle to a SALT II agreement.

The meeting had gone so well that a number of American officials hoped that Vance and Gromyko might be able to tie up the loose ends in SALT in a matter of days. As Warnke had hinted to the Russians already, Carter indicated to Gromyko that he might compromise on the average number of cruise missiles per bomber if the Soviets would accept the American position that the MX be allowed ten warheads. The President signaled flexibility on some of the other outstanding issues, too. Gromyko cabled back to Moscow a report of his Saturday session with Carter, and on Sunday he held a previously unscheduled meeting with Vance at the State Department. That, too, was encouraging. The U.S. negotiators remembered how the year before, Gromyko had come back to see the President a second time, bringing with him a number of important concessions from the Politburo. But there was to be no repetition this time. Instead of staying in the U.S. to await instructions from the Kremlin for another round of talks then and there, Gromyko flew home after the Sunday meeting. "We were annoyed as hell that Gromyko left the way he did," said one of the principal American negotiators afterward. "Carter had made some courageous decisions. Gromyko should have stayed and seen it through. It was just one more instance of his playing poker for its own sake."

Carter himself was disappointed and angry. He commented in a meeting with his staff that the Soviets seemed to be "dragging it out" and that he was "impatient and frustrated—do the Russians want it or don't they?" Yes, the Russians wanted a SALT agreement, but they must have sensed Carter's impatience. They may have calculated that he wanted it so badly that they could extract a few more concessions just by waiting him out, applying what veteran American negotiators called the eleventh-hour squeeze. Also, while the remaining issues were few and Carter had signaled flexibility on some of them, it is difficult to see in retrospect how Gromyko could have resolved all of them, even with the most forthcoming of replies from the Kremlin. Therefore it may have been disappointing, but it should not have been so surprising that there would have to be at least one more Vance-Gromyko round—the eighth such meeting since the beginning of the administration.

A Treaty or an Agreement?

With every meeting that failed to produce an agreement, the President's political advisers became more worried about ratification. Hamilton Jordan and Frank Moore, the White House's chief lobbyist, began to think more and more about the possibility of sending SALT II to the Congress as an agreement, requiring a simple majority of both houses, rather than a treaty, requiring approval by two thirds of the Senate. Walter Mondale had always been concerned that submitting SALT II as a treaty would put the administration in the uncomfortable, and possibly unwinnable, position of having to woo a handful of conservative senators whose support, however expensive politically, might be crucial to passage of the treaty. Many members of the House of Representatives—including Robert Carr and Thomas Downey as well as Clement Zablocki of Wisconsin, the chairman of the International Relations Committee—had urged Carter to let both chambers pass judgment on the agreement. There was certainly a compelling precedent. The SALT I interim accord on offensive strategic weapons had been approved as an agreement. Its duration had been five years. SALT II, if it was finally signed and approved in 1979, would last only six years, until 1985. Even Senator Alan Cranston, one of the leading supporters of SALT, once suggested to Cyrus Vance and his assistant for congressional affairs, Douglas Bennet, that they consider sending SALT up as an agreement to both houses in order to prevent a minority of the Senate from being able to block passage, although Cranston later changed his mind about the wisdom of the idea. Carter himself had wanted all along at least to have the option of submitting SALT II as an agreement, requiring only simple-majority approval. At the State Department and the Arms Control Agency, however, it had been a foregone conclusion since early 1977 that SALT II could only be a treaty, requiring endorsement by two-thirds of the Senate. It was designated as such in the Joint Draft Text under negotiation in Geneva —a fact that angered Carter when he saw the document. "How come it says 'treaty' here?" he demanded in a meeting. "Didn't I say a hundred times I might want to send it up as an agreement?" Mondale once exploded at what he called the "yahoos at the State Department who'd better learn the difference between a treaty and an agreement if they're going to keep working for this administration." One of the "yahoos," of course, was Vance himself. He and Warnke both favored submitting SALT II as a treaty. They figured that to do otherwise would be politically counterproductive. It would antagonize virtually the entire Senate. Friends and foes of SALT alike would see it as a cowardly and possibly unconstitutional ploy to circumvent their collective veto. Nevertheless, Jordan and Moore prevailed on the President to make sure that the document being negotiated in Geneva could be submitted either as a treaty or as an agreement. The interagency SALT Backstopping Committee fired off a cable to the delegation ordering the insertion of an asterisk after the first reference to "treaty" in the heading of the JDT. The asterisk called attention to a footnote saying that the term "agreement/treaty" was used "without prejudice to the form of the document, which will be decided by the governments." The Soviets did not take the matter terribly seriously. They saw the asterisk as a symbol of what they regarded as the basic capriciousness of American democracy.*

---

*As Vance and Warnke had predicted, most senators, including Alan Cranston, were outraged when they learned that the administration was reserving the right to submit the document as an agreement. The asterisk remained in the JDT until the last weeks of the negotiating, but Carter finally committed himself publicly to sending it up to the Hill as a treaty requiring two-thirds approval for ratification.

The Anticlimactic Meeting

Vance agreed to try again with Gromyko in Moscow in October. He accepted the Soviet invitation without checking with Carter first. The President was angry that the secretary of state had not insisted that the next meeting be in Geneva. In Carter's view, if the Soviets were going to drag their feet, then let them do it on neutral ground. But Vance had already accepted the Soviets' invitation, and he hoped that the physical proximity of the negotiations to the Politburo might make it easier to get quick and favorable Soviet decisions during the talks. His aides were billing the mission in advance as "the last mile," "the final round," "the climactic meeting," "a real showdown." It was a curious mixture of impatience, bluff and optimism. Some officials, like Leslie Gelb, were saying, in effect, that this time it really was all or nothing, make or break—and success or failure was up to the Russians; this time the outcome of the meeting depended on what Gromyko was carrying in *his* briefcase. "The U.S. can simply make no new movement," said one of the negotiators shortly before leaving. "We're going to hear what the Russians have to say now that they've thought over what we had to say last month. This time it's really their turn, once and for all." Others, like Paul Warnke, were saying that there was room for movement on both sides and that just a little compromise would bring the two together. The seasonal motto "SALT by Christmas!" was again in the air along the Potomac.

But the Soviets, who no more believed in Christmas in 1978 than they had in 1977, did not feel in the least bound by any American deadline. A Russian diplomat commented at the time, with a mixture of bemusement and contempt: "Your government is really quite extraordinary. It works itself into a frenzy of public expectations and then blames us when those expectations are proved unrealistic. Does your President really think that we are going to compromise our principles so that he can give the American people a great big Christmas present? If he's that anxious, then let him compromise *his* principles and pay for the present that way. We're not going to buy it for him. We don't owe him anything."

When Vance arrived at the negotiating table in the Kremlin, Gromyko had, as usual, one largely symbolic giveaway to demonstrate his government's magnanimity and commitment to the lofty goals of arms control. The concession involved prior notification of missile tests. In one of his very first press conferences, in February 1977, Carter had set as part of his goal in SALT an agreement whereby each side would notify the other in advance of ICBM tests. Such a provision was designed to decrease the chances that a test—especially a test in which a number of rockets were launched at once—might be mistaken for the beginning of an attack. Prior notification would also make it easier for the two sides to monitor each other's ICBM programs. The Soviets resisted the idea for the same reason they resisted an agreed data base and a modified ban on encryption: it ran against their grain to make the work of American intelligence easier. So for nearly two years, the U.S. and the Soviet negotiators had been haggling over whether advance notification should be required for test flights that stayed within national boundaries or just for "extraterritorial" launches into the Pacific Ocean, for single launches or just for multiple ones—and over the minimum permissible interval between launches that were to be considered separate rather than simultaneous. At the Moscow meeting, the Soviets agreed to give advance notification of all extraterritorial launches and all tests that would involve more than one ICBM in flight at the same time. In acceding to the Americans on this "confidence-building measure," the Soviets made clear that they were going out of their way to accommodate President Carter on something about which he personally felt strongly and in which he had invested his prestige. Thus, by underscoring the importance they attached to a leader's word, the Soviets were using the advance notification issue to score points for their own position— and Leonid Brezhnev's promise—on Backfire.

There was progress on other matters too, but it was, in a way so characteristic of SALT, progress accompanied by problems. Gromyko told Vance that the Soviets had decided to accept the American "averaging approach" to the number of air-launched cruise missiles allowed on heavy bombers rather than the strict limit of 20 ALCMs per plane that Moscow had insisted on earlier. In response, the U.S. lowered its proposal for the average number from 35 to 30, and the Soviets inched upward from 20 to 25. But while moving two steps forward on the issue of bomber fractionation, the Soviets moved one big step backward on the related issue of missile fractionation. Gromyko reminded his guests that the Soviet acceptance of a warhead freeze on existing types of ICBMs in July had been conditional; it had depended on American acceptance of a strict limit on ALCMs per bomber rather than the averaging approach. Since the Russians were now yielding to the U.S. on the averaging approach, Gromyko continued, their earlier concession on the MIRV freeze was no longer operative. At first the Soviets planted themselves firmly on their earlier position that the SS-17, currently with four warheads, should be allowed as many as the other "light" Soviet ICBM, the SS-19, with six —and that the American MX should be limited to six warheads too, since it was required to be a light missile. By the end of the meeting, the U.S.S.R. had modified its position so as to allow ten warheads on the MX—but also to allow ten for the SS-17 and SS-19. Said a Soviet shortly afterward: "Your government argued that it needed the MX as an answer to our SS-18. Well, from our standpoint, we needed the SS-19 as an answer to your MX."

The Soviets had confronted the U.S. with a choice between two alternatives, neither acceptable: a fractionation freeze that allowed the Russians to add two warheads to the SS-17 but did not allow the U.S. as many warheads on its new type of ICBM as the Russians had on their largest existing ICBM—or a fractionation freeze that allowed both sides to go as high as ten warheads on both existing and new types. That would mean no meaningful freeze at all. "Allowing ten RVs [reentry vehicles] across the board would shoot down the whole new-types provision in flames," commented one American negotiator. "You'd have promiscuous fractionation—fractionation run amok." The whole Soviet performance, sighed another haggard American official, "was like one good news/bad news joke after another."

The U.S. response to these Soviet maneuvers was to treat as agreed in principle those aspects of the Soviet position that suited the U.S. position and to reject or ignore those that the U.S. did not like. Thus, the Americans chose to interpret the Soviet negotiating position then on the table as including: *(a)* acceptance of an averaging approach to bomber fractionation; *(b)* acceptance of a freeze of MIRVs at the number already tested on existing types of ICBMs; and *(c)* acceptance of the principle that the one allotted new type of ICBM could have as many warheads as the largest existing type—i.e., ten reentry vehicles for the MX. Never mind that the Soviets had agreed to those three elements only provisionally, at different times and in combination with other elements that the U.S. considered unacceptable. "The Russians," commented one American, "were confronting us with a challenge; we would now have to test the proposition that once they'd accepted something, they couldn't unaccept it." A number of Americans were reasonably confident that the U.S. would ultimately get its

way on all three points—an averaging approach to bomber fractionation, a meaningful MIRV freeze on existing types of ICBMs, and the
freedom to put ten warheads on the MX. They calculated that the
Soviets would not have agreed to any of those provisions, even tentatively and conditionally, unless the Kremlin had decided it could live
with them as part of the final agreement.

The option of MIRVing the MX with ten warheads was, it should
be recalled, an important political selling point for SALT II. The
Carter administration wanted to be able to tell the Congress that while
the Soviets had a one-sided right to rockets as big as the SS-18, the U.S.
had the right to as many warheads on the MX as the Soviets could put
on the SS-18. The MX, whether it was deployed in a mobile mode or
in fixed sites, would be considerably smaller than the SS-18 and classified as a "light" missile. Nullifying the perceived Soviet advantage in
"heavy" missiles had been of constant concern to the administration.
At a Special Coordination Committee meeting early in 1978, Paul
Warnke had asked whether the Defense Department and the Joint
Chiefs wanted him and his fellow negotiators to keep open the option
of deploying a mobile heavy missile under SALT II. The SALT I ban
on new heavy missiles that was to be carried over into SALT II applied
to fixed-site heavies. The deployment of intercontinental mobile missiles of any size was to be banned only in the SALT II protocol. After
the expiration of the protocol, the U.S. could—under the treaty as it
was drafted in early 1978—deploy a monster rocket as big as the SS-18
aboard a submarine or a giant airplane or on an underground track or
in any other mobile basing mode that the Pentagon could devise. Did
Harold Brown and the Joint Chiefs want such a thing? Should the
negotiators protect such an option? The Defense Department studied
the matter for months and finally came back to Warnke with an answer: no, the U.S. military could see no use for a mobile heavy missile
of its own, so SALT should ban such a thing for the entire treaty
period, lest the Soviets develop one. It was the answer that Warnke
had been hoping for. It vindicated his position, and Leslie Gelb's, that
despite the grumbling of American generals and admirals, the Soviet
"advantage" in heavy missiles was all but meaningless. Whatever its
political unseemliness, the apparent asymmetry in "heaviness" per se
was of little military importance. What mattered in the strategic balance was the number of warheads, not the brute size of the rocket.
The U.S. was determined to have the right to as many warheads on
the MX as the Soviets had on the SS-18. The Soviets had finally ac-

cepted that principle. So at the Moscow meeting in October 1978, the U.S. proposed—and the Soviets agreed to—a ban in the treaty on heavy mobiles.

Untying the Knot

On the increasingly contentious and vital matter of the encryption of telemetry, the Moscow meeting was marked by a large and awkward Soviet step backward. The move seemed to be related, in a way that was not entirely clear at the time, to mounting Soviet annoyance over the U.S. proposal for a definition of cruise missiles that permitted the unconstrained deployment of conventionally armed ALCMs after the expiration of the protocol. Since Gromyko's visit to New York and Washington the month before, Vladimir Semyonov had been taking a hard line on the outstanding issues at the permanent negotiations in Geneva—particularly on the issue of cruise missile definition: the U.S.S.R. was as determined as ever to treat nuclear-armed and conventional ALCMs alike. At the same time, he adopted the ploy of pretending that the related issue of cruise missile range definition had been disposed of between Gromyko and Carter in September, much as the U.S. pretended that the Soviets had irrevocably accepted the American proposal for a fractionation freeze. "Since we've agreed on cruise missile range . . ." Semyonov would say. Ralph Earle would have to correct him: "No, Mr. Minister, we haven't agreed on that yet. The resolution of that issue, you'll recall, remains contingent on the satisfactory resolution of some others." The U.S. would agree to calculate cruise missile range strictly by the odometer, without an allowance for evasive action, if the Russians agreed to an exemption for conventionally armed ALCMs in the treaty. Yet Semyonov was as firm as ever in rejecting such an exemption. "Each time we address this subject," he said, "we are trying to find stronger words."

On the issue of telemetry, the Soviets had pulled back to the stronghold of their earlier complaint that by seeking a modified restriction on encryption, the U.S. was overstepping the bounds between arms control and espionage, between monitoring compliance and prying into legitimate military secrets. A few days before Vance was to meet Gromyko in Moscow, Warnke joined Earle in Geneva and together they faced down Semyonov on the issue: the treaty must spell out, in a "common understanding," that some telemetry is relevant to some provisions of SALT and therefore encryption of telemetry should be banned as a deliberate concealment measure "whenever it impedes" verification. The word "whenever" was carefully chosen to imply that encryption does indeed sometimes impede. Had the key three words been "*if* it impedes," the Soviets might have found it easier to accept the provision and then argue that in fact encryption never impedes and is therefore always permitted. For that reason the Americans made a point of always saying "when," not "if," in discussing encryption as a deliberate concealment measure. Without a limited ban cast in those terms, said Warnke to Semyonov sternly, the treaty could not be properly verified; moreover, it could not—indeed, should not—be ratified. "I'm prepared to be criticized," said the much criticized Warnke, who had already announced his intention to return to private law practice, "but I'm not prepared to be ridiculed." In the course of a two-and-a-half-hour meeting, Semyonov finally conceded that insofar as telemetry is relevant to the verification of SALT, its encryption could be prohibited by SALT.

But an extraordinary thing happened in Moscow a few days later when Vance arrived there for another round of talks with Gromyko. Semyonov was repudiated by his own bosses. When Vance referred to the exchange that Warnke and Earle had had with Semyonov a few days before in Geneva, Semyonov suddenly appeared very worried and started shuffling through his notes, looking for a memorandum with which to refute the American version of what he had said. Gromyko told Vance that the Soviet government still maintained that the telemetry of missile tests was irrelevant to the provisions of SALT. Georgy Kornienko told Warnke that on this question Semyonov "didn't understand our position." Over lunch, Warnke sat next to Gromyko and the subject came up again. "You can encrypt as long as it doesn't impede," said Warnke, "but you can't carve out an exemption for encryption altogether." Gromyko replied in English: "On this question I am like a stone wall." Warnke told the foreign minister, "Well, you'd better stop being like a stone wall, because this is an extremely important issue if the agreement is to be verified and ratified."

The Americans were puzzled that the Soviet policy-makers would so bluntly undercut their own negotiator. When the Kremlin announced shortly afterward that Semyonov was being transferred from the post of chief SALT negotiator to that of ambassador to West Germany, there was even speculation in Washington that he was being demoted for exceeding his instructions on the encryption issue. That speculation seemed ill founded. The ambassadorship to the Federal Republic is an important and prestigious assignment in the Soviet foreign service. The embassy in Bonn is hardly a diplomatic exile. Semyonov had been chief SALT negotiator since the dawn of the negotiations in 1969. He had spent much of his career in Germany and prided himself on his knowledge of German culture. He would quote Goethe at any excuse. His transfer was more likely a reward than a punishment, and it was probably occasioned by the fact that his American opposite number, Warnke, was also about to step down. Semyonov's successor was Victor Karpov, the Foreign Ministry representative on the delegation, and Warnke's replacement as chief negotiator was Ralph Earle.

The apparent confusion of signals—all too common on the American side but virtually unprecedented on the Soviet side—could be explained as a bargaining tactic, or so the American negotiators hoped. Perhaps the Kremlin had, as Semyonov indicated, decided to accept a common understanding that prohibited encryption whenever it impeded verification, but Gromyko and Kornienko were holding out on formal acceptance until the U.S. conceded on the issue of cruise missile definition; the Soviets would give up on an exemption for encryption if and when the Americans gave up on an exemption for conventionally armed cruise missiles. Both were issues of verification and therefore tied together in Gromyko's proverbial ball of twine.

In the weeks after Vance's return from Moscow, the Carter administration underwent an agonizing reappraisal over whether to try, through further negotiation and compromise, to untie the knot or whether, through an outright American concession, to cut the string. Cyrus Vance was more convinced than ever that the U.S. position on cruise missile definition not only was dubious on its merits, but was contributing to Soviet inflexibility on the other outstanding issues, particularly encryption. Paul Warnke fully agreed with Vance—but Warnke was now out of the government, although he was still serving as a consultant to the administration on SALT. Vance, Warnke, Earle, Gelb and most other high officials of the Arms Control Agency and the State Department felt that Carter and Harold Brown should never have let Henry Jackson and Sam Nunn persuade them of the political importance of the issue to the European allies. "Cruise missile definition was important to NATO only insofar as we made it seem important by making such a big deal out of it in the negotiations," said an American diplomat who was instructed to reassure the West Europeans that the U.S. would stand firm in protecting conventionally armed cruise missiles. "A fool is somebody who formulates a problem in such a way that he can't solve it except by backing down," said a State Department official. "And it was in just that sense that our definition of cruise missiles was foolish."

Zbigniew Brzezinski was having some second thoughts—indeed, third thoughts—about his own position on the issue. Originally, in 1977, he had worried about the difficulty of verifying a distinction between conventional and nuclear warheads on cruise missiles. Then he had come around to the Pentagon view that the verification of such a distinction was a Soviet problem, not an American one, because of the U.S. superiority in cruise missile technology. Having changed his mind once, he was now coming full circle to his original position: what if the Soviets developed long-range ALCMs more quickly than the intelligence community expected and deployed them on the Backfire bomber, claiming they were conventionally armed? Under the American definition, since the Backfire was to be treated in SALT as an aircraft other than a heavy bomber, Backfires armed with long-range conventional ALCMs could "run free" after the expiration of the protocol—and the U.S. would have little confidence that the ALCMs aboard those Backfires were really conventional. Walter Mondale was worried about the same thing. "Someday the Soviets will have a cruise missile and paint it with a big 'C' and load it on a Backfire," said the Vice-President, "and then where will we be? It's a distinction that can't be verified and therefore shouldn't be in the treaty."

In late November, Brzezinski and Mondale went to the President separately and argued that a concession would not only help move the negotiations along—it was also prudent, given the danger of the Soviets' using the U.S. provision to cheat. Harold Brown, the principal sponsor of the exemption for conventional ALCMs, reluctantly came around to the same conclusion. He, Brzezinski and Mondale consulted with Sam Nunn, who said he still felt it was important to protect all conventional cruise missiles from being constrained by SALT, but that his primary concern was with ground-launched and sea-launched cruise missiles. The Joint Chiefs made much the same point in a meeting with Carter. The Chiefs said they did not care so much about an agreed statement on conventional ALCMs per se as they did about the principle that SALT should not limit conventional weapons; they wanted assurances that the blanket prohibition contained in the protocol would not be treated as a precedent to be extended after the expiration of the protocol. Carter responded, "That's not going to happen as long as I'm President." Since the press was full of speculation that Carter would be a one-term President—and since the protocol would not expire until well after the next presidential election—Carter's promise did not fully allay the Chiefs' misgivings, but it was the best he could offer. At a White House meeting at the end of November, Carter told Mondale, Vance, Brown, Brzezinski and Hamilton Jordan that he had decided once and for all to concede on the issue of cruise missile definition. He said he realized that in some respects he was damned if he did and damned if he didn't; if he stuck with the definition, he would be criticized on the grounds that it was not verifiable, and if he abandoned it, he would be criticized for "caving in" to the Soviets in their dogged effort to prevent the U.S. from reaping the benefits of a program in which it had a genuine and significant technological advantage. Carter said he would rather live with the latter criticism; the principle of verifiability was more important to defend than the appearance of hanging tough, and he now saw more merit in the argument that the cruise missile definition as originally proposed by the U.S. was unverifiable.

Shortly afterward, Vance met with Dobrynin and told him that the U.S. was prepared to withdraw its proposed exemption for conventionally armed cruise missiles on aircraft other than heavy bombers. The secretary of state made clear in that meeting, and in a series of follow-up meetings, that the administration hoped the Kremlin would reciprocate with some concessions of its own—particularly on a common understanding prohibiting the encryption of telemetry when it impeded verification, but also on a fractionation freeze for existing ICBMs and on the average number of ALCMs allowed aboard heavy bombers. Without committing his government to an explicit set of compromises, Dobrynin indicated that the next Vance-Gromyko meeting—in Geneva just before Christmas—should be productive and might permit the two sides to announce a date for a summit meeting at which Carter and Brezhnev could sign the agreement. Officials in Washington and Moscow began to make tentative plans for a summit in mid January.

13 Another Christmas, Another Snag

"When you get down to the end in something like SALT," David Aaron once observed, "it gets harder and harder to move the negotiations forward because it is harder and harder for either side to move off positions it has staked out as being of life-or-death, do-or-die importance. Neither guy wants to be the one who made the last big concession." When Jimmy Carter decided at the end of November to abandon his preferred cruise missile definition, with its exemption for conventionally armed ALCMs, he was authorizing what he thought might well be the last big concession in SALT II. He justified the concession because he believed it would trigger the chain reaction of final compromises on lesser issues that he had been hoping for since the summer.

But then, in early December, the Soviets changed their position in a way that would ultimately shift the onus of making one of the last important concessions from Carter back to the Kremlin. It concerned the issue of defining new types of ICBMs. Each side was to be allowed one new type before the treaty expired in 1985. Modification of existing types was to be permitted within narrow parameters. The Soviets had already indicated a willingness to accept an American "short list" of parameters—length and diameter of the booster, number of stages, fuel type, throw-weight and launch-weight—and the U.S. was seeking the addition of a few more. The Soviets had also indicated as far back as May 1978 that they would accept the American proposal of plus or minus 5 percent as the maximum permissible change in the length, diameter, throw-weight and launch-weight of an existing type of ICBM. But in early December, at a private meeting between the two new chief negotiators in Geneva, Victor Karpov told Ralph Earle that while the Soviet Union still accepted a 5 percent limit on the increase within any of the parameters, it wanted no limit on "downsizing." After the meeting Earle told a colleague, "I'm afraid we're a good deal further apart than people thought we were."

That was an understatement. By backing off their earlier acceptance of the plus or minus 5 percent rule and accepting instead only the upper limit, the Soviets were trying to recapture the right to modify an existing missile by making it considerably smaller. At first blush, the Soviet shift may have seemed out of character and perhaps even to be encouraged. After all, it was the big Soviet ICBMs that had traditionally bedeviled American defense planners. Why shouldn't SALT be used to "push" the Soviets toward smaller ICBMs in the same way that it was being used to "force them out to sea" (i.e., toward a greater reliance on submarine-launched rockets)? The answer was that the Soviet ICBM program was already moving in the direction of somewhat smaller, more efficient and more accurate missiles anyway. The design bureaus of the Strategic Rocket Forces were improving propulsion and guidance systems, learning to build boosters more compactly and to miniaturize electronics. With the monstrous SS-18, the Russian designers seemed to have reached the limits of what they felt they could accomplish with brute size. With the smaller SS-19, they had turned the corner, and some of their projected fifth-generation rockets were believed to be smaller still. By trying to rewrite the new-types definition in a way that would permit unlimited downsizing, Karpov was seeking to open up in SALT II a loophole every bit as gaping as the one the Soviets had managed to keep open in SALT I by avoiding a precise definition of a heavy missile. A plus-5-percent/minus-infinity definition would make a mockery out of the new-types rule as a whole. Instead of being limited to one new, significantly different, substantially modernized ICBM, the Russians would be able to build as many as they wished, keeping a vigorous ICBM research and development program alive indefinitely. For that reason, Karpov's message to Earle in early December came as an extremely unpleasant surprise.

Why had the Soviets changed their position? Possibly the Soviet policy-makers and negotiators had agreed to the plus or minus 5 percent provision before the military designers had had a chance to study its implications. The Soviets may have experienced something comparable to the incident in 1977 when the Pentagon realized belatedly that an American proposal severely restricting changes in reentry vehicles would hinder the development of maneuverable warheads, so Harold Brown had insisted that the proposal be rescinded. When Earle's cable with the bad news from Karpov circulated among the weapons experts in Washington, they scratched their heads and tried to figure out what sort of new ICBM it was the Soviets were trying to protect. One theory was that the American success in preserving the right to develop an MX with ten warheads and in freezing the number of warheads on the SS-17 and SS-19 would force the Soviets to scrap their plan for a single-warhead, solid-fuel follow-on to the aging SS-11. Instead, the Russians would use their allowance of one new type to develop a big, new MIRVed rocket, and they would try to shoehorn a more reliable and potent successor to the SS-11 into the category of a smaller, modified existing type. Another theory was that the Soviets wanted a more compact version of an existing fixed-site ICBM that could eventually be converted into a mobile missile to take the place of the SS-16, which SALT had forced them to give up. This line of speculation was known around the corridors of the Pentagon and the CIA as "fitting the SS-11 successor into the SS-16 envelope." Whatever the Soviets' motive for trying to stretch the new-types definition downward, their position was unacceptable to the U.S., and Earle was instructed to tell Karpov so in strong terms.

The China Card

New problems in the text of SALT II were accompanied by a sudden complication in the context. On Friday December 15, President Carter and Chairman Hua Guofeng simultaneously released a joint Sino-American statement in Washington and Peking announcing the normalization of diplomatic relations between the U.S. and the People's Republic of China. Carter also announced that Deputy Premier Deng Xiaoping, the most powerful of the Chinese leaders, would visit the U.S. at the end of January. The announcement came as a shock to almost everyone, even though it was consistent with American policy of the previous seven years and two administrations. There had been high-level contacts between the U.S. and the Communist Chinese since 1971, when Henry Kissinger made a secret trip to Peking to prepare the way for Richard Nixon a year later. The Shanghai Communiqué, signed by Nixon in 1972, was in effect a declaration of mutual intent to normalize relations someday. Jimmy Carter had made no secret of his hope to establish full diplomatic ties with Peking during his first term, even though doing so would probably mean severing formal government-to-government relations with Taiwan. But for nearly two years it was conventional wisdom in Washington, encouraged by many officials of the administration, that Carter would wait to normalize relations with Peking until he had signed SALT II with Leonid Brezhnev.

The Kremlin had watched the accelerating rapprochement between its two most threatening potential adversaries, the U.S. and China, with acute apprehension. Since May 1978, when Zbigniew Brzezinski had used the occasion of his first visit to Peking to make a number of inflammatory anti-Soviet pronouncements, the Soviets worried all the more that the U.S. might be laying the ground for what someday would be a military pact with China, perhaps even a multilateral alliance uniting the U.S., China, Japan and Western Europe. Encirclement by its enemies was a recurring nightmare for the Soviet Union, and Brzezinski's new-found proprietary interest in Sino-American normalization suggested to the Kremlin that he nurtured just such a dream. Secret negotiations between the Carter administration and the Chinese leadership had been going on for many months over the terms and timing of normalization. Cyrus Vance was one of a handful of American officials involved, but he was by no means the moving force. That distinction was Brzezinski's. He was personally impatient to get on with normalization and felt it was a mistake to delay out of deference to the Russians. The Chinese leaders, too, were impatient to get on with it. Moreover, they probably liked the idea that normalization would come before a SALT II signing and that their deputy premier would visit Washington ahead of Brezhnev. The Chinese managed to make their own impatience an imperative in the negotiations over normalization, and they played skillfully on Brzezinski's difficulty in resisting the temptation to rattle the Soviets. In the midst of the climactic stage of the secret negotiations between Washington and Peking, in early December, senior administration officials had leaked word to the press that plans were under way for Brezhnev to come to Washington for a SALT II signing the week of January 15.

The week of December 11, while Brzezinski was supervising the final exchanges between Washington and Peking, Vance was in the Middle East trying, once again in vain, to breathe new life into the Camp David accord. He was in Jerusalem when President Carter called to notify him that he was about to announce normalization.

Vance had to cut short his trip and fly home, with barely enough time to helicopter from Andrews Air Force Base to the White House to be present for the President's announcement. Nothing could have better dramatized the extent to which Vance was peripheral, and Brzezinski central, to the making of U.S. policy toward China at that decisive moment. To compound the secretary of state's political discomfiture, to say nothing of his jet lag, he was due to fly back to Geneva less than a week later for another meeting with Gromyko on SALT.

The suspense preceding that meeting was greater than ever: now that the famous China card was on the table, would the Soviets up the ante in SALT? Brzezinski said absolutely not. When he summoned Anatoly Dobrynin to the White House for a courtesy briefing a few hours before the President's announcement, the ambassador shrugged off the news in a debonair way. Brzezinski and others at the White House concluded that the official reaction of Dobrynin's superiors back in Moscow would be much the same. Henry Kissinger, too, predicted that Carter's announcement on China would have no effect on SALT. Soviet officials in Moscow, in background interviews with reporters and in private conversations with U.S. diplomats, said their government would be watching Sino-American developments more closely than ever, but that the Soviet leaders were too statesmanlike and too much committed to the cause of peace to let the announcement of normalization get in the way of the conclusion of a treaty. Cyrus Vance, Marshall Shulman and some other State Department advisers were not so sure, but they kept their fingers crossed.

New Worries over Old Issues

The first two days of meetings in Geneva went fairly smoothly, although they were not without their ritualistic reiterations of old complaints. In the opening session on Thursday, December 21, Gromyko as usual reviewed the record of what the Soviets regarded as American unreasonableness. Vance pressed for agreement on a launcher distinguishability rule. This was the provision requiring that any new Soviet MIRV launcher look different from a single-warhead launcher. The U.S. had, at the instigation of the Pentagon and the intelligence community, been seeking such a rule in order to prevent the recurrence of an ambiguity like the one at Derazhnya and Pervomaisk. Gromyko responded by dredging up the matter of the Minuteman silos at Malmstrom Air Force Base in Montana. He claimed that the "environmental shelters" protecting the workmen who were hardening those silos still made it impossible for Soviet national technical means to distinguish between the MIRVed and unMIRVed Minutemen. In view of the failure of the Air Force to correct the problem of the shelters, he warned, it might be necessary to count all silos as MIRVed after all—just as the U.S. had insisted on doing at D-and-P. Gromyko's warning went beyond Malmstrom. He hinted that the Soviets might reopen the question of whether MIRVed and unMIRVed Minutemen in general were distinguishable—whether all 450 Minuteman IIs deployed in the U.S. might not have to count against the MIRV subceiling. It was assumed on the American side that Gromyko was not seriously threatening such a thing. Rather he was making the U.S. pay a price, in time and negotiating energy, for its failure to remove the Malmstrom shelters and for its continuing fixation with D-and-P. An exasperated Vance said that the Air Force would eliminate the problem at Malmstrom once and for all, adding that he hoped the Soviets would, also once and for all, stop raising questions about Minuteman distinguishability. Gromyko replied that once the Malmstrom shelters were removed, Soviet national technical means would determine if there was any problem in differentiating between the MIRVed and unMIRVed Minutemen there. It seemed to be Gromyko's face-saving way of saying to the U.S.: get rid of those shelters as you promised, and we'll stop pretending that they impede verification. Afterward, Vance told an aide, "I hope I never hear the word Malmstrom again as long as I live." It was a wish that was not to be granted.

During the first two days of the meeting, another pair of problems arose which had never before come up as a significant issue at the Vance-Gromyko level in the negotiations. It concerned two exotic forms of cruise missiles—a multiple-warhead version and an unarmed version used for reconnaissance. The Soviets, naturally, wanted to ban both, and the U.S. military, just as naturally, wanted to protect both.

Multiple-warhead cruise missiles were the object of one of the more burlesque digressions of SALT. The Soviets, in their passion to hinder the U.S. from developing and deploying cruise missiles in any conceivable form, proposed a ban on what they called "MIRVed cruise missiles" in 1977. The American negotiators in Geneva were nonplused. They had never heard of such a thing. They asked Washington for instructions. Harold Brown joked that the Soviets clearly did not know what they were talking about since the phrase "MIRVed cruise missile" was a contradiction in terms: the "R" in the acronym MIRV stands for "reentry" and refers to the fact that an ICBM warhead reenters the atmosphere on a ballistic trajectory. Cruise missiles, by definition, never leave the atmosphere. They "cruise" like an airplane to their target. But some of Brown's uniformed colleagues at the Pentagon considered the proposed Soviet ban no joke. There was a feeling around the Defense Department that whatever a multiple-warhead cruise missile might be, if the Soviets wanted to prohibit it, then there must be some good reason to have one. The closest thing to a "MIRVed cruise missile" then in the works was a drone that the Pentagon tested in early 1978. It was armed with multiple (but not independently targetable) conventional warheads and designed to attack an enemy airfield; the device would zoom down the main runway, spewing small explosives that would wreak destruction much more extensive and difficult to repair than bomb craters. When the U.S. accepted a limit in SALT on the average number of cruise missiles to be permitted on heavy bombers, the idea of a multiple-warhead air-launched cruise missile became especially attractive to the Air Force in its unending pursuit of "maxflex" (maximum flexibility). The multiple-warhead cruise missile even acquired its own acronym, MWCM (pronounced "Mewcum" or, alternatively, "Mwickum"). Its detractors—who were many and scornful—called it by such nicknames as "son of ALCM," "the mini-MIRV" and "the pilotless peashooter." They were contemptuous of the idea because the U.S. had no plans to deploy bombers with more than twenty cruise missiles during the SALT II treaty period anyway, yet the treaty would allow the U.S. an average of well over twenty ALCMs per plane. Therefore there seemed little sense in trying to cram extra, independently targetable warheads onto those ALCMs.

The best that one of Harold Brown's top civilian aides could say for the MWCM was, "There is a case for not giving it away forever"—in other words, not allowing a ban in the treaty to be extended by precedent after 1985. Harold Brown and Walter Slocombe argued in the Special Coordination Committee and other interagency groups that even though the U.S. had no plans for such a system, the Geneva delegation should resist Soviet attempts to impose a ban on the testing of multiple-warhead ALCMs as part of the treaty. It was a point of contention that dogged the negotiators in Geneva but was considered too minor—"trivial" was the word American officials often used—to be brought to the ministerial level. But on the Thursday and Friday of the Vance-Gromyko meeting, it reached that level when the Soviets protested—to the utter bafflement of the Americans—that the U.S. had "reneged" on an earlier agreement to ban the testing of "MIRVed ALCMs" in the treaty. U.S. officials had no idea what the Russians were talking about, and for months afterward, they combed the negotiating record, looking for some exchange in Geneva that the Russians might have construed as representing American acceptance of such a ban.*

The other variation on the discordant theme of cruise missiles concerned long-range reconnaissance drones, or cruise missiles fitted with cameras instead of warheads, and other unmanned—but also unarmed—aircraft. The U.S. had sought at the delegation level to distinguish between armed cruise missiles, which it called "weapon delivery vehicles," and "unarmed pilotless vehicles" (UPVs); only the former would be covered by SALT. That terminology did not satisfy the Russians. They were afraid the U.S. might transfer to its allies UPVs—which the allies would then convert into "weapon delivery vehicles" simply by fitting them with warheads instead of cameras. On Friday, the second day of the Geneva meeting, Ralph Earle took Victor Karpov aside and proposed solving the problem with a "type rule": once a drone of a certain type had been tested as a weapon delivery vehicle, all individuals of that type would count as weapon delivery vehicles. That was not enough, said Karpov. The Soviets wanted a strict limit on the number of UPVs each side could deploy.

The negotiators also threshed out the long-standing twin problems of which aircraft must count as heavy bombers and which heavy bombers must count as cruise missile carriers. The Russians had redesigned a number of their old workhorse intercontinental bombers, the Bears and Bisons, to serve as reconnaissance planes, tankers for midair refueling and submarine hunters. As such, they were not, strictly speaking, any longer bombers. The Russians had maintained for a long time that these "bomber variants" should not count against the SALT ceiling on total strategic nuclear launch vehicles. The U.S. disagreed. It maintained that even if a Bison tanker had been fitted with a hose-reel probe for midair refueling, as long as the aircraft in question still had bomb bays, then it must count as a bomber. In the terminology of SALT, it was not enough for there merely to be "observable differ-

---

*At one point, the American negotiators in Geneva had been authorized to tell the Soviets orally that the U.S. might consider a ban on the deployment but not on the testing of multiple-warhead air-launched cruise missiles. It is possible that the Soviets simply misunderstood, thinking that the Americans had accepted a ban on deployment *and* testing.

ences" between a tanker and a bomber (the presence of a refueling probe was an observable difference). There must also be "functionally related observable differences"—i.e., the absence of bomb bays. Bomb bays were related to the bomber's function of dropping bombs; in order to avoid counting these bomber variants as strategic nuclear launch vehicles, the Soviets would have to eliminate the bomb bays.

The U.S. had already agreed to the same principle of functionally related observable differences—inevitably abbreviated as FRODs— with regard to wide-bodied cruise missile carriers: if the Air Force ever did develop a modified 747 or some other jumbo jet for carrying ALCMs, the aircraft would have to be distinguished by FRODs. It would also have to be built from scratch; it could not simply be a converted airliner or transport plane. But the Soviets had a more immediate objection involving the use of B-52s. The Air Force had already tested an early version of cruise missile, the ALCM-A, on two models of B-52, the B-52G and the B-52H. There were about 270 planes of those models. The Russians were holding out for a launcher counting rule whereby all B-52Gs and B-52Hs must count against the 1,320 subceiling, even though the U.S. had decided not to deploy the ALCM-A at all and intended to mount cruise missiles on only about 140 B-52s. To make matters even more complicated—and more closely interrelated—the Soviets had a similar problem. They had launched what they said was a short-range air-to-surface missile, the AS-3, from the Bear bomber. The U.S. questioned the range of the AS-3, saying that if it had a range of more than 600 kilometers, then the Bears would have to count as cruise missile carriers.

These were truly minor issues—the small change of SALT—and the trade-offs necessary to resolve them were obvious and relatively painless. For instance, the Soviets would stop pretending that the testing of the discarded ALCM-A transformed all B-52Gs and B-52Hs into cruise missile carriers, and the Americans would stop pretending that the primitive AS-3 made a cruise missile carrier out of the Bear. But already during the first two days of the Vance-Gromyko meeting, the Soviet negotiators began to rattle the small change in a way that suggested the final bargains might be more difficult to strike and ultimately perhaps more expensive than the Americans had assumed.

Another neatly paired, almost symmetrical set of sticking points concerned, on the one hand, the deadline by which the Soviets must dismantle enough strategic systems to be within the new ceilings and, on the other, the duration of the three-year protocol. The Russians had approximately 2,500 ICBM launchers, submarine missile tubes and heavy bombers. That meant that about six months after SALT II came into effect, they would have to get rid of about 100 systems—mostly older Bears and Bisons—in order to be within the Vladivostok limit of 2,400. At issue still in December was when exactly they would have to dismantle another 150 systems in order to be in compliance with the reduced ceiling of 2,250. Naturally, the Soviets wanted the deadline to be as far in the future and as flexible as possible, and just as naturally, the Americans wanted it to be sooner rather than later. On the issue of the duration of the protocol, the Americans similarly favored haste while the Soviets sought to delay—although for very different reasons. Since the protocol served primarily to curtail the American cruise missile program, the U.S. wanted to get it over with as soon as possible while the Soviets wanted to drag it out. Originally the U.S. had proposed in effect backdating the protocol, so that it would start with the expiration of SALT I in October 1977, run for three years and expire in October 1980. Later the U.S. offered to let the expiration slip until December 31, 1980. The Soviets resisted agreeing to a date-certain before the negotiations were concluded. They maintained that the longer the negotiations continued, the later the protocol should end. According to their position, the protocol would run for three years starting from the "date of entry into force" of the SALT II treaty. This not only served their purpose of prolonging constraints on cruise missiles, but it was meant as a negotiating tactic, to put the U.S. under additional pressure to come to terms quickly. By the time Vance and Gromyko met in Geneva in December 1978, the Soviets were saying that if SALT II was in force by March 31, 1979— which would mean that under their scheme the protocol would expire March 31, 1982—they would commit themselves to dismantling excess systems between the first and last day of 1981. That was not good enough for the American side. The U.S. wanted to make sure that the Russians came down to the new ceiling of 2,250 total strategic launchers by a much more clearly defined schedule. Specifically, said the Americans, by the middle of 1981—June 30—"all systems that are to be dismantled must be in a state of irreversible inoperability." That was the phrase favored by the Pentagon; it offended the ear and the logic of most members of the Geneva delegation—it struck them as awkward and redundant. But the point was that the U.S. did not want to leave the Soviet Union the freedom to wait until the end of 1981 to go about its dismantling in earnest. Since the protocol was to expire shortly afterward—and with it would end the restrictions on the deployment and transfer of long-range ground-launched and sea-launched cruise missiles—the Americans were afraid that the Russians might procrastinate their dismantling of old bombers in order to put pressure on the U.S. to exercise self-restraint in its cruise missile program even after the expiration of the protocol. Explained a U.S. official in Geneva: "We didn't want the Russians to be unduly tempted to use the pace at which they dismantled as a subtle sort of blackmail over us. The situation we wanted to avoid was one in which, once the protocol was coming to an end, as we speeded up our deployment of fancy new GLCMs and SLCMs, they slowed down the decommissioning of decrepit old bombers and launchers. It would hardly be of great military strategic significance, but it could be tricky politically."

A Proposal of Marriage

On other, more important questions there was considerable progress. Now that the U.S. was no longer holding out for an exemption for conventionally armed cruise missiles, the American negotiators were free to accept the strict Soviet definition of the 600-kilometer lower limit for cruise missile range that Gromyko had insisted on in exchange for doing away with the 2,500-kilometer upper limit. The U.S. agreed to define cruise missile range as the maximum distance that a missile can fly before its fuel runs out; that definition left the drone some extra room to maneuver vertically to get over mountains but none to zig and zag laterally. For their part, the Soviets agreed to a missile fractionation freeze that would hold the SS-17 to four warheads and the SS-19 to six. They had accepted such a freeze once before, in July, but they had done so on the condition that the U.S. concede to the Soviet position on the treatment of cruise missiles aboard bombers, which the U.S. had refused to do. This time Gromyko's agreement to a fractionation freeze seemed firm, and it was accompanied by acceptance of the American right to put ten warheads on the MX, although both concessions were technically contingent on the satisfactory resolution of a number of other issues. On one of these, the average number of ALCMs per bomber, the gap was further narrowed. Gromyko came up from 25 to 27, and Vance—even though American officials had said repeatedly the U.S. could go no lower than 30—came down to 28. Gromyko offered a compromise on another sticking point: he proposed 20 percent as the permissible bounds for downsizing an existing type of ICBM. That was an improvement over the Soviet position of two weeks before, when Karpov had told Earle that the Russians wanted no lower limit at all. But 20 percent was still unacceptable to the U.S. Vance told Gromyko that there must be no more than a 5 percent change in either direction within the agreed parameters for the SALT II curtailment of modernization to be "meaningful."

The two diplomats also spent considerable time on the thorny issue of telemetry encryption. After the Moscow meeting in October, at which Gromyko had rejected the American contention that SALT must explicitly ban any encryption which hindered the monitoring of compliance, the problem was remanded to the delegations in Geneva. But it was clearly a problem of such exquisite complexity and sensitivity that it could only be resolved at what the negotiators called "the political level"—between Vance and Gromyko themselves. They alone would have to agree on the wording of a "common understanding" in the Joint Draft Text that addressed the question of encryption. The American-preferred provision would have stressed what was forbidden—i.e., encryption "whenever it impeded" verification. Gromyko brought with him to Geneva, and gave to Vance on the first day of their talks, Soviet-preferred language that would have stressed what was permitted—i.e., encryption that did *not* impede verification. Vance emerged from the session hopeful. While the emphasis was different, the Soviet position was not incompatible with the American one. Most importantly, the Soviets seemed implicitly to be accepting a critical aspect of the American position: the *only* criterion for determining the permissibility or impermissibility of encryption should be whether or not the encryption in question impeded verification; there should be no burden on the U.S. to establish that a particular instance of Soviet encryption was deliberately intended to impede verification. The U.S. side wanted to avoid cases in the Standing Consultative Commission in which the American representatives would challenge the use of code and their Soviet counterparts could defend the practice by responding that the code was intended to protect legitimate military secrets, not to thwart American monitoring of SALT. According to the American formulation of the limited encryption ban, which the Soviets now seemed tacitly to accept, the intent of encryption was irrelevant to its permissibility; only its effect mattered. If its effect was to impede, then it would be forbidden, regardless of intent. That did not solve the potential problem of how to establish in the Standing Consultative Commission that a given use of code had impeded verification without at the same time telling the Russians more than they ought to know about American sources and methods of intelligence gathering. But Vance was still encouraged.

In a meeting of the American side after Vance and Gromyko had met one on one, George Seignious, the retired Army general and former member of the SALT delegation who had taken Warnke's place as director of the Arms Control and Disarmament Agency, proposed what he called a "marriage" of the two positions. Vance instructed James Timbie, ACDA's principal technical expert, to draft a new common understanding incorporating the Soviet and American versions. The result was a provision whereby any method of transmitting telemetry, "including its encryption," would be banned whenever it impeded verification; then, as a nod to the Soviets, the new American language added that any method of transmitting telemetry would be permitted as long as it did not impede verification. Vance had Ralph Earle try out the new version on Victor Karpov in a private session of their own. Karpov was noncommittal but passed the proposal along to Gromyko. In his next meeting with Vance, the Soviet foreign minister said he would relay the proposed compromise back to Moscow with his recommendation that it be accepted on one condition—that the three-word phrase "including its encryption" appear not once but twice; those three words must also be inserted into the sentence about methods of transmitting telemetry that did not impede. The Russians did not want the once taboo word "encryption" to be used exclusively in the context of prohibition. That would invite the inference, they feared, that the practice in general was prohibited. If the U.S. was going to demand an explicit reference to encryption as something that was to be forbidden in some circumstances, then the Soviets were going to insist that it be accompanied by an explicit reference to encryption as something that was to be permitted in other circumstances.

Vance's "talking points" included instructions for him to raise the matter of the Soviets' use of code in the telemetry of their SS-18 tests. The secretary of state did so in private with Gromyko, referring to the test of July 29, 1978, in which the Soviet had encrypted the telemetry channels containing data on the reentry vehicle. The SS-18 was an "existing type" of ICBM. The testing of such missiles would not be limited by SALT. But the U.S. could be sure that the modernization of an existing type was within the bounds set by the new-types rule only if U.S. national technical means had access to SALT-related telemetry. Vance told Gromyko that once the treaty was in force, any missile not previously tested would be deemed a system that had to be verified. The U.S. must be able to determine to its own satisfaction that the system was indeed "old" and that any of its modifications fell within the permissible, though still disputed, parameters of the new-types rule. Under such an interpretation, the only instances in which the Soviets would be able to engage in substantial encryption would be those in which they would have the least interest in doing so—the firings of operational missiles to make sure they were still reliable and to train their crews. Vance cited the July 29 launch as a case in point of a test that must be verifiable, since the U.S. would need to satisfy itself that the individual rocket had not been upgraded in ways that should classify it as a new type.

The secretary of state might have cited a second example—a similar test, with a similar degree of encryption, which had taken place only the day before, on Thursday. The CIA representative in Geneva told Vance about the December 21 test as the American negotiators were meeting among themselves at the Botanic Building on Friday. However, Vance did not mention the December 21 test to Gromyko. For one thing, U.S. intelligence had only a preliminary, incomplete readout on the test. For another, the U.S. did not want the Russians to know how quickly American national technical means were able to run a check on which channels of telemetry in a test were encrypted. Gromyko's response to Vance's point about the July 29 test was oblique but—Vance believed—positive and satisfactory: he asserted that the common understanding he and Vance had agreed upon would be adequate to cover any specific case that might arise. He said that the Soviet government would be prepared to settle any case on the basis of the common understanding. To Vance, the fact that Gromyko had chosen not to say anything in direct response to the American position on the July 29 test implied acquiescence.

At the end of the Friday afternoon session, the mood on the American side was buoyant. Under Vance's supervision, Ralph Earle, Leslie Gelb, Reginald Bartholomew and Walter Slocombe got together to draft a cable to Washington, over Vance's name, reporting on the day's proceedings and requesting permission to accept the compromise common understanding on encryption, as amended by the Soviets with the repetition of three words. The American party hoped that the next morning's session would produce formal agreement on the encryption issue and a further Soviet concession on the permissible degree of downsizing in the modification of an existing type of ICBM. With those problems resolved, there would be nothing in dispute but what the Americans still considered the minor issues of reconnaissance drones and multiple-warhead cruise missiles, as well as a handful of other details. These, it was believed, could be left to the permanent delegations to dispose of while the secretary of state and the foreign minister announced a mid-January summit at which Carter and Brezhnev would sign SALT II. Seignious told Vance that he had found Gromyko far more flexible and agreeable than veterans of past encounters with the foreign minister had led him to expect. Seignious and Paul Warnke, who was now serving the administration as a part-time consultant on SALT, were sufficiently confident that the next morning's meeting would be *pro forma* and upbeat that they decided to miss it and to catch an early flight back to the U.S. so they would have some extra time with their families over Christmas weekend. Vance's chief press spokesman, Hodding Carter, cautioned newsmen that there was still no final agreement, but he reflected the mood of the delegation and thus encouraged the press to expect one the next day. "We are close to the end of the road," he said, echoing a line Vance himself was using to characterize the progress he felt had been made.

The wire services transmitted dispatches from Geneva suggesting that SALT was at hand. As soon as these stories reached the White House teletype machines, they were flashed to Air Force One, which was en route to Georgia. The President was going home to Plains for Christmas. Hamilton Jordan and Jody Powell were with him. Before leaving Washington, Jordan and Powell, along with Gerald Rafshoon, the White House media adviser, and Frank Moore, chief of congressional liaison, had held a series of meetings to prepare briefings on the agreement for the press and the Congress in the event that Vance and Gromyko were able to announce a date for the summit after their final session Saturday. The extremely positive wire service stories from Geneva suggested that an announcement was indeed imminent, yet the presidential party had still heard nothing directly from Vance.

Vance Is Overruled

In the early evening that Friday, when Vance's reporting cable finally arrived, Zbigniew Brzezinski convened a meeting in his office in the corner of the White House west wing. In addition to Brzezinski

and David Aaron there were Harold Brown, Stansfield Turner, Warren Christopher, the deputy secretary of state, and Spurgeon Keeny,
the deputy director of ACDA. It was supposed to be a short session.
Brzezinski and Aaron were due at the British ambassador's for a
Christmas party. Their wives were waiting for them outside the office.
But the meeting continued until nearly 11 P.M. It turned out to be long
and contentious, primarily because of the way Vance proposed to deal
with the encryption issue. In his cable from Geneva, the secretary of
state explained that he and Gromyko had worked out language explicitly banning encryption "whenever it impedes" verification while explicitly permitting it when it does not impede verification. Stansfield
Turner was already unhappy with the administration's decision not to
seek an across-the-board ban on encryption. He felt the limited ban
on which the U.S. had settled was a half measure at best. Furthermore,
he objected to the notion that the SALT II document would go so far
as to stipulate, in black and white, that encryption was allowed. In
view of what he felt was the noncommittal nature of Gromyko's response to Vance's point about the July 29 test, Turner argued that the
Soviets would have far too much leeway to decide for themselves
when encryption impeded verification and when it did not; indeed,
the Russians might well take the position that in actual practice,
telemetry was never really necessary to verification and its encryption
was therefore never really impermissible. After a lengthy, sometimes
heated discussion, Turner said he could live with the common understanding on encryption that Vance and Gromyko had worked out if
Vance stated the American objection to the July 29 test more bluntly
and if Gromyko responded more satisfactorily. The director of Central
Intelligence proposed that at the next day's meeting in Geneva, Vance
should raise the matter of the July 29 test again, this time seeking
Gromyko's "concrete affirmation" that a repetition of such a test
would be illegal under SALT II. Warren Christopher, referring to his
own experience as a lawyer, warned against using the July 29 test as
a bench mark for the legality of encryption; all the Soviets would have
to do would be to encrypt one less channel than they had encrypted
on July 29, still scrambling many others, and they could then claim
they were staying within the bounds on which the Americans had
insisted. "Whenever I've cited a specific example in pursuit of a general principle," said Christopher, "I've always regretted it later on."
David Aaron agreed. He once remarked that no less a SALT personage
than Paul Nitze, during his term as a negotiator in Geneva, had laid

down a stern warning: "Never try to establish principles by citing examples. Otherwise the examples will come back and bite you later on." Roger Molander, who was consulted during the Friday night meeting, pointed out that if the U.S. tried to tie Gromyko down to a more precise agreement about the July 29 test, the Saturday session in Geneva could only be inconclusive, since Gromyko would have no negotiating instructions on how to respond, nor would he be able to get new instructions on so sensitive and complex a matter from Moscow fast enough to salvage the hoped-for announcement of a summit.

Finally, the meeting produced what Brzezinski felt was an acceptable compromise. Vance would not seek an affirmative response from Gromyko. Instead, he would confront Gromyko with the American interpretation that a repetition of the July 29 test would be in violation of the agreement; then he would say, in effect, "if you disagree with our interpretation, speak now or forever hold your peace." According to diplomatic practice, Gromyko's "noncontradiction" would be considered tantamount to assent, and it would become part of the negotiating record that would accompany and amplify the treaty.

Brzezinski telephoned Jimmy Carter, who was by now at his family home in Plains. Brzezinski told the President it was the consensus of the group in his office that Vance should go back to Gromyko and get his tacit agreement on the impermissibility of the encryption used in the July 29 test. Carter authorized Brzezinski to instruct Vance accordingly. The night-shift communications experts in the White House Situation Room transmitted Brzezinski's cable to Vance shortly before midnight Washington time. That was just before 6 A.M. in Geneva. The secretary of state saw the cable just after he woke up. He was, according to an associate, "as angry as I've ever seen him. He was being told that he hadn't done it right the first time and that he should go back and do it again. Cy Vance is not given to temper tantrums or questioning his orders. He's very cool, very stoical, and very, very much a good soldier. But on this occasion he was livid and close to mutiny."

Vance telephoned Brzezinski on a secure line from the Botanic Building and protested his instructions in the strongest terms. For him to go through the whole exercise with Gromyko on the matter of the July 29 test again would be pointless and provocative. It would accomplish nothing, he said, except to arouse Soviet recalcitrance on encryption and very likely on other issues as well. He was appealing his new instructions, and he needed an answer right away, since he was due at the Soviet mission within an hour. Brzezinski put through a conference call to Stansfield Turner and Harold Brown, waking them up. They said it was important as a matter of principle that Gromyko acknowledge the impermissibility of encryption such as that used on July 29. Brzezinski then phoned Jody Powell in Plains. They decided to awaken the President, even though he had been suffering from acute hemorrhoids and, said Powell, was badly in need of rest. Brzezinski reported Vance's misgivings to Carter, but the national security adviser left no doubt that he felt Vance should do as he had been told. The President agreed.

When Brzezinski tried to relay that message back to the secretary of state, Vance was already at the Soviet mission in Geneva, beginning a private meeting with Gromyko. Marshall Shulman, who had accompanied Vance to the mission, came on the line. "Do you know where you've reached us, Zbig?" he asked. "Do you still want to talk to Cy?"

"Considering the circumstances, yes," replied Brzezinski. Both men knew that since they were talking on a Soviet phone, there was a good chance the Russians were listening in. Therefore when Shulman fetched Vance to the phone, Brzezinski was careful not to specify the subject at hand. Instead he said, "With reference to that particular item we discussed in our earlier conversation, the previous instructions stand." Assuming that the conversation was being monitored, Brzezinski took a degree of pleasure in imagining how the Soviet eavesdroppers would bridle at the sound of his distinctively accented voice and rapid-fire delivery, not to mention his tough message to Vance. With a slight extra ingredient of melodrama, Brzezinski told the secretary that Carter considered encryption "a critical issue for ratification."* Vance obeyed those instructions. He confronted Gromyko with the American interpretation that "encryption of telemetry such as that practiced on July 29, if extended to modified or new systems, would be a violation" of the agreement. Then he said, "If you disagree, tell me now." Gromyko did not flatly contradict Vance, but by his testy manner and dyspeptic expression he made

---

*Subsequently, Soviet officials involved in the negotiations indicated that they may not actually have known what Brzezinski said to Vance after all—or they may have misunderstood the subject of the telephone conversation. The Soviets believed, or at least professed to believe, that Vance had received a phone call from Brzezinski in which the national security adviser ordered the secretary of state to toughen the American position on multiple-warhead cruise missiles—and that it was U.S. obstreperousness on that issue that led to the lack of progress on Saturday.

clear that he was unhappy with the American refusal to leave well
enough alone. Subsequently, another Soviet official explained
Gromyko's reaction: the foreign minister still felt that the common
understanding he and Vance had already worked out was an adequate
basis for the Standing Consultative Commission to adjudicate any dispute over the permissibility of a coded test. Moreover, he resented
what seemed an American attempt to apply retroactively a provision
of a treaty that was not yet concluded, much less in force. It seemed
an attempt to get the Russians in effect to confess that they had done
something wrong—that they had sinned against the spirit of SALT.
Vance could tell that by carrying out his unwelcome new instructions,
he had—just as he had feared—aroused Soviet hypersensitivity.

Things Fall Apart

Vance had jarred Gromyko with an unpleasant surprise, and the
Soviet foreign minister fully reciprocated. He told Vance that before
they could set a date for a Carter-Brezhnev summit, there must be
agreement on the outstanding problems of unarmed drones, multiple-
warhead cruise missiles, bomber definitions, the duration of the protocol and the schedule for dismantling excess Soviet systems. It was not
enough to leave the permanent delegations to close the gap on those
details while preparations for a summit proceeded. First must come
resolution of all the outstanding matters. Only then would the Soviet
leadership commit itself to a date for the Carter-Brezhnev meeting.

At the end of their tête-à-tête, Vance and Gromyko rejoined their
colleagues. Ralph Earle, Marshall Shulman and Malcolm Toon could
see from Vance's expression as he approached that the talks had hit
a big snag. After three and a half hours at the Soviet mission, the two
sides broke for lunch, then tried again for another three and a half
hours at the Botanic Building. Back in the U.S., among Carter's inner
circle, the suspense was now laced with apprehension. "What the hell
is going on over there?" asked Hamilton Jordan at one point. "Why is
it taking so long? Where's the announcement?" The White House had
alerted the television networks that President Carter might have a
major statement to be broadcast live. As Saturday wore on, the President's political and media advisers feared that they might have stage-
managed an embarrassing anticlimax. Vance and Toon both had U.S.
Air Force jets standing by at Geneva airport, ready for early getaways.
Everyone wanted to be home by Christmas Eve, the next day, and

Vance had one more stop—in Brussels to meet with the Israeli foreign minister and the Egyptian prime minister, on the stalled Middle East settlement. Shortly after lunch the pilots were told that their departures would be delayed.

Much of the afternoon session was spent figuring out how to put the best possible face on the failure to reach an agreement. When they finally emerged blinking into the fresh air and sunlight to face the reporters and the cameras, Vance and Gromyko made separate statements. "Foreign Minister Gromyko and I have essentially reached agreement on most of the questions on which differences have existed," said Vance. "We will continue to work on those questions that have not been resolved through our regular diplomatic channels." Gromyko struck the same note: "A lot of work has indeed been done. We can really say that most of the questions on which there was no agreement have essentially been agreed. But there is still some work to be done." As to the elusive summit, added Vance, "We are agreed in principle on a meeting of the heads of our two states." But it would come, Gromyko repeated for the public record, only after everything had been settled. With that, the two men parted.

Vance barely made it back to the U.S. in time for Christmas Eve with his family—and another Christmas without SALT. Ralph Earle and the other members of the permanent delegation were not even that fortunate. Their Christmas home leaves had already been canceled, in anticipation that the Vance-Gromyko meeting would end in the announcement of a summit and that the delegations would be charged with cleaning up the last details of an agreement. Now they were ordered back to the negotiating table with the much more daunting assignment of chipping away at the major stumbling blocks that the secretary of state and the foreign minister had been unable to overcome.

What had happened? For one thing, the Americans had, once again, been badly served by their own optimism. Gromyko and Dobrynin had warned repeatedly that there could be no summit until everything had been settled by the negotiators. But Vance and other American officials seemed unwilling to believe that everything meant *every*thing. Up until the last day of the meeting in Geneva, there was a working assumption on the American side that if the secretary of state and the foreign minister could resolve the primary issues—notably fractionation and encryption—the secondary issues, which had only

just reached the ministerial level for the first time, could be remanded
back to the delegations, where they belonged, and would not be allowed to stand in the way of the summit. After all, the negotiation of
the SALT I agreements had reached its climax *at* the summit. Nixon
and Brezhnev engaged in tough, suspenseful and highly substantive
bargaining, primarily over the status of submarine-launched missiles
in the interim agreement, during their meeting in Moscow in May
1972. Moreover, Nixon had played his own China card only three
months before when he paid the first presidential visit to the People's
Republic and signed the Shanghai Communiqué. And in April 1972,
Nixon had in effect dared the Soviets to impose linkage on SALT by
bombing North Vietnam and mining Haiphong harbor on the eve of
his departure for Moscow.

But much had changed since 1972. Whatever his political health,
the decline of Brezhnev's physical vigor made it imprudent for his
advisers to send him into a summit meeting with Carter at which there
were serious SALT issues outstanding. Also, the nature of the triangular relationship among Washington, Moscow and Peking had changed
fundamentally since 1972. The atmosphere of the interplay was no
longer conducive to SALT and Soviet-American summitry. Nixon and
Kissinger had solemnly denied that they were playing off China and
Russia against each other, although they were doing precisely that—
and the Soviets knew it. Carter and Brzezinski likewise denied that
they were consolidating the U.S. relationship with Peking as a
geopolitical counterbalance to Soviet power, although they were
doing precisely that—and the Soviets knew it. The important difference was that Nixon and Kissinger had pursued Soviet-American détente and Sino-American rapprochement more or less simultaneously,
as parallel policies, while Carter and Brzezinski presided—also more
or less simultaneously—over the *deterioration* of Soviet-American relations and the consummation of Sino-American ties. Largely for that
reason, the Carter administration's policy appeared hostile to the
Kremlin in a way that the Nixon administration's had not.

Viewed from that Soviet perspective, the American handling of
normalization with Peking and timing of the forthcoming visit by
Deng Xiaoping seemed downright provocative. During Vance's pre-
Christmas meeting with Gromyko in Geneva, aides of the two men
talked informally about Carter's December 15 announcement of normalization and its probable impact on SALT. This so-called corridor
conversation produced no direct confirmation that the Kremlin had

—its own disclaimers to the contrary notwithstanding—decided to stall in the negotiations. But a number of Soviet officials complained, both in Geneva and subsequently, that the Carter administration was "taking the Soviet Union for granted," "trifling with us," "trying to trick us." Their complaints centered on the press leak—which they were convinced could only have been sanctioned at the highest level —of the January 15 date for the Carter-Brezhnev summit. That leak, followed by Carter's surprise announcement that Deng would be coming at the end of January, looked to Soviet eyes like a deliberate American attempt to catch the Kremlin in a double trap: the Soviets would be under new pressure from "world public opinion" to conclude an agreement by the January 15 deadline, and Brezhnev would be in the uncomfortable position of preceding Deng to the U.S. That timetable alone would give Deng an opportunity to upstage Brezhnev. Visits by Soviet leaders to the U.S., after all, were becoming commonplace. Brezhnev would be coming for the second time, a full twenty years after Nikita Khrushchev's pioneering journey. Deng's visit, by contrast, would be a momentous first. Thus, the timetable that the Americans had in mind was, in the words of a Soviet diplomat, "so thoroughly unappealing as to be unacceptable."

At first, Zbigniew Brzezinski dismissed out of hand the possibility that Soviet irritation over normalization and apprehension over the Deng visit had influenced the course of SALT. He reasoned that since the Soviets had inveighed against American talk of linkage between SALT and the Russian-Cuban involvement in Africa, it would be "utterly illogical" for the Kremlin now to forge a link between SALT and Sino-American relations. Rather, Brzezinski interpreted the delay in Geneva as a "typical Soviet bargaining tactic"—an eleventh-hour holdout for a few more American concessions. But later, after meeting with Dobrynin and after talking to the U.S. officials who had been in Geneva, Brzezinski rather reluctantly came to agree with Vance, Marshall Shulman and others that the administration's China policy had complicated SALT after all. There was a consensus, which everyone admitted was speculative, that Gromyko might have moved to settle the outstanding issues on Saturday if it had not been for the China factor. Instead, the Kremlin may have instructed him to use the secondary issues of multiple-warhead cruise missile, reconnaissance drones, bomber variants, duration of the protocol and a schedule for dismantling as "regulators" to control the timing of the Brezhnev visit. Dickering over the final details of the agreement would give the Russians a chance to assess Deng's American debut, to measure its anti-Soviet content, and then to decide when—perhaps even whether—to proceed with a SALT signing and a Carter-Brezhnev summit.

14 Playing to a Draw

It took more than four months—from before New Year's until after May Day—to close the gap left by Cyrus Vance and Andrei Gromyko at their meeting in December 1978 in Geneva. The apparatchiks and advocates of SALT sometimes found themselves under almost unbearable strain and suspense. The critics had a heyday. It was a period of linkage run wild—the most negative sort of linkage. Political events of early 1979 seemed to be conspiring to scuttle not just the treaty but the talks.

Deng Xiaoping's nine-day visit to the U.S. at the end of January and beginning of February lived up to the Soviets' worst expectations. Sino-Soviet enmity was at least as prominent a theme of Deng's rhetoric as Sino-American friendship. In one appearance after another, the Chinese deputy premier denounced the Soviet Union for its aggressiveness and untrustworthiness, noting pointedly that SALT and similar bilateral agreements between the superpowers would do nothing to inhibit the "polar bear." As managed by the administration, the Deng visit was clearly Zbigniew Brzezinski's operation, just as the mid-December surprise announcement of Sino-American normalization had been. His first night in the U.S., Deng dined informally—and with much publicity—at Brzezinski's home. Vance was there too, but both literally and figuratively as just another guest rather than as a cohost. In the days that followed, the secretary of state was as publicly visible as the presidential national security adviser, but while Brzezinski looked as though he was having the time of his life, Vance looked more than usually uncomfortable and apprehensive. At the conclusion of Deng's stay in Washington, Brzezinski worked out a press communiqué with the Chinese visitors, declaring among other things that the U.S. and China "reaffirm they are opposed to efforts by any country or group of countries to establish hegemony or domination over others." The use of the anti-Soviet code word "hegemony" had the predictable effect of infuriating the Soviets. The same day the communiqué was released, Vance called in Anatoly Dobrynin to assure him that the new relationship between Washington and Peking was not aimed against Moscow. "Perhaps the administration doth protest too much," said a Soviet diplomat at the time.

From the Russian perspective, the administration protested altogether too little when Deng used his American tour as a platform to warn that China might strike militarily against Vietnam, a Soviet ally. While sounding anti-Soviet alarms around the country, Deng said repeatedly that China might have to "teach a lesson" to the Vietnamese, whom he called "the Cubans of the Orient," for their invasion of Cambodia and for recurring skirmishes on the Sino-Vietnamese border. Fearing what was coming, the State Department issued a statement shortly after Deng's departure expressing concern about the possibility of "a Chinese attack on Vietnam" and insisting that the U.S. was "not taking sides in the struggle between two Communist states in Asia." Stiffer warnings were sounded from Moscow. China was in danger of "overstepping the forbidden line in Vietnam," said the Soviet press. "The snubbed dragon wants to show its claws." The Russians made clear that they would hold the U.S. responsible if Deng carried out the threats he had made against Vietnam while in the U.S.

Deng wasted little time in doing just that. In mid February, less than two weeks after the end of his American visit, Deng ordered Chinese troops into Vietnam. For over two weeks, they wreaked havoc north of Hanoi. They captured a disputed frontier area, temporarily occupied a number of towns, and then did what some Americans had advocated during the U.S.'s own military involvement in Vietnam: China declared itself the winner and withdrew. The Chinese could—and did—take satisfaction from the fact that the Soviet Union never intervened directly, either in the defense of Vietnam or in a diversionary or punitive attack on China's northern border. The Kremlin had confined itself to increased arms shipments to Hanoi and to warnings that the Chinese "stop before it is too late." But the whole episode was hardly a military or diplomatic triumph for Deng. The invasion did nothing to pry the Vietnamese out of Cambodia; it left Vietnam a formidable power in the region and more dependent than ever on Soviet assistance; and China was widely criticized for aggression, while the Soviet Union got international credit for its self-restraint.

There was nothing ambiguous about the effect of China's behavior on Soviet-American relations and on SALT. It was unquestionably and unmitigatedly damaging. In public, the Soviets accused the U.S. of at least tacitly approving the Chinese invasion of Vietnam. After years of rejecting the concept of U.S.-imposed linkage between SALT and human rights, SALT and Africa, SALT and the Middle East—after years of lecturing Washington that SALT should be nurtured in antiseptic isolation from other issues of dispute between the two countries —the Kremlin now made clearer than ever that from its own standpoint, linkage was very much in order where China was concerned. In a speech in late February, while the Chinese were still inside Vietnam, Gromyko declared: "The Central Committee of the Communist Party and the Soviet government have drawn attention more than once to the fact that such actions by the U.S. as . . . playing 'the China card,' which has become so dear to those in Washington who think little of the future, in no way meet the purposes of the [SALT] agreement [or] the goals of peace in general."

In private, the warning was even more stark. A Soviet diplomat in Washington said, "We are now in the post-Deng era of Soviet-American relations. This means that things that were possible two months ago in SALT are no longer possible now." Gromyko told Ambassador Malcolm Toon that the Deng visit to the U.S. and its aftermath represented an attempt by China to "undermine" SALT and détente and that Chinese influence was "obstructing the development of Soviet-American relations." The foreign minister alluded to the much publicized disagreement between Vance and Brzezinski over how to manage the triangular relationship among China, Russia and America. Complaining that U.S. official attitudes "change as quickly as the weather in the North Atlantic," Gromyko made clear he was concerned that Brzezinski's position was ascendant. In back-channel conversation both in Washington and Moscow, there were dark hints that the Soviet leadership might be undertaking a fundamental reassessment of its policy toward the U.S., including a reassessment of the desirability of concluding a SALT agreement at all. Carter administration officials, especially those in the State Department, took these signals seriously. They allowed for the possibility that the Soviets were engaging in a certain amount of psychological warfare, seeking to exploit the Vance-Brzezinski rift. But even making allowances for Russian bluff and wile, some Americans detected what they felt were signs of genuine consternation on the part of their Soviet interlocutors about how the Kremlin would ultimately respond. By all accounts and certainly by all appearances, Leonid Brezhnev's health was worse than ever. It was increasingly difficult to imagine him speaking out forcefully in Politburo meetings on behalf of the policy and the treaty with which he so dearly wanted to be identified.

SALT had been in the doldrums before, but there was, in late February 1979, a new note of despair at the State Department. Officials who had previously confined their worries to the danger that the Senate might reject the treaty now, for the first time, began to talk about the possibility that there would be no treaty for the Senate to consider—that at the eleventh hour and fifty-ninth minute, SALT would be overtaken by events.

The Lost Listening Posts

Among those adverse events was the upheaval in Iran. The revolutionary wave that swept Shah Mohammad Reza Pahlavi off the Peacock throne and into exile contained strong currents of anti-Americanism. The loose alliance of Moslem fundamentalists and leftists who rode that wave to power saw American military installations in their country as symbols of American backing for the Shah, and the departure of the Shah in January, followed almost immediately by the triumphal return from exile of his archenemy, the Ayatollah Khomeini, left little doubt that the U.S. would lose its intelligence-gathering stations near the Caspian Sea, with their giant antennas pointed north toward the U.S.S.R. The CIA dismantled one of the posts as the political turmoil was coming to a head; a second, more important facility was abandoned in late February. The closings were widely reported in the American press in a manner that could not have come as worse news for the administration. Just at a time when the excruciatingly sensitive and complex issue of encryption was finding its own way into newspaper articles—and into the arguments of SALT skeptics—here was more reason to doubt whether the new treaty could be verified. Reporters had no difficulty finding anonymous administration officials who conceded that the loss of the Iranian posts would, for the time being, roughly double the margin of error in the CIA's estimates of key features of Soviet missile tests. Repeated statements to the contrary from the White House and the State Department did little to dispel the widespread impression that it would be easier now for the Soviets to cheat on SALT II in significant respects and not get caught. Senator Henry Jackson charged that the loss in Iran had done "irreparable harm" to America's ability to monitor Soviet compliance.

The facts were considerably more complicated—and less alarming —than the newspaper stories and the politicians' speeches suggested. They were also more complicated than the administration cared to explain. The Iran stations were part of a varied and far-reaching network of American facilities that keep track of Soviet military activity, including missile tests. These facilities include airplanes, satellites, ships and ground stations outfitted with an array of equipment for taking photographs, detecting launches by infrared sensors, intercepting radio messages and tracking missiles and their warheads by radar. Many of these functions are overlapping. Redundancy is a deliberately designed and highly prized feature of the system. As a Soviet missile lifts out of its silo, it can be watched simultaneously by an American satellite specially positioned overhead and by radar hundreds of miles away. During the propulsion phase, when the booster heaves the rocket into its ballistic trajectory, the craft sends telemetric signals back to earth; these can be picked up by both aerial reconnaissance and ground stations. Before reentry, the post-boost vehicle or bus dispenses each of its dummy warheads on its own trajectory to a target in "impact areas" on the Kamchatka Peninsula of eastern Siberia or in the Pacific Ocean. Reentry itself can be closely observed by American installations in the Aleutian Islands and aboard ships at sea. The posts in Iran were valuable, though not indispensable, components of this interlocking network. They had the geographical advantage of relative proximity to the Soviet ICBM test launchers at Tyuratam near the Aral Sea and the antiballistic missile test site at Sary-Shagan near Lake Balkhash. It is from Tyuratam that the Soviets test many of the missiles to be covered by SALT. The Iranian posts were well situated to watch the lift-off and listen in on signals that pass between the rocket and its ground control. This data would help ensure that modifications in existing types of ICBMs stayed within the parameters set by the new-types rule for length, diameter, launch-weight and throw-weight. It was primarily American ability to monitor compliance with that provision of SALT II—the new-types rule—that suffered as a result of the loss of the Iranian posts. Adherence to other crucial limits in SALT, such as deployment of launchers and the warhead fractionation freeze, would be verified with information from other sources, primarily spy satellites and surface facilities near the Kamchatka and Pacific impact areas. Thus, the technical damage done in Iran was not as sweeping as some press accounts and politicians suggested. Nor was it by any means permanent. The administration moved quickly to upgrade other existing means of collection, such as ground stations in Turkey, and to reinforce them with new facilities in order to monitor launches from Tyuratam.

However, the political and public relations damage was more difficult to repair. For one thing, the administration was in a predicament over how to boast about the cherished redundancy of its intelligence-gathering system without jeopardizing secrets. This was a bind similar to the one in which the U.S. had found itself in 1978 as it drew the Russians into a negotiation about the permissibility of telemetry encryption. How does the President or the director of Central Intelligence tell Senate skeptics of SALT what they want to hear in order to support the treaty without inadvertently telling the Soviets what they want to hear in order to improve countermeasures that thwart American intelligence? Verifying SALT, after all, was only a part of the task performed by the Iranian stations and all the other pieces in the system. The larger task is espionage—such as spying on the development of guidance systems for the Soviets' increasingly accurate ICBMs, a technological innovation that was not to be constrained by the new-types rule, and on the development of intermediate-range missiles, which are exempt from SALT altogether.

These mitigating—and complicating—considerations were, for the most part, ignored in the furor over the loss in Iran. What seemed to matter politically were the simple and indisputable facts that Iran had been a friend, and now it was at best neutral; American outposts there had had something to do with keeping an eye on the Russians, and now they were out of commission. The loss of Iran was a setback to American geopolitical interests; the loss of the listening posts there was a setback to the American ability to know its potential enemy. Thus, the political atmosphere in which SALT in general, and its verifiability in particular, were to be judged was more sour than ever. The administration acknowledged that if SALT was to be concluded and ratified, that atmosphere would have to improve. The Soviets had now, more bluntly than ever, linked the fate of the negotiations to Washington's conduct of its new association with China. On the American side, while the Democratic administration continued to disavow linkage, the Republican opposition embraced the notion and made it doctrine. Senate Minority Leader Howard Baker told Brezhnev himself in January 1979 that the treaty would have to be weighed by the Senate "in the overall context of Soviet-American relations." In February, Baker delivered on behalf of most Republican senators and many Democrats as well a curt, clear and irrefutable message to the administration when he said at a GOP conference in Easton, Maryland, "Linkage is a fact of life."

Cyrus Vance was sufficiently concerned about the escalation of tensions between Washington and Moscow that in late February he momentarily put aside the business of SALT per se and raised with Anatoly Dobrynin the problem of the deteriorating political climate. The two men discussed the fact that Brezhnev, in his capacity as unopposed candidate for reelection to the Supreme Soviet from the Bauman district of Moscow, was due to make a "campaign speech" on foreign policy. Vance was eager to use Dobrynin as a channel through which to influence the tone and substance of Brezhnev's speech. Vance took Dobrynin to meet with Carter. For twenty-five minutes in the Oval Office, the President delivered a carefully prepared message that combined an admonition with an appeal. He told Dobrynin that the Soviet leadership should have accepted his original suggestion of annual "consultative" meetings at the highest level, independent of treaty signings; the Kremlin's insistence on linking SALT and summitry had exacerbated the problem of linkage as a whole. Carter pointed out that while the Soviets might allege—falsely—American complicity in the Chinese invasion of Vietnam, the U.S. had a much more valid grievance over the recent attack by South Yemen, a Soviet client state, against North Yemen. But Carter's main point to Dobrynin was that relations between the U.S. and Russia must be set right before the strain got out of control; Sino-American normalization and the Sino-Vietnamese border war must not determine the course of Soviet-American relations; and most immediately and urgently, SALT must be concluded.

Two days later, Brezhnev in effect said he agreed. In a surprisingly mild and moderate speech, the Soviet leader repeated what had become the ritualistic warning for China to get out of Vietnam, but he did not couple it with the charge that the U.S. had instigated or approved the invasion, nor did he imply that SALT would be held hostage until the Chinese withdrew. SALT, he said, "will probably be

signed during my meeting with President Carter in the near future."
He called the agreement "a reasonable compromise that takes into
consideration the interests of both sides." In Washington, there was a
chorus of sighs of relief.

The Brezhnev-Carter Correspondence

But the compromise to which Brezhnev referred was not yet complete. In addition to the welter of disagreements over Indochina and
the Middle East, the U.S. and the Soviet Union were still embroiled
in substantive disputes over SALT itself. On what had already become
one of the thorniest of all the final sticking points, encryption of
telemetry, neither side was satisfied with the negotiating record as it
then stood. Vance and Gromyko had struck a bargain in Geneva just
before Christmas to include in the treaty a common understanding
that banned encryption when it impeded verification and permitted
it when it did not. Vance had been pleased with that formulation
because it meant the U.S. would have grounds for protesting any
encryption that constituted an impediment, regardless of whether the
Soviets were deliberately trying to impede verification or, as they
would surely claim, merely trying to protect legitimate military secrets. However, Stansfield Turner and to a lesser extent Harold Brown
and Zbigniew Brzezinski had not been content with the common
understanding all by itself. They felt it left the Soviets too much latitude to argue that while hypothetically some telemetry might be
relevant to SALT and hypothetically some encryption might be impermissible, in actual practice neither of those conditions had ever
arisen, or was likely to arise. Therefore Turner, Brown and Brzezinski
wanted the common understanding in the treaty reinforced by a formal exchange in the negotiating record. In this exchange the Russians
would acknowledge that Soviet encryption *as already practiced* had
met the criterion of impermissibility stipulated by the common understanding and that a repetition of that practice would be a violation.
Under unexpected and unwelcome last-minute instructions from the
White House, Vance had sought Gromyko's "noncontradiction" of the
American position that encryption such as that used in the July 29,
1978, SS-18 test, if extended to a new or modified system, would be
a violation. Gromyko's response had been testy but not an outright
contradiction.

In January, Ralph Earle went through the same exercise with Victor Karpov in Geneva. Earle cited not only the July 29 test but the similar December 21 test as well. "If you disagree" with the American position, said Earle, concluding the ritual, "tell me now." Karpov, like Gromyko before, was being given a chance to speak now or forever hold his peace. He held his peace, but not forever. One trouble with the diplomatic device of noncontradiction is that an understanding arrived at by the silence of one party is easily undone; all that party has to do is break silence. That is exactly what Karpov did. On February 14— Valentine's Day—he came back to Earle and told him he was "under instructions from my government" to state that the previously agreed common understanding on encryption was adequate to cover any case that might arise and that there was "no need for further interpretation." It was the Soviets' way of saying that they neither accepted nor rejected the American position—and that they didn't want to hear the subject raised again.

Back in Washington, where Karpov's statement was known in some offices as "the Kremlin's Valentine," the interagency squabble over how to handle the encryption issue started all over again. At the State Department and Arms Control and Disarmament Agency, there was little dismay, and even less surprise, that the Soviets were still refusing to admit that they had done anything wrong on July 29 and December 21. One official, who had opposed the attempt to get Soviet "noncontradiction" all along, commented sardonically, "The whole episode was just another example of how you can always find trouble if you're imaginative and persistent enough in the way you look for it. If you keep pressing the Russians for greater and greater specificity, sooner or later they're going to balk and you're going to end up jeopardizing a very useful general agreement. Frankly, I don't blame the Russians one bit for throwing our interpretation right back in our faces."

But even those who felt a degree of sympathy with the Soviet position recognized that Karpov's latest statement raised a serious political problem. In its upcoming effort to win the support of John Glenn and other senators, the administration had been counting on demonstrating that it had extracted from the Soviets what amounted to a promise never again to encrypt as much telemetry as they had on July 29 and December 21, and specifically not to encrypt the telemetry from the reentry vehicles. Karpov's statement had the predictable effect of throwing Stansfield Turner into a relapse of agitation on the issue. Having never really made his peace with the common understanding and still regarding the noncontradiction device as a half measure at best, he now felt justified in trying again to get an across-the-board prohibition of encryption. At a Special Coordination Committee meeting on March 5, Turner suggested a number of options for handling the problem now that Karpov had reopened the issue, and the option obviously closest to Turner's heart was to "ban all telemetry denial, including encryption," in the testing of any missile covered by SALT.

The other members of the SCC, notably Brown and Brzezinski, shared Turner's concern but did not believe there was any hope of getting the Soviets to accept an outright ban on encryption. As one official involved in the deliberations recalled: "The essence of the problem was that under the harshest interpretation, the Soviets might be leaving open the implication that 'telemetry relevant to SALT' and 'encryption which impedes verification' are null sets. We had to find some way of closing off that implication. That meant getting the Soviets to acknowledge unambiguously that verification requires access to telemetry in some instances, such as the July 29 and December 21 tests." The SCC drafted a letter from Carter to Brezhnev. The President approved the text, but he remarked at one point that the U.S. might be trying too hard to "cross every t and dot every i"—and that the pursuit of precision in this matter reminded him of Menachem Begin's doggedness about semantic technicalities in the negotiations over the Egyptian-Israeli peace treaty. The Carter letter sought, in effect, to do in writing what Vance had tried to do with Gromyko—and Earle had tried to do with Karpov—orally. It elicited a Soviet response, also in writing, that was more quarrelsome than ever. The Brezhnev reply was in one respect a mirror image of the American complaint. Just as the U.S. argued that the Soviet position was ambiguous in a way that implied all encryption was permissible, so the Kremlin argued that the American position was ambiguous in a way that implied all encryption should be banned. Clearly, the Russians were most riled by the repeated American citation of the two encoded SS-18 tests in 1978: What was the U.S. trying to say by harping on those tests? That encryption of precisely the same set of channels should be forbidden? Or, as the Russians professed to suspect, that all encryption should be forbidden? Brezhnev's reply was extremely closely held. Harold Brown, for example, was not even given a copy of his own. A White House aide went to the Pentagon and showed him the letter on an "eyes only" basis.

Once again, the Americans went back to the drawing board. The week of March 19, there was a series of meetings that produced a new approach to the problem. The deputies of the cabinet-level SCC members gathered for a "Mini-SCC" meeting. This, and a number of other, more informal brainstorming sessions, involving the second-echelon technical experts, produced a recommendation for a second Carter letter to Brezhnev. This one would focus on the general point that some telemetry is, in fact—not just in theory—relevant to SALT, and that some encryption *as practiced* impedes verification. The new letter would not address the two controversial 1978 tests at all. That omission was fine with Aaron, Gelb, Timbie, Molander and other experts who had never been happy with Brown's and Brzezinski's willingness to indulge Turner in his fixation with those tests.

However, the omission was not acceptable to Brown, Brzezinski and Turner themselves. At a "principals only" (no deputies invited) SCC meeting on March 21, Turner said that the Brezhnev letter was insulting in the way it distorted the American position on the two 1978 tests; he felt that Carter should not let Brezhnev have the last word on that subject. Harold Brown supported the idea, suggested by David Aaron, that the Carter letter be accompanied by a "note" from Vance to Dobrynin clarifying—and thus, ever so politely, reiterating—the U.S. position on the tests. The note would explain that contrary to the Soviet interpretation, the U.S. was not suggesting that SALT should forbid all encryption; rather, it should ban only encryption that impedes verification, as it sometimes does— as, indeed, it did on July 29 and December 21.

Before trying out the letter-and-note combination on the Kremlin, Carter wanted to make sure the plan had the backing of the Joint Chiefs of Staff. He had the chairman of JCS, General David Jones, explain to his colleagues the reason for the new approach; then the President summoned the Chiefs and Harold Brown to the White House for a discussion of encryption and the other outstanding issues in SALT. The next day, March 29, Vance gave Dobrynin the new letter from Carter to Brezhnev and the accompanying note. For more than a week the administration waited for the Kremlin's response. On Saturday April 7, it came. During a forty-minute meeting at the State Department, when the discussion turned to encryption, Dobrynin uttered the words Vance had been waiting for: "This issue has now been resolved on the basis of these exchanges."

Whittling Them Down

In the midst of their negotiations over encryption, Vance and Dobrynin also chipped away at the lingering disagreement over the degree of downsizing that would be permissible in the modification of an existing ICBM. For nearly a year, the U.S. had held firm to the position that no change of more or less than 5 percent should be allowed in any of the parameters used to distinguish between an existing type and the one new type allowed each side. The Soviets had appeared to accept the plus or minus 5 percent rule in early 1978; then in December they tried first to do away with the lower limit altogether, later to extend it to minus 20 percent. The matter had been left unresolved when Vance returned home, disappointed and discouraged, from his pre-Christmas meeting with Gromyko in Geneva.

In early January the Special Coordination Committee met largely to discuss this issue, which was termed on the agenda "new-types definition." Zbigniew Brzezinski was the chairman. He argued that the U.S. "must not give a single inch, not a single percentage point" on the plus or minus 5 percent rule. There was not much disagreement. Everyone felt that allowing the Russians 20 percent downsizing would make a mockery of the claim that SALT contained an exemption for only one new type of ICBM. "Minus 20 percent is out of the question," said Brzezinski, "because it would effectively give them a second, or even a third, fourth and fifth, new-types exemption."

That SCC meeting did, however, result in granting the American delegation in Geneva some flexibility to negotiate the list of parameters which would be used in the new-types definition—that is, the parameters to which the plus or minus 5 percent rule would apply. The Soviets had already agreed to a short list or hard core of six parameters: (1) length of the booster, (2) maximum diameter of the booster, (3) number of stages of the rocket, (4) fuel type of the booster, (5) throw-weight and (6) launch-weight. The Soviets had also recently accepted a prohibition on decreasing the weight of individual reentry vehicles. But the U.S. persisted in its effort to add restrictions on the initial weight and power (total impulse) of each stage of the rocket and on the initial weight, power and fuel type of the post-boost vehicle, or "bus," which dispenses reentry vehicles that hurtle back into the atmosphere. The U.S. delegation in Geneva was authorized to bargain away some of those extra parameters in exchange for Soviet acceptance of plus or minus 5 percent to govern the parameters that were finally agreed on. The first ones to fall by the wayside were those governing the initial weights of the individual stages and of the bus.

The same sort of dickering went on back in Washington. In early February, Vance met with Dobrynin to review the outstanding problems in SALT. The Soviet ambassador said there were two problems with the Americans' new-types definition: "You ask for more parameters than we do, and they go beyond our ability to verify them by national technical means. Second, we need more than 5 percent downsizing." Dobrynin added, however, "But we are willing to compromise short of 20 percent." Vance took it as an encouraging sign of flexibility. He and other American officials suspected they could probably close a deal at 10 percent on the spot, but they felt that even a 10 percent downsizing allowance in all parameters would give the Soviets too much latitude to modernize existing rockets. So the dickering continued.

On February 12, the Special Coordination Committee met again and decided to "sweeten" the American new-types definition by coupling it with a concession on one of the minor sticking points in SALT —multiple-warhead, or MIRVed, cruise missiles. The U.S. had already agreed to a ban on the testing of such things in the protocol; the Soviets wanted to extend the ban for the life of the treaty, until 1985. The SCC decided Vance should propose to Dobrynin an explicit trade-off. As one of the American principals put it at the time, "We said we'd ban the testing of MIRVed ALCMs in exchange for getting our way on the new-types definition." The next afternoon Vance put the proposition to Dobrynin, and the Americans sat back to wait for the Soviet reply. Dobrynin returned with a counterproposal that was predictable but unacceptable: a downsizing limit of "10 or 12 percent." His compatriots at the negotiating table in Geneva formally proposed 12 percent, but the Carter administration chose to regard 10 percent as the new Soviet offer, since Dobrynin had let that number pass his lips.

Even by their own standards, the Soviets were yielding ground glacially. The frustrated and puzzled Americans began to reexamine their own analysis—and to probe the Russians—for some indication of why the design bureaus of the Soviet Strategic Rocket Forces felt they needed more than 5 percent downsizing. The assumption on the American side since December had been that the Russians belatedly realized 5 percent would prevent them from proceeding with the development of some modernized, more compact successors to some of their existing ICBMs. Alexander Shchukin seemed obliquely to be confirming that suspicion when he remarked in Geneva, "We need it [the extra downsizing] for flexibility in design." But there were some other hints that perhaps the Soviet effort to stretch the downsizing rule also had something to do with the Russians' testing practices and that they were primarily interested in stretching the limit in only one or two parameters rather than in all of them.

Victor Karpov once asked Ralph Earle in Geneva, "Is it the U.S. position that no more than minus 5 percent should be permitted in changes in launch-weight and throw-weight?" Earle replied firmly that it was. When he transmitted the exchange back to Washington in a "memcon," analysts there deduced that perhaps the Soviets were particularly eager for extra flexibility in those two parameters. Then, on a different occasion in Geneva, Shchukin suggested informally to his opposite number, Gerald Johnson, a scientist who represented the office of the Secretary of Defense, that in testing ICBMs from Tyura-tam, the Soviets needed to experiment with ballast in the top stage of the rocket and with varying amounts of fuel in the bottom stage. Ballast would affect both the throw-weight and the launch-weight; the amount of fuel on board the booster would affect the launch-weight. A memcon of that conversation sent the experts in Washington back to their maps and pocket calculators to figure out what Shchukin might have been talking about. They speculated along the following lines. The Tyuratam test site—the facility on which the lost Iranian posts had been focused—conducts two sorts of ICBM tests. There are full-range tests into the mid-Pacific. (Under SALT II, the Soviets would be obliged to give the U.S. advance notice of these "extraterritorial" launches.) Then there are truncated flight tests into an impact area on the Kamchatka Peninsula in eastern Siberia. In the latter case, the Soviets could get what the technicians call a "full burn" out of the rocket booster—that is, they could simulate a full-range test—by add-ing ballast to the payload, or they could adjust other aspects of the missile's performance by reducing fuel. Presumably, the Russians were interested in a plus 5 percent/minus 10 percent rule in order to give themselves a 15 percent spread within which to experiment with the equations involving weight and range.

The Carter administration was prepared to consider a carefully defined exception to the new-types definition allowing the Soviets extra downsizing in throw-weight and possibly launch-weight as well.

But the administration was willing to do so only if the Soviet negotiators could present a convincing case that such an exception was necessary for legitimate test practices and that it would not be used to circumvent the constraints on modernization—that it would not be used, in short, to develop a significantly smaller, better missile.

In early March, just before heading off to Cairo and Jerusalem with President Carter for a desperate and ultimately successful attempt to save the Camp David peace treaty, Vance held another meeting with Dobrynin and told him that the U.S. wanted to hear a formal, persuasive rationale for the Soviet position on downsizing. Then, at a principals-only Special Coordination Committee meeting on March 21 (the same meeting that produced the second Carter letter to Brezhnev on encryption), Vance said it was time to resolve the downsizing issue once and for all; the Geneva delegations had tried and failed to whittle the Soviets down to minus 5 percent in exchange for the U.S.'s willingness to whittle down the list of parameters. Now it was time to make the trade-off in one fell swoop. In his session with Dobrynin a week later, Vance proposed a straightforward swap of a firm plus or minus 5 percent rule for the elimination of the last three extra parameters (the power, or total impulse, of each stage, the power of the bus, and the fuel type of the bus). That left the 5 percent limit to apply to changes in length, diameter, launch-weight and throw-weight. The U.S. would agree, however, to one exception: reductions of more than 5 percent would be allowed for launch-weight and throw-weight as long as the reduction was accounted for exclusively and entirely by the offloading of reentry vehicles or decoy warheads and a corresponding amount of fuel.* In other words, no structural change of more than 5 percent would be allowed. This exception apparently went part-way in helping the Soviets meet their need to test ICBMs at less than full range with less than a full load of reentry vehicles, for at his breakthrough meeting with Vance on Saturday, April 7, Dobrynin accepted the American position.

Bus Stops

That breakthrough, however, was not conclusive. The resolution of encryption and downsizing cleared the docket of the principal pieces

---

*The formulation of this exception was largely based on a long-standing American proposal that the Pentagon had advocated because it facilitated certain of its own testing and deployment practices.

of old business left over from before Christmas. But there was now one major piece of new business. It concerned the SS-18, the MIRVed heavy missile, and whether the Soviets were developing a version of that rocket that could carry more warheads than the ten allowed by the fractionation freeze—the provision whereby no existing type of ICBM could be tested with more reentry vehicles than the maximum already tested on that type.

At issue this time were two SS-18 tests at the end of 1978, one shortly before and the other shortly after the pre-Christmas Vance-Gromyko meeting in Geneva. In each of these tests, the post-boost vehicle dispensed the permissible maximum of ten dummy warheads or reentry vehicles; but it went through at least two additional war-head-dispensing maneuvers or feints. In the jargon of MIRVed mis-silry, the PBV engaged in two "release simulations." More plainly, the bus made two extra stops even though no extra reentry vehicles got off. If the type of missile involved had been other than the SS-18, American officials would have been less concerned. They really had to worry only insofar as the extra release simulations suggested an actual capacity to carry extra reentry vehicles aboard the bus. The Soviets had recently accepted as part of the new-types definition a prohibition against making the reentry vehicles smaller and lighter than those already tested. Part of the reason for this rule was precisely to prevent the Soviets from developing highly accurate mini-MIRVs that could be stuffed in large numbers onto the SS-17, SS-19 and SS-18 in place of the big, heavy, high-yield blockbuster warheads that had been the traditional Russian specialty. That provision, which was known suc-cinctly if inelegantly as the no-lighter-RV rule, would give the Ameri-cans confidence that even if Soviet MIRVed missiles engaged in re-lease simulations, the SS-17s and SS-19s were not being tested with extra, unreleased warheads over and above the four and six that they were to be allowed by the fractionation freeze. Close observation of past tests had established that with most Soviet ICBMs, as with Ameri-can missiles, the weight of the warhead cluster accounts for approxi-mately half the total throw-weight. The other half is bus, guidance system and propellant. That meant the U.S. technicians monitoring a test could add up the weight of the reentry vehicles dispensed, and if the sum was equal to approximately half the throw-weight, they could be fairly sure there were no extra ones on board.

But the SS-18 was an exception to this rule. The ratio of total RV weight to total throw-weight was unusually low. That anomaly had made U.S. experts a bit uneasy, but they had written it off to an inefficiently designed, excessively bulky bus. That explanation made more sense than the suspicion that the Soviets were saving room on board for more than ten warheads. Before December, the Soviets had tested the SS-18 with nine RVs released and one release simulation. Then, to the consternation and alarm of the Americans, the SS-18 was tested with ten RVs and two release simulations. At the worst, these maneuvers suggested that the SS-18 might be learning to carry and release twelve warheads. That was nothing compared to the twenty-five to forty warheads that many Pentagon analysts believed the SS-18 might be capable of launching in the absence of SALT, but it was still a serious political problem. For the Soviets to be showing an interest in developing a missile with a capacity to launch more warheads than it would be allowed to carry raised the suspicion that they might be preparing for a "breakout," an opportunity to cheat on the treaty or abrogate it suddenly and in a way that significantly affected the strategic balance. Also, the fractionation freeze was a key selling point for the administration in its upcoming struggle for ratification, and release simulations of the sort carried out in the two December tests seemed to violate the spirit if not the letter of the fractionation freeze. So the administration gave a heavy sigh and set about trying to tighten the letter of the provision so as to prohibit such practices in the future.

There were a number of similarities between this wrinkle in the fabric of SALT and the problems caused by the Soviets' use of encryption on July 29 and December 21, 1978. In both cases the missile involved was the SS-18, although the encryption episode involved a single-warhead version while the release simulations occurred in MIRV tests. In both cases, the Soviets had altered their test practices in a way that seemed, inexplicably, almost calculated to complicate not only the negotiations themselves but also the ratification debate in the Senate. In both cases, the U.S. response was to tell the Russians that a repetition of the practice would be an infringement of SALT II (indeed, Alexander Shchukin complained in Geneva in early 1979 that the U.S. was developing the rude and unconstructive habit of "accusing the Soviet Union of violating this treaty in advance"). Finally, in both cases—encryption and release simulation—the American position was encumbered by twin complications: the U.S. had to be careful not to reveal intelligence secrets by telling the Russians too much in the course of the negotiations, and it had to be careful not to rewrite the strictures of SALT in a way that obtruded on American programs and practices.

Part of the problem was that the Pentagon had for a long time taken pains to ensure that SALT did not forbid the use of "penetration aids" on its ICBMs. These were devices that would increase the chances of the warheads penetrating Soviet antimissile defenses and reaching their targets. Penetration aids might be decoy warheads that would draw enemy fire away from the live ones, or they might be bursts of metal chaff that would make it harder for the radar in the Soviet antiballistic missile system to track the incoming warheads. The U.S. had experimented with both sorts of penetration aids, including at least one test with two reentry vehicles and ten decoys on a Minuteman III. But the state of the art on the American side contained an important difference between the procedure used to release a MIRV warhead and that used to release a decoy or chaff. The acronym MIRV, it should be recalled, stands for multiple *independently targetable* reentry vehicle. In order to start a warhead on its way toward its independent target with the necessary accuracy, the bus must place it on the proper trajectory with great precision. That means the bus must aim the warhead in the right direction, turn it loose, then back off slowly and carefully in order not to interfere in any way with the warhead's flight. Since accuracy is not so important for decoys or chaff, they can be spring loaded; the release mechanisms are far simpler— and the procedures are distinctive when they show up in telemetry beamed back to earth—and intercepted by the other side.

To make the issue even more delicate in the negotiations, some Navy and Air Force designers had been planning for American missiles to engage in practices virtually identical to the Soviet release simulations that had suddenly become so worrisome from a political standpoint. "Release simulations can themselves be penetration aids," explained a military specialist (the terminology of his profession had begun to sound curiously like that of a sex therapist). Since an antiballistic missile system takes aim at an incoming warhead partly by drawing a bead on the bus at the time of release, feints of the sort that the SS-18 had conducted in December would make it more difficult for the ABM system to intercept the warheads actually released. Some Air Force enthusiasts for the MX, America's drawing-board replacement for the Minuteman, wanted the missile to have the capacity to engage in release simulations over and above the ten warheads it would be allowed to carry under SALT II. More immediately, the designers of the Trident-I submarine-launched ballistic missile had already provided for such a capacity in their handiwork. The Trident would carry a full complement of eight warheads—six less than allowed under the

SALT fractionation freeze of fourteen reentry vehicles per SLBM. But the Trident bus had been designed to stop as many as twenty times, dispensing warheads at eight stops, and engaging in feint-type release simulations at the other twelve in order to confuse Soviet defenders. That would mean six stops over and above the SLBM fractionation limit of fourteen. So before the Carter administration could go back to the negotiating table and tell the Russians no more than ten stops for the SS-18 bus, it had first to tell the Air Force no more than ten stops for the MX bus and the Navy no more than fourteen for the Trident.

Decoys and other sorts of penetration aids, however, had still to be protected in the treaty. So the new American position as presented to the Russians in early 1979 was somewhat convoluted: the language of the fractionation freeze would have to be tightened in a way that the sum of reentry vehicles actually released plus feint-type release simulations could not exceed the maximum fractionation of that type of missile (ten for the MX and SS-18, fourteen for the Trident, etc.); furthermore, any maneuver relating to penetration aids over and above that maximum must be "different" from the "procedure" used to dispense warheads. The vagueness of that formulation was an invitation for the Soviet negotiators to ask what the U.S. meant by "different." For that matter, what did it mean by "procedure"? Having asked those innocent-sounding questions, the Soviets could sit back and watch the Americans squirm. The U.S. did not want to elaborate on either word because to do so would be to give the Russians hints about how American monitors had caught the SS-18 engaging in release simulations; too much explanation and precision would compromise "sources and methods" of intelligence.

The performance of the intelligence community in this episode was already a matter of extreme sensitivity, overlaid with controversy, within the U.S. government. The tests in question had taken place in December. Yet it took more than two months for the policy-makers at the Pentagon and the White House to find out what had happened. The CIA justified itself by explaining that time-consuming and painstaking analysis were required to determine exactly what the Russians had been up to in those tests.

To make matters worse, the intelligence community's findings reached the readers of the *New York Times* only a few days after Cyrus Vance, Harold Brown and Zbigniew Brzezinski found out about the December tests in top-secret briefings. Richard Burt, the national security affairs correspondent of the *Times*, had been giving the Carter administration fits for two years.* He had been the first reporter to print the details of the September 1977 breakthrough in SALT II. That story had inflamed Henry Jackson's anger at the administration decision to abandon a new, lower limit on Soviet heavy missiles. Burt had been the first to report Carter's decision to defer production of the neutron bomb, a story that had exacerbated U.S.–West German tensions over that subject. But his most impressive scoop—regarded within the administration as his most damaging— was an article in the *Times* on March 14, 1979, reporting that the top level of the Pentagon had learned only the week before about the SS-18 release simulations. The headline was misleading—or at least it presumed more than U.S. experts had concluded: "Soviet [Union] Reported to Add to Load Missile Can Fire." But the article laid out the details of the testing incident in a way that touched off precisely the sort of congressional challenges about the validity of the fractionation freeze that the administration feared.

The Soviets apparently appreciated the severity of the political problem caused by their use of feints. They may have realized that, given the importance the administration attached to the fractionation freeze, stonewalling on their part might stall the negotiations indefinitely—and if the administration failed to get its way on the issue, that failure alone could contribute significantly to the rejection of the treaty by the Senate. On May 1, Dobrynin gave Vance an "oral note"**—a list of the latest Kremlin positions on the outstanding issues. When Vance glanced down at the list, he saw that it included Soviet acceptance of the American-proposed restriction on release simulations. The Soviets had agreed to ban release simulations as practiced in the two tests in December. Marshall Shulman was sitting in on the meeting. After Dobrynin left, Shulman settled into the rocking chair that Vance, who suffered from chronic back trouble, kept in the hideaway study off his spacious main office. The secretary sat at his desk. Talking over the meeting, the two men agreed that the last problem of major significance—the last issue that had the potential of blocking an agreement forever—had been solved. But they also knew

---

*Burt was one of the few true defense scholastics on the SALT beat. Before joining the *Times*, he was an assistant director of the International Institute for Strategic Studies in London.

**In diplomatic exchanges, oral notes are sometimes, but not always, read aloud before they are handed over.

that elation would be premature. Minor problems remained, problems that could delay a treaty for weeks—and every week that passed without announcement of agreement in principle probably meant the Senate debate would last a week longer, carrying the issue of SALT deeper into the perilous season of presidential politics which would begin in earnest in the fall.

15 The End of the Game

In the final phase of SALT II, virtually every issue, major and minor, was under intensive negotiation between Vance and Dobrynin as well as between the delegations in Geneva. The two-track approach was largely at the Soviets' behest. In all, the secretary of state and the Soviet ambassador met twenty-five times between January 1 and May 7. They would meet at the State Department, usually in Vance's hideaway study, often with Marshall Shulman and Leslie Gelb or Jerome Kahan present. If it was late in the day, Vance and Dobrynin would wind down from their formal exchanges of set pieces and oral notes by sipping Scotch and talking about problems extraneous to the substance of SALT but relevant to the atmosphere of the talks. Dobrynin, for example, protested on a number of occasions about news articles in the American press that quoted anonymous government officials speculating in a way that Dobrynin found insulting on whether Brezhnev would be physically and mentally competent to negotiate with Carter at a summit. Other times, Dobrynin said his government was worried that the U.S. seemed to be deliberately stalling in the negotiations, holding out intractably for what the Russians considered unreasonable positions. But in the American view, it was the Soviets who were dragging their feet. Initially, American officials had hoped that the Russians' preference for parallel talks in Washington and Geneva meant that the Kremlin was serious about closing the gap quickly. However, for months the progress on major issues—encryption, downsizing and release simulation—had come slowly and painfully, and the progress on minor issues was often accompanied by new complications.

For example, in late January Dobrynin gave Vance an oral note on "bomber fractionation," or the average number of cruise missiles to be permitted on airplanes. At their December meeting in Geneva, Vance and Gromyko had narrowed the disagreement to a difference of one; the U.S. had come down from 30 to 28, and the U.S.S.R. had come up from 25 to 27. Now Dobrynin told Vance that Moscow would accept 28 for the average. But there was a hitch. The Soviets wanted the administration to make a statement saying that the U.S. had no plan to deploy a cruise missile carrier with more than 20 ALCMs. This undertaking would not be an integral part of the SALT agreement. Rather, it would be a separate but accompanying statement, somewhat like the assurances the Soviets had agreed to furnish on the production rate and range of the Backfire. Dobrynin explained that the Kremlin leaders needed to allay the concern of the Soviet military about cruise missiles in much the same way that the American leaders had to take account of the Joint Chiefs' stubborn worries over Backfire. In fact, the U.S. Air Force had no plans to deploy any bombers with more than 20 ALCMs per plane for the entire treaty period, since the B-52 was the designated cruise missile carrier and 20 ALCMs was the maximum load for a B-52. Harold Brown said as much in his annual report to the Congress for 1979. But the Carter administration did not want to address itself directly to the Kremlin on the matter. That would make it appear—to the political detriment of SALT II—that the administration's deployment plans were governed in some measure by Soviet pressure. Therefore the Soviets would have to content themselves with the declaration of American intentions contained in Brown's annual report, in the congressional testimony of Air Force officials, and other on-the-record statements by members of the executive branch for the benefit of the legislative branch; there need not be any separate statement for the benefit of the Soviet government. But Dobrynin persisted, and in the end the administration agreed to an agreed statement as part of the SALT treaty, in which both sides would promise not to put more than 20 ALCMs on their "current types" of heavy bomber—in the U.S.'s case, the B-52. That technically left the Air Force free under SALT to accelerate the development of a new, built-from-scratch wide-bodied cruise missile carrier before 1985 with an average of 28 ALCMs per plane if the U.S. ever felt such an acceleration was necessary.

The U.S. also agreed to what it considered a mostly cosmetic concession on the deadline for the dismantling of the 150 Soviet strategic

launch vehicles that made the difference between the Vladivostok
ceiling of 2,400 and the newly agreed reduced ceiling of 2,250. For
many months, the American negotiators had been seeking a precise
timetable, whereby at regular intervals during the year 1981 set per-
centages of the weapons would have to be dismantled, and by mid
1981 all 150 would have to be "in a state of irreversible inoperability"
(an abominable phrase that was later improved somewhat to read
"observably inoperable"). But in early February, Vance told Dobrynin
that the U.S. would no longer insist on so rigid a timetable, as long as
the Soviets agreed that the dismantling would take place at a steady
rate during 1981 and would be complete by the last day of that year.
The Russians agreed, and made a concession of their own, accepting
December 31, 1981, as the termination date of the protocol—earlier
than they had originally wanted. As long as the expiration of the
protocol and the deadline for dismantling were coterminous, American officials calculated, there would be little danger of the Soviets'
using the pace at which they dismantled to pressure the U.S. into
extending the restrictions on cruise missiles contained in the protocol.

As the brackets symbolizing disagreement fell away from the Joint
Draft Text of the treaty, so did the asterisk at the beginning of the
document. That asterisk symbolized the dispute within the Carter
administration in 1978 over whether to keep open the option of submitting SALT II as an agreement requiring a simple majority in both
houses of Congress rather than a treaty requiring two thirds of the
Senate. Now that Carter had publicly committed himself to submitting it as a treaty, in one of the last weeks of the negotiations an order
went out from the SALT Backstopping Committee to the delegation
in Geneva to strike the asterisk and the footnote to which it was
attached. Some brackets remained until the very end as typographical
monuments to ancient points of contention that neither side had both-
ered to tear down. For example, one passage of American-preferred
language still contained a definition of the Backfire as a heavy bomber
to be counted against the new 2,250 ceiling of total nuclear strategic
launch vehicles. Jimmy Carter, like Henry Kissinger before him, had
long since given up on trying to count the Backfire under SALT, but
it remained for the Geneva negotiators to expunge from the Joint
Draft Text the last evidence of a long-abandoned American position.

Dobrynin and Vance decided to leave a number of minor but
substantive issues for the delegations to thresh out between the time
Vance and Dobrynin reached agreement in principle on the treaty

and the time Carter and Brezhnev signed the document at the summit. There were about a dozen such issues. They included the drafting of precise language in the plus or minus 5 percent new-types definition for a narrowly defined exception to facilitate certain legitimate Soviet testing practices. Other still open questions were whether the 18 heavy launchers at the Tyuratam test site would count against the SALT ceiling (the Soviets had by now indicated they would be willing to dismantle twelve of those silos and convert the others into test launchers that were clearly different from operational ones)* and whether long-range target drones were to be treated in the same way as reconnaissance drones. The latter would be covered by a common understanding saying that neither side had plans to test or deploy unarmed pilotless vehicles (UPVs) with ranges greater than 600 kilometers. Both sides had been thinking primarily of reconnaissance drones when the UPV issue arose as a last spasm of the Soviet fixation with cruise missiles. In deciding whether it could afford to sacrifice UPVs, the Pentagon took an inventory of its own fleet. Belatedly, the U.S. realized it had left target drones out of the survey and therefore wanted them left out of the ban. It was an issue of such utter pettiness that neither the U.S. nor the U.S.S.R. had done its homework properly or formulated the problem with sufficient precision before settling on the statement of "nonintention" to test or deploy. It also came to be considered a wrangle unworthy of further discussion between Vance and Dobrynin. (In the end, target drones were exempted.)

Thus, slowly but surely, as the high-stakes issues were resolved, the penny-ante problems, too, fell into place. They were relegated to Geneva for final dickering. The pile of small change on the table between Vance and Dobrynin had been reduced to two pieces—and they were both plug nickels. That is, they were both phony issues, having to do not with some monstrous Soviet silo buster but with the U.S. Minuteman.

One problem involved the perennially aggravating "environmental" shelters over the Minuteman silos at Malmstrom Air Force Base in Montana, over which so much ill will had already been generated in Geneva and Washington. At the pre-Christmas meeting, Gromyko had reiterated the five-year-old Soviet complaint that despite their modification in 1977, the shelters were still a concealment measure

*When the chief CIA representative in Geneva returned to Washington in the spring of 1979, he gave his KGB opposite number a T-shirt emblazoned with the slogan, "Free the Tyuratam Eighteen!"

that impeded Soviet verification of the mix between unMIRVed Minuteman IIs and MIRVed Minuteman IIIs at Malmstrom. Moreover,
Gromyko had continued, the Soviets were now uncertain about their
ability to distinguish between all 450 Minuteman IIs and all 550 Minuteman IIIs, throughout the U.S. Vance had sought to do away with
the red herring then and there by promising that the U.S. would
remove the shelters forthwith if the Russians would stop pretending
to have difficulty distinguishing between MIRVed and unMIRVed
Minutemen. But subsequently Vance's effort to solve the problem was
undermined by the Pentagon and the National Security Council.
Malmstrom had long been an issue of passionate obduracy on the part
of the Air Force and the Joint Chiefs of Staff. The American missile-
men had always considered the Soviet position on Malmstrom a sham
—which Vance would be the first to agree it was. But the military also
considered it an important issue of principle—which Vance felt it was
not; he saw it as a thoroughly expendable negotiating point.

The Air Force and the JCS had successfully resisted Henry Kissinger's attempt at conceding to the Soviets on the Malmstrom shelters,
and they had resented the Carter administration's order in 1977 to
shrink the shelters by half. After the Vance-Gromyko exchange before
Christmas, under pressure from the Chiefs and the Pentagon as a
whole, the National Security Council issued a presidential order to
Ralph Earle in early 1979: he was instructed to tell Victor Karpov that
the U.S. would give the Soviets a date-certain for removing the shelters *if and when* they dropped the issue of Minuteman distinguishability. "If and when" clearly meant "if and after." Hearing this, Karpov
arched his brow reprovingly and reminded Earle that Vance had, in
his pre-Christmas exchange with Gromyko, said nothing about the
resolution of Minuteman distinguishability being a precondition for
resolution of the Malmstrom problem. Karpov was right; Vance had
not. The American position had stiffened, and so, naturally, the Soviet
position did the same. For the four long months between January and
early May, the U.S. and the Soviet Union went through a sort of
reverse Alphonse-and-Gaston act, with the Russians saying, "You get
rid of the shelters, then we'll shut up about distinguishability," and the
Americans saying, "No, you shut up first, then we'll get rid of the
shelters." In February, Earle was authorized to give Karpov a date-
certain for removal. It was April 30. But the precondition was still
there. April 30 came and went, and the shelters were still in place—
even though the Montana snows had melted. The shelters stayed

because the Soviets were still complaining about Minuteman distinguishability, demanding that the U.S. provide "convincing data that will allow us to distinguish Minuteman IIs from Minuteman IIIs by national technical means."

The other equally phony but not so exasperating or contentious Minuteman issue concerned the fractionation freeze and how many MIRVs would be allowed on the Minuteman III. Neither the Air Force nor anyone else in a responsible position in the government proposed increasing the MIRV load of Minuteman from three. But the fractionation freeze was drafted in terms of the maximum number of warheads with which a given type of ICBM had already been tested, and there had been a test, code-named Pave Pepper, during the Ford administration, in which the Minuteman III had been fired with seven reentry vehicles ("to see how many eggs you could squeeze out of that kind of bird"). Ideally, strictly for reasons of political appearance, the Carter administration would have liked to leave open the Pave Pepper loophole in SALT II. But during the first week in May, at Vance's urging, the Special Coordination Committee approved a fallback position: he could concede to the Soviets on this militarily insignificant point and close the loophole.

Vance told the SCC that with the last of the important, substantive problems—release simulation—finally out of the way, he and Dobrynin could probably hammer out a trade-off on the two Minuteman problems, distinguishability and fractionation, that very week. But negotiating the time and place for the Brezhnev-Carter summit would take longer. Carter, Mondale, Vance, Brzezinski, Aaron, Jordan and others held a series of meetings, formal and informal, to discuss the desirability of coupling the announcement of agreement in principle on SALT with announcement of a summit. The consensus was that it would look better if both announcements could be made simultaneously or within a short time of each other. Another possibility would have been for Vance and Dobrynin to push hard to resolve the twin Minuteman problems at their next session that same week, but defer an announcement of SALT until an accompanying summit announcement was ready. The trouble with that plan was that it raised the danger of a leak; the press might find out SALT was finally in the bag and report the fact before the administration announced it. Better, therefore, to leave something unresolved over the weekend, so that Vance's aides, when they were called by reporters, could honestly say there was still some "substance" to be worked out in SALT. "We don't have to bite the bullet on this one this week," Vance told the SCC. So he and Dobrynin drew out their negotiation of the Minuteman sticking points until Monday, May 7. Thus, ironically, after months and months of official impatience and overoptimism, of thwarted predictions and time-consuming snags, at the very last minute the two sides in effect rigged a final delay in order to enhance the political impact of the announcement. But after six and a half years of SALT II, one more week seemed like a small price to pay if it would increase, even by an iota, the treaty's chances of surviving the upcoming fight for ratification in the Senate.

Vance's meeting with Dobrynin on Monday morning, May 7, went well. The Soviet ambassador asked for fifteen minutes at the outset to talk to Vance alone, before Marshall Shulman joined them. The one-on-one session was devoted to the exceedingly sensitive subject of where and when Brezhnev could meet Carter with minimum strain on his fragile health. Then they cut the knot tying the two Minuteman issues. Dobrynin held firm for closing the Pave Pepper loophole, and Vance went to his fallback, agreeing that Minuteman III would be explicitly frozen at three warheads. As a mutually face-saving device on the other outstanding problem, the two men agreed that the Soviets would drop their complaint about Minuteman distinguishability provided the U.S. gave the Soviet Union a formal statement on the numerical breakdown between Minuteman IIs and Minuteman IIIs (450 and 550, as the Soviets and every newspaper reader in America knew perfectly well); Vance also committed the U.S. to giving the Soviets formal notification if Minuteman IIIs were ever put into Minuteman II holes. As for Malmstrom, yet again Vance promised that the troublesome shelters would come down. But this time he was determined to follow up on that promise quickly and forcefully. He resolved to ask Harold Brown the next day to give the necessary order to the Air Force. Walter Slocombe had already drafted an order to be issued in Brown's name. The shelters were down within a matter of days.

That same climactic Monday afternoon, Vance went to report to the White House. "We're at the end of the road," he told Carter, Mondale, Brzezinski, Jordan and Powell. Shortly afterward, Brzezinski passed the news to David Aaron, who had been chairing a SALT Working Group meeting. Aaron was glad to hear that the Vance-Dobrynin session had gone well, but he felt no sudden swell of euphoria or relief. The final moves of the endgame of SALT II had been so excruciatingly protracted—the last mile of the road had been so strewn with small stones that caused big jolts—Aaron could not believe that there wouldn't be some rough spots and unpleasant surprises ahead, between the announcement and the summit. And after the summit loomed a whole new set of difficult negotiations—between the Carter administration and the United States Senate. In case those went well and SALT II was ratified, there were administration task forces already at work on the daunting business of preparing for SALT III. Monday evening Aaron raided the refrigerator in Brzezinski's office and found a nearly empty bottle of Polish vodka. He poured small shots into paper coffee cups for himself, Roger Molander and Brzezinski's press spokesman, Jerrold Schecter. Aaron then proposed a toast: "Here's to what's been done—and to what's left still to do!"

Aaron's weariness, apprehension and even disbelief were widely shared by colleagues elsewhere in the government. At the Pentagon, Slocombe remarked with a wry smile, "I'll believe it when I see it." The treaty had yet to be signed by the President and ratified by the Senate. Slocombe's military assistant, Colonel Richard Klass, summed up the mixture of anxiety and anticlimax that dampened the feeling of accomplishment on both sides of the Potomac: "We've been approaching this asymptotically for so long—getting closer and closer but never quite seeming to arrive."

Marshall Shulman felt deep satisfaction, especially on behalf of his friend and boss Vance; particularly since the departure of Paul Warnke in late 1978, Vance had borne the brunt of the day-by-day, issue-by-issue negotiating through so many moments of what seemed like hopeless impasse or imminent collapse. But Shulman and a number of other veteran and dedicated participants in the enterprise also felt a sense of heaviness, a sense that the whole SALT process—while it had, once again, added a major and basically sound treaty to its track record—was becoming parlously complicated and cumbersome. In the short run, Shulman knew that there was some delicate and demanding bargaining of treaty language and other details still to be done in Geneva, and at his suggestion Ralph Earle was summoned home just for one day—the Monday that the final pieces fell into place. After Vance's conclusive exchanges with Dobrynin, Earle met with the secretary, Shulman and George Seignious to plan for the upcoming "crash effort" to polish the Joint Draft Text for signing by Carter and Brezhnev. Then Earle went straight back to the airport to catch the transatlantic red-eye to Geneva. Cables were prepared to notify Malcolm Toon in Moscow and the leaders of allied governments that

Vance would be announcing the agreement at the White House Wednesday afternoon. Late Monday, the secretary told one of his assistants, Peter Tarnoff, to telephone Leslie Gelb at a hotel in Italy, where he was attending an international conference with his wife. Because they were speaking on an open phone line, the conversation between Tarnoff and Gelb was brief, elliptical and devoid of any note of celebration, although Gelb may have had more cause for relief than others for whom a whole new round of hard work was just beginning. After countless bureaucratic battles against what had often seemed like the Pentagon-NSC-CIA axis—battles that often had been draining and sometimes losing—Gelb had recently announced his intention to leave the government after SALT was signed in mid June. He would be able to observe the suspenseful, knock-down-drag-out aftermath from the sidelines. Gelb's mentor and comrade in arms control, Paul Warnke, did not hear about Monday's final breakthrough until Tuesday morning. He heard it on the news over his car radio. He was taking a day off from his law practice to drive to Juniata College in Huntingdon, Pennsylvania, to give a speech on SALT.

Appendix: The SALT II Agreement

TREATY
BETWEEN THE UNITED STATES OF AMERICA
AND
THE UNION OF SOVIET SOCIALIST REPUBLICS
ON THE LIMITATION OF STRATEGIC OFFENSIVE ARMS

The United States of America and the Union of Soviet Socialist Republics, hereinafter referred to as the Parties,

Conscious that nuclear war would have devastating consequences for all mankind,

Proceeding from the Basic Principles of Relations Between the United States of America and the Union of Soviet Socialist Republics of May 29, 1972,

Attaching particular significance to the limitation of strategic arms and determined to continue their efforts begun with the Treaty on the Limitation of Anti-Ballistic Missile Systems and the Interim Agreement on Certain Measures with Respect to the Limitation of Strategic Offensive Arms, of May 26, 1972,

Convinced that the additional measures limiting strategic offensive arms provided for in this Treaty will contribute to the improvement of relations between the Parties, help to reduce the risk of outbreak of nuclear war and strengthen international peace and security,

Mindful of their obligations under Article VI of the Treaty on the Non-Proliferation of Nuclear Weapons,

Guided by the principle of equality and equal security,

Recognizing that the strengthening of strategic stability meets the interests of the Parties and the interests of international security,

Reaffirming their desire to take measures for the further limitation and for the further reduction of strategic arms, having in mind the goal of achieving general and complete disarmament,

Declaring their intention to undertake in the near future negotiations further to limit and further to reduce strategic offensive arms,

Have agreed as follows:

Article I

Each Party undertakes, in accordance with the provisions of this Treaty, to limit strategic offensive arms quantitatively and qualitatively, to exercise restraint in the development of new types of strategic offensive arms, and to adopt other measures provided for in this Treaty.

Article II

For the purposes of this Treaty:

1. Intercontinental ballistic missile (ICBM) launchers are land-based launchers of ballistic missiles capable of a range in excess of the shortest distance between the northeastern border of the continental part of the territory of the United States of America and the northwestern border of the continental part of the territory of the Union of Soviet Socialist Republics, that is, a range in excess of 5,500 kilometers.

2. Submarine-launched ballistic missile (SLBM) launchers are launchers of ballistic missiles installed on any nuclear-powered submarine or launchers of modern ballistic missiles installed on any submarine, regardless of its type.

3. Heavy bombers are considered to be:

   (a) currently, for the United States of America, bombers of the B-52 and B-1 types, and for the Union of Soviet Socialist Republics, bombers of the Tupolev-95 and Myasishchev types;

   (b) in the future, types of bombers which can carry out the mission of a heavy bomber in a manner similar or superior to that of bombers listed in subparagraph (a) above;

   (c) types of bombers equipped for cruise missiles capable of a range in excess of 600 kilometers; and

   (d) types of bombers equipped for ASBMs.

4. Air-to-surface ballistic missiles (ASBMs) are any such missiles capable of a range in excess of 600 kilometers and installed in an aircraft or on its external mountings.

5. Launchers of ICBMs and SLBMs equipped with multiple independently targetable reentry vehicles (MIRVs) are launchers of the types developed and tested for launching ICBMs or SLBMs equipped with MIRVs.

6. ASBMs equipped with MIRVs are ASBMs of the types which have been flight-tested with MIRVs.

7. Heavy ICBMs are ICBMs which have a launch-weight greater or a throw-weight greater than that of the heaviest, in terms of either launch-weight or throw-weight, respectively, of the light ICBMs deployed by either Party as of the date of signature of this Treaty.

8. Cruise missiles are unmanned, self-propelled, guided, weapon-delivery vehicles which sustain flight through the use of aerodynamic lift over most of their flight path and which are flight-tested from or deployed on aircraft, that is, air-launched cruise missiles, or such vehicles which are referred to as cruise missiles in subparagraph 1(b) of Article IX.

Article III

1. Upon entry into force of this Treaty, each Party undertakes to limit ICBM launchers, SLBM launchers, heavy bombers, and ASBMs to an aggregate number not to exceed 2,400.

2. Each Party undertakes to limit, from January 1, 1981, strategic offensive arms referred to in paragraph 1 of this Article to an aggregate number not to exceed 2,250, and to initiate reductions of those arms which as of that date would be in excess of this aggregate number.

3. Within the aggregate numbers provided for in paragraphs 1 and 2 of this Article and subject to the provisions of this Treaty, each Party has the right to determine the composition of these aggregates.

4. For each bomber of a type equipped for ASBMs, the aggregate numbers provided for in paragraphs 1 and 2 of this Article shall include the maximum number of such missiles for which a bomber of that type is equipped for one operational mission.

5. A heavy bomber equipped only for ASBMs shall not itself be included in the aggregate numbers provided for in paragraphs 1 and 2 of this Article.

6. Reductions of the numbers of strategic offensive arms required to comply with the provisions of paragraphs 1 and 2 of this Article shall be carried out as provided for in Article XI.

Article IV

1. Each Party undertakes not to start construction of additional fixed ICBM launchers.

2. Each Party undertakes not to relocate fixed ICBM launchers.

3. Each Party undertakes not to convert launchers of light ICBMs, or of ICBMs of older types deployed prior to 1964, into launchers of heavy ICBMs of types deployed after that time.

4. Each Party undertakes in the process of modernization and replacement of ICBM silo launchers not to increase the original internal volume of an ICBM silo launcher by more than thirty-two percent. Within this limit each Party has the right to determine whether such an increase will be made through an increase in the original diameter or in the original depth of an ICBM silo launcher, or in both of these dimensions.

5. Each Party undertakes:

   (a) not to supply ICBM launcher deployment areas with intercontinental ballistic missiles in excess of a number consistent with normal deployment, maintenance, training, and replacement requirements;
   (b) not to provide storage facilities for or to store ICBMs in excess of normal deployment requirements at launch sites of ICBM launchers;
   (c) not to develop, test, or deploy systems for rapid reload of ICBM launchers.

6. Subject to the provisions of this Treaty, each Party undertakes not to have under construction at any time strategic offensive arms referred to in paragraph 1 of Article III in excess of numbers consistent with a normal construction schedule.

7. Each Party undertakes not to develop, test, or deploy ICBMs which have a launch-weight greater or a throw-weight greater than that of the heaviest, in terms of either launch-weight or throw-weight, respectively, of the heavy ICBMs deployed by either Party as of the date of signature of this Treaty.

8. Each Party undertakes not to convert land-based launchers of ballistic missiles which are not ICBMs into launchers for launching ICBMs, and not to test them for this purpose.

9. Each Party undertakes not to flight-test or deploy new types of ICBMs, that is, types of ICBMs not flight-tested as of May 1, 1979, except that each Party may flight-test and deploy one new type of light ICBM.

10. Each Party undertakes not to flight-test or deploy ICBMs of a type flight-tested as of May 1, 1979 with a number of reentry vehicles greater than the maximum number of reentry vehicles with which an ICBM of that type has been flight-tested as of that date.

11. Each Party undertakes not to flight-test or deploy ICBMs of the one new type permitted pursuant to paragraph 9 of this Article with a number of reentry vehicles greater than the maximum number of reentry vehicles with which an ICBM of either Party has been flight-tested as of May 1, 1979, that is, ten.

12. Each Party undertakes not to flight-test or deploy SLBMs with a number of reentry vehicles greater than the maximum number of reentry vehicles with which an SLBM of either Party has been flight-tested as of May 1, 1979, that is, fourteen.

13. Each Party undertakes not to flight-test or deploy ASBMs with a number of reentry vehicles greater than the maximum number of reentry vehicles with which an ICBM of either Party has been flight-tested as of May 1, 1979, that is, ten.

14. Each Party undertakes not to deploy at any one time on heavy bombers equipped for cruise missiles capable of a range in excess of 600 kilometers a number of such cruise missiles which exceeds the product of 28 and the number of such heavy bombers.

Article V

1. Within the aggregate numbers provided for in paragraphs 1 and 2 of Article III, each Party undertakes to limit launchers of ICBMs and SLBMs equipped with MIRVs, ASBMs equipped with MIRVs, and heavy bombers equipped for cruise missiles capable of a range in excess of 600 kilometers to an aggregate number not to exceed 1,320.

2. Within the aggregate number provided for in paragraph 1 of this Article, each Party undertakes to limit launchers of ICBMs and SLBMs equipped with MIRVs, and ASBMs equipped with MIRVs to an aggregate number not to exceed 1,200.

3. Within the aggregate number provided for in paragraph 2 of this Article, each Party undertakes to limit launchers of ICBMs equipped with MIRVs to an aggregate number not to exceed 820.

4. For each bomber of a type equipped for ASBMs equipped with MIRVs, the aggregate numbers provided for in paragraphs 1 and 2 of this Article shall include the maximum number of ASBMs for which a bomber of that type is equipped for one operational mission.

5. Within the aggregate numbers provided for in paragraphs 1, 2, and 3 of this Article and subject to the provisions of this Treaty, each Party has the right to determine the composition of these aggregates.

Article VI

1. The limitations provided for in this Treaty shall apply to those arms which are:

    (a) operational;
    (b) in the final stage of construction;
    (c) in reserve, in storage, or mothballed;
    (d) undergoing overhaul, repair, modernization, or conversion.

2. Those arms in the final stage of construction are:

    (a) SLBM launchers on submarines which have begun sea trials;
    (b) ASBMs after a bomber of a type equipped for such missiles has been brought out of the shop, plant, or other facility where its final assembly or conversion for the purpose of equipping it for such missiles has been performed;
    (c) other strategic offensive arms which are finally assembled in a shop, plant, or other facility after they have been brought out of the shop, plant, or other facility where their final assembly has been performed.

3. ICBM and SLBM launchers of a type not subject to the limitation provided for in Article V, which undergo conversion into launchers of a type subject to that limitation, shall become subject to that limitation as follows:

    (a) fixed ICBM launchers when work on their conversion reaches the stage which first definitely indicates that they are being so converted;
    (b) SLBM launchers on a submarine when that submarine first goes to sea after their conversion has been performed.

4. ASBMs on a bomber which undergoes conversion from a bomber of a type equipped for ASBMs which are not subject to the limitation provided for in Article V into a bomber of a type equipped for ASBMs which are subject to that limitation shall become subject to that limitation when the bomber is brought out of the shop, plant, or other facility where such conversion has been performed.

5. A heavy bomber of a type not subject to the limitation provided for in paragraph 1 of Article V shall become subject to that limitation when it is brought out of the shop, plant, or other facility where it has been converted into a heavy bomber of a type equipped for cruise missiles capable of a range in excess of 600 kilometers. A bomber of a type not subject to the limitation provided for in paragraph 1 or 2 of Article III shall become subject to that limitation and to the limitation provided for in paragraph 1 of Article V when it is brought out of the shop, plant, or other facility where it has been converted into a bomber of a type equipped for cruise missiles capable of a range in excess of 600 kilometers.

6. The arms subject to the limitations provided for in this Treaty shall

continue to be subject to these limitations until they are dismantled, are destroyed, or otherwise cease to be subject to these limitations under procedures to be agreed upon.

7. In accordance with the provisions of Article XVII, the Parties will agree in the Standing Consultative Commission upon procedures to implement the provisions of this Article.

Article VII

1. The limitations provided for in Article III shall not apply to ICBM and SLBM test and training launchers or to space vehicle launchers for exploration and use of outer space. ICBM and SLBM test and training launchers are ICBM and SLBM launchers used only for testing or training.

2. The Parties agree that:

    (a) there shall be no significant increase in the number of ICBM or SLBM test and training launchers or in the number of such launchers of heavy ICBMs;

    (b) construction or conversion of ICBM launchers at test ranges shall be undertaken only for purposes of testing and training;

    (c) there shall be no conversion of ICBM test and training launchers or of space vehicle launchers into ICBM launchers subject to the limitations provided for in Article III.

Article VIII

1. Each Party undertakes not to flight-test cruise missiles capable of a range in excess of 600 kilometers or ASBMs from aircraft other than bombers or to convert such aircraft into aircraft equipped for such missiles.

2. Each Party undertakes not to convert aircraft other than bombers into aircraft which can carry out the mission of a heavy bomber as referred to in subparagraph 3(b) of Article II.

Article IX

1. Each Party undertakes not to develop, test, or deploy:

    (a) ballistic missiles capable of a range in excess of 600 kilometers for installation on waterborne vehicles other than submarines, or launchers of such missiles;

    (b) fixed ballistic or cruise missile launchers for emplacement on the ocean floor, on the seabed, or on the beds of internal waters and inland waters, or in the subsoil thereof, or mobile launchers of such missiles, which move only in contact with the ocean floor, the seabed, or the beds of internal waters and inland waters, or missiles for such launchers;

    (c) systems for placing into Earth orbit nuclear weapons or any other kind of weapons of mass destruction, including fractional orbital missiles;

    (d) mobile launchers of heavy ICBMs;

    (e) SLBMs which have a launch-weight greater or a throw-weight greater than that of the heaviest, in terms of either launch-weight or throw-weight, respectively, of the light ICBMs deployed by either Party as of the date of signature of this Treaty, or launchers of such SLBMs; or

(f) ASBMs which have a launch-weight greater or a throw-weight greater than that of the heaviest, in terms of either launch-weight or throw-weight, respectively, of the light ICBMs deployed by either Party as of the date of signature of this Treaty.

2. Each Party undertakes not to flight-test from aircraft cruise missiles capable of a range in excess of 600 kilometers which are equipped with multiple independently targetable warheads and not to deploy such cruise missiles on aircraft.

Article X

Subject to the provisions of this Treaty, modernization and replacement of strategic offensive arms may be carried out.

Article XI

1. Strategic offensive arms which would be in excess of the aggregate numbers provided for in this Treaty as well as strategic offensive arms prohibited by this Treaty shall be dismantled or destroyed under procedures to be agreed upon in the Standing Consultative Commission.

2. Dismantling or destruction of strategic offensive arms which would be in excess of the aggregate number provided for in paragraph 1 of Article III shall begin on the date of the entry into force of this Treaty and shall be completed within the following periods from that date: four months for ICBM launchers; six months for SLBM launchers; and three months for heavy bombers.

3. Dismantling or destruction of strategic offensive arms which would be in excess of the aggregate number provided for in paragraph 2 of Article III shall be initiated no later than January 1, 1981, shall be carried out throughout the ensuing twelve-month period, and shall be completed no later than December 31, 1981.

4. Dismantling or destruction of strategic offensive arms prohibited by this Treaty shall be completed within the shortest possible agreed period of time, but not later than six months after the entry into force of this Treaty.

Article XII

In order to ensure the viability and effectiveness of this Treaty, each Party undertakes not to circumvent the provisions of this Treaty, through any other state or states, or in any other manner.

Article XIII

Each Party undertakes not to assume any international obligations which would conflict with this Treaty.

Article XIV

The Parties undertake to begin, promptly after the entry into force of this Treaty, active negotiations with the objective of achieving, as soon as possible, agreement on further measures for the limitation and reduction of strategic arms. It is also the objective of the Parties to conclude well in advance of 1985 an agreement limiting strategic offensive arms to replace this Treaty upon its expiration.

Article XV

1. For the purpose of providing assurance of compliance with the provisions of this Treaty, each Party shall use national technical means of verification at its disposal in a manner consistent with generally recognized principles of international law.

2. Each Party undertakes not to interfere with the national technical means of verification of the other Party operating in accordance with paragraph 1 of this Article.

3. Each Party undertakes not to use deliberate concealment measures which impede verification by national technical means of compliance with the provisions of this Treaty. This obligation shall not require changes in current construction, assembly, conversion, or overhaul practices.

Article XVI

1. Each Party undertakes, before conducting each planned ICBM launch, to notify the other Party well in advance on a case-by-case basis that such a launch will occur, except for single ICBM launches from test ranges or from ICBM launcher deployment areas, which are not planned to extend beyond its national territory.

2. The Parties shall agree in the Standing Consultative Commission upon procedures to implement the provisions of this Article.

Article XVII

1. To promote the objectives and implementation of the provisions of this Treaty, the Parties shall use the Standing Consultative Commission established by the Memorandum of Understanding Between the Government of the United States of America and the Government of the Union of Soviet Socialist Republics Regarding the Establishment of a Standing Consultative Commission of December 21, 1972.

2. Within the framework of the Standing Consultative Commission, with respect to this Treaty, the Parties will:

   (a) consider questions concerning compliance with the obligations assumed and related situations which may be considered ambiguous;
   (b) provide on a voluntary basis such information as either Party considers necessary to assure confidence in compliance with the obligations assumed;
   (c) consider questions involving unintended interference with national

technical means of verification, and questions involving unintended impeding of verification by national technical means of compliance with the provisions of this Treaty;

(d) consider possible changes in the strategic situation which have a bearing on the provisions of this Treaty;

(e) agree upon procedures for replacement, conversion, and dismantling or destruction, of strategic offensive arms in cases provided for in the provisions of this Treaty and upon procedures for removal of such arms from the aggregate numbers when they otherwise cease to be subject to the limitations provided for in this Treaty, and at regular sessions of the Standing Consultative Commission, notify each other in accordance with the aforementioned procedures, at least twice annually, of actions completed and those in process;

(f) consider, as appropriate, possible proposals for further increasing the viability of this Treaty, including proposals for amendments in accordance with the provisions of this Treaty;

(g) consider, as appropriate, proposals for further measures limiting strategic offensive arms.

3. In the Standing Consultative Commission the Parties shall maintain by category the agreed data base on the numbers of strategic offensive arms established by the Memorandum of Understanding Between the United States of America and the Union of Soviet Socialist Republics Regarding the Establishment of a Data Base on the Numbers of Strategic Offensive Arms of June 18, 1979.

Article XVIII

Each Party may propose amendments to this Treaty. Agreed amendments shall enter into force in accordance with the procedures governing the entry into force of this Treaty.

Article XIX

1. This Treaty shall be subject to ratification in accordance with the constitutional procedures of each Party. This Treaty shall enter into force on the day of the exchange of instruments of ratification and shall remain in force through December 31, 1985, unless replaced earlier by an agreement further limiting strategic offensive arms.

2. This Treaty shall be registered pursuant to Article 102 of the Charter of the United Nations.

3. Each Party shall, in exercising its national sovereignty, have the right to withdraw from this Treaty if it decides that extraordinary events related to the subject matter of this Treaty have jeopardized its supreme interests. It shall give notice of its decision to the other Party six months prior to withdrawal from the Treaty. Such notice shall include a statement of the extraordinary events the notifying Party regards as having jeopardized its supreme interests.

Done at Vienna on June 18, 1979, in two copies, each in the English and Russian languages, both texts being equally authentic.

FOR THE
UNITED STATES OF AMERICA

FOR THE
UNION OF SOVIET SOCIALIST
REPUBLICS

PRESIDENT

OF THE UNITED STATES

OF AMERICA

GENERAL SECRETARY OF THE
CPSU,
CHAIRMAN OF THE PRESIDIUM
OF THE
SUPREME SOVIET OF THE USSR

PROTOCOL TO THE TREATY
BETWEEN THE UNITED STATES OF AMERICA
AND
THE UNION OF SOVIET SOCIALIST REPUBLICS
ON THE LIMITATION OF STRATEGIC OFFENSIVE ARMS

The United States of America and the Union of Soviet Socialist Republics, hereinafter referred to as the Parties,

Having agreed on limitations on strategic offensive arms in the Treaty,

Have agreed on additional limitations for the period during which this Protocol remains in force, as follows:

Article I

Each Party undertakes not to deploy mobile ICBM launchers or to flight-test ICBMs from such launchers.

Article II

1. Each Party undertakes not to deploy cruise missiles capable of a range in excess of 600 kilometers on sea-based launchers or on land-based launchers.

2. Each Party undertakes not to flight-test cruise missiles capable of a range in excess of 600 kilometers which are equipped with multiple independently targetable warheads from sea-based launchers or from land-based launchers.

3. For the purposes of this Protocol, cruise missiles are unmanned, self-propelled, guided, weapon-delivery vehicles which sustain flight through the use of aerodynamic lift over most of their flight path and which are flight-tested from or deployed on sea-based or land-based launchers, that is, sea-launched cruise missiles and ground-launched cruise missiles, respectively.

Article III

Each Party undertakes not to flight-test or deploy ASBMs.

Article IV

This Protocol shall be considered an integral part of the Treaty. It shall enter into force on the day of the entry into force of the Treaty and shall remain in force through December 31, 1981, unless replaced earlier by an agreement on further measures limiting strategic offensive arms.

Done at Vienna on June 18, 1979, in two copies, each in the English and Russian languages, both texts being equally authentic.

<table>
<tr><td align="center">FOR THE
UNITED STATES OF AMERICA</td><td align="center">FOR THE
UNION OF SOVIET SOCIALIST
REPUBLICS</td></tr>
<tr><td align="center">PRESIDENT</td><td align="center">GENERAL SECRETARY OF THE
CPSU,</td></tr>
<tr><td align="center">OF THE UNITED STATES</td><td align="center">CHAIRMAN OF THE PRESIDIUM
OF THE</td></tr>
<tr><td align="center">OF AMERICA</td><td align="center">SUPREME SOVIET OF THE USSR</td></tr>
</table>

AGREED STATEMENTS AND COMMON UNDERSTANDINGS REGARDING THE TREATY BETWEEN THE UNITED STATES OF AMERICA AND THE UNION OF SOVIET SOCIALIST REPUBLICS ON THE LIMITATION OF STRATEGIC OFFENSIVE ARMS

In connection with the Treaty Between the United States of America and the Union of Soviet Socialist Republics on the Limitation of Strategic Offensive Arms, the Parties have agreed on the following Agreed Statements and Common Understandings undertaken on behalf of the Government of the United States of America and the Government of the Union of Soviet Socialist Republics:

To paragraph 1 of Article II of the Treaty

First Agreed Statement. The term "intercontinental ballistic missile launchers," as defined in paragraph 1 of Article II of the Treaty, includes all launchers which have been developed and tested for launching ICBMs. If a launcher has been developed and tested for launching an ICBM, all launchers of that type shall be considered to have been developed and tested for launching ICBMs.

First Common Understanding. If a launcher contains or launches an ICBM, that launcher shall be considered to have been developed and tested for launching ICBMs.

Second Common Understanding. If a launcher has been developed and tested for launching an ICBM, all launchers of that type, except for ICBM test and training launchers, shall be included in the aggregate numbers of strategic offensive arms provided for in Article III of the Treaty, pursuant to the provisions of Article VI of the Treaty.

Third Common Understanding. The one hundred and seventy-seven former Atlas and Titan I ICBM launchers of the United States of America, which are no longer operational and are partially dismantled, shall not be considered as subject to the limitations provided for in the Treaty.

Second Agreed Statement. After the date on which the Protocol ceases to be in force, mobile ICBM launchers shall be subject to the relevant limitations provided for in the Treaty which are applicable to ICBM launchers, unless the Parties agree that mobile ICBM launchers shall not be deployed after that date.

To Paragraph 2 of Article II of the Treaty

Agreed Statement. Modern submarine-launched ballistic missiles are: for the United States of America, missiles installed in all nuclear-powered submarines; for the Union of Soviet Socialist Republics, missiles of the type installed in nuclear-powered submarines made operational since 1965; and for both Parties, submarine-launched ballistic missiles first flight-tested since 1965 and installed in any submarine, regardless of its type.

To Paragraph 3 of Article II of the Treaty

First Agreed Statement. The term "bombers," as used in paragraph 3 of Article II and other provisions of the Treaty, means airplanes of types initially constructed to be equipped for bombs or missiles.

Second Agreed Statement. The Parties shall notify each other on a case-by-case basis in the Standing Consultative Commission of inclusion of types of bombers as heavy bombers pursuant to the provisions of paragraph 3 of Article II of the Treaty; in this connection the Parties shall hold consultations, as appropriate, consistent with the provisions of paragraph 2 of Article XVII of the Treaty.

Third Agreed Statement. The criteria the Parties shall use to make case-by-case determinations of which types of bombers in the future can carry out the mission of a heavy bomber in a manner similar or superior to that of current heavy bombers, as referred to in subparagraph 3(b) of Article II of the Treaty, shall be agreed upon in the Standing Consultative Commission.

Fourth Agreed Statement. Having agreed that every bomber of a type included in paragraph 3 of Article II of the Treaty is to be considered a heavy bomber, the Parties further agree that:

   (a) airplanes which otherwise would be bombers of a heavy bomber type shall not be considered to be bombers of a heavy bomber type if they have functionally related observable differences which indicate that they cannot perform the mission of a heavy bomber;

   (b) airplanes which otherwise would be bombers of a type equipped for cruise missiles capable of a range in excess of 600 kilometers shall not be considered to be bombers of a type equipped for cruise missiles capable of a range in excess of 600 kilometers if they have functionally related observable differences which indicate that they cannot perform the mission of a bomber equipped for cruise missiles capable of a range in excess of 600 kilometers, except that heavy bombers of current types, as designated in subparagraph 3(a) of Article II of the Treaty, which otherwise would be of a type equipped for cruise missiles capable of a range in excess of 600 kilometers shall not be considered to be heavy bombers of a type equipped for cruise missiles capable of a range in excess of 600 kilometers if they are distinguishable on the basis of externally ob-

servable differences from heavy bombers of a type equipped for cruise missiles capable of a range in excess of 600 kilometers; and
(c) airplanes which otherwise would be bombers of a type equipped for ASBMs shall not be considered to be bombers of a type equipped for ASBMs if they have functionally related observable differences which indicate that they cannot perform the mission of a bomber equipped for ASBMs, except that heavy bombers of current types, as designated in subparagraph 3(a) of Article II of the Treaty, which otherwise would be of a type equipped for ASBMs shall not be considered to be heavy bombers of a type equipped for ASBMs if they are distinguishable on the basis of externally observable differences from heavy bombers of a type equipped for ASBMs.

First Common Understanding. Functionally related observable differences are differences in the observable features of airplanes which indicate whether or not these airplanes can perform the mission of a heavy bomber, or whether or not they can perform the mission of a bomber equipped for cruise missiles capable of a range in excess of 600 kilometers or whether or not they can perform the mission of a bomber equipped for ASBMs. Functionally related observable differences shall be verifiable by national technical means. To this end, the Parties may take, as appropriate, cooperative measures contributing to the effectiveness of verification by national technical means.

Fifth Agreed Statement. Tupolev-142 airplanes in their current configuration, that is, in the configuration for anti-submarine warfare, are considered to be airplanes of a type different from types of heavy bombers referred to in subparagraph 3(a) of Article II of the Treaty and not subject to the Fourth Agreed Statement to paragraph 3 of Article II of the Treaty. This Agreed Statement does not preclude improvement of Tupolev-142 airplanes as an anti-submarine system, and does not prejudice or set a precedent for designation in the future of types of airplanes as heavy bombers pursuant to subparagraph 3(b) of Article II of the Treaty or for application of the Fourth Agreed Statement to paragraph 3 of Article II of the Treaty to such airplanes.

Second Common Understanding. Not later than six months after entry into force of the Treaty the Union of Soviet Socialist Republics will give its thirty-one Myasishchev airplanes used as tankers in existence as of the date of signature of the Treaty functionally related observable differences which indicate that they cannot perform the mission of a heavy bomber.

Third Common Understanding. The designations by the United States of America and by the Union of Soviet Socialist Republics for heavy bombers referred to in subparagraph 3(a) of Article II of the Treaty correspond in the following manner:

Heavy bombers of the types designated by the United States of America as the B-52 and the B-1 are known to the Union of Soviet Socialist Republics by the same designations;

Heavy bombers of the type designated by the Union of Soviet Socialist Republics as the Tupolev-95 [alternatively Tu-20] are known to the United States of America as heavy bombers of the Bear type; and

Heavy bombers of the type designated by the Union of Soviet Socialist Republics as the Myasishchev are known to the United States of America as heavy bombers of the Bison type.

To Paragraph 5 of Article II of the Treaty

First Agreed Statement. If a launcher has been developed and tested for launching an ICBM or an SLBM equipped with MIRVs, all launchers of that type shall be considered to have been developed and tested for launching ICBMs or SLBMs equipped with MIRVs.

First Common Understanding. If a launcher contains or launches an ICBM or an SLBM equipped with MIRVs, that launcher shall be considered to have been developed and tested for launching ICBMs or SLBMs equipped with MIRVs.

Second Common Understanding. If a launcher has been developed and tested for launching an ICBM or an SLBM equipped with MIRVs, all launchers of that type, except for ICBM and SLBM test and training launchers, shall be included in the corresponding aggregate numbers provided for in Article V of the Treaty, pursuant to the provisions of Article VI of the Treaty.

Second Agreed Statement. ICBMs and SLBMs equipped with MIRVs are ICBMs and SLBMs of the types which have been flight-tested with two or more independently targetable reentry vehicles, regardless of whether or not they have also been flight-tested with a single reentry vehicle or with multiple reentry vehicles which are not independently targetable. As of the date of signature of the Treaty, such ICBMs and SLBMs are: for the United States of America, Minuteman III ICBMs, Poseidon C-3 SLBMs, and Trident C-4 SLBMs; and for the Union of Soviet Socialist Republics, RS-16 [SS-17], RS-18 [SS-19], RS-20 [SS-18] ICBMs and RSM-50 [SS-N-18] SLBMs.

Each Party will notify the other Party in the Standing Consultative Commission on a case-by-case basis of the designation of the one new type of light ICBM, if equipped with MIRVs, permitted pursuant to paragraph 9 of Article IV of the Treaty when first flight-tested; of designations of additional types of SLBMs equipped with MIRVs when first installed on a submarine; and of designations of types of ASBMs equipped with MIRVs when first flight-tested.

Third Common Understanding. The designations by the United States of America and by the Union of Soviet Socialist Republics for ICBMs and SLBMs equipped with MIRVs correspond in the following manner:

Missiles of the type designated by the United States of America as the Minuteman III and known to the Union of Soviet Socialist Republics by the same designation, a light ICBM that has been flight-tested with multiple independently targetable reentry vehicles;

Missiles of the type designated by the United States of America as the Poseidon C-3 and known to the Union of Soviet Socialist Republics by the same designation, an SLBM that was first flight-tested in 1968 and that has been flight-tested with multiple independently targetable reentry vehicles;

Missiles of the type designated by the United States of America as the Trident C-4 and known to the Union of Soviet Socialist Republics by the same designation, an SLBM that was first flight-tested in 1977 and that has been flight-tested with multiple independently targetable reentry vehicles;

Missiles of the type designated by the Union of Soviet Socialist Republics as the RS-16 and known to the United States of America as the SS-17, a light ICBM that has been flight-tested with a single reentry vehicle and with multiple independently targetable reentry vehicles;

Missiles of the type designated by the Union of Soviet Socialist Republics as the RS-18 and known to the United States of America as the SS-19, the heaviest in terms of launch-weight and throw-weight of light ICBMs, which has been flight-tested with a single reentry vehicle and with multiple independently targetable reentry vehicles;

Missiles of the type designated by the Union of Soviet Socialist Republics as the RS-20 and known to the United States of America as the SS-18, the heaviest in terms of launch-weight and throw-weight of heavy ICBMs, which has been flight-tested with a single reentry vehicle and with multiple independently targetable reentry vehicles;

Missiles of the type designated by the Union of Soviet Socialist Republics as the RSM-50 and known to the United States of America as the SS-N-18, an SLBM that has been flight-tested with a single reentry vehicle and with multiple independently targetable reentry vehicles.

Third Agreed Statement. Reentry vehicles are independently targetable:

(a) if, after separation from the booster, maneuvering and targeting of the reentry vehicles to separate aim points along trajectories which are unrelated to each other are accomplished by means of devices which are installed in a self-contained dispensing mechanism or on the reentry vehicles, and which are based on the use of electronic or other computers in combination with devices using jet engines, including rocket engines, or aerodynamic systems;

(b) if maneuvering and targeting of the reentry vehicles to separate aim points along trajectories which are unrelated to each other are accomplished by means of other devices which may be developed in the future.

Fourth Common Understanding. For the purposes of this Treaty, all ICBM launchers in the Derazhnya and Pervomaisk areas in the Union of Soviet Socialist Republics are included in the aggregate numbers provided for in Article V of the Treaty.

Fifth Common Understanding. If ICBM or SLBM launchers are converted, constructed or undergo significant changes to their principal observable structural design features after entry into force of the Treaty, any such launchers which are launchers of missiles equipped with MIRVs shall be distinguishable from launchers of missiles not equipped with MIRVs, and any such launchers which are launchers of missiles not equipped with MIRVs shall be distinguishable from launchers of missiles equipped with MIRVs, on the basis of externally observable design features of the launchers. Submarines with launchers of SLBMs equipped with MIRVs shall be distinguishable from submarines with launchers of SLBMs not equipped with MIRVs on the basis of externally observable design features of the submarines.

This Common Understanding does not require changes to launcher conversion or construction programs, or to programs including significant changes to the principal observable structural design features of launchers, underway as of the date of signature of the Treaty.

To Paragraph 6 of Article II of the Treaty

First Agreed Statement. ASBMs of the types which have been flight-tested with MIRVs are all ASBMs of the types which have been flight-tested with two or more independently targetable reentry vehicles, regardless of whether or not they have also been flight-tested with a single reentry vehicle or with multiple reentry vehicles which are not independently targetable.

Second Agreed Statement. Reentry vehicles are independently targetable:

  (a) if, after separation from the booster, maneuvering and targeting of the reentry vehicles to separate aim points along trajectories which are unrelated to each other are accomplished by means of devices which are installed in a self-contained dispensing mechanism or on the reentry vehicles, and which are based on the use of electronic or other computers in combination with devices using jet engines, including rocket engines, or aerodynamic systems;

  (b) if maneuvering and targeting of the reentry vehicles to separate aim points along trajectories which are unrelated to each other are accomplished by means of other devices which may be developed in the future.

To Paragraph 7 of Article II of the Treaty

First Agreed Statement. The launch-weight of an ICBM is the weight of the fully loaded missile itself at the time of launch.

Second Agreed Statement. The throw-weight of an ICBM is the sum of the weight of:

  (a) its reentry vehicle or reentry vehicles;

  (b) any self-contained dispensing mechanisms or other appropriate devices for targeting one reentry vehicle, or for releasing or for dispensing and targeting two or more reentry vehicles; and

  (c) its penetration aids, including devices for their release.

Common Understanding. The term "other appropriate devices," as used in the definition of the throw-weight of an ICBM in the Second Agreed Statement to paragraph 7 of Article II of the Treaty, means any devices for dispensing and targeting two or more reentry vehicles; and any devices for releasing two or more reentry vehicles or for targeting one reentry vehicles, which cannot provide their reentry vehicles or reentry vehicle with additional velocity of more than 1,000 meters per second.

To Paragraph 8 of Article II of the Treaty

First Agreed Statement. If a cruise missile is capable of a range in excess of 600 kilometers, all cruise missiles of that type shall be considered to be cruise missiles capable of a range in excess of 600 kilometers.

First Common Understanding. If a cruise missile has been flight-tested to a range in excess of 600 kilometers, it shall be considered to be a cruise missile capable of a range in excess of 600 kilometers.

Second Common Understanding. Cruise missiles not capable of a range in excess of 600 kilometers shall not be considered to be of a type capable of a range in excess of 600 kilometers if they are distinguishable on the basis of externally observable design features from cruise missiles of types capable of a range in excess of 600 kilometers.

Second Agreed Statement. The range of which a cruise missile is capable is the maximum distance which can be covered by the missile in its standard design mode flying until fuel exhaustion, determined by projecting its flight path onto the Earth's sphere from the point of launch to the point of impact.

Third Agreed Statement. If an unmanned, self-propelled, guided vehicle which sustains flight through the use of aerodynamic lift over most of its flight path has been flight-tested or deployed for weapon delivery, all vehicles of that type shall be considered to be weapon-delivery vehicles.

Third Common Understanding. Unmanned, self-propelled, guided vehicles which sustain flight through the use of aerodynamic lift over most of their flight path and are not weapon-delivery vehicles, that is, unarmed, pilotless, guided vehicles, shall not be considered to be cruise missiles if such vehicles are distinguishable from cruise missiles on the basis of externally observable design features.

Fourth Common Understanding. Neither Party shall convert unarmed, pilotless, guided vehicles into cruise missiles capable of a range in excess of 600 kilometers, nor shall either Party convert cruise missiles capable of a range in excess of 600 kilometers into unarmed, pilotless, guided vehicles.

Fifth Common Understanding. Neither Party has plans during the term of the Treaty to flight-test from or deploy on aircraft unarmed, pilotless, guided vehicles which are capable of a range in excess of 600 kilometers. In the future, should a Party have such plans, that Party will provide notification thereof to the other Party well in advance of such flight-testing or deployment. This Common Understanding does not apply to target drones.

To Paragraph 4 of Article IV of the Treaty

Agreed Statement. The word "original" in paragraph 4 of Article IV of the Treaty refers to the internal dimensions of an ICBM silo launcher, including its internal volume, as of May 26, 1972, or as of the date on which such launcher becomes operational, whichever is later.

Common Understanding. The obligations provided for in paragraph 4 of Article IV of the Treaty and in the Agreed Statement thereto mean that the original diameter or the original depth of an ICBM silo launcher may not be increased by an amount greater than that which would result in an increase in the original internal volume of the ICBM silo launcher by thirty-two percent solely through an increase in one of these dimensions.

To Paragraph 5 of Article IV of the Treaty

Agreed Statement. The term "normal deployment requirements," as used in paragraph 5 of Article IV of the Treaty, means the deployment of one missile at each ICBM launcher.

To Paragraph 6 of Article IV of the Treaty

Common Understanding. A normal construction schedule, in paragraph 6 of Article IV of the Treaty, is understood to be one consistent with the past or present construction practices of each Party.

To Paragraph 7 of Article IV of the Treaty

First Agreed Statement. The launch-weight of an ICBM is the weight of the fully loaded missile itself at the time of launch.

Second Agreed Statement. The throw-weight of an ICBM is the sum of the weight of:

(a) its reentry vehicle or reentry vehicles;
(b) any self-contined dispensing mechanisms or other appropriate devices for targeting one reentry vehicle, or for releasing or for dispensing and targeting two or more reentry vehicles; and
(c) its penetration aids, including devices for their release.

Common Understanding. The term "other appropriate devices," as used in the definition of the throw-weight of an ICBM in the Second Agreed Statement to paragraph 7 of Article IV of the Treaty, means any devices for dispensing and targeting two or more reentry vehicles; and any devices for releasing two or more reentry vehicles or for targeting one reentry vehicle, which cannot provide their reentry vehicles or reentry vehicle with additional velocity of more than 1,000 meters per second.

To Paragraph 8 of Article IV of the Treaty

Common Understanding. During the term of the Treaty, the Union of Soviet Socialist Republics will not produce, test, or deploy ICBMs of the type designated by the Union of Soviet Socialist Republics as the RS-14 and known to the United States of America as the SS-16, a light ICBM first flight-tested after 1970 and flight-tested only with a single reentry vehicle; this Common Understanding also means that the Union of Soviet Socialist Republics will not produce the third stage of that missile, the reentry vehicle of that missile, or the appropriate device for targeting the reentry vehicle of that missile.

To Paragraph 9 of Article IV of the Treaty

First Agreed Statement. The term "new types of ICBMs," as used in paragraph 9 of Article IV of the Treaty, refers to any ICBM which is different from those ICBMs flight-tested as of May 1, 1979 in any one or more of the following respects:

(a) the number of stages, the length, the largest diameter, the launch-weight, or the throw-weight, of the missile;
(b) the type of propellant (that is, liquid or solid) of any of its stages.

First Common Understanding. As used in the First Agreed Statement to paragraph 9 of Article IV of the Treaty, the term "different," referring to the length, the diameter, the launch-weight, and the throw-weight, of the missile, means a difference in excess of five percent.

Second Agreed Statement. Every ICBM of the one new type of light ICBM permitted to each Party pursuant to paragraph 9 of Article IV of the Treaty shall have the same number of stages and the same type of propellant (that is, liquid or solid) of each stage as the first ICBM of the one new type of light ICBM launched by that Party. In addition, after the twenty-fifth launch of an ICBM of that type, or after the last launch before deployment begins of ICBMs of that type, whichever occurs earlier, ICBMs of the one new type of light ICBM permitted to that Party shall not be different in any one or more of the following respects: the length, the largest diameter, the launch-weight, or the throw-weight, of the missile.

A Party which launches ICBMs of the one new type of light ICBM permitted pursuant to paragraph 9 of Article IV of the Treaty shall promptly notify the other Party of the date of the first launch and of the date of either the twenty-fifth or the last launch before deployment begins of ICBMs of that type, whichever occurs earlier.

Second Common Understanding. As used in the Second Agreed Statement to paragraph 9 of Article IV of the Treaty, the term "different," referring to the length, the diameter, the launch-weight, and the throw-weight, of the missile, means a difference in excess of five percent from the value established for each of the above parameters as of the twenty-fifth launch or as of the last launch before deployment begins, whichever occurs earlier. The values demonstrated in each of the above parameters during the last twelve of the twenty-five launches or during the last twelve launches before deployment begins, whichever twelve launches occur earlier, shall not vary by more than ten percent from any other of the corresponding values demonstrated during those twelve launches.

Third Common Understanding. The limitations with respect to launch-weight and throw-weight, provided for in the First Agreed Statement and the First Common Understanding to paragraph 9 of Article IV of the Treaty, do not preclude the flight-testing or the deployment of ICBMs with fewer reentry vehicles, or fewer penetration aids, or both, than the maximum number of reentry vehicles and the maximum number of penetration aids with which ICBMs of that type have been flight-tested as of May 1, 1979, even if this results in a decrease in launch-weight or in throw-weight in excess of five percent.

In addition to the aforementioned cases, those limitations do not preclude a decrease in launch-weight or in throw-weight in excess of five percent, in the case of the flight-testing or the deployment of ICBMs with a lesser quantity of propellant, including the propellant of a self-contained dispensing mechanism or other appropriate device, than the maximum quantity of propellant, including the propellant of a self-contained dispensing mechanism or other appropriate device, with which ICBMs of that type have been flight-tested as of May 1, 1979, provided that such an ICBM is at the same time flight-tested or deployed with fewer reentry vehicles, or fewer penetration aids, or both, than the maximum number of reentry vehicles and the maximum number of penetration aids with which ICBMs of that type have been flight-tested as of May 1, 1979, and the decrease in launch-weight and throw-weight in such cases results only from the reduction in the number of reentry vehicles, or penetration aids, or both, and the reduction in the quantity of propellant.

Fourth Common Understanding. The limitations with respect to launch-weight and throw-weight, provided for in the Second Agreed Statement and the Second Common Understanding to paragraph 9 of Article IV of the Treaty, do not preclude the flight-testing or the deployment of ICBMs of the one new type of light ICBM permitted to each Party pursuant to paragraph 9 of Article IV of the Treaty with fewer reentry vehicles, or fewer penetration aids, or both, than the maximum number of reentry vehicles and the maximum number of penetration aids with which ICBMs of that type have been flight-tested, even if this results in a decrease in launch-weight or in throw-weight in excess of five percent.

In addition to the aforementioned cases, those limitations do not preclude a decrease in launch-weight or in throw-weight in excess of five percent, in the case of the flight-testing or the deployment of ICBMs of that type with a lesser quantity of propellant, including the propellant of a self-contained dispensing mechanism or other appropriate device, than the maximum quantity of propellant, including the propellant of a self-contained dispensing mechanism or other appropriate device, with which ICBMs of that type have been flight-tested, provided that such an ICBM is at the same time flight-tested or deployed with fewer reentry vehicles, or fewer penetration aids, or both, than the maximum number of reentry vehicles and the maximum number of penetration aids with which ICBMs of that type have been flight-tested, and the decrease in launch-weight and throw-weight in such cases results only from the reduction in the number of reentry vehicles, or penetration aids, or both, and the reduction in the quantity of propellant.

To Paragraph 10 of Article IV of the Treaty

First Agreed Statement. The following types of ICBMs and SLBMs equipped with MIRVs have been flight-tested with the maximum number of reentry vehicles set forth below:

For the United States of America

ICBMs of the Minuteman III type—seven reentry vehicles;
SLBMs of the Poseidon C-3 type—fourteen reentry vehicles;
SLBMs of the Trident C-4 type—seven reentry vehicles;

For the Union of Soviet Socialist Republics

ICBMs of the RS-16 type[SS-17]—four reentry vehicles;
ICBMs of the RS-18 type[SS-19]—six reentry vehicles;
ICBMs of the RS-20 type[SS-18]—ten reentry vehicles;
SLBMs of the RSM-50 type[SS-N-18]—seven reentry vehicles.

Common Understanding. Minuteman III ICBMs of the United States of America have been deployed with no more than three reentry vehicles. During the term of the Treaty, the United States of America has no plans to and will not flight-test or deploy missiles of this type with more than three reentry vehicles.

Second Agreed Statement. During the flight-testing of any ICBM, SLBM, or ASBM after May 1, 1979 the number of procedures for releasing or for dispensing may not exceed the maximum number of reentry vehicles established for missiles of corresponding types as provided for in paragraphs 10, 11, 12, and 13 of Article IV of the Treaty. In this Agreed Statement "procedures for releasing or for dispensing" are understood to mean maneuvers of a missile associated with targeting and releasing or dispensing its reentry vehicles to aim points, whether or not a reentry vehicle is actually released or dispensed. Procedures for releasing anti-missile defense penetration aids will not be considered to be procedures for releasing or for dispensing a reentry vehicle so long as the procedures for releasing anti-missile defense penetration aids differ from those for releasing or for dispensing reentry vehicles.

Third Agreed Statement. Each Party undertakes:

(a) not to flight-test or deploy ICBMs equipped with multiple reentry vehicles, of a type flight-tested as of May 1, 1979, with reentry vehicles the weight of any of which is less than the weight of the lightest of those reentry vehicles with which an ICBM of that type has been flight-tested as of that date;

(b) not to flight-test or deploy ICBMs equipped with a single reentry vehicle and without an appropriate device for targeting a reentry vehicle, of a type flight-tested as of May 1, 1979, with a reentry vehicle the weight of which is less than the weight of the lightest reentry vehicle on an ICBM of a type equipped with MIRVs and flight-tested by that Party as of May 1, 1979; and

(c) not to flight-test or deploy ICBMs equipped with a single reentry vehicle and with an appropriate device for targeting a reentry vehicle, of a type flight-tested as of May 1, 1979, with a reentry vehicle the weight of which is less than fifty percent of the throw-weight of that ICBM.

To Paragraph 11 of Article IV of the Treaty

First Agreed Statement. Each Party undertakes not to flight-test or deploy the one new type of light ICBM permitted to each Party pursuant to paragraph 9 of Article IV of the Treaty with a number of reentry vehicles greater than the maximum number of reentry vehicles with which an ICBM of that type has been flight-tested as of the twenty-fifth launch or the last launch before deployment begins of ICBMs of that type, whichever occurs earlier.

Second Agreed Statement. During the flight-testing of any ICBM, SLBM, or ASBM after May 1, 1979 the number of procedures for releasing or for dispensing may not exceed the maximum number of reentry vehicles established for missiles of corresponding types as provided for in paragraphs 10, 11, 12, and 13 of Article IV of the Treaty. In this Agreed Statement "procedures for releasing or for dispensing" are understood to mean maneuvers of a missile associated with targeting and releasing or dispensing its reentry vehicles to aim points, whether or not a reentry vehicle is actually released or dispensed. Procedures for releasing anti-missile defense penetration aids will not be considered to be procedures for releasing or for dispensing a reentry vehicle so long as the procedures for releasing anti-missile defense penetration aids differ from those for releasing or for dispensing reentry vehicles.

To Paragraph 12 of Article IV of the Treaty

First Agreed Statement. The following types of ICBMs and SLBMs equipped with MIRVs have been flight-tested with the maximum number of reentry vehicles set forth below:

For the United States of America

ICBMs of the Minuteman III type—seven reentry vehicles;
SLBMs of the Poseidon C-3 type—fourteen reentry vehicles;
SLBMs of the Trident C-4 type—seven reentry vehicles;

For the Union of Soviet Socialist Republics

ICBMs of the RS-16 type[SS-17]—four reentry vehicles;
ICBMs of the RS-18 type [SS-19]—six reentry vehicles;
ICBMs of the RS-20 type[SS-18]—ten reentry vehicles;
SLBMs of the RSM-50 type[SS-N-18]—seven reentry vehicles.

Second Agreed Statement. During the flight-testing of any ICBM, SLBM, or ASBM after May 1, 1979, the number of procedures for releasing or for dispensing may not exceed the maximum number of reentry vehicles established for missiles of corresponding types as provided for in paragraphs 10, 11, 12, and 13 of Article IV of the Treaty. In this Agreed Statement "procedures for releasing or for dispensing" are understood to mean maneuvers of a missile associated with targeting and releasing or dispensing its reentry vehicles to aim points, whether or not a reentry vehicle is actually released or dispensed. Procedures for releasing anti-missile defense penetration aids will not be considered to be procedures for releasing or for dispensing a reentry vehicle so long as the procedures for releasing anti-missile defense penetration aids differ from those for releasing or for dispensing reentry vehicles.

To Paragraph 13 of Article IV of the Treaty

Agreed Statement. During the flight-testing of any ICBM, SLBM, or ASBM after May 1, 1979 the number of procedures for releasing or for dispensing may not exceed the maximum number of reentry vehicles established for missiles of corresponding types as provided for in paragraphs 10, 11, 12, and 13 of Article IV of the Treaty. In this Agreed Statement "procedures for releasing or for dispensing" are understood to mean maneuvers of a missile associated with targeting and releasing or dispensing its reentry vehicles to aim points, whether or not a reentry vehicle is actually released or dispensed. Procedures for releasing anti-missile defense penetration aids will not be considered to be procedures for releasing or for dispensing a reentry vehicle so long as the procedures for releasing anti-missile defense penetration aids differ from those for releasing or for dispensing reentry vehicles.

To Paragraph 14 of Article IV of the Treaty

First Agreed Statement. For the purposes of the limitation provided for in paragraph 14 of Article IV of the Treaty, there shall be considered to be deployed on each heavy bomber of a type equipped for cruise missiles capable of a range in excess of 600 kilometers the maximum number of such missiles for which any bomber of that type is equipped for one operational mission.

Second Agreed Statement. During the term of the Treaty no bomber of the B-52 or B-1 types of the United States of America and no bomber of the Tupolev-95 [Tu-20] or Myasishchev types of the Union of Soviet Socialist Republics will be equipped for more than twenty cruise missiles capable of a range in excess of 600 kilometers.

To Paragraph 4 of Article V of the Treaty

Agreed Statement. If a bomber is equipped for ASBMs equipped with MIRVs, all bombers of that type shall be considered to be equipped for ASBMs equipped with MIRVs.

To Paragraph 3 of Article VI of the Treaty

Agreed Statement. The procedures referred to in paragraph 7 of Article VI of the Treaty shall include procedures determining the manner in which mobile ICBM launchers of a type not subject to the limitation provided for in Article V of the Treaty, which undergo conversion into launchers of a type subject to that limitation, shall become subject to that limitation, unless the Parties agree that mobile ICBM launchers shall not be deployed after the date on which the Protocol ceases to be in force.

To Paragraph 6 of Article VI of the Treaty

Agreed Statement. The procedures for removal of strategic offensive arms from the aggregate numbers provided for in the Treaty, which are referred to in paragraph 6 of Article VI of the Treaty, and which are to be agreed upon in the Standing Consultative Commission, shall include:

(a) procedures for removal from the aggregate numbers, provided for in Article V of the Treaty, of ICBM and SLBM launchers which are being converted from launchers of a type subject to the limitation provided for in Article V of the Treaty, into launchers of a type not subject to that limitation;

(b) procedures for removal from the aggregate numbers, provided for in Articles III and V of the Treaty, of bombers which are being converted from bombers of a type subject to the limitations provided for in Article III of the Treaty or in Articles III and V of the Treaty into airplanes or bombers of a type not so subject.

Common Understanding. The procedures referred to in subparagraph (b) of the Agreed Statement to paragraph 6 of Article VI of the Treaty for removal of bombers from the aggregate numbers provided for in Articles III and V of the Treaty shall be based upon the existence of functionally related observable differences which indicate whether or not they can perform the mission of a heavy bomber, or whether or not they can perform the mission of a bomber equipped for cruise missiles capable of a range in excess of 600 kilometers.

To Paragraph 1 of Article VII of the Treaty

Common Understanding. The term "testing," as used in Article VII of the Treaty, includes research and development.

To Paragraph 2 of Article VII of the Treaty

First Agreed Statement. The term "significant increase," as used in subparagraph 2(a) of Article VII of the Treaty, means an increase of fifteen percent or more. Any new ICBM test and training launchers which replace ICBM test and training launchers at test ranges will be located only at test ranges.

Second Agreed Statement. Current test ranges where ICBMs are tested are located: for the United States of America, near Santa Maria, California, and at Cape Canaveral, Florida; and for the Union of Soviet Socialist Republics, in the areas of Tyura-Tam and Plesetskaya. In the future, each Party shall provide notification in the Standing Consultative Commission of the location of any other test range used by that Party to test ICBMs.

First Common Understanding. At test ranges where ICBMs are tested, other arms, including those not limited by the Treaty, may also be tested.

Second Common Understanding. Of the eighteen launchers of fractional orbital missiles at the test range where ICBMs are tested in the area of Tyura-Tam, twelve launchers shall be dismantled or destroyed and six launchers may be converted to launchers for testing missiles undergoing modernization.

Dismantling or destruction of the twelve launchers shall begin upon entry into force of the Treaty and shall be completed within eight months, under procedures for dismantling or destruction of these launchers to be agreed upon in the Standing Consultative Commission. These twelve launchers shall not be replaced.

Conversion of the six launchers may be carried out after entry into force of the Treaty. After entry into force of the Treaty, fractional orbital missiles shall be removed and shall be destroyed pursuant to the provisions of subparagraph 1(c) of Article IX and of Article XI of the Treaty and shall not be replaced by other missiles, except in the case of conversion of these six launchers for testing missiles undergoing modernization. After removal of the fractional orbital missiles, and prior to such conversion, any activities associated with these launchers shall be limited to normal maintenance requirements for launchers in which missiles are not deployed. These six launchers shall be subject to the provisions of Article VII of the Treaty and, if converted, to the provisions of the Fifth Common Understanding to paragraph 5 of Article II of the Treaty.

To Paragraph 1 of Article VIII of the Treaty

Agreed Statement. For purposes of testing only, each Party has the right, through initial construction or, as an exception to the provisions of paragraph 1 of Article VIII of the Treaty, by conversion, to equip for cruise missiles capable of a range in excess of 600 kilometers or for ASBMs no more than sixteen airplanes, including airplanes which are prototypes of bombers equipped for such missiles. Each Party also has the right, as an exception to the provisions of paragraph 1 of Article VIII of the Treaty, to flight-test from such airplanes cruise missiles capable of a range in excess of 600 kilometers and, after the date on which the Protocol ceases to be in force, to flight-test ASBMs from such airplanes as well, unless the Parties agree that they will not flight-test ASBMs after that date. The limitations provided for in Article III of the Treaty shall not apply to such airplanes.

The aforementioned airplanes may include only:

(a) airplanes other than bombers which, as an exception to the provisions of paragraph 1 of Article VIII of the Treaty, have been converted into airplanes equipped for cruise missiles capable of a range in excess of 600 kilometers or for ASBMs;

(b) airplanes considered to be heavy bombers pursuant to subparagraph 3(c) or 3(d) of Article II of the Treaty; and

(c) airplanes other than heavy bombers which, prior to March 7, 1979, were used for testing cruise missiles capable of a range in excess of 600 kilometers.

The airplanes referred to in subparagraphs (a) and (b) of this Agreed Statement shall be distinguishable on the basis of functionally related observable differences from airplanes which otherwise would be of the same type but cannot perform the mission of a bomber equipped for cruise missiles capable of a range in excess of 600 kilometers or for ASBMs.

The airplanes referred to in subparagraph (c) of this Agreed Statement shall not be used for testing cruise missiles capable of a range in excess of 600 kilometers after the expiration of a six-month period from the date of entry into force of the Treaty, unless by the expiration of that period they are distinguishable on the basis of functionally related observable differences from airplanes which otherwise would be of the same type but cannot perform the mission of a bomber equipped for cruise missiles capable of a range in excess of 600 kilometers.

First Common Understanding. The term "testing," as used in the Agreed Statement in paragraph 1 of Article VIII of the Treaty, includes research and development.

Second Common Understanding. The Parties shall notify each other in the Standing Consultative Commission of the number of airplanes, according to type, used for testing pursuant to the Agreed Statement to paragraph 1 of Article VIII of the Treaty. Such notification shall be provided at the first regular session of the Standing Consultative Commission held after an airplane has been used for such testing.

Third Common Understanding. None of the sixteen airplanes referred to in the Agreed Statement to paragraph 1 of Article VIII of the Treaty may be replaced, except in the event of the involuntary destruction of any such airplane or in the case of the dismantling or destruction of any such airplane. The procedures for such replacement and for removal of any such airplane from that number, in case of its conversion, shall be agreed upon in the Standing Consultative Commission.

To Paragraph 1 of Article IX of the Treaty

Common Understanding to subparagraph (a). The obligations provided for in subparagraph 1(a) of Article IX of the Treaty do not affect current practices for transporting ballistic missiles.

Agreed Statement to subparagraph (b). The obligations provided for in subparagraph 1(b) of Article IX of the Treaty shall apply to all areas of the ocean floor and the seabed, including the seabed zone referred to in Articles I and II of the 1971 Treaty on the Prohibition of the Emplacement of Nuclear Weapons and Other Weapons of Mass Destruction on the Seabed and the Ocean Floor and in the Subsoil Thereof.

Common Understanding to subparagraph (c). The provisions of subparagraph 1(c) of Article IX of the Treaty do not require the dismantling or destruction of any existing launchers of either Party.

First Agreed Statement to subparagraphs (e) and (f). The launch-weight of an SLBM or of an ASBM is the weight of the fully loaded missile itself at the time of launch.

Second Agreed Statement to subparagraphs (e) and (f). The throw-weight of an SLBM or of an ASBM is the sum of the weight of:

(a) its reentry vehicle or reentry vehicles;
(b) any self-contained dispensing mechanisms or other appropriate devices for targeting one reentry vehicle, or for releasing or for dispensing and targeting two or more reentry vehicles; and
(c) its penetration aids, including devices for their release.

Common Understanding to subparagraphs (e) and (f). The term "other appropriate devices," as used in the definition of the throw-weight of an SLBM or of an ASBM in the Second Agreed Statement to subparagraphs 1(e) and 1(f) of Article IX of the Treaty, means any devices for dispensing and targeting two or more reentry vehicles; and any devices for releasing two or more reentry vehicles or for targeting one reentry vehicle, which cannot provide their reentry vehicles or reentry vehicle with additional velocity of more than 1,000 meters per second.

To Paragraph 2 of Article IX of the Treaty

Agreed Statement. Warheads of a cruise missile are independently targetable if maneuvering or targeting of the warheads to separate aim points along ballistic trajectories or any other flight paths, which are unrelated to each other, is accomplished during a flight of a cruise missile.

To Paragraph 3 of Article XV of the Treaty

First Agreed Statement. Deliberate concealment measures, as referred to in paragraph 3 of Article XV of the Treaty, are measures carried out deliberately to hinder or deliberately to impede verification by national technical means of compliance with the provisions of the Treaty.

Second Agreed Statement. The obligation not to use deliberate concealment measures, provided for in paragraph 3 of Article XV of the Treaty, does not preclude the testing of anti-missile defense penetration aids.

First Common Understanding. The provisions of paragraph 3 of Article XV of the Treaty and the First Agreed Statement thereto apply to all provisions of the Treaty, including provisions associated with testing. In this connection, the obligation not to use deliberate concealment measures includes the obligation not to use deliberate concealment measures associated with testing, including those measures aimed at concealing the association between ICBMs and launchers during testing.

Second Common Understanding. Each Party is free to use various methods of transmitting telemetric information during testing, including its encryption, except that, in accordance with the provisions of paragraph 3 of Article XV of the Treaty, neither Party shall engage in deliberate denial of telemetric information, such as through the use of telemetry encryption, whenever such denial impedes verification of compliance with the provisions of the Treaty.

Third Common Understanding. In addition to the obligations provided for in paragraph 3 of Article XV of the Treaty, no shelters which impede verification by national technical means of compliance with the provisions of the Treaty shall be used over ICBM silo launchers.

To Paragraph 1 of Article XVI of the Treaty

First Common Understanding. ICBM launches to which the obligations provided for in Article XVI of the Treaty apply, include, among others, those ICBM launches for which advance notification is required pursuant to the provisions of the Agreement on Measures to Reduce the Risk of Outbreak of Nuclear War Between the United States of America and the Union of Soviet Socialist Republics, signed September 30, 1971, and the Agreement Between the Government of the United States of America and the Government of the Union of Soviet Socialist Republics on the Prevention of Incidents On and Over the High Seas, signed May 25, 1972. Nothing in Article XVI of the Treaty is intended to inhibit advance notification, on a voluntary basis, of any ICBM launches not subject to its provisions, the advance notification of which would enhance confidence between the Parties.

Second Common Understanding. A multiple ICBM launch conducted by a Party, as distinct from single ICBM launches referred to in Article XVI of the Treaty, is a launch which would result in two or more of its ICBMs being in flight at the same time.

Third Common Understanding. The test ranges referred to in Article XVI of the Treaty are those covered by the Second Agreed Statement of paragraph 2 of Article VII of the Treaty.

To Paragraph 3 of Article XVII of the Treaty

Agreed Statement. In order to maintain the agreed data base on the numbers of strategic offensive arms subject to the limitations provided for in the Treaty in accordance with paragraph 3 of Article XVII of the Treaty, at each regular session of the Standing Consultative Commission the Parties will notify each other of and consider changes in those numbers in the following categories: launchers of ICBMs; fixed launchers of ICBMs; launchers of ICBMs equipped with MIRVs; launchers of SLBMs; launchers of SLBMs equipped with MIRVs; heavy bombers; heavy bombers equipped for cruise missiles capable of a range in excess of 600 kilometers; heavy bombers equipped only for ASBMs; ASBMs; and ASBMs equipped with MIRVs.

To Paragraph 2 of Article II of the Protocol

Agreed Statement. Warheads of a cruise missile are independently targetable if maneuvering or targeting of the warheads to separate aim points along ballistic trajectories or any other flight paths, which are unrelated to each other, is accomplished during a flight of a cruise missile.

To Paragraph 3 of Article II of the Protocol

First Agreed Statement. If a cruise missile is capable of a range in excess of 600 kilometers, all cruise missiles of that type shall be considered to be cruise missiles capable of a range in excess of 600 kilometers.

First Common Understanding. If a cruise missile has been flight-tested to a range in excess of 600 kilometers, it shall be considered to be a cruise missile capable of a range in excess of 600 kilometers.

Second Common Understanding. Cruise missiles not capable of a range in excess of 600 kilometers shall not be considered to be of a type capable of a range in excess of 600 kilometers if they are distinguishable on the basis of externally observable design features from cruise missiles of types capable of a range in excess of 600 kilometers.

Second Agreed Statement. The range of which a cruise missile is capable is the maximum distance which can be covered by the missile in its standard design mode flying until fuel exhaustion, determined by projecting its flight path onto the Earth's sphere from the point of launch to the point of impact.

Third Agreed Statement. If an unmanned, self-propelled, guided vehicle which sustains flight through the use of aerodynamic lift over most of its flight path has been flight-tested or deployed for weapon delivery, all vehicles of that type shall be considered to be weapon-delivery vehicles.

Third Common Understanding. Unmanned, self-propelled, guided vehicles which sustain flight through the use of aerodynamic lift over most of their flight path and are not weapon-delivery vehicles, that is, unarmed, pilotless, guided vehicles, shall not be considered to be cruise missiles if such vehicles are distinguishable from cruise missiles on the basis of externally observable design features.

Fourth Common Understanding. Neither Party shall convert unarmed, pilotless, guided vehicles into cruise missiles capable of a range in excess of 600 kilometers, nor shall either Party convert cruise missiles capable of a range in excess of 600 kilometers into unarmed, pilotless, guided vehicles.

Fifth Common Understanding. Neither Party has plans during the term of the Protocol to flight-test from or deploy on sea-based or land-based launchers unarmed, pilotless, guided vehicles which are capable of a range in excess of 600 kilometers. In the future, should a Party have such plans, that Party will provide notification thereof to the other Party well in advance of such flight-testing or deployment. This Common Understanding does not apply to target drones.

Done at Vienna, on June 18, 1979, in two copies, each in the English and Russian languages, both texts being equally authentic.

FOR THE	FOR THE
UNITED STATES OF AMERICA	UNION OF SOVIET SOCIALIST REPUBLICS
PRESIDENT	GENERAL SECRETARY OF THE CPSU,
OF THE UNITED STATES	CHAIRMAN OF THE PRESIDIUM OF THE
OF AMERICA	SUPREME SOVIET OF THE USSR

SOVIET BACKFIRE STATEMENT

On June 16, 1979, President Brezhnev handed President Carter the following written statement:

"The Soviet side informs the U.S. side that the Soviet 'Tu-22M' [alternatively designated Tu-26] airplane, called 'Backfire' in the U.S.A., is a medium-range bomber and that it does not intend to give this airplane the capability of operating at intercontinental distances. In this connection, the Soviet side states that it will not increase the radius of action of this airplane in such a way as to enable it to strike targets on the territory of the U.S.A. Nor does it intend to give it such a capability in any other manner, including by in-flight refueling. At the same time, the Soviet side states that it will not increase the production rate of this airplane as compared to the present rate."

President Brezhnev confirmed that the Soviet Backfire production rate would not exceed 30 per year.

President Carter stated that the United States enters into the SALT II agreement on the basis of the commitments contained in the Soviet statement and that it considers the carrying out of these commitments to be essential to the obligations assumed under the Treaty.

MEMORANDUM
OF UNDERSTANDING BETWEEN
THE UNITED STATES OF AMERICA
AND
THE UNION OF SOVIET SOCIALIST REPUBLICS
REGARDING THE ESTABLISHMENT OF
A DATA BASE ON THE NUMBERS OF STRATEGIC OFFENSIVE
ARMS

For the purposes of the Treaty Between the United States of America and the Union of Soviet Socialist Republics on the Limitation of Strategic Offensive Arms, the Parties have considered data on numbers of strategic offensive arms and agree that as of November 1, 1978 there existed the following numbers of strategic offensive arms subject to the limitations provided for in the Treaty which is being signed today.

	U.S.A.	U.S.S.R.
Launchers of ICBMs	1,054	1,398
Fixed launchers of ICBMs	1,054	1,398
Launchers of ICBMs equipped with MIRVs	550	576
Launchers of SLBMs	656	950
Launchers of SLBMs equipped with MIRVs	496	128
Heavy bombers	574	156
Heavy bombers equipped for cruise missiles capable of a range in excess of 600 kilometers	0	0
Heavy bombers equipped only for ASBMs	0	0
ASBMs	0	0
ASBMs equipped with MIRVs	0	0

At the time of entry into force of the Treaty the Parties will update the above agreed data in the categories listed in this Memorandum.

Done at Vienna on June 18, 1979, in two copies, each in the English and Russian languages, both texts being equally authentic.

FOR THE
UNITED STATES OF AMERICA

FOR THE
UNION OF SOVIET SOCIALIST
REPUBLICS

CHIEF OF THE
UNITED STATES DELEGATION
TO THE STRATEGIC ARMS
LIMITATION TALKS

CHIEF OF THE
U.S.S.R. DELEGATION
TO THE STRATEGIC ARMS
LIMITATION TALKS

STATEMENT OF DATA ON THE NUMBERS OF STRATEGIC OFFENSIVE ARMS AS OF THE DATE OF SIGNATURE OF THE TREATY

The United States of America declares that as of June 18, 1979 it possesses the following numbers of strategic offensive arms subject to the limitations provided for in the Treaty which is being signed today:

Launchers of ICBMs	1,054
Fixed launchers of ICBMs	1,054
Launchers of ICBMs equipped with MIRVs	550
Launchers of SLBMs	656
Launchers of SLBMs equipped with MIRVs	496
Heavy bombers	573
Heavy bombers equipped for cruise missiles capable of a range in excess of 600 kilometers	3
Heavy bombers equipped only for ASBMs	0
ASBMs	0
ASBMs equipped with MIRVs	0

June 18, 1979

CHIEF OF THE
UNITED STATES DELEGATION
TO THE STRATEGIC ARMS
LIMITATION TALKS

STATEMENT OF DATA ON THE NUMBERS OF STRATEGIC OFFENSIVE ARMS AS OF THE DATE OF SIGNATURE OF THE TREATY

The Union of Soviet Socialist Republics declares that as of June 18, 1979 it possesses the following numbers of strategic offensive arms subject to the limitations provided for in the Treaty which is being signed today:

Launchers of ICBMs	1,398
Fixed launchers of ICBMs	1,398
Launchers of ICBMs equipped with MIRVs	608
Launchers of SLBMs	950
Launchers of SLBMs equipped with MIRVs	144
Heavy Bombers	156
Heavy bombers equipped for cruise missiles capable of a range in excess of 600 kilometers	0
Heavy bombers equipped only for ASBMs	0
ASBMs	0
ASBMs equipped with MIRVs	0

June 18, 1979

CHIEF OF THE
U.S.S.R. DELEGATION
TO THE STRATEGIC ARMS
LIMITATION TALKS

JOINT STATEMENT
OF PRINCIPLES AND BASIC GUIDELINES
FOR SUBSEQUENT NEGOTIATIONS
ON THE LIMITATION OF STRATEGIC ARMS

The United States of America and the Union of Soviet Socialist Republics, hereinafter referred to as the Parties,

Having concluded the Treaty on the Limitation of Strategic Offensive Arms,

Reaffirming that the strengthening of strategic stability meets the interests of the Parties and the interests of international security,

Convinced that early agreement on the further limitation and further reduction of strategic arms would serve to strengthen international peace and security and to reduce the risk of outbreak of nuclear war,

Have agreed as follows:

First. The Parties will continue to pursue negotiations, in accordance with the principle of equality and equal security, on measures for the further limitation and reduction in the numbers of strategic arms, as well as for their further qualitative limitation.

In furtherance of existing agreements between the Parties on the limitation and reduction of strategic arms, the Parties will continue, for the purposes of reducing and averting the risk of outbreak of nuclear war, to seek measures to strengthen strategic stability by, among other things, limitations on strategic offensive arms most destabilizing to the strategic balance and by measures to reduce and to avert the risk of surprise attack.

Second. Further limitations and reductions of strategic arms must be subject to adequate verification by national technical means, using additionally, as appropriate, cooperative measures contributing to the effectiveness of verification by national technical means. The Parties will seek to strengthen verification and to perfect the operation of the Standing Consultative Commission in order to promote assurance of compliance with the obligations assumed by the Parties.

Third. The Parties shall pursue in the course of these negotiations, taking into consideration factors that determine the strategic situation, the following objectives:

1) significant and substantial reductions in the numbers of strategic offensive arms;

2) qualitative limitations on strategic offensive arms, including restrictions on the development, testing, and deployment of new types of strategic offensive arms and on the modernization of existing strategic offensive arms;

3) resolution of the issues included in the Protocol to the Treaty Between the United States of America and the Union of Soviet Socialist Republics on the Limitation of Strategic Offensive Arms in the context of the negotiations relating to the implementation of the principles and objectives set out herein.

Fourth. The Parties will consider other steps to ensure and enhance strategic stability, to ensure the equality and equal security of the Parties, and to implement the above principles and objectives. Each Party will be free to raise any issue relative to the further limitation of strategic arms. The Parties will also consider further joint measures, as appropriate, to strengthen international peace and security and to reduce the risk of outbreak of nuclear war.

Vienna, June 18, 1979

FOR THE
UNITED STATES OF AMERICA

PRESIDENT

OF THE UNITED STATES

OF AMERICA

FOR THE
UNION OF SOVIET SOCIALIST
REPUBLICS

GENERAL SECRETARY OF THE
CPSU,
CHAIRMAN OF THE PRESIDIUM
OF THE
SUPREME SOVIET OF THE USSR

Index